PSYCHOTHERAPY
FOR WOMEN

PSYCHOTHERAPY FOR WOMEN

Treatment Toward Equality

Edited By

EDNA I. RAWLINGS, Ph.D.

University of Cincinnati
Cincinnati, Ohio

DIANNE K. CARTER, Ph.D.

University of Iowa
Iowa City, Iowa

CHARLES   C   THOMAS   •   PUBLISHER

Springfield • *Illinois* • *U.S.A.*

Published and Distributed Throughout the World by
CHARLES C THOMAS ● PUBLISHER
Bannerstone House
301-327 East Lawrence Avenue, Springfield, Illinois, U.S.A.

© *1977, by* CHARLES C THOMAS ● PUBLISHER
ISBN 0-398-03584-9
Library of Congress Catalog Card Number: 76-23165

With THOMAS BOOKS *careful attention is given to all details of
manufacturing and design. It is the Publisher's desire to present books that
are satisfactory as to their physical qualities and artistic possibilities and
appropriate for their particular use.* THOMAS BOOKS *will be true to those
laws of quality that assure a good name and good will.*

Printed in the United States of America
RN-1

Library of Congress Cataloging in Publication Data
Main entry under title:
Psychotherapy for women.

Includes bibliographies and index.
1. Psychotherapy. 2. Radical therapy. 3. Sex
discrimination against women. I. Rawlings, Edna I.
II. Carter, Dianne K. [DNLM: 1. Psychotherapy.
2. Women. 3. Social conditions--United States.
WM420 P975]
RC480.5.P77   616.8′914   76-23165
ISBN 0-398-03584-9

Affectionately dedicated to our parents who encouraged our achievements, supported our independence, and allowed us to be whoever we would be.

the late Paul Porter Innerarity
Jane Elizabeth Nichols Innerarity Boone

Elsie Laura Wickers Knotts
Hugh Knotts

CONTRIBUTORS

Harold Adams received his Ph.D. from the University of Michigan and has been on the faculty of the University of Iowa since 1968. He is on the editorial board of *The Humanist Educator* and is a member of the New American Movement which shares his goal of building socialism in the United States.

Lois Brien received her Ph.D. from the University of Iowa in 1959. She is currently a Gestalt therapist in private practice in San Francisco, and a member of the faculty of the California School of Professional Psychology. She is an active feminist both in her therapeutic work with women and in the larger community. She recently finished a year's appointment on the Marin County Commission on the Status of Women, and is at work on a book about women and inequality/equality/androgyny.

Annette M. Brodsky received her Ph.D. in Clinical Psychology from the University of Florida in 1970. Currently, she is Assistant Professor of Psychology at the University of Alabama and on the staff of the psychological clinic involved in training students in psychotherapy and personality assessment. She is chairperson of the Southeastern Psychological Association Commission on the Status of Women, co-chairperson of the American Psychological Association Task Force on Sex Bias and Sex Role Stereotyping in Psychotherapeutic Practice, and a member of the executive committee of Div. 35, APA (The Psychology of Women). Her current research is on women in mental hospitals and prisons. Her interest in the clinical applications of women's issues is reflected in her development of women's studies programs at Southern Illinois University and Alabama, in her work on The Feminist Therapist Roster for the Association for Women in Psychology, in forming and consulting with consciousness-raising (C-R) groups, in presentations at conferences on women, and in publications in professional journals.

Dianne K. Carter received her Ph.D. from the University of Utah in Counseling-Clinical Psychology. She has been at the University of Iowa since 1971 where she is involved in teaching, clinical training, and the practice of feminist therapy. Her clinical emphasis is feminist therapy groups for divorced women. Her research interests include value changes as the essential ingredient of therapy and the formulation of the values and strategies of feminist therapy.

Cindy Rice Dewey received her M.Ed. and Ed.S. degrees in 1972 from the University of Florida. She was a Vocational Specialist and Codirector of the Women's Walk-In Counseling Service at the University of Florida. She was involved in building a home with her husband, Doug, who is a pottery craftsman, and her eight-year-old son, Todd. She played banjo with the Possum Trot String Band, and enjoyed gardening. Tragically, in January, 1976, Cindy died.

Leona Durham is a student in the College of Law and a prospective candidate for Ph.D. in the Department of Mass Communications at the University of Iowa. She is active in the National Lawyers Guild. She is interested in building socialism as an alternative to the economic and psychological oppression of a capitalist system whose burden is borne primarily by women and minority groups.

Jossette Escamilla-Mondanaro received her M.D. degree in 1971 from Syracuse Medical College. She is now living in San Francisco where she is a member of the faculty of the California School of Professional Psychology, director of the Pregnant Addicts Program, and medical director of the Adolescent and Young Adult Alcohol Program. She is actively involved in general practice, office gynecology, and therapy with women at the Haight-Asbury Women's Clinic and the Ching Min Asian Women's Clinic.

Norma B. Gluckstern received her Ed.D. degree from the University of Massachusetts. Currently she is Assistant Professor of Psychology at The Catholic University of America. She is also director of the Model Education Program at the Berkshire County House of Correction and codirector of Microtraining Associates, Inc. She helped to found the Everywoman's Center in the University and has been active in a number of Counseling programs for women. In addition to coediting a special feature on corrections for the American Personnel and Guidance Journal, she has coauthored a series of video tapes and manuals on microcounseling.

Marie Celeste Guzell was born in Lloydell, Pennsylvania and received her Bachelor's degree at the Pennsylvania State University and her Ph.D. in Clinical Psychology at Louisiana State University. She has taught psychology at California State University (Sacramento), the University of Northern Iowa, and is currently at Indiana State University. She has done research in the characteristics of creative adolescents, personality correlates of aesthetic preferences, sex factors in honesty and deceit, sex bias in psychological testing, sex bias in teacher evaluations, and personality changes of women in women's studies courses.

Lenore. W. Harmon obtained her Ph.D. in Psychology from the University of Minnesota in 1965. Since then, she has been a counselor, teacher, and researcher, devoting much of her energy to the problems of counseling women. Currently, she is Professor of Educational Psychology and coordinator of Women's Studies at the University of Wisconsin (Milwaukee). She is active in the American Psychological Association and the American Personnel and Guidance Association. She edits the *Journal of Vocational Behavior*.

Patricia Jakubowski received her Ed.D. in Counseling from the University of Illinois. She conducted her own behavioral counseling firm in Chicago for two years. Presently she is Associate Professor of Education at the University of Missouri (St. Louis). She has given workshops on assertion training, has participated in numerous university conferences on assertion, and has spoken on assertion training before the American Council on Education, the Michigan and Kansas Associations of Women Deans and Counselors, the Wisconsin Spring Groups Conference, and the Las Vegas Humanistic Behavior Modification Conference. She is Associate Editor of *Counselor Education and Supervision* and has been selected to be one of ten National Consultants for the American Personnel and Guidance Association project on Sex Equality in Guidance Practices. In addition to assertion training and behavior modification, she has done research in the area of human expectancy.

Anica Vesel Mander is a teacher of languages, literature, and women's studies. She was one of the founders of Alyssum, a center for feminist consciousness in San Francisco, and is coauthor with Anne Kent Rush of *Feminism as Therapy* (Bookworks/Random House). She is presently working on a historical autobiography of three generations of women which will be published by Moon Books, San Francisco.

Edna I. Rawlings received her Ph.D. in Clinical Psychology from the University of Wisconsin (Madison) in 1966. She was formerly at the University of Iowa College of Medicine and Indiana State University. She currently is Associate Professor of Psychology at the University of Cincinnati. She has extensive experience in training members of all helping professions in individual and group therapy skills, including natural helpers in rural communities. Her professional publications include the areas of personality research and group psychotherapy research and practice. Feminist therapy, female sexuality and mental imagery are her current professional and research interests.

C. Jane Sanders received her M.A. in Rehabilitation Counseling at the University of Iowa and is now a Ph.D. candidate in Counseling Psychology. Her research interests include the psychology of receiving aid, the psychological aspects of women, the effects of feminist training and courses on psychological androgyny, assertive behavior training, and counselor education as training for social change.

Barbara E. Sang received her Ph.D. from Yeshiva University in 1970. She is currently living in New York where she is a clinical psychologist in private practice and an artist. Since 1968 she has been active in the gay and women's movements; she is chairwoman of the board of the Homosexual Counseling Center, a book reviewer for the *Homosexual Counseling Journal,* an active member of the Association of Gay Psychologists, a member of the newly created Task Force on the Status of Gay and Lesbian Psychologists, and a member of the Association for Women in Psychology. During the summer of 1975 she served on the faculty of Sagaris, an institute for the study of feminist thought.

Ardelle Poletti Schultz. As Director of Treatment at TODAY, Inc. (Bucks County, Pa.), Ardelle Poletti Schultz uses empirical knowledge she has gained from over six years of working with addicted women. Her experience as cotherapist in marathon groups of recovered alcoholic women led her into the treatment field where she became leader of the first women's group at Eagleville Hospital & Rehabilitation Center. She brings to therapy a commitment to the struggles for women's rights. She is in constant demand as lecturer and workshop leader and has presented several papers to national and state conferences on women's needs: "Radical Feminism," "Women and Addiction: An Overview," and "The Non-Sexist Approach to Treatment."

Robert Seidenberg received his medical training at Syracuse University and his psychoanalytic training at the Institute for Psychoanalysis (Chicago). He is a practicing psychiatrist and psychoanalyst in Syracuse, New York, and is also Clinical Professor of Psychiatry at the Upstate Medical Center, SUNY. He is a member of the American Psychiatric Association (Fellow) and of the American Psychoanalytic Association. He is past-president of the Western New York Psychoanalytic Association and was a founding member of the Central New York Chapter of the National Organization for Women (N.O.W.). He is author of over a hundred articles. His books include *Mind and Destiny, Marriage Between Equals,* and *Corporate Wives — Cor-*

porate Casualties? He is married to civil rights' attorney, Faith A. Seidenberg; they have three children.

Natalie Shainess is a Board-Diplomate in Psychiatry who received her psychiatric training at the New York State Psychiatric Institute and Hospital, and her Certificate in Psychoanalysis from the William Alanson White Institute of Psychiatry, Psychoanalysis and Psychology in New York City, where she is on the faculty. She is also a Lecturer in Psychiatry at Columbia University College of Physicians and Surgeons. Though primarily in private practice, she has held a number of teaching appointments including that of Assistant Clinical Professor of Psychiatry at the New York School of Psychiatry, the State Residency Training Program. Specializing in feminine psychology, she has over one hundred publications. Among the most recent are a chapter on "The Effect of Changing Cultural Values upon Women," in the revised edition of the *American Handbook of Psychiatry,* Ed. S. Arieti, 1974 (a basic psychiatric text), and "Authentic Feminine Orgastic Response," in *Sexuality and Psychoanalysis,* Ed. Adelson, 1975.

Cynthia Sheldon, M.S.W., received her degree in 1962 from the University of California, Berkeley. She trained with the late Fritz Perls in Big Sur and then founded the Gestalt Institute of San Francisco in 1967 where she is presently a trainer. In addition to her private practice, Gestalt teaching the workshops in the U. S. and abroad, she developed The Melange Institute in San Anselmo, California, a center for teaching family therapy with a Gestalt and Teichian approach. Over the past five years she has participated in numerous workshops and groups for women; three years ago she helped organize Alyssum, a feminist drop-in center in San Francisco. Her feminist work has influenced her Gestalt and family teaching. All have influenced her personal life-style.

Dorothy Cox Stewart received her M.A. in Psychology from Columbia University and is now a Ph.D. candidate in Counseling Psychology at the University of Iowa. Her research interests include training for feminist therapists, the effect of faith on mental health, assertion training, and the causes and effects of sex-role stereotyping.

Theodora Wells received her M.B.A. from the University of Southern California in 1965. She now heads Wells Associates, a consulting firm for organizations, groups, individuals, and affirmative action programs. She designs programs to develop interpersonal competence and nondefensive communication which focus on personal growth from learned sex-role behaviors to self-chosen behavior patterns. She is coauthor of *Breakthrough: Women into Management,* author of "Woman — Which Includes Man, Of Course," and many management and training articles. She has taught a U.C.L.A. extension course, "Management Development for Women," since 1968 and is active in professional associations for management, psychology, training and feminist consulting.

Hogie Wyckoff received a B.A. in Philosophy at U. C. Berkeley, and then trained extensively with Dr. Claude Steiner at the Berkeley Radical Psychiatry Center. A radical feminist, she has been facilitating and teaching Radical Psychiatry problem-solving for women in Berkeley for five years. She is the coauthor of *Scripts People Live, Readings in Radical Psychiatry,* and has written a number of articles about feminist therapy. She is a member of the collective that puts out the quarterly journal *Issues in Radical Therapy.* Currently, she is working on a book called *Radical Psychiatry for Women* and is learning to incorporate body-related therapies into her work. She shares a large house in Berkeley with six other people committed to cooperative living. A major concern for her is how to deal with the problems involved in being a nonmonogamous bisexual woman in this culture.

PREFACE

THE goal of this book is to provide the professional community with a guide to psychotherapeutic treatment which encourages women to develop as complete human beings. Psychotherapy, as empirical evidence and published opinion now show, does not occur without the therapist's own values and attitudes having an impact upon the client. We believe that the attitudes and beliefs which many therapists have about women are sufficiently erroneous and restricting that treatment has been more debilitating than therapeutic. It is this antitherapeutic situation for women which gave us the impetus to create this book. The direction for its creation has come from feminists and radical therapists; we acknowledge our debt to those groups.

In this book we examine the ways in which sexism is represented in the theories and practices of psychotherapists. However, unlike some of the current writers criticizing psychotherapy for women, we do not merely add to the list of complaints against the male-dominated therapeutic community. Rather, we take positive steps toward correction by presenting some concepts and procedures which we and our contributors have found to be useful in aiding women to liberate themselves.

Because there are so many recent innovative developments in nonsexist and feminist therapeutic approaches for women, we invited psychotherapists, counselors, educators, and other professionals who are experts in the particular areas we wanted represented, to submit original papers for this book. The papers selected were edited within the context of our own values as feminists and as therapists. This editing resulted in some lively exchanges between ourselves and our contributors. Most of the differences were resolved amicably with compromise on both sides, though we lost two contributors in the process.

Feminist thought at this historical stage, is not a tightly knit, closely agreed philosophy; so while a feminist view is common to all papers, each makes a unique contribution: in concept, insight, technique, or application. Section I discusses the importance of therapists' values in the treatment of women. This section explores the nature of the personal and professional values therapists have about women, and then it examines the ways therapists' values are imposed during therapy. Section II differentiates between nonsexist and feminist therapy and details ten assumptions and twenty strategies of feminist therapy. Comparative sexist and feminist analyses of two case histories is the companion chapter. In Section III several nonsexist approaches which are helpful to women in realizing equality and their human potential are described. One is a scathing indictment of marriage counseling; the other two are women-centered approaches to treatment. Section IV discusses clinical problems and applications appropriate for assertion training. Perhaps more than any other one technique, this material teaches women how to liberate themselves. Section V presents career counseling as therapy which can help in liberating women from economic dependence on men. The first chapter is an original theoretical conception of the occupational position of women, the second offers an entirely new vocational counseling technique, and the third provides a guide to doing therapy with professional women. Section VI is a rare disclosure for therapists. It contains selections on the therapeutic treatment of lesbians written by women therapists who are themselves lesbians. This section is a consciousness-raising experience for the entire "straight" community, women as well as men.

The previously described sections offer new ways of thinking about women so that accepted techniques are applied more therapeutically. The following sections not only contribute new thinking about women, but they also challenge traditional techniques and suggest approaches either not sanctioned by the professional community or not previously understood or acknowledged as therapy. Section VII describes the ways in which feminist ideology is therapeutic for women. This view is documented within the context of two different settings: consciousness-raising and women's studies courses. This section also contains a carefully selected and annotated bibliography to serve as bibliotherapy for clients not acquainted with feminist thought. In Section VIII radical feminist therapists challenge the power and the beneficial effect of that therapy provided by the mental health community. They also propose alternative treatments. Section IX suggests that participating in social activism which promotes feminist goals for society is also related to beneficial personal change for the participants. Section X, the Epilogue, examines the role of the mental health professions in perpetuating the *status quo* for women. Optimistically, the Epilogue, also investigates ways in which psychotherapists can participate in social change for a more humanistic and egalitarian society.

The term *therapy* is used in the text in a broad sense to connote not only symptom removal but also the positive growth and development of full human functioning. In this latter sense, editing this book has been therapeutic for us in our professional and personal lives. In working on this book we have become increasingly dedicated to feminism and convinced of the importance of its contribution to psychotherapy for women.

We would like to acknowledge the assistance of the women who devoted considerable time, energy and care to the myriad tasks associated with the creation of a book. Susan McQuinn was our copy editor, Ellen Piel and Dorothy Stewart were our research and editorial assistants and Karen Jackson, Cathy Carter and Joyce Hampsher were our typists. We are grateful for the invaluable help of these competent women. Complete responsibility for the quality of the final product must, of course, rest with us.

Edna I. Rawlings
Dianne K. Carter

CONTENTS

PSYCHOTHERAPY FOR WOMEN

Section I

INTRODUCTION

Chapter 1

VALUES AND VALUE CHANGE
IN PSYCHOTHERAPY

INTRODUCTION

"VALUE-FREE psychotherapy is a myth" (Bart, 1971). All systems of psychotherapy contain implicit value systems (Halleck, 1971). In deciding who to treat, what diagnostic categories to assign, which treatment goals to set, and which techniques or strategies to employ, therapists are exercising value judgments. London (1964) described psychotherapy as a moral exchange. Pepinsky and Karst (1964) hypothesized a *convergence* phenomenon in which clients' values shift closer to the norms and standards of their therapists. This hypothesized shift was confirmed by Rosenthal (1955) who demonstrated that clients judged most improved in therapy had modified their values to more clearly resemble those of their therapists, whereas unimproved clients' values had become less like their therapists' values.

Rokeach went beyond merely acknowledging the occurrence of value shifts in psychotherapy; he maintained that the phenomena was not only a legitimate but a crucial aspect of psychotherapy:

> ... the aim of psychotherapy can be conceptualized, at least in part, as an attempt to bring about change or value reeducation in a client or patient ... If therapy is to be successful, it surely must be manifested as changes or rearrangement of value priorities and as changes in the degree of integration of the client's or patient's value system (1973, p. 333).

Rokeach also presented evidence that changes in values produce changes in attitudes and behavior; changes in behavior were temporary unless accompanied by modification in values. Like Rokeach, we also believe that the nature of therapy is in large part a change in the client's values.

While some writers are now acknowledging the pivotal place of value change in therapy, few have focused on the source of influence for change. We believe that one source of influence is political; values which are in the best interests of the dominant power group to alter get altered. Typically, the interest of the dominant group is to keep things constant.

> Most psychiatrists are unaware . . . of their impact upon the social order; therefore, they fail to grasp the political implications of their work. The net effect of psychiatric practice based on the illusion of political

5

neutrality is to conceal the existence of social conflict and to preserve the *status quo* (Halleck, 1971, p. 30).

The "illusion of political neutrality" particularly works against the interests of disenfranchised and minority people. It is especially harmful to women who are a majority in numbers but a minority in power and status. Women are the largest consumers of psychotherapy (Chesler, 1972b) and so are the largest consumers of a "service" that works against their best interests, i.e. the maintenance of the *status quo.*

Therapist values, both personal and professional, influence value change in their clients. Professional values stem from the personality theory with which therapists identify, their models of psychotherapy, and their models of mental health. These professional values converge to determine technique and goals.

Therapists' values and the political implications, especially as these affect women and other minority groups, are hard to separate. In the following pages we will describe some sources of therapists' private and professional values, and how these relate to women and the treatment of them. In the instances when women are valued negatively or are valued highly for their subordinate role to men, the political implications are obvious and we will not draw them out in the present discussion. (See the Epilogue for further discussion of the political implications of psychotherapy.)

PERSONAL SOURCES OF PSYCHOTHERAPIST'S VALUES ABOUT WOMEN*

Several studies of the attitudes of women and men toward women's changing roles provide a background for understanding influences on therapists' personal values. Before discussing therapists' values, we will review the findings of these studies.

Individual differences in men's personalitites have been found to be related to reactions to female sex roles (Dufresne, 1972). Men who react negatively to the women's movement are conservative thinkers and are dogmatic and authoritarian, valuing obedience and respect for authority (Ellis and Bentler, 1972; Defresne, 1972; Worell, 1971). Generally, they are self-protective and avoid taking risks (Worell, 1971). Miller (1973) has shown that to some extent male self-esteem is related to attitudes towards women's rights. On some small college campuses, conservative attitudes towards women's rights were correlated with low self-esteem. Low self-esteem in men has also been found to be highly correlated with the need to maintain distance from individuals considered outgroups (Dempe-

---

*We wish to acknowledge the assistance of Ellen Piel in the review of the literature and in many of the conclusions in this section. (Eds.)

wolff, 1974) and with the treatment of women as sex objects (Vavrick and Jurich, 1971). On the other hand, high self-esteem men are more likely to view females as persons (Dempewolff, 1974; Vavrick and Jurich, 1971) and to view them in more humanistic terms (Daly, 1969). Other characteristics of men associated with positive reactions to the women's movement are self-reliance, independence, low authoritarianism, adaptability, being politically liberal, and showing flexibility toward sex roles (Defresne, 1972; Johnson & MacDonnell, 1974).

A stereotypic view of masculine identity and the security a man feels about his work may color his reactions to women. Success with work has been a major source of masculine identity for middle-class men (Bardwick, 1973). Men who have stereotypic notions of masculinity and who have doubts about the usefulness of their work, may be vulnerable to feeling threatened by women, especially competitive, competent women. Such men need some group over which to feel superior. Competent women reduce these men's feelings of self-approval because, in being unable to confirm their superiority to women, they are unable to confirm their masculinity (Brenton, 1966). The more secure a man is in his personal identity and feelings of competence, the less likely he is to be threatened by competent women.

Other women labelled as threatening by stereotypic men are those who are sexually assertive. Tavris (1973) found that men who attribute sex-role differences to biology react negatively to women who take the sexual initiative, find them sexually unattractive and label them "threatening." Biological determinists view women in the women's movement as deviants: frustrated, aggressive, and neurotic (Tavris, 1973).

The biological determinists in Tavris' (1973) study who subscribe to stereotypic ideas of sex-roles were also found to deceive women in order to have sexual intercourse with them. Similarly, in their surveys of sex-calloused attitudes and actual sex-aggression, Kanin (1971) and Mosher (undated) noted a relationship between traditional masculinity in college men and sexual exploitation of women. Again, men who were less concerned with projecting a *macho* image were more accepting of egalitatian relationships and less inclined to sexual exploitation of women.

> Some antifeminists of both sexes simply have the characteristics of people who oppose most forms of social change: They tend to be politically conservative, religious, less educated, and older. Age ... brings resistance to change because the individual has a longer investment in the traditional ways, and because of the personal difficulty in changing deeply ingrained habits and beliefs (Staines, Tavris, & Jayaratne, 1974, p. 55).

Many women oppose tenets of the women's movement. One particular group of antifeminist women have the roots of their opposition in their personal success within the system: both professional success (a high-status job with good pay) and social success (popularity with men, attractiveness and a good marriage). These are the Queen Bees. Queen Bees have typically worked very hard to get where they are. They do not want competition for their jobs any more than men do; nondiscriminatory policies toward other women are threatening to them (Staines, Tavris, & Jayaratne, 1974).

Queen Bees relish the fact that they are "special," that they have unique qualifications that allow them high-ranking positions normally denied to women. These antifeminists prefer the individual explanation of their success because it enhances their self-esteem (Staines, Tavris, & Jayaratne, 1974). They, therefore, reject one of the key assumptions underlying the women's movement, which is that women's problems are external in origin. These successful women (some women therapists are in this group) do not question the attitude that "any woman could do it if she had the ability and was willing to work hard" (Bird, 1969).

Before extrapolating from the above studies to the treatment of women, we should explore the clinical evidence for whether or not the therapist's personality affects her/his therapy. Therapist personality has long been intuitively recognized as one of the most important ingredients in therapy. Cutler (1958) attempted to explore the effect of a therapists' personality in therapy by studying countertransference effects. Based on a reformulation of Bruner's (1951) theory of perception, Cutler examined two hypotheses: (1) There is a systematic relationship between the therapist's conflicts, and his/her tendency to over- or underreport the occurrence of similar behavior in him/herself and the patient in psychotherapy. (2) The therapists' therapeutic handling of material which is conflict-relevant for him/her will be less adequate than his/her handling of material which is relatively conflict-free. Both hypotheses were confirmed. Cutler also determined that "varying levels of experience in therapy and of increased self-awareness brought about by personal analysis do not seem to make a difference" (1958, p. 335).

Assuming, then, that the therapist's personality conflicts do affect the adequacy of the therapy, we might speculate as to how male therapists' conflicts about women might affect their female clients. Drawing from the literature reviewed above on attitudes toward women, we might conclude that male therapists who are conservative, dogmatic, and authoritarian would have difficulty achieving rapport and be minimally self-disclosing to a strong female client. Positive regard for her would be lacking. Other male therapists with traditional notions of masculinity who are unsure about the usefulness of their work (perhaps not an unusual reaction for psychotherapists) may be especially threatened by competent female clients. We could speculate that such therapists would be inclined to discourage competent women from seeking careers and becoming vocationally and financially independent.

In the same vein, therapists who take a biological deterministic view of sex-role behaviors are likely to label intelligent assertive women as frustrated, aggressive (castrating), and neurotic. Treatment by such therapists would surely be to aid these women to accept their feminine identity by accepting a subordinate mode of behavior ("You don't have to try so hard to be acceptable."). Such therapists, in dealing with sexual assault or sexual exploitation suffered by a female client, are not likely to give her much moral support or to encourage her to assert herself in future situations. Rather, they are likely to blame her for tempting her assailant. Such responses are "crazy-making" because it is difficult for a woman to avoid situations in which a male does not feel tempted. This therapist attitude prohibits women from acknowledging the trauma of such an event and thereby processing it. Conversely, male therapists with high self-esteem and secure sexual identity who are more egalitarian and more accepting of women as persons will likely offer support and, consequently, facilitate processing. However, even these therapists might convey unintentional biases, particularly of a subtle nature due to their unconscious acceptance of cultural values and roles for women.

Some role-identified female therapists can be as uncomprehending of women's plight as their male counterparts. Since they have proved that women can succeed, they deny discrimination. Queen Bees, described earlier, would fit into this category. These women therapists have found it to be in their personal interests to be cooperative and nonthreatening to their male colleagues (Staines, Jayaratne, & Tavris, 1974). They think either that women really are inferior (they identify with the dominant groups and think they are exceptions) or that women are not really motivated to succeed. Accordingly, investigations of therapist's attitudes have revealed no differences between female and male therapists in their acceptance of sex-role stereotypes (Broverman et al., 1970; Chesler, 1972, a).

PROFESSIONAL SOURCES OF PSYCHOTHERAPIST'S VALUES ABOUT WOMEN

Other sources of psychotherapists' values about women are the personality theories they adopt (their view of human nature), their models of psychopathology (what problems should be treated), and their models of mental health (the goals of treatment). We propose to examine each of these aspects in order to understand the values that affect the treatment women receive in psychotherapy.

Personality Theory

To examine the effects of personality theory on therapists' values regarding women requires extrapolation since most personality theories are really theories of men; personality theory conveys little about the psychology of women except in those areas in which the function of women is viewed as complementary to the function of men:

> It would be incorrect to assume that the psychology of women existed as a separate speciality within the discipline (of psychology). The female was discussed only in relation to the male, and the function of the female was thought to be distinctly different from and complementary to the function of the male (Shields, 1975, p. 739).

Insofar as Freud had a great deal to say about women, his theory of personality is an exception to the statement that personality theories include little about the psychology of women. It is true that he discusses the female, though only in relation to the male.

There are two diametrically opposed approaches to the psychology of women: (1) biological determinism represented by Freud and Erikson; and (2) cultural determinism represented by Horney and Thompson, neo-Freudians, and Hacker and Allport, sociologists.

Biological Determinism Theories of Personality

First, let us consider biological determinism as represented by Freud and Erikson.

FREUD'S PSYCHOLOGY OF WOMEN. Since Freud's views of women have had widespread impact on psychotherapists, we will consider his psychology of women in particular detail. Freud's influence on culture in general and systems of psychotherapy in particular is tremendous. Within the last 100 years, Freud's ideas are second only to Darwin's in influence and impact on the American intellectual community; and, in the area of psychotherapy which he originated, almost all of our current concepts and techniques are derived either directly from Freud or from one of his disciples.

Freud has much to say about women; unfortunately, he was an anti-feminist and a male-supremacist. His impact on feminine psychology is unrivaled. Perhaps more than any other one source, Freud's writings on women have kept women down by lending scientific validity to the insidious relationship between the sexes.

The fundamental basis of Freud's conception of the female personality is the idea of penis envy. Freud assumed that a female's discovery of her lack of a penis is a catastrophe of such vast proportions that it haunts her all through life and accounts for most aspects of her temperament. His entire psychology of women, from which much of modern psychology and psychoanalysis derives heavily, is built upon this original tragic experience. To quote Freud:

> They [little girls] notice the penis of a brother or playmate, strikingly visible and of large proportions, at once recognize it as the superior counterpart of their own small and inconspicuous organ, and from that time forward fall victim to envy of the penis (1925, p. 190). After a woman has become aware of the wound of her narcissism, she develops, like a scar, a sense of inferiority. When she has passed beyond her first attempt at explaining her lack of a penis as being a punishment personal to herself and has realized that sexual character is a universal one, she begins to share the contempt felt by men for a sex which is the lesser in so important a respect (1925, p. 192).

The mother is "almost always held responsible for her [little girls's] lack of a penis" because the mother sent her daughter "into the world so insufficiently equipped" (1925, p. 192). The girl is said to assume her female parent has mutilated her as a judgment on her general unworthiness, or possibly for the crime of masturbation. She then turns her anxious attention to her father. At first, the little girl expects her father to be magnanimous and award her a penis. Later, disappointed in this hope, she consoles herself with the hope of bearing his baby. "Her happiness is great if later on this wish for a baby finds fulfillment in reality, and quite especially so if the baby is a little boy who brings the longed-for penis with him" (1925, p. 128). (Freudian logic converts childbirth, an impressive female accomplishment, into little more than a hunt for a male organ.)

In a girl whose development is fortunate, there are still many obstacles: "she acknowledges the fact of her castration, the consequent superiority of the male and her own inferiority, but she also rebels against these unpleasant facts" (1925, p. 257). And so, while healthy, complete women seek fulfillment in a life devoted to maternity and reproduction, other women aspire to an existence outside the biological area, falling into the error Freud calls "the masculinity complex." These women do not seek the penis openly and honestly in maternity, but instead desire to enter universities, pursue an independent life, or take up feminism. They grow restless and require treatment as "neurotics." Freud castigated such "immature" women as "regressive" or incomplete persons, clinical cases of "arrested development" (1925, p. 128).

MODESTY AND SHAME. Freud believed that two aspects of women's character are directly related to penis envy: modesty and shame. It is a woman's self-despair over the "defect" of her "castration" which gives rise to the well-known shame of women. Freud designated shame as a feminine characteristic *par excellence*. Its purpose, in his view, is simply the concealment of her defect. The women hides her parts to hide her wound.

PRESERVATION OF THE HUMAN RACE. Freud entrusted the preservation of the human race to the male —

> Nature has paid less careful attention to the demands of the female function than to those of masculinity ... the achievement of the biological aim is entrusted to the aggressiveness of the male, and is to some extent independent of the cooperation of the female (1933,b).

Male libido or sexual drive is interpreted by Freud as a power in the service of life; it must, therefore, be permitted to wreak its will on the female whether or not she has the desire to cooperate. The frigid woman and woman's presumed lower sexual drive is presented as an example of the male's superior regard for posterity. The whole balance and justification for male sexual aggression toward the female is hereby subsumed under the issue of the continuation of the species. This view has since given rise to the diction which psychology has ever since employed to describe sexuality: surrender (by the female), and dominance or mastery (by the male).

PASSIVITY, MASOCHISM, AND NARCISSISM. The three most distinguishing traits of the female personality were, in Freud's view, passivity, masochism, and narcissism. Masochism and passivity, Freud would have us understand, are not only feminine, but also dynamically interrelated: Masochism comprises all passive attitudes to sexual life. Of course, for Freud to describe a woman's nature as essentially masochistic justifies any conceivable domination or humiliation forced upon her. Nearly any atrocity committed against women can be exonerated on the theory of her innate masochism.

THE INFERIOR MENTALITY OF THE FEMALE. It is difficult to continue to describe the female as an incomplete male without implicating the quality of her intellect relative to his. According to Freud, men sublimate and transcend their sexuality, thereby supplying the energy source from which civilizations are built. In contrast, women are intimidated from pursuing the strongest interest they are capable of entertaining, that is, sexuality and are directed away from any study until "all mental effort and knowledge in general is depreciated in their eyes" (1908, p. 94). To quote Freud directly:

> ... the undoubted fact of the intellectual inferiority of so many women can be traced to that inhibition of thought necessitated by sexual suppression (1908, p. 94).

According to Freud, women have contributed little to civilization for civilization is made through sublimation, and "women are endowed with the power to sublimate only in a limited degree" (1908, p. 78). Moreover, as Freud emphasized, the female is not required to conceal and transcend her Oedipal complex. She does not fear castration, thus she fails to develop a sufficient superego. The male, in contrast, makes his contribution to civilization through sublimation and the development of a strong superego goaded on by fear of castration — as a result of possessing a penis and the possibility of losing it. Never having had a penis and so, unafraid to lose it, the female has far less superego than the male. This is why, Freud explains, she is largely without moral sense, inclined to be less ethically rigorous, has little perception of justice, is more subject to emotional bias, and unable to contribute to culture.

In summary, Freud's psychology of women portrays women as inferior and incomplete males, suffering from lack of a penis. The resultant penis envy of women is the fundamental postulate upon which every other detail of her assumed nature (including her inferior intellect) is built. The theory of penis envy shifts the blame of women's suffering back upon herself for daring to aspire to a biologically impossible state. Any hankering for a less humiliating and circumscribed existence is immediately ascribed to unnatural and unrealistic deviation from her genetic identity and her fate. A woman who resists "femininity," that is, feminine temperament, status, and role, is thought to court neurosis, for femininity is her fate as "anatomy is her destiny."

We admit to a bias against Freud's psychology of women. Our reaction is captured in the following quote from Deckard:

> One is tempted to dismiss Freud and his theories as a sick joke. One wonders what happened during his childhood to produce such a penis fixation. Anyone who considers half the human race to be "mutilated" creatures" on the basis of the characteristics that makes the continuation of the species possible, has got to be sick.
>
> Unfortunately, we cannot dismiss him so easily. He has had too much effect on our thinking. That his theories could have been and, in many quarters, still are taken seriously illustrates the incredible misogyny prevalent in Western society (1975, pp. 17-18).

One of Freud's disciples, Erik Erikson (1967) concluded that while women are biologically different from men, they are not necessarily inferior. He argued that the psychology of women was determined by their "productive inner space" (the womb) which conditions them to be conserving and nurturent. In contrast, men, because of their external genitalia, exploit and manipulate the external world. Obviously, Erikson was drawing a parallel between the reproductive system and the psychological characteristics of the sexes, a variation of the Freudian thesis that the nature of the sex organs produced personality differences between the sexes. The data Erikson presents to establish his theory are observations that a group of ten-year-old girls built enclosed structures while a group of ten-year-old boys constructed open structures. For those who accept this data as support of Erikson's theory, a reminder: By age ten, children have been socialized into gender roles so that learning is confounded with whatever innate differences may exist.

Psychotherapists make the same error in reasoning that Freud and Erikson did; because the behaviors they observed in women occurred with high frequency, they assumed that these behaviors must be innate.

Because of Freud's remarkable impact upon Western intellectual thought and culture generally, his views on women have also received wide acceptance. They persist despite the fact that there has never been *any* empirical, scientific substantiation of them. They were based on observations he made of his female patients. Observations of people who present themselves for therapy are not generalizable to normal, nonpatient populations. This is a basic scientific rule which Freud generally ignored.

The gravest distortion in Freud's theory of female psychology stems from his failure to separate two radically different phenomena, feminine biology and feminine status. By inferring that feminine status is the product of feminine biology, and therefore, inevitable rather than the social situation, he conveys the impression that woman's status is only what nature planned for her. Freud fails to fully consider that definitions of "masculine" and "feminine" are elaborate behavioral constructs originating from cultural norms. Instead, he equates such behavior with inherited innate qualities.

In Freud's defense, we must admit that later in life he confessed that he did not understand women (Freud, 1933a); however, his honest self-appraisal of his psychology of women has been conveniently overlooked by most of his followers.

Sociocultural Theories of Personality

NeoFreudians' Revision of Freud's Psychology of Women. Karen Horney and Clara Thompson are two outstanding examples of psychoanalysts who rejected Freud's biological explanations of feminine character in favor of sociocultural theory. They contended that the psychological attributes Freud observed in women were not due to women's biological inferiority but represented the outcome of cultural prejudices against women and their inferior social status. Penis envy, in their opinion, was merely symbolic of women's envy of male prerogatives and privileges in society. They questioned the innateness of such personality traits as passivity, masochism, and narcissism, preferring to explain the presence of these traits in women in terms of women's inferior social status, economic dependency on men and the social inhibition of sexual and aggressive behavior.

In discussing feminine masochism, Horney (1963) suggested that any culture which contained one or more of the following factors would predispose the appearance of masochism in women:

1. blocking of outlets in women for expansiveness and sexuality;
2. restriction in the number of children, especially when children are the measure of a woman's social and personal contribution;
3. an estimation of women as inferior to men;
4. economic dependence of women on men or on family;
5. restriction of women to spheres of life built chiefly upon emotional bonds such as family life, religion, or charity work; and
6. a surplus of marriageable women, particularly when marriage offers the principal opportunity for sexual gratification, children, security, and social recognition.

When some or all of these six elements are present in a culture, Horney believes that there may appear certain fixed ideologies concerning the "nature" of women. For example, woman is likely to be considered innately weak, emotional, dependent, and limited in capacities for independent work and autonomous thinking. Included in this category is the psychoananlytic belief that women are masochistic by nature. It is obvious, Horney says, that these ideologies about women function not only to reconcile women to their subordinate role by presenting it as an unalterable one, but also to plant the belief that it represents a fulfillment they crave, or an ideal for which it is commendable and desirable to strive. The influence that these ideologies exert on women is materially strengthened by the fact that women showing the specified traits are more frequently chosen by men.

In a similar vein, Thompson (1963) noted that women's alleged narcissism and greater need to be loved could be accounted for by economic necessity. Their primary security and social position came from establishing a permanent love relationship; love, in essence, became women's profession. Thompson also dismissed Freud's contention that women have weaker superegos due to the differential outcome of the Oedipus complex for boys and girls. As an alternative explanation she wrote:

> ... the character trait of having no strong beliefs or convictions is not found universally in women and it also occurs frequently in men in this culture ... It is an attitude typical of people whose security depends on the approval of some powerful person or group (1963, p. 77).

Concerning Freud's idea that women are more intellectually rigid and lose the capacity for intellectual and emotional growth earlier than men, Thompson postulated that lack of opportunity for continued personality development and dependency on sexuality for security reduced flexibility and diminished growth. In summarizing her observations of women,

Thompson concluded:

> I have pointed out that characteristics and inferiority feelings which
> Freud considered to be specifically female and biologically determined
> can be explained as developments arising in and growing out of Western
> woman's historic situation of underprivilege, restriction of development,
> insincere attitude toward the sexual nature, and social and economic
> dependence. The basic nature of woman is still unknown (1963, p. 84).

Horney's and Thompson's efforts to correct the sexist bias in Freud's
theory of women was a major contribution to the psychology of women,
but those efforts were limited by the confinement of their work within the
framework of psychoanalysis. Looking at the factors that contribute to
women's psychology in the context of social-psychological formulations
of prejudice against minority groups provides some additional understanding on this subject.

THE MINORITY STATUS OF WOMEN. As we have seen, Horney and
Thompson characterized women as victims of sexist oppression, devoid of
power in their personal lives as well as in the social structure, subjects of
prejudice and discrimination. In discussing women as a minority group,
Hacker distinguishes between two kinds of minority people: those who
are aware of their minority group status, and those who do not know they
are being discriminated against.

> No empirical study of the frequency of minority-group feelings among
> women has yet been made, but common observations would suggest
> that, consciously at least, few women believe themselves to be members
> of a minority group in the way in which some Negroes, Jews, Italians,
> etc., may so conceive themselves (Hacker, 1951, p. 61).

Women feel no minority-group consciousness; they harbor no resentment. Hacker observes that a group that has no minority-group consciousness cannot properly be said to belong to a minority group. She,
therefore, uses the term "minority group status" to apply to women. She
continues: "If it is conceded that women have a minority-group status,
what may be learned from applying to women various theoretical constructs in the field of intergroup relations?" (Hacker, 1953, p. 63)

One of the most authoritative writers on the subject of prejudice and
the effects of minority group status is Gordon Allport. He observed that
minority persons subject to discrimination developed certain characteristic ego defenses (Allport, 1954). (Allport also noted that not every
member of the group will develop every defense and that not all the ego
defenses adopted will be negative or unpleasant.) Carter (1974) demonstrated correspondence between ego defenses observed in minority groups
as described by Allport and ego defenses exhibited by women (Table 1-I.).

DENIAL OF MEMBERSHIP. Perhaps the simplest ego defense a victim can
make is to deny her/his membership in a disparaged group. This denial

comes easily for those who have no distinctive color, appearance, or accent and who do not feel any loyalty or attachments to their group. It is not possible for women to deny their sex-role membership. They may engage in partial denial by dropping from their behavior any qualities which are identified as "feminine." These are the women who feel rewarded when someone observes that they "think like a man" or who prefer the company of men to that of women.

Deliberate denials of one's membership are not always easy to distinguish from the normal adaptations that one must make to the practices of the dominant majority. Women who belong to the male-dominated profession may have no intention of discarding their alliances with women, but assimilation of the characteristics of their profession may be a type of denial.

WITHDRAWAL AND PASSIVITY. Freud regarded women's passivity as innate. Passive acquiescence is sometimes the only way in which minority group members can survive. By agreeing with one's adversaries, minority people avoid being conspicuous, and have no cause for fear. Women who develop a withdrawn and supine manner are often rewarded by men with protection. So well are women conditioned with this characteristic that they have much difficulty in expressing appropriate anger, even when they choose to. Note, for example, the felt need for assertion training in many women's groups.

Rebellion and aggression in minority people would certainly be met by punishment, and constant anxiety and anger could induce sufficient stress to cause mental illness. At best, aggressive, angry women are labeled as "deviant." Sometimes they are hospitalized.

SLYNESS AND CUNNING. The less powerful group is primarily concerned with survival. Direct, honest reactions to destructive treatment are avoided. For many minority people open action in their own self-interest could literally result in death. For women, open reaction may mean economic hardship, social ostracism, psychological isolation, and the diagnosis of neuroticism or personality disorder by psychotherapists. These threats to open interaction encourage sly, cunning, and manipulative behavior — a third kind of ego defense.

Minority group members resort to various disguised reactions; they "put on" the oppressor while appearing to please him. Jewish stories and various folk tales are full of such humorous examples. The television family situation comedies in which father is absurdly manipulated by mother is a continuation of such folk "wisdom."

Sneaky traits may also develop as a means of gaining petty revenge. The weaker undermines the stronger. It entails all sorts of pretense. One ingratiates oneself, flatters, gains favors, seduces and generally cheapens the ethics of human relations in the interests of both survival and revenge.

IDENTIFICATION WITH THE DOMINANT GROUP: SELF-HATE. A more subtle mechanism is involved in cases where the victim instead of pretending to agree with her/his "betters," actually does agree with them, and sees her/his own group through their eyes. This is the almost classical case with women. This is a mysterious phenomenon because women are hopelessly barred from total assimulation and yet they mentally identify with the outlook and prejudices of the male culture toward women. An example of this is a study by Goldberg (1968). Goldberg investigated prejudice among women toward women in the area of intellectual and professional competence. The results confirmed the hypothesis that college women value the professional work of men more highly than the identical work of women.

Another study in a different area demonstrates the same phenomenon among women. Rosenkrantz, Vogel, Bee, Broverman, and Broverman (1968) asked college students to rate the typical adult female and male on 122 bipolar adjectives. The results indicated that the traits attributed to males by both sexes were the most socially desirable. Furthermore, the women described themselves as high on feminine traits which were not socially desirable, and low on masculine but socially desirable traits such as independent, objective, logical, direct, self-confident, and ambitious.

Both test studies indicate that women identify with the prejudices toward women of the male culture and accept their inferior state as natural. The primary reason for women's acceptance of their "inferiority" is that, in our western culture, we believe in the doctrine of individual responsibility. It is the individual who shapes her/his world, or so we believe. When things go wrong, the individual is to blame. Hence, women are ashamed of their lack of assertion, their dependence, their readiness to tears, and their ignorance in financial and political matters.

SUMMARY OF EGO DEFENSES. Let us consider a summary of ego defenses among victims of discrimination. Charted on Table 1-I this information is adapted from Allport's *The Nature of Prejudice* (1954, p. 157). The boldface type is directly from Allport. The lower case is our addition and represents the defensive behaviors of victimized women. The left-hand column contains ego defenses displayed by intropunitive individuals (anger turned inward). The middle- and right-hand columns contain ego defenses of extropunitive individuals (anger turned outward).

Except for manipulation, narcissism, and competitiveness (middle column), the defensive behaviors of traditional women are intropunitive. The defensive behaviors of feminist women are extropunitive. When the defensive behaviors of women are compared with the defensive behaviors of other discriminated groups, it is clear that these female behaviors are not innate or biologically fixed as myth or professional and popular

TABLE 1 - I

TYPES OF EGO DEFENSES AMONG VICTIMS OF DISCRIMINATION*

INTROPUNITIVE INDIVIDUALS Traditional Women	EXTROPUNITIVE INDIVIDUALS Traditional Women	EXTROPUNITIVE INDIVIDUALS Feminist Women
DENIAL OF MEMBERSHIP IN OWN GROUP	SLYNESS AND CUNNING	OBSESSIVE CONCERN AND SUSPICION
Deriving pleasure from "thinking like a man"	Manipulation of men	Hypersensitivity to sexist remarks
Preferring the company of men	NEUROTICISM	STRENGTHENING IN-GROUP TIES
WITHDRAWAL AND PASSIVITY	Narcissism	Consciousness-raising groups
Indecision	COMPETITIVENESS	Support groups
Misdirected anger to persons of less power	Put men down, either directly or indirectly ("castrating female")	Campus and community women's centers
Difficulty in expressing anger	Derive satisfaction only from competing with men	Financial and professional and self-help collectives
Avoidance of conflict		Cooperative political action
CLOWNING		PREJUDICE AGAINST OTHER GROUPS
Giggling		Anger towards men
Being coy and cute		
Humorous self-depreciation		

SELF-HATE

Acceptance of own "natural inferiority"

Building a man's egos, especially at a woman's own expense

Assuming the door-mat posture with men

Chronic depression

IN-GROUP AGGRESSION

Competitive with other women

Back-biting and gossiping

Putting down other women

SYMPATHY WITH ALL VICTIMS

Sentimentality

Volunteer and charity work

SYMBOLIC STATUS STRIVING

Expensive house, beautiful clothes, professional husband and his financial success, well-behaved children and their accomplishments

NEUROTICISM

Helplessness, phobias, and hysteria

AGGRESSION AND REVOLT

Divorce

Individual and class action law suits against employers

Radical feminism

COMPETITIVENESS

Compete for the prize, not to put down men or other women

ENHANCED STRIVING

Striving for better jobs, for better salaries, and for higher academic degrees

*Adapted from Gordon Allport, *The Nature of Prejudice*, 1954, p. 157.

literature conclude; they are the result of women's oppression and their minority status.

DIFFERENCES BETWEEN SELF-IDENTIFIED MINORITY PERSONS AND WOMEN. Because women are discriminated against on the basis of their sex rather than because of their ethnic or racial origin, they must cope with additional disadvantages to which other discriminated people are not subjected.

1. Women actually live with their oppressors. This is true of no other minority group except slaves. The point of view a woman hears expressed most frequently is that of the dominant group and so that point of view becomes her reality. In this situation, the most likely ego defense she would develop is identification with the dominant group and self-hate.

2. Women have no in-group ties with their own kind. There are no female ghettos. This physical isolation prevents them from knowing that many women feel unhappy about similar things; each blames herself for her own unhappiness. Most important, it prevents women from giving one another support for any changes they wish to make. Few people (who lack support from at least one other person) can act in opposition to the *status quo* without feeling alienated and a little crazy.

3. Women must compete for men against their own kind for economic and social survival. The result is that they regard all other women, at best, with suspicion and, usually, as an enemy. Competition reinforces the physical barriers between women with psychological isolation.

4. Sex is a woman's most valuable asset. Since it is her most potent bargaining power, she must use it manipulatively. For her own social and economic survival, she cannot afford to allow her sexual behavior to be guided by her emotional responses.

5. The treatment women receive from men is not usually overtly abusive. On the contrary, sometimes they receive special privileges. The receipt of special privileges fosters a false consciousness in women and coopts their feelings of anger and resentment. Acting in terms of their *subjective* best interests is not always in their *objective* best interests.

IMPLICATIONS OF PERSONALITY THEORIES FOR THE TREATMENT OF WOMEN. Whether a therapist believes in a Freudian-derived theory of personality with a biological basis or in a sociocultural theory of personality has tremendous implications for the treatment of women. Freudians and biological determinists consider the inferiority of women as innate and appropriate. They view women who do not express inferiority or submissiveness to men as needing assistance in working through an acceptance of their "femininity" (femininity, in this case, meaning a subordinate position to men). In contrast, therapists accepting a sociocultural theory of personality would view women's display of inferiority, not as innate, but socially caused and correctable. Their therapeutic goals would be to enable women to develop their human potential, not merely their feminine potential, and to encourage them to assume a personal and political stance equal to men.

Models of Psychopathology

The mental illness model of psychopathology is comprised of biologically based theories which lead to a search for causes of pathology within a person. This model evokes images of scientific objectivity and neutrality which obscure the value implications of psychotherapists' ministrations. The environmental model consists of socially based theories which lead to a search for sources of pathology within the environment. These favor a "problems in living" approach (Szasz, 1960). The environmental model clearly labels psychotherapy as an activity which imposes ethical and political choices. Halleck observed that no theory of psychotherapy is ethically or politically neutral:

> ... by the very nature of his practice, the psychiatrist consistently takes positions on issues that involve the distribution of power within social systems — issues that have political implications ... The psychiatrist either encourages the patient to accept existing distributions of power or encourages the patient to change them. Every encounter with any psychotherapist, therefore, has political implications (Halleck, 1971, p. 32).

Mental Illness Model

The term "mental illness" produces a misleading parallel between individual unhappiness or socially deviant behavior and a physical disease that has an etiology of neurological and/or chemical imbalances. The use of the term confuses behavior disorders which have a physical etiology, e.g. syphillis with those that involve no demonstrable organic basic, e.g. neurosis or character disorder. The logic underlying the parallel is faulty and circular. Initially used to describe behavior that was personally or socially disruptive, "mental illness" has gradually become reified into a thing or object. It is now used to explain the very phenomena it was coined to describe: "X's suspiciousness is paranoid (sick) behavior; the reason X's behavior is suspicious is because he is paranoid (sick)."

The term "mental illness" forces one's thinking about behavior problems into a medical analogue. A medical analogue implies a medical cure, but aside from prescribing psychotropic drugs, very little of the activity that psychotherapists engage in could be considered medical practice.

Finally, the most serious objection to the term is that its use obscures the moral conflicts of socially deviant and undesirable behavior inherent in the social context. Without attention to the social context, psychotherapy legitimizes and reinforces the existing power structure, psychotherapists become the agents of social control. Politically alert groups have made similar observations. Hence, Brown, a radical therapist, describes the implications of the medical model:

> ... psychotherapy, as the new star chamber, has been utilized in this country more than anywhere in the interests of social control ... [everyone is crazy, and the cause is in their heads rather than in the environment (1973, p. 450)].

Psychotherapists who subscribe to the medical model by encouraging women to think of their anger and unhappiness as an emotional illness exert social control over women. Brown concurs that the implications of the medical model of psychopathology are particularly dangerous for women:

> ... in order to keep them [women] tied to socially determined roles, they bear the brunt of psychopathological classification — not only in terms of being more relatively diagnosed (and mistreated) as "mentally ill," but also in terms of special illnesses being invented just for them; e.g. puerperal (childbirth) and menopausal neurosis and psychosis (1973, p. 450.)

Implications of Models of Psychopathology for the Treatment of Women

The mental-illness model personalizes social problems. Clients are seen as victims of their internal impulses which they should learn to master through psychotherapy, or perhaps through a somatotherapy, for example, drugs. Women's rebellion against restrictive and stultifying roles is dismissed by medical-model adherents. They label the rebellion as a projection of women's personal inadequacies and further proof of illness. Thus, psychoanalyst Marynia Farnham passed the following judgment of *feminism*:

> This ideology, to come directly to the point, we regard as expression of emotional sickness, of neurosis ... Feminism ... was at its core a deep illness (Lundberg and Farnham, 1947, p. 143).

Lundberg and Farnham accused feminists of inducing vast individual suffering in women and men and for creating public disorder. Not only feminists, but even nonfeminist, discontented women, in the opinion of these authors, share in causing disastrous consequences for the new generation.

The insidious result of labelling women's misery and/or revolt as "mental illness" is to lay the blame for society's ills on women's shoulders. Women thus become societal scapegoats; this allows the roots of their oppression and social disorganization to remain unexamined.

The environmental model politicalizes personal problems. Viewing personal problems as the result of social problems does not, as some fear, foster or excuse apathy or irresponsibility in the client. The purpose of psychotherapy based on the environmental model is "to enable the individual to function as a responsible actor rather than a powerless victim" (Bart, 1971, p. 126).

Radical therapists insist that the professional responsibilities of therapists go beyond their responsibilities to individual clients; therapists also have a responsibility to use their positions of power and expertise to make society aware of the social etiology of personal problems and to participate in political and social action to create a society which promotes, rather than stifles, the growth of women and other minority persons as whole human beings (see Adams and Durham, Chapter 22, and Epilogue).

Models of Mental Health

The public expects that mental health professionals who claim to know when someone needs psychotherapy or hospitalization for mental illness have rather explicit notions of what constitutes mental health. Actually, this assumption is false. Ehrlich and Abraham-Magdamo quote the definition of mental health of the American Psychiatric Association:

> A state of being rather than absolute, in which a person has effected a reasonably satisfactory integration of his instinctual drives. His integration is acceptable to himself and to his social milieu as reflected in his interpersonal relationships, his actual achievement, his flexibility, and the level of maturity he has attained (1974, pp. 65-66).

Ehrlich and Abraham-Magdamo criticize that definition given by the APA for apparently applying only to men, for using unscientific concepts such as "instinctual drives," for employing vague undefined terms such as "maturity" and "flexibility" whose meaning would vary from one psychiatrist to another and, finally, for heavily emphasizing social adjustment. The APA emphasis on social adjustment is confusing since it contradicts the mental illness model. The mental illness model is based on absolute rather than relativistic criteria; pathology is presumably located in organ-system dysfunction, and, thus, should not depend on the social setting or the cultural system.

It is relevant to our purpose here to examine three models of mental health which have generated considerable controversy with respect to the treatment women receive in psychotherapy. We have labelled these models: (1) the normative, (2) the androcentric, and (3) the androgynous.

Normative Model

The normative model of mental health is widely accepted by the general public. This model defines mental health as behavior in accordance with the values and role prescription of society, particularly sex-role prescription.

Since cultural role prescriptions and values are different for women and men, the normative model implies a double standard of mental health. That a double standard of mental health for the sexes exists can be demonstrated by examining the counseling readiness scale which is a subscale of the Adjective Check List (ACL) (Gough and Heilbrun, 1965), a frequently used personality measure. The ACL is empirically derived and lists sex separately. The adjectives on the *Positive* list are a composite self-description of people who were responsive to counseling, or who saw themselves in need of counseling. The adjectives on the *Negative* list are a composite self-description of people who were not responsive to counseling, or who did not see themselves in need of counseling (Heilbrun and Sullivan, 1962).

The women who said they needed counseling described themselves as aggressive, assertive, autocratic, bossy, coy, cynical, dignified, discrete, effeminate, enterprising, formal, independent, individualistic, inhibited, intelligent, moody, noisy, opportunistic, painstaking, rigid, self-centered, serious, soft-hearted, stingy, tense, thorough, unaffected, unemotional, and unrealistic.* Look at a few adjectives whose appearance on the *Positive* list are noteworthy: assertive, dignified, discrete, enterprising, formal, independent, individualistic, intelligent, serious, and thorough. These adjectives do not immediatley strike one as unhealthy characteristics. Rather, they appear to describe a person who behaves as if she considered herself equal in status to anyone. Such a woman however, would *not* fit the cultural sex-role stereotype for women. Failing to fit societal expectations, such a woman apparently does not perceive herself to be emotionally sound (Carter, 1974).

Understanding of the effect of women on societal expectations becomes complete when we look at the self-description of women who did *not* see themselves needing therapy. This is the *Negative* list: energetic, honest, jolly, patient, peaceable, slow, sociable, suggestive, trusting, wholesome. Except for the first two items, energetic and honest, the rest of the items

---

*For a listing of the male as well as the female adjectives, see Chapter 17.

suggest a person with rather childlike qualities: jolly, patient, peaceable, slow, sociable, suggestible, trusting and wholesome. That this is a healthy way for an adult female to describe herself is debatable; it does fit the sex role for women.

If a woman decides to enter therapy, most likely her therapist will agree with the standards of mental health portrayed in the ACL Counseling Readiness Scale. The widely quoted study of Broverman and associates (1970) provides evidence that most psychotherapists also operate on a double standard of mental health for men and women. Broverman and her associates sent a 122-item questionnaire to seventy-nine actively functioning clinicians (33 women and 46 men) with one of three sets of instructions: describe a healthy, mature, socially competent (a) adult, sex unspecified, (b) man, or (c) woman. It was hypothesized that clinical judgments about the characteristics of healthy individuals would differ as a function of the sex of the person judged. A second hypothesis predicted that behaviors judged healthy for an adult, sex unspecified, which are presumed to reflect an ideal standard of health, would resemble behaviors judged healthy for men, but differ from behaviors judged healthy for women.

Both hypotheses were confirmed. The clinicians judged healthy women differently from healthy men by saying they were more submissive, less independent, less adventurous, more easily influenced, less aggressive, less competitive, more excitable in minor crisis, having their feelings more easily hurt, being more emotional, more conceited about their appearance, and less objective. As the investigators pointed out, this constellation seems a most unusual way of describing *any* mature, healthy individual. These results confirm the hypothesis that for psychotherapists a double standard of health exists for men and women; that is, the general standard of health is actually applied only to men, while healthy women are perceived by therapists as significantly less healthy by adult standards.

Broverman et al. suggested that the origin of the double standard of mental health lay in the clinicians acceptance of an "adjustment" notion of mental health. According to the adjustment viewpoint, a woman must conform to the behavioral norms for her sex even though they are less socially desirable and less healthy by generalized adult standards. For many therapists the client's adequate sexual identity, i.e. conforming to the cultural feminine sex role, is the *sine qua non* of mental health. As Keller observed, "treatment is less geared to challenging cultural definitions of mental health than to improving women's capacity to live up to them!" (1974, p. 414)

In discussing the close correspondence between therapists' notions of healthy male and healthy adult traits, Broverman et al. drew the following implications for women:

> Acceptance of an adjustment notion of health, then, places women in the conflictual position of having to decide whether to exhibit those positive characteristics considered desirable for men and adults, and thus have their "femininity" questioned, that is, be deviant in terms of being a woman; or to behave in the prescribed feminine manner, accept second-class adult status, and possibly live a lie to boot (1970, p. 6).

Androcentric Model

The androcentric or male-centered model, implicit in the above Broverman statement, is a single standard of mental health for both sexes, the male standard. Most psychotherapists consider women who exhibit masculine traits as neurotic. Evidence exists, however, that having the traits of a healthy man are beneficial for women, particularly women in pursuit of a career and that such women are not emotionally disturbed. Career women higher in masculine traits are the ones most likely to succeed professionally (Block, 1973).

Stewart and Winter (1974) studied a group of career-oriented college women whom they described as "self-defining." (In the opinion of the investigators these women were personally well-adjusted with no evidence of neurosis.) These self-defining women resembled males in the (TAT) fantasy stories they constructed. Their fantasies were organized around themes of action and causality and contained characters who determined their own fate. (Traditional, marriage-oriented, other-defining women told stories expressing much feeling but little action.) Displaying another trait characteristic of males, the self-defining women were most ashamed of their feelings of weakness and vulnerability. (Traditional women were ashamed of their feelings of hostility.) The authors concluded that both the self-defining women and the traditional women were clinging to rigid sex-role stereotypes; however, in the cases of self-defining women the stereotype they clung to was primarily masculine.

Feminists by and large reject the androcentric model. They resent the bias in society that interprets masculine associated activities and traits as superior and denigrates whatever is feminine. Feminists do not view acquiring male-associated traits and behaviors and curtailing female-associated behaviors as leading to enhanced mental health in women or men. In reviewing the Broverman et al. (1970) criteria for a healthy adult, Silveria portrays one dimension of the feminist point of view of healthy behavior when she asks:

> Where is the ability to interact positively with others? Where is gentleness, love, awareness of others, the ability to express feelings, empathy? ... I *am* saying that a major version of mental health, advanced by

psychology for years reveals a lack of understanding of what makes for a full and human life (1973, p. 102).

The Androgyny Model

The association of certain human traits with particular sex roles has produced a psychological *set*, i.e. a predisposition to view human behavior in a constricted way. As Adler (1963) noted, since the culture only admits two possible sex roles, rejection of one leads the individual to act in the opposite manner (sex-role reversal). Only recently have we seriously considered alternative roles for people that are neither masculine or feminine. Continuing to think of traits in terms of the masculine-feminine dichotomy perpetuates the old *set*. Conceptualizing trait constellation other than the usual constellation of masculine and feminine, Block (1973) employs Bakan's concepts of *agency* and *communion*. Bakan asserts that the concepts *agency* and *communion* contain characteristics of all living forms. Block defines Bakan's concepts as follows:

> Agency ... manifests itself in self-protection, self-assertion, and self-expansion. Communion ... manifests itself in the being at one with other organisms (1973, p. 515).

Adjectives that reflect agency include: adventurous, self-confident, assertive, dominating, restless, ambitious, self-centered, shrewd, and competitive. Adjectives reflecting communion include: sympathetic, responsive, idealistic, loving, generous, artistic, and considerate. The overlap between agency and the masculine mode and communion and the feminine mode is apparent. Bakan's major contribution is that he defined the major developmental task of an organism as integrating and balancing agency with communion. The androgyny model depicts an integration and balance of feminine and masculine. From the standpoint of other models of optimal behavior — humanistic, self-actualization, and ego maturity — there are definite benefits to be derived from the androgyny model. Evidence of these benefits is summarized below:

1. *Moral judgment.* Greater maturity as measured on the Kohlberg's Moral Judgment Test was "accompanied by more androgynous, less sex-typed definitions of self" (Block, 1973). This was true for both females and males, but the effect was greatest for males.

2. *Ego maturity.* Women scoring at higher levels of ego maturity on the Loevinger Sentence Completion method were more balanced with respect to agentic and communion concerns (Block, 1973).

3. *Cognitive functioning.* Optimal cognitive functioning in children of both sexes depends on an optimal balance between feminine-active and masculine-passive orientation (Maccoby, 1966).

4. *Creativity.* In both sexes, greater creativity depends on a balance of masculine and feminine traits (Hammer, 1964 & Helson, 1966).

5. *Sex-role adaptability.* Androgynous males and females showed appropriate "masculine" behavior in resisting pressure to conform and appropriate "feminine" behavior in playing with a kitten. Nonandrogynous persons, particularly feminine females, exhibited some sort of behavior deficits (Bem, 1975).

On the basis of research evidence, Block (1975) concluded that the current socialization process has a differential outcome for females and males. Contemporary social values increase experiential options for males and encourage more androgynous behavior among them since some feminine concerns are emphasized, e.g. conscientiousness, while there is pressure to give up some of the negative aspects of the masculine role, e.g. self-centeredness. In the socialization of women, however, traditional feminine values continue to be stressed and masculine values discouraged. Block reminds the reader of costs of sex role specialization and points out the value of androgyny:

> If our social aim can become both collectively and individually, the integration of agency and communion, the behavioral and experiential options of men and women alike will be broadened and enriched and we all can become more truly whole, more truly human (Block, 1973, p. 526).

Implications of Models of Mental Health for the Treatment of Women

What we choose to believe about the nature of (wo)man has social consequences. Models of psychopathology indicate what the therapeutic treatment will be; models of mental health indicate what the therapeutic goal will be. If a therapist values the institution of masculinity-femininity with all its associate behavioral prescriptions, then the goal of therapy will be to enable a woman to adjust to those behaviors prescribed by her sex role. If a therapist has been able to give up institutionalized sexism, this is a cause for celebration among feminists. Frequently overlooked, however, is the nature of the replacement. For many people there is a growing appreciation for strong women. Strong women are admired and reinforced for their decisiveness, straight thinking, confrontation style, political and professional success, in short, for all the characteristics for which men have always been admired. Therapists with this point of view hold the androcentric model of mental health. Their therapeutic goal for women would be to develop strength and eradicate soft "womanliness."

The women's movement had been underway for several years before some feminists realized that what institutional sexism was being replaced

with, the androcentric model, was not much better than what it was
replacing.* These feminist were able to overcome constricted thinking
about behavior based on only what was valued in the male-dominated
culture, and concluded that the best of all possible worlds would be one
in which women and men possessed the best of both male-associated and
female-associated characteristics. It was this thinking that prepared the
way and formed the basis of the androgyny model of mental health.
Therapists who adhere to this model would have as treatment goals the
ability of their women clients to feel and express both very tender, soft,
gentle emotions as well as angry, assertive, decisive, behaviors — an
integration and balance of female-associated and male-associated characteristics.

SUMMARY

The central theme of this chapter is that much of therapy is changing
clients' values. Clients' values become more similar to the therapist's
values. Therapist's values and personality conflicts regarding women
affect the adequacy of their therapy. Male therapists who are conservative,
dogmatic, and authoritarian would have difficulty achieving rapport and
would be minimally self-disclosing to a strong female client. Male therapists with traditional notions of masculinity who are unsure about the
usefulness of their work would also be threatened by competent female
clients. Therapists who take a biological-deterministic view of sex-role
behaviors are likely to label intelligent, assertive women as frustrated,
aggressive (castrating), and neurotic. Similarly, some women therapists
have conflicts regarding other women and value them negatively. They
think either that women really are inferior or that women are not motivated to succeed. Treatment by any of these groups would be more
harmful to women than no treatment at all.

Freudians and biological determinists view the inferiority of women as
innate and appropriate. Treatment of women by these therapists would
be to assist their working through an acceptance of their femininity, that
is, their subordinate position to men. In contrast, social-cultural therapists do not view women's display of inferiority as innate but socially
caused and correctable. Treatment would focus on correcting this inferiority and enabling women to develop their human as well as their feminine potential.

Therapists who hold to the mental illness model personalize social
problems. They label women's rebellion as a projection of their personal

---

*Cultural feminists eulogize feminine traits and offer a matriarchal model of mental health for
women. [See Mander, Chapter 15, and Bardwick (1957)] This viewpoint has not had widespread
acceptance among feminists (Deckard, 1975).

inadequacies and further proof of illness. In contrast, the environmental therapists politicalize women's personal problems. The purpose is to "enable the individual to function as a responsible actor rather than as a powerless victim" (Bart, 1971, p. 126). Radical therapists insist that as professionals, therapists have social responsibilities: to use their power and expertise to make society aware of the social etiology of personal problems and to participate in social and political action to create a society which promotes the growth of women and other minority groups.

We have identified three models of mental health: the normative, the androcentric, and the androgynous. The normative model is the one widely accepted by the general public. This model defines mental health as behavior in accordance with the values and role prescription of society, particularly sex-role prescription. This model carries a double standard of mental health for males and females. The androcentric model is a single standard of mental health, the male standard. Feminists, by and large, reject the androcentric model. Feminists believe that the best of all worlds would be one in which men and women possessed the best of both female-associated and male-associated characteristics. This is the androgynous model.

REFERENCES

Adler, Alfred: Sex. In Miller, Jean Baker (Ed.): *Psychoanalysis and Women*. Baltimore, Penguin, 1963.

Allport, Gordon, W.: *The Nature of Prejudice*. Garden City, Doubleday Anchor Edition, 1958.

Bardwick, Judith M.: Future directions of the movement. Paper presented at American Psychological Association, Chicago, September, 1975.

Bardwick, Judith M.: Women's liberation: nice idea, but it won't be easy. *Psychology Today, 6*:26, 1973.

Bart, Pauline, B.: The myth of a value-free psychotherapy. In Bell, Wendell and Mau, James A. (Eds.): *The Sociology of the Future*. New York, Russell Sage Foundation, 1971, pp. 113-159.

Bem, Sandra L.: Sex-role adaptability: one consequence of psychological androgyny. *Journal of Personality and Social Psychology, 31*:634, 1975.

Bird, Caroline: *Born Female*. New York, Pocket, 1969.

Block, Jeanne H.: Conceptions of sex role: some cross-cultural and longitudinal perspectives. *American Psychologist 28*:512, 1973.

Brenton, M.: *The American Male*. London, George Allen and Unwin LTD, 1966.

Broverman, Inge K., Broverman, Donald M., Rosenkrantz, Paul S., and Vogel, Susan R.: Sex-role stereotypes and clinical judgments of mental health. *Journal of Consulting and Clinical Psychology, 34*:1, 1970.

Brown, Phil: Male supremacy in Freud. In Brown, Phil (Ed.): *Radical Psychology*. New York, Harper & Row, 1973.

Bruner, Jerome: Personality dynamics and the process of perceiving. In Blake, R. N. and Ramsey, G. V. (Eds.): *Perception: An Approach To Personality*. New York, Ronald, 1951, pp. 121-147.

Carter, Dianne K.: Ego defenses of women: consequences of minority status. Keynote address presented at the University of Tennessee conference, Innovations in Counseling Women, November, 1974.

Chesler, Phyllis: Patient and patriarch: women in the psychotherapeutic relationship. In Gornick, Vivian and Moran, Barbara K. (Eds.): *Women in Sexist Society.* New York, Signet, 1972. (a)

Chesler, Phyllis: *Women and Madness.* New York, Doubleday, 1972. (b)

Cutler, Richard L.: Countertransference effects in psychotherapy. *Journal of Consulting Psychology, 22:*349, 1958.

Daly, E. J. : Projected sex blame and religiosity in college men. *Dissertation Abstracts, 29*(9-B)3480, 1969.

Deckard, Barbara S.: *The Women's Movement: Political, Socioeconomic, and Psychological Issues.* New York, Harper & Row, 1975.

Dempewolff, J.: Feminism and its correlates. *Dissertation Abstracts International, 33B:*3113, 1973.

Dufresne, M. J.: Differential reactions of males to three different female sex roles. *Dissertation Abstracts International, 32B:*6642, 1972.

Ehrlich, Annette and Abraham-Magdam, Fred: Caution: mental health may be hazardous. *Human Behavior, 3:*64, 1974.

Ellis, L. J. and Bentler, P. M.: Traditional sex-determined role standards and sex stereotypes. *Personality and Social Psychology, 25:*28, 1973.

Erikson, Erik H.: Inner and outer space: reflections on womanhood. In Lifton, Robert Jay (Ed): *The Woman in America.* Boston, Beacon, 1967.

Freud, Sigmund: *New Introductory Lectures on Psychoanalysis.* Sprott, W. J. H., translator. New York, Norton, 1933. (a)

Freud, Sigmund: Femininity. In Sprott, W. J. H.'s translation: *The Psychology of Women,* 1933. (b)
Also in Jones, Ernest (Ed.): *The Collected Papers of Sigmund Freud.* New York, Basic, 1959, Vol. V.

Freud, Sigmund: Some psychological consequences of the anatomical distinctions between the sexes, 1925.
Also in Jones, Ernest (Ed.): *The Collected Papers of Sigmund Freud.* New York, Basic, 1959, Vol. V.

Freud, Sigmund: "Civilized" sexual morality and modern nervousnous, 1908. Also in Jones, Ernest (Ed.): *The Collected Papers of Sigmund Freud.* New York, Basic, 1959, Vol. II.

Goldberg, Philip A.: Are women prejudiced against women? *Transaction.* April:28-30, 1968.

Gough, Harrison G. and Heilbrun, Alfred B. Jr.: *The Adjective Check List Manual.* Palo Alto, Consulting Psychologists, 1965.

Hacker, Helen M.: Women as a minority group. *Social Forces, 30:*60, 1951.

Halleck, Seymour: Therapy is the handmaiden of the status quo. *Psychology Today, 4:*30, 1971.

Hammer, E.: Creativity and feminine ingredients in young male artists. *Perceptual and Motor Skills, 19:*414, 1964.

Heilbrun, Alfred B. Jr. and Sullivan, Donald J.: The prediction of counseling readiness. *Personnel and Guidance Journal, 41:*112, 1962.

Helson, Ravanna: Personality of women with imaginative and artistic interests; the role of masculinity, orginality, and other characteristics in their creativity. *Journal of*

Personality, 34:1, 1966.

Horney, Karen: The problem of feminine masochism. In Miller, Jean Baker (Ed.): *Psychoanalysis and Women*. Baltimore, Penguin, 1963, pp. 21-38.

Johnson, Ronald W. and MacDonnell, Joan: The relationship between conformity and male and female attitudes toward women. *Journal of Social Psychology, 94*:155, 1974.

Kanin, E.: Sexually aggressive college males. *The Journal of College Student Personnel, 12*:107, 1971.

Keller, Suzanne: The female role: constants and change. In Franks, Violet and Burtle, Vasant (Eds.): *Women in Therapy*. New York, Brunner/Mazel, 1974.

London, Perry: *The Modes and Morals of Psychotherapy*. New York, Holt, Rinehart & Winston, 1964.

Lundberg, Ferdinand and Farnham, Marynia: *Modern Women: The Lost Sex*. New York, The Universal Library, 1947.

Maccoby, Eleanor E.: *The Development of Sex Differences*. Stanford, Stanford University, 1966.

Miller, T. E.: Male attitudes towards women's rights as a function of their level of self-esteem. Paper presented at the meeting of the American Psychological Association, Honolulu, September, 1972.

Mosher, D. L.: Sex callousness toward women. U. S. Commission On Obscenity and Pornography, pp. 313-325 (undated).

Pepinsky, H. B. and Karst, Thomas O.: Convergence: A phenomenon in counseling and in psychotherapy. *American Psychologist, 19*:333, 1964.

Rokeach, Milton: *The Nature of Human Values*. New York, Free Press, 1973.

Rosenkrantz, Paul S., Vogel, Susan R., Bee, Helen, Broverman, Inge K., and Broverman, Donald M.: Sex-role stereotypes and self-concepts in college sutdents. *Journal of Consulting and Clinical Psychology, 32*:287, 1968.

Rosenthal, David: Changes in some moral values following psychotherapy. *Journal of Consulting Psychology, 19*:431, 1955.

Shields, Stephanie A.: Functionalism, Darwinism, and the psychology of women: a study in social myth. *The American Psychologist, 30*:739, 1975.

Silveira, Jeanette: Male bias in psychology. In Leppaluouto, Jean R., Acker, Joan, Naffziger, Claudeen, Brown, Karla J. H., Porter, Catherine M., Mitchell, Barbara A. and Hanna, Roberta (Eds.): *Women on the Move: Feminist Perspective*. Eugene, Oregon, University of Oregon, 1973, pp. 95-110.

Staines, Graham, Tavris, Carol and Jayaratne, Toby E.: The queen bee syndrome. *Psychology Today, 1*:55, 1974.

Stewart, Abigail J. and Winter, David G.: Self-definition and social definition in women. *Journal of Personality, 42*:238, 1974.

Szasz, Thomas S.: The myth of mental illness. *American Psychologist, 15*:113, 1960.

Tavris, Carol: Who likes women's liberation and why; the case of the unliberated liberals. *Journal of Social Issues, 29*:175, 1973.

Thompson, Clara: Cultural pressures in the psychology of women. In Miller, Jean Baker (Ed.): *Psychoanalysis and Women*. Baltimore, Penguin, 1963.

Vavrik, Julie and Jurich, Anthony P.: Self-concept and attitude toward acceptance of females; a note. *The Family Coordinator, 20*:151, 1971.

Worell, J.: Supporters and opposers of women's liberation: some personality correlates. Paper presented at the meeting of the American Psychological Association, Washington, D. C., September, 1971.

Chapter 2

UNILATERAL AND RECIPROCAL INFLUENCE IN PSYCHOTHERAPY

Argyris documented the differences between theories which people espouse, i.e. theories which people *say* they use and theories which people use, i.e. theories inferred from how people *actually* behave. He then formulated a general theoretical model which accounted for the behaviors in which people actually engage. He called this model *theories-in-use* or Model 1. Data for the formation of Argyris's theories-in-use model was taken from video- or audiotapes and other instruments that collect directly observable behavior.

To confirm his formulation of Model 1, Argyris (1975) examined research conducted by experimental social psychologists whose primary purpose was to describe the world as it is. He found Model 1 to be congruent with the models of persons and society described by those researchers. In addition, Argyris also found that:

> The experimental method . . . represents a technical theory of action that is also congruent with Model 1. . . . The result is the production of generalizations, which when they are translated into statements about effective action become statements that remain within the constraints of and reinforce a Model 1 world (1975, p. 481).

The researchers whose methods Argyris investigated did not question their approach and, therefore, did not discover other possibilities in human nature.

In Model 1 the influencing agent exercised *unilateral control*. (See Table 2-I for summary of Model 1.) The governing variables for the model are as follows: achieve the purpose or goal as the agent defines it; win, do not lose; suppress negative feelings and emphasize rationally. Model 1 reduces free choice by reducing information. The person being influenced is not given valid feedback by the agent. At the same time the agent discourages responses from the influenced person which would confront the agent's actions. The hypotheses generated by the agent become self-sealing, self-fulfilling prophecies. Argyris called this *single-loop learning*. Whatever learning situation the agent develops will be within the confines of what is acceptable within her/his model. The agent can judge her/his success within the model but has no means to objectively evaluate the values implicit in the situation. The thesis of this chapter is that there are differences between psychotherapists' espoused

TABLE 2 - I

MODEL I*

Governing variables	Action strategies	Consequences for the behavioral world	Consequences for learning	Effectiveness
1. Define goals and try to achieve them.	1. Design and manage the environment unilaterally (be persuasive, appeal to larger goals).	1. Actor seen as defensive, inconsistent, incongruent, competitive, controlling, fearful of being vulnerable, manipulative, withholding of feelings, overly concerned about self and others or underconcerned about others.	1. Self-sealing	
2. Maximize winning and minimize losing.	2. Own and control the task (claim ownership of the task, be guardian of definition and execution of task).	2. Defensive interpersonal and group relationship (dependence upon actor, little additivity, little helping others).	2. Single-loop learning.	Decreased Effectiveness.

Governing variables	Action strategies	Consequences for the behavioral world	Consequences for learning	Effectiveness
3. Minimize generating or expressing negative feelings.	3. Unilaterally protect yourself (speak with inferred categories accompanied by little or no directly observable behavior, be blind to impact on others and to the incongruity between rhetoric and behavior, reduce incongruity by defensive actions such as blaming, stereotyping, suppressing feelings, intellectualizing).	3. Defensive norms (mistrust, lack of risk-taking, conformity, external commitment, emphasis on diplomacy, power-centered competition, and rivalry).	3. Little testing of theories publicly. Much testing of theories privately.	
4. Be rational.	4. Unilaterally protect others from being hurt (withhold information, create rules to censor information and behavior, hold private meetings).	4. Low freedom of choice, internal commitment, and risk-taking.		

*Table reproduced from *Theory in Practice: Increasing Professional Effectiveness*, by Chris Argyris and Donald A. Schön, San Francisco: Jossey-Bass, 1975, pp. 68-69. Used with permission of Jossey - Bass, Chris Argyris and Donald A. Schön.

theories of psychotherapy and therapy as actually practiced, and that therapy as actually practiced parallels Argyris' Model 1.

There are many schools of psychotherapy. Harper (1974) describes thirty-six and his list is not exhaustive. Each school gives the client a new perspective from which to understand her/his distress and also suggests a remedy. For example, Freudians will explain the client's problems in light of childhood trauma or unresolved Oedipal complexes; cure will necessarily involve working through transference of childhood authority figures with the therapist. Mowrer's integrity theory explains the client's suffering as guilt due to "sin." The cure is confession and atonement to reintegrate the client with her/his community. Each school of psychotherapy claims to have the most effective techniques; claims are primarily supported by the therapist's beliefs and a few case histories. Since human behavior is complex and multidimensional, the therapist can always find some aspect of the client's behavior to point to as evidence of therapeutic improvement.

In commenting on the profusion of different schools of psychotherapy, London said: "The very profusion can be considered symptomatic of the poverty of psychotherapy as an applied science, for it does not represent different assaults on different kinds of problems but *competing tactics in the same battle*" (1964, p. 24). (Italics added.)

Are there many different ways of treating behavior, or are there many different ways to espouse what are basically similar procedures? Objectively observed, therapists' influencing procedures (theories-in-use) appear more similar than different. One of the most important of the similarities fits squarely within the confines of Argyris' Model 1. That similarity is manipulation. "Psychotherapy is: ... the name we give to a particular kind of personal influence: by means of communications, one person, identified as 'the psychotherapist', exerts an ostensibly therapeutic influence on another, identified as 'the patient' " (Szasz, 1975, p. vii).

There is increasing consensus among psychotherapists that the therapist is a manipulator of behavior (Krasner, 1964; Gillis, 1974). This position is abhorrent to some therapists. Carl Rogers (Rogers & Skinner, 1966), for example, argues that as a therapist he has a choice between controlling, manipulating and destroying, on the one hand, and understanding, embracing, and enriching, on the other. Humanistically oriented psychotherapists pride themselves on their spontaneity, permissiveness, and warmth (London, 1964). Krasner suggests, however, that of all the techniques therapists use to manipulate behavior, spontaneity may be the most effective. He writes: "The therapist is an individual programmed by his training into a fairly effective behavior control machine. Most likely the machine is most effective when it least appears like a machine" (1964, p. 200). Krasner (1964) believes that therapists avoid the issue of behavior control because they realize it would raise numerous moral, ethical and legal issues which they are ill-prepared to confront.

And yet, responsible therapists cannot evade the control issue. As London cogently points out:

> Either therapists can successfully influence behavior or they cannot, and they have little choice of what to claim. If they wish to say they cannot do so, or may not do so in just those areas where human concern is greatest, and are therefore not at all responsible for the behavior of their clients, one must ask what right they have to be in business ... But if, on the other hand, they affirm some technical expertise and wish to claim a genuine ability to influence people, then they must also assume some responsibility for the nature of that influence. In that event, they must ultimately see themselves as moral agents as they are confronted with moral problems ... It is not clear that psychotherapists are suited to assume this role, but it seems certain they cannot escape it (1964, p. 14-15).

For psychotherapists to claim that they do not control behavior appears to be a naive and, perhaps, irresponsible position. Influence exerted without awarenss is not more morally defensible than that exercised with full awareness.

If manipulation of behavior by therapists is characteristic of most therapists, then the methods describing how manipulation occurs should embrace the characteristics of all schools of psychotherapy. In fact, it does. An examination of therapists' influencing techniques does not require reference to any particular school of therapy. An understanding of the similarities in manipulation techniques can be gained from a study of the persuasion (social influence) literature.

Frank was one of the pioneers in conceptualizing therapy as social influence. In his classic study, *Persuasion and Healing* (1961), he drew primarily from the persuasion literature to integrate such diverse phenomena as faith-healing, primitive magic, brainwashing and psychotherapy. Recently, Gillis (1974) has supplemented Frank's original thesis of psychotherapy as social influence. Gillis reduced therapy to the following simplistic formula:

> First, the therapist attains a position of acendency or power over the patient.
> Second, s/he pushes her/his client to examine her/his problems in a new light.
> Third, s/he convinces her/his client that the therapy is definitely working, apart from any objective evidence of change.

Gillis identified two major sources of therapist's power: command and friendship.

COMMAND POWER. The credibility and legitimate authority of the therapist is in part established by her/his title or position and made more salient by the display of diplomas and certificates plus a certain ambience established by dress and office furnishing. The therapist's behavior — using technical jargon, diagnostic labels and paradigmatic responses* — contributes to the command power of the therapist. (Since males have greater power in our society, male therapists probably have more command power than female therapists.)

FRIENDSHIP POWER. Friendship power is established by the therapist's presenting her/himself as an attractive, decent person whose approval the client wants to keep and increase. Therapists speak of friendship power as "establishing rapport."

The characteristics of clients that make clients more susceptible to influence are feelings of helplessness (dependency), low self-esteem, and a moderately high state of affective arousal. The client's feeling of helplessness is generated by a state of suffering which brings her/him to the therapist to seek relief. The usual ambiguity of most therapy situations and the confusion tactics of the therapist heighten the client's emotional reactivity, thereby making her/him even more susceptible to influence.

PLACEBO EFFECT. Command power (control, authority) and friendship power (concern, caring) both mobilize the distressed client's expectation of help and create what Frank (1973) called "the placebo effect" of therapy.†

The placebo effect (expectation of help) is a nonspecific, but essential ingredient in all therapy situations. Once the client's positive expectation is mobilized, almost any strategy — esoteric interpretation to hard sell — has been reported to work (Gillis, 1974).

COGNITIVE DISSONANCE. Another nonspecific but effective strategy in all therapies is the generation of cognitive dissonance. Cognitive dissonance is produced whenever therapists get clients to act in ways that are inconsistent with the client's habitual beliefs and feelings. Engaging in discrepant behaviors causes psychological tension. Psychological tension provides motivation for clients to change their attitudes in order to reduce the discrepancies between their attitudes and feelings and their new behavior (See Festinger, 1957). Cognitive dissonance theory explains, for example, how severe initiation into therapy makes therapy appear more valuable to the client and, therefore, renders her/him more susceptible to

---

*Paradigmatic responses have dissimilar overt and covert messages. The overt message is an apparent social response to the client; the covert message is an asocial response, the intent of which is to "call the patient's bluff" or to "exaggerate his worse fears." The effect is said to produce beneficial (?) confusion and anxiety for the client (Beier, 1966; Nelson, 1962).

†In medicine, a *placebo* is a chemically inert substance whose curative powers are ascribed to the patient's expectation (faith, hope) of cure. In psychotherapy the "placebo effect," refers to any aspect of therapy which mobilizes the client's expectations of help (Shapiro, 1971).

a therapist's influence. Severe initiation into therapy includes things like taking stressful psychological tests, being placed on a long waiting list, paying high fees, and driving long distances to therapy sessions. Putting oneself through such inconvenience is inconsistent with attitudes that one does not need therapy or that therapy is not really very useful. The more severe the initiation, the more the client will probably feel that s/he must persuade the therapist that s/he is a worthy candidate for attention.

Cognitive dissonance theory also predicts that clients "benefit" most from therapy when they are forced to work hard and exert effort. Effortful behavior is inconsistent with the attitude that therapy is not helpful. Clients are encouraged to exert effort by carrying out extensive homework assignments between sessions, doing most of the talking, and engaging in self-disclosure. It is likely that the greater the ambiguity of the therapist, the greater will seem the effort to self-disclose by the client. To justify the effort expended in these therapy tasks, the client must convince her/himself that s/he is indeed improving.

Techniques Making New Values and Beliefs Resistant to Change. Argyris (1975) summarized the principles articulated by McGuire (1964) for making new beliefs and values resistant to later tactics to change them. Such techniques are important in therapy to insure continuation of new beliefs and values after therapy termination. These techniques are:

1. Have the client make a behavioral commitment.

2. Anchor the beliefs to other cognitions. It will be more difficult for the client to change the belief without changing the entire network of beliefs in which the new belief is embedded.

3. Induce resistant cognitive states by increasing the client's anxiety about the issues; s/he will be less willing to expose her/himself to counter-persuasion.

4. Innoculate the client by giving her/him mild doses of opposition argument to stimulate her/his defenses against counter-persuasion.

5. Give the client prior training, e.g. behavioral rehearsal, in resisting persuasive attempts.

This description of therapists' methods of influence embraces almost all schools of psychotherapy and suggests that manipulation is a similarity which most therapies share. Therapists' techniques of social influence also resemble Argyris' Model 1 governing variables:

1. Achieve the purpose as the agent (therapist) defines it.
2. Win, do not lose.
3. Suppress negative feelings.
4. Emphasize rationality (1975, p. 469).

In Argyris' Model 1 the agent exercises *unilateral control*. In therapy as commonly practiced, the therapist also exercises *unilateral control.*

Women, Therapy, and Unilateral Control

Unilateral control in therapy is incompatible with feminist values. The superordinate values that feminists hold for women are equality and freedom: equality that females and males will have equal access to opportunity for personal development and power over their own lives; freedom for increased choice of alternative life-styles.

Wyckoff (Ch. 20) argues that the mystification (confusion) of women by psychotherapists prevents women from learning and confronting the true sources of their oppression, i.e. society. Chesler attacks the usefulness of most treatment for women: "For most women the psychotherapeutic encounter is just one more instance of an unequal relationship, just one more opportunity to be rewarded for expressing distress and to be 'helped' by being (expertly) dominated" (1972a, p. 373). Many women are enraged with psychotherapists for treating them within the context of Model 1 and imposing unilateral control over them.

Safeguards Against Misuse of Influence

What safeguards does the public, including women, have against the misuse of influence by therapists? Some psychotherapists have argued that the best safeguard against the misuse of influence by therapists is increased public awareness of influencing techniques. Others, like Bandura think that "awareness alone, however, is a weak counter-valence" (1974, p. 868). Bandura summarizes his position on reliable safeguards as follows:

> The most reliable source of opposition to manipulative control resides in the reciprocal consequences of human interactions ... If protection against exploitation relied solely upon individual safeguards, people would be continually subjected to coercive pressures. Accordingly, they create institutional sanction which set limits on the control of human behavior. The integrity of individuals is largely secured by societal safeguards that place constraints on improper means and foster reciprocity through balancing of interests (1974, p. 868).

If, as Argyris maintains, Model 1 (unilateral control) describes the world and people as they are, then we have few models available to provide direction in fostering reciprocity. But, is the world so invariant regarding Model 1 behavior that a style of unilateral control is innate and unchangeable? Argyris doubts that it is. He has found, empirically, that many of his subjects *espouse* a model of reciprocity, and persons who tend to be high on Model 1, e.g. corporation presidents can develop changes towards reciprocity within four weeks of full-time education. Argyris concludes, therefore, that:

> ... much social behavior is not innate, that it is highly influenced by the environment, and that the environment (culture) is an artifact created by (wo)man to fulfill (her) his basic predisposition to create orderly rule-dominated worlds (Israel & Tajfel, 1972 cited in Argyris, 1975, p. 485). (parentheses added)

He states further that: "The time has arrived for social psychology to conduct research that provides (wo)mankind with insight into new cultures and new rules" (1975, p. 485). (parentheses added). He then outlines an alternative model of behavior that embodies *reciprocal influence*. He calls it Model 2 (Argyris, 1975).

Reciprocal Influence: Argyris' Model 2

The governing variables in Model 2 are "valid information, free and informed choice, and internal commitment" (Argyris, 1975, p. 482). (See Table 2-II for a summary of Model 2.) The behavioral strategies in the reciprocal influence model (Model 2) are as follows:

1. Clearly and precisely articulate one's goals and values.
2. Invite others to confront one's views, allowing those views to be altered in order that the position generated be based on the most complete and valid information possible.
3. Obtain the maximum contribution of each person involved in order to assure the widest possible exploration of views.
4. Share power with anyone who has competence and who is relevant in deciding or implementing the action.
5. Do not make decisions for others.
6. Do not compete with others or use one-upmanship ploys for the purpose of self-gratification.
7. If new concepts are created, the meaning given them by the creator and the inference processes used to develop them are open to scrutiny by those expected to use them.
8. Evaluations and attributions are minimized.
9. If evaluations and attributions are used, they are coupled with the observable behavior that led to their formulation.
10. If evaluations and attributions are used, they are presented in such a way as to encourage open and constructive confrontation.

TABLE 2 - II

MODEL II*

Governing variables	Action strategies	Consequences for the behavioral world	Consequences for learning	Consequences for quality of life	Effectiveness
1. Valid information	1. Design situations or environments where participants can be origins and can experience high personal causation (psychological success, confirmation, essentiality).	1. Actor experienced as minimally defensive (facilitator, collaborator, choice creator).	1. Disconfirmable processes.	1. Quality of life will be more positive than negative (high authenticity and high freedom of choice).	Increased long-run effectiveness.
2. Free and informed choice.	2. Task is controlled jointly.	2. Minimally defensive interpersonal relations and group dynamics.	2. Double-loop learning	2. Effectiveness of problem solving and decision making will be great, especially for difficult problems.	
3. Internal commitment to the choice and constant monitoring of its implementation.	3. Protection of self is a joint enterprise and oriented toward growth (speak in directly observable categories, seek to reduce blindness about own inconsistency and incongruity). 4. Bilateral protection of others.	3. Learning-oriented norms (trust, individuality, open confrontation on difficult issues).	3. Public testing of theories.		

*Table reproduced from *Theory in Practice: Increasing Professional Effectiveness*, by Chris Argyris and Donald A. Schön, San Francisco: Jossey-Bass, 1975, pp. 68-69. Used with permission of Jossey - Bass, Chris Argyris and Donald Schön.

The consequences of Model 1 are opposite those of Model 2. The consequences of Model 2 include an increase in free choice, feelings of internal commitment and essentiality. Model 2 emphasizes *double-loop learning* — influence is reciprocal. The basic ideas behind the articulated views are confronted and tested publicly. Results are *not* self-confirming as in Model 1; the ideas are subject to disconformation. New information concerning human nature can flow from Model 2, hopefully leading to a new image of what it means to be human.

Feminist therapy also envisions a new image of what it means to be human: its strategies have many parallels with the strategies of Model 2. In the next chapter which describes feminist therapy, we will integrate the strategies used in feminist therapy with Argyris' Model 2, the reciprocal influence model.

REFERENCES

Argyris, Chris: Dangers in applying results from experimental social psychology. *American Psychologist, 30*:469, 1975.

Argyris, Chris and Schön, Donald A.: *Theory in Practice: Increasing Professional Effectiveness.* San Francisco, Jossey-Bass, 1974.

Bandura, Albert: Behavior theory and the models of man. *American Psychologist, 29*:859, 1974.

Beier, Ernst G.: *The Silent Language of Psychotherapy.* Chicago, Aldine, 1966.

Chesler, Phyllis: Patient and patriarch: women in the psychotherapeutic relationship. In Gornick, Vivian & Moran, Barbara K. (Eds.): *Women in Sexist Society.* New York, Signet, 1972 (a).

Frank, Jerome D.: *Persuasion and Healing.* Baltimore, The John Hopkins Press, 1961.

Gillis, John S.: Social influence therapy: the therapist as manipulator, *Psychology Today, 8*:91, 1974.

Harper, Robert A.: *Psychoanalysis and Psychotherapy 36 Systems.* New York, Jason Aronson, 1974.

Israel, Joachim and Tajfel, Henri (Eds.): *The Context of Social Psychology,* New York, Academic Press, 1972.

Krasner, Leonard: Behavior control and social responsibility. *American Psychologist, 17*:199, 1964.

London, Perry: *The Modes and Morals of Psychotherapy.* New York, Holt, Rinehart & Winston, 1964.

McGuire, W. J.: Inducing resistance to persuasion. In Berkowitz, L. (Eds.): *Advances in Experimental Social Psychology* (Vol. 1). New York, Academic Press, 1964.

Nelson, Marie C.: *Paradigmatic Approaches to Psychoanalysis: Four Papers.* New York, Department of Psychology, Stuyvestant Poliyclinic, 1962.

Rogers, Carl R. and Skinner, Buris Frederick: Some issues concerning the control of human behavior: A symposium. *Science, 124*:1057, 1956.

Rosenthal, David: Changes in some moral values following psychotherapy. *Journal of Consulting Psychology, 19*:431, 1955.

Shapiro, Arthur K.: Placebo effects in medicine, psychotherapy, and psychoanalysis. In

Bergin, Allen E. & Garfield, Sol L. (Eds.): *Handbook of Psychotherapy and Behavior Change: An Empirical Analysis.* New York, Wiley, 1971.

Szasz, Thomas S.: *The Ethics of Psychoanalysis: The Theory and Method of Autonomous Psychotherapy.* New York, Dell Publishing Co., 1965.

Section II

FEMINIST AND NONSEXIST PSYCHOTHERAPY

—— *Chapter 3* ——

FEMINIST AND NONSEXIST
PSYCHOTHERAPY*

THE values, structure, and goals of sexist therapy are destructive to women. In the preceding chapters we have presented evidence that clients in therapy move closer to the values of their therapists (see Ch. 1). Sexist therapists accept the traditional/cultural definitions of women as essential to an adequate sexual identity, the *sine qua non* of mental health. However, we feel the traditional role of women in our culture is demeaning, powerless and negatively valued. Internalization of this role leads to low self-esteem and self-hatred. If sexist values are learned from a therapist, a woman client will be discouraged from expressing assertion, independence and power.

The structure of sexist therapy is based on a patriarchal model. Women are encouraged by sexist therapists to be helpless and dependent; this therapy perpetuates childlike behavior and works against women learning skills to be independent and self-directing. Sexist therapy places the blame for women's problems on intrapsychic factors, an analysis which increases the client's sense of inadequacy and self-abnegation. Clients are led to believe that individual solutions for their difficulties may be obtained by adjusting to the very roles and behaviors that are oppressing them, thwarting their self-growth and self-actualization. Sexist therapy is not only destructive to individual women but also to women as a group. Society and private therapy isolates women from each other (Chesler, 1972). By insisting on individual solutions to women's problems and adjustment to the *status quo*, sexist therapy prevents women from confronting and dealing with the social and political causes of their unhappiness.

In reaction against sexist therapies, the therapeutic approaches presented in this volume endeavor to facilitate women's assuming equality in society. All the approaches do not fit the model of feminist psycho-

*We wish to acknowledge the assistance of Joan Saks Berman, Joy Kenworthy, and Elaine Sachnoff for their criticisms and comments. All are feminist therapists in private practice: Joy Kenworthy in Madison, Wisconsin; Joan Saks Berman and Elaine Sachnoff in Chicago. Joy Kenworthy is also associated with the Women's Research Institute of Wisconsin, Inc. and Joan Saks Berman teaches women's studies in the Sociology Department, Northeastern Illinois State University.

therapy, though some do. However, all do fit a nonsexist model.

FEMINIST AND NONSEXIST THERAPIES DEFINED

Nonsexist and feminist therapies are similar in that they do not represent a particular set of therapeutic techniques. Except for Freudian Analysis,* almost any existing technique can be accommodated by nonsexist or feminist therapies. Both therapies assume that women and men by nature may be different from one another, but they do not speculate upon what those differences are since behaviors are heavily influenced by culture. Therefore, feminist and nonsexist therapies allow clients to determine their own destinies without the construction of culturally prescribed sex-role stereotypes based upon assumed biological differences. Both approaches attempt to facilitate equality (in personal power) between females and males.

Although feminist and nonsexist therapies are often used interchangeably, we make a distinction between the two. The major distinction is that feminist therapy incorporates the political values and philosophy of feminism from the women's movement in its therapeutic values and strategies while nonsexist therapy does not. Feminism insists that (1) males and females should have equal opportunities for gaining personal, political-institutional, *and* economic power;† and that (2) interaction between persons should be egalitarian. Feminist therapists, therefore, are intolerant of the mysticism and authoritarian power of traditional therapists. Nonsexist therapists may function in an egalitarian model also, but they do so from humanistic motivations and not, as feminist therapists, from a political position.

Feminist-therapy strategies are compatible with Argyris' reciprocal influence model described in Chapter 2. Feminist therapists also endorse cultural determinism, the environmental model of psychopathology, and the androgynous model of mental health discussed in Chapter 1. Because of the endorsement of an androgynous model of mental health, feminist therapists are specialists in sex-role socialization, especially, but not exclusively, in the sex-role socialization of women.

In regarding feminist and nonsexist therapies as different, we do not imply that one is better than the other. Rather, we believe that one may be more appropriate than the other, depending upon the client. Nonsexist therapy should be used with traditional female clients for whom

---

*Traditional psychoanalysis, guided rigidly by Freud's psychology of women, is by definition sexist and is not acceptable to feminists (see Ch. 1).

†"In the women's movement we believe that the personal and the political cannot be separated" (Bart, undated).

the tenets of feminism are threatening; feminist therapy should be used for female clients who are dissatisfied with the constriction of the culturally defined role for women and are seeking alternatives.

Dependent, passive women who, perhaps, were sent to therapy by their husbands, and women with especially demanding or uncooperative husbands may be helped most by nonsexist therapy. Such women come into therapy feeling badly about themselves and powerless. They will often view feminism as a threat to what they consider the benefits of their feminine role. However, many other women who appear in therapy are women for whom the traditional sex-role is no longer working: divorced women; women thirty or older; women whose children have grown; women who feel vaguely dissatisfied even though they have "everything" (home, husband, and children); strong, competent women who believe themselves to be insufficiently feminine and, therefore, deviant. Feminist therapy can be particularly helpful to such women.

The higher the woman's level of consciousness, the more appropriate feminist therapy is for her. As a woman's consciousness develops, treatment may evolve from nonsexist to feminist therapy. Good therapy always starts where the client is and keeps pace with her progress.

NONSEXIST THERAPY

Values (Assumptions) of Nonsexist Therapy

The following are nonsexist values or assumptions which feminist therapy also incorporates:

THE THERAPIST IS AWARE OF HER/HIS OWN VALUES. It is not enough that a therapist believes that males and females are equal. S/he must also learn what the sexist issues are and work to heighten her/his own culturally burdened awareness. S/he examines her/his own expectations for female-male behavior and becomes aware of which of her/his values were consciously chosen and which s/he unconsciously introjected from cultural values. S/he carefully examines the cultural values and discards those which are inconsistent with her/his other values and a nonsexist philosophy. This necessitates taking time for attending training workshops in nonsexist and feminist therapies, consulting with nonsexist or feminist therapists, reading the women's literature, and *periodically participating* in values clarification workshops.* The therapist should

---

*Values clarification is a systematic method of examining one's attitudes and beliefs in order to define more specifically those beliefs which are important. It is concerned not with content but with the valuing process. Values-clarification exercises or workshops help people to learn this process of making conscious choices by careful generation and consideration of alternative values (Simon, Howe, & Kirschenbaum, 1972).

also participate in a women's (or men's) consciousness-raising group or a feminist support group and in other ways expose her/himself to self-criticism.

THERE ARE NO PRESCRIBED SEX-ROLE BEHAVIORS. The nonsexist therapist assumes that clients should make decisions about their behavior based on what they want for and from themselves and not on what is expected because of their sex.

Lesbians and male homosexuals are not considered emotionally or sexually maladjusted, solely on the basis of sexual preference. Alternate sexual lifestyles are accepted by nonsexist therapists as perfectly healthy. Nonsexist therapists believe that much of the emotional stress experienced by homosexuals is not due to internal psychic conflicts but to external social pressures to conform to the prevailing heterosexual norm and to fears of criticism for not conforming.

SEX-ROLE REVERSALS IN LIFE-STYLE ARE NOT LABELED PATHOLOGICAL. The nonsexist therapist is comfortable with sex-role reversals. If s/he counsels a couple who have reversed sex-roles, (for instance, she being more assertive and he being more passive, or she being the bread-winner, and he taking care of things at home), the therapist thinks that it is fortunate that two people are able to work out behavioral styles and an assignment of tasks which gives each of them satisfaction.

MARRIAGE IS NOT REGARDED AS ANY BETTER AN OUTCOME OF THERAPY FOR A FEMALE THAN FOR A MALE. Because of the cultural expectation that women be dependent, most therapists assume therapy has a good outcome when their female clients marry. If a male client marries, most therapists first consider whether or not he made the choice out of weakness (he needed someone to lean on) or out of strength (he has stabilized his emotions and accepts himself; his commitment to a relationship is an expression of his new integration). A nonsexist therapist would go through the same concerns regarding the marriage of a woman.

FEMALES ARE EXPECTED TO BE AS AUTONOMOUS AND ASSERTIVE AS MALES; MALES ARE EXPECTED TO BE AS EXPRESSIVE AND TENDER AS FEMALES. The nonsexist therapist believes that the best emotional balance is achieved by a person, female or male, who has a blend of assertiveness and tenderness. (See Ch. 1 for a discussion of androgyny.)

THEORIES OF BEHAVIORS BASED ON ANATOMICAL DIFFERENCES ARE REJECTED. Freud, as discussed earlier, built his theory of the "innate" superiority of males compared to females upon the fact that males have penises and females do not. Similarly, Erikson also insisted that the female's anatomy is destiny (and personality as well). In his essay "Inner and Outer Space: Reflections on Womanhood," Erikson (1967) argues that by reason of the presence of a womb in females, femininity is equated with passivity. Nonsexist therapists reject such ideas.

Strategies of Nonsexist Psychotherapy

The following strategies are used by both nonsexist and feminist therapists:

THE THERAPIST DOES NOT USE THE POWER OF HER/HIS POSITION TO SUBTLY REINFORCE OR PUNISH CLIENTS FOR EXHIBITING "APPROPRIATE" OR "INAPPROPRIATE" FEMININE OR MASCULINE BEHAVIORS. The nonsexist therapist accepts expressions of dependency, tenderness and emotionality in male clients and is personally comfortable with men who place relationships and family values above occupational or professional achievement. S/he is as comfortable with female clients who do not want children, who think most of the men they know are inadequate, and who express a desire for leadership, achievement, dominance, and power, as s/he is with a traditional "suburban housewife."

DIAGNOSES ARE NOT BASED ON A CLIENT'S FAILURE TO ACHIEVE CULTURALLY PRESCRIBED SEX-ROLE BEHAVIORS. If a housewife, who did not have a good relationship with her own mother or whose mother was absent, came to therapy complaining of depression and headaches, which began three months after marriage, the nonsexist therapist would not assume that faulty sex-role identification was the cause of the depression. Instead s/he would explore the client's present circumstances to determine what are the current environmental pressures and the client's social assumptions. S/he would determine whether the client is living a life-style she finds comfortable, or whether she is engaged in a life-style she believes is necessary in order to be acceptable to others. The therapist would explore what the client can do to make her life more fulfilling. If the client decides she would prefer to return to school to study engineering and not have children, the therapist would not assume faulty sex-role identification. Rather, s/he would assume that this person prefers a life-style different from that which traditional women choose.

SEX-BIASED TESTING INSTRUMENTS ARE NOT USED.* In a practical sense, this means that the nonsexist therapist may use no instruments at all since none are without sex-bias. Projective tests are less offensive since the bias rests with the interpreter rather than the instrument. Even with projective tests, however, there is a danger of bias if established criteria for interpretation are used. Since such criteria or normative data reflect the *status quo*, interpretations based on normative data are, by definition, sexist.

FEMINIST THERAPY

The roots of feminist therapy are in the new concepts in social

---

*See further discussion of testing under Feminist Strategy No. 14.

thinking provided by the women's movement, in the protests of women against sexist bias among psychotherapists, and in the research on women that the current feminist movement has brought to psychology and psychotherapy (Brodsky, 1975).

Feminist therapy does not have or claim any therapeutic techniques except, perhaps, sex-role analysis.* Brodsky and Task Force colleagues (Brodsky, Holroyd, Payton, Rubinstein, Rosenkrantz, Sherman, & Zell, 1975) reported that the APA Task Force on Sex Bias and Sex-Role Stereo-typing in Psychotherapeutic Practice surveyed women therapists in the American Psychological Association regarding the therapeutic techniques they used with women. The respondents reported beneficial effects with a number of techniques. Psychoanalysis was the only treatment technique which the Task Force labeled sexist in and of itself, regardless of the values of the therapist.†

While feminist therapists come from diverse schools of psychotherapy and use different techniques in their work, they do have common bonds of values and strategies. However, there is no official set of guidelines for feminist therapy. We have generated the guidelines which follow through our work with female clients, teaching women's studies courses, associating with other feminist therapists and writing and editing this book.

Values (Assumptions) of Feminist Therapy

THE INFERIOR STATUS OF WOMEN IS DUE TO THEIR HAVING LESS POLIT-ICAL AND ECONOMIC POWER THAN MEN. Feminist therapists focus on social rather than hormonal or anatomical factors to explain why women are treated as a minority with little power (see Ch. 1 on the minority status of women). Feminists all agree that the basic problem is the power differential between males and females. However, they disagree on which social factors account for the power difference. Feminist therapists emphasize different personal-political issues in therapy, depending upon which feminist philosophy they identify with most strongly.

Polk (1974) explored the power differential between males and females from four theoretical perspectives within the women's movement. These perspectives are summarized from Polk as follows:

1. *Sex-role socialization:* Society assigns different personality character-istics to each sex; different societies assign different characteristics. Sex-roles are learned as part of the individual's socialization and form a core

---

*See the end of this chapter for a list of techniques useful with feminist therapy.

†We agree that Freudian theory is sexist, but we regard the psychoanalysts who contributed to this book, Seidenberg, (Ch. 7) and Shainess (Ch. 5), as nonsexist therapists according to the definition we presented at the beginning of this chapter. Neither of these psychoanalysts accepts the Freudian theory of personality on which the inferiority of women is based (Eds.).

identity. Higher status and greater power are almost always part of the male role.

2. *Conflicting cultures approach:* Values are dichotomized by sex just as roles are. Masculine values have higher status and women are devalued because they represent an alternate culture. The dominant visible culture reflects masculine values. Feminists who accept this postion are identified as "cultural feminists."

3. *Socialist perspective:* Socialist feminists see sexism as functional for capitalism and contend that capitalism oppresses both sexes. Their goal is to change the basic political and economic structure of society in order to redistribute power and wealth more equally between men and women. They believe that nothing short of a revolution will change the existing inequalities (see Deckard, 1975, for a more detailed description of this position).

4. *Power analysis:* This perspective does not ignore the preceding perspectives but views sex roles and values as symptomatic of a broader problem, i.e. the domination of female by males. Power analysis is concerned with *how* men oppress women rather than the origins of the oppression. The power-analysis position is taken by radical feminists.

Drawing primarily from the power-analysis perspective, Polk (1974) identified the following sources of male power: (1) Normative power: Men control tradition sex-role definitions. (2) Institutional power: Men control the basic institutions of socialization and social control, i.e. the media, religion, and the educational institutions. (3) Reward power: Through their normative and institutional power, men reward women who conform to traditional sex-roles and withhold reward from those who do not conform. (4) Expertise power: Men are the experts in every field; thus, they function as "gatekeepers" of knowledge. (5) Psychological power: The social conditioning of men molds them to fit the value structure of institutions better than women's social conditioning does. (6) Brute force: Men have more strength and more confidence in their physical strength than do women. Beatings and rape, as expressions of masculine strength, are forms of social control over women.

A FEMINIST THERAPIST DOES NOT VALUE AN UPPER- OR MIDDLE-CLASS CLIENT MORE THAN A WORKING-CLASS CLIENT. This assumption reflects the radical-socialist origins of feminist therapy. It is assumed that differences among women can stimulate them to learn from one another. There may be some difficulty in implementing this learning since some working-class women find it difficult to empathize with the problems of middle-class women.

THE PRIMARY SOURCE OF WOMEN'S PATHOLOGY IS SOCIAL, NOT PERSONAL: EXTERNAL, NOT INTERNAL. The design of cultures and the resulting environmental stress is the chief cause of most of women's tensions, anxieties, neuroses and psychoses. That portion of pathology which is internal has been conditioned by parents who have themselves been conditioned and shaped by the sexist values in their environment.*

THE FOCUS ON ENVIRONMENTAL STRESS AS A MAJOR SOURCE OF PATHOLOGY IS NOT USED AS AN AVENUE OF ESCAPE FROM INDIVIDUAL RESPONSIBILITY. Individual responsibility is an important part of feminist therapy, though in practice it is almost never necessary to remind a female client of this value. So elementary is the value of autonomy and so debilitating is the state of dependency that clients who seek feminist therapy rarely need to be reminded of the need for them to take responsibility for themselves. It may happen that a client will stagnate at the completion of a cathartic stage by continuing to focus on the agents of her injustice rather than moving on to what she intends to do about the consequences of the injustice. If she is fortunate enough to be in a women's therapy group, the other members will remind her that she must go on with her life. This means taking responsibility for initiating action to get what she wants for herself. The therapy group's impatience with this woman would contrast sharply to their tolerance for women not in therapy who are mired in roles of helpless dependency. The group would expect more from the client because she understands the source of her oppression, has the philosophy of feminism to help her conceptualize her alternatives, and has the support of other women.

FEMINIST THERAPY IS OPPOSED TO PERSONAL ADJUSTMENT TO SOCIAL CONDITIONS; THE GOAL IS SOCIAL AND POLITICAL CHANGE (Agel, 1971). Most traditional therapies function to promote or even enforce the *status quo*. The effect is to create and perpetuate the inferior status of women. The submissive, dependent, narcissistic female is considered normal and well-adjusted not only by Freudians but by traditional therapists (Broverman, Broverman, Clarkson, Rosenkrantz, & Vogel, 1970). Few traditional therapists question the cultural belief that women's lives should be centered around love and service to others. Women who do not aspire to become wives and mothers are usually characterized as disturbed in their sexual identification.

OTHER WOMEN ARE NOT THE ENEMY. Without isolation from one another and without the need to compete for men in order to survive economically, women trust and feel close to other women. Other women become important sources of emotional support. This increases the personal warmth and pleasure in the lives of all women and reduces their emotional dependence on men.

MEN ARE NOT THE ENEMY EITHER. Some radical feminists do identify men as the enemy. They contend that sexism serves the power needs of

*This observation was suggested by Elaine Sachnoff.

the male ego (Deckard, 1975). Reversing discrimination and oppression does not appear to us to be a satisfactory solution to human ills. Both sexes are victims of sex-role socialization. There are many negative aspects to the male sex role (Jourard, 1964; Kaye, 1974). However, since men benefit more from sexism than women do and since most men are loath to give up their position of privilege, women cannot count on help from men in changing the social role system. Women will have to liberate themselves.

WOMEN MUST BE ECONOMICALLY AND PSYCHOLOGICALLY AUTONOMOUS. Absolute psychological autonomy is not possible nor desirable; however, no adult person can afford to be wholly or one-sidely dependent upon another person. Autonomy can be accomplished only if women assume responsibility for their own behavior. Women must take responsibility for deciding what they want from life and for themselves and must devise ways to achieve their goals within a realistic framework.

Marriage should not be used as an escape from responsibility for self. Marriage is a partnership of equals, not a dropout haven for women to avoid the need to make hard decisions about what they value and what they want their lives to mean.

Economic autonomy will be difficult to implement for some women.* These are women who married out of high school and skipped job-skills training in order to have children. Without cooperation from a husband or aid from welfare, the only alternative to economic dependence for such women is a lower standard of living or giving their husbands custody of the children. Economic autonomy is a value which always needs to be considered in relationship to hard reality.

RELATIONSHIPS OF FRIENDSHIP, LOVE, AND MARRIAGE SHOULD BE EQUAL IN PERSONAL POWER. It is not politically just nor emotionally sound for a female to be passive and dependent or for a male to be dominant and strong. To upset this traditional interaction, females and males must drop their covert agreement in which "he protects her" and, in exchange, "she supports his ego."

MAJOR DIFFERENCES BETWEEN "APPROPRIATE" SEX-ROLE BEHAVIORS MUST DISAPPEAR. This is necessary in order to avoid sex-role expectations and stereotyping. Sex-roles should become androgynous (see Ch.1). Women should assume the best characteristics of men's roles while keeping the best of their own, and men should assume the best characteristics of women's roles while keeping the best of their own. For example, women can be assertive, decisive, and comfortable with the use of power for the benefit of others as well as sensitive, emotionally expressive, and

---

*We wish to acknowledge the assistance of Joan Saks Berman in this discussion of economic autonomy. (Eds.)

nurturing. Men can be tender and responsive to the emotions of others, as well as analytical and competent.

Strategies of Feminist Psychotherapy

BEFORE THERAPY BEGINS, THERAPISTS HAVE AN OBLIGATION TO MAKE EXPLICIT THEIR VALUES REGARDING WOMEN'S ROLES (OR ANY OTHER RELEVANT VALUES) TO THE CLIENT. A therapist's personal values are even more important than her/his clinical effectiveness. The personal values of the therapist influence which behaviors a client will value in herself. An ineffective therapist with nonsexist or feminist values will do minimum harm to female clients. In contrast, a skillful sexist therapist can do a great deal of damage to women. There are occasions, however, when it will be difficult for the therapist to explain her/his values. When the client is in crisis, the therapist must be sensitive to the client's pain and not intrude too much. When the client is very suspicious of feminism or other "radical" movements it might be difficult for the therapist to adequately explain her/his values. Such clients require great skill from the therapist in honestly conveying her/his beliefs relevant to her/his work. It may not be possible for the therapist to convey everything of importance during the first session. By the third session the basic issues at least should have been covered.*

WHENEVER POSSIBLE, THE PERSONAL POWER BETWEEN THE CLIENT AND THERAPIST APPROACHES EQUALITY. The client will attribute power to the therapist because of her/his expertise. However, the therapist does not exaggerate the power difference. For example, the therapist does not use her/his objective vantage point in a style which puts the client down. Nor does the therapist pose as an omnipotent figure by using other one-upmanship ploys. The therapist does not mystify the client by withholding her/his impression of the client's situation. Impressions are shared and are presented as the therapist's own perceptions which require confirmation by the client. The therapist does not couch her/his impressions in exotic clinical explanations of the client's "conditions" but in terms of desirable behaviors and in words and concepts that the client can easily understand.

WOMEN ARE ENCOURAGED TO BE AUTONOMOUS PEOPLE. They are encouraged to determine what they want for themselves and then to put events in motion to get what they want. It is often harder for a woman *to know* what she wants than *to get* what she wants. This is especially true for married women; the longer they have been married, the harder it is for

---

*We wish to acknowledge the assistance of Joy Kenworthy in this discussion of the difficulty of therapists' sharing their values with clients. (Eds.)

them; they have been so vigilant to other people's wants, they are by now unable to identify their own.

Women begin to discover that *they* can decide what they want in life and then can act to get it. They no longer depend on someone else to initiate those decisions and actions. They no longer react automatically to social pressures, but choose their behaviors freely and consciously. They work on developing power to carry things through and stop expecting that they will need to be rescued by a person wiser or stronger. They increasingly see themselves as self-sufficient and as free to develop intimacy, awareness, spontaineity, and joy.*

BEFORE THERAPY BEGINS, THE CLIENT AND THERAPIST ENTER INTO A CONTRACT SPECIFYING THE BEHAVIOR THE CLIENT WANTS TO CHANGE. The client decides what she wants to work on and makes an agreement with the therapist (and group members if she is in group therapy) specifying what concrete, observable behavior she wants to change. Having a contract helps both client and therapist focus on the client's goals and makes progress easy to measure. A contract also minimizes the risk that the therapist (or group) will manipulate the client and it enables the client to be responsible for what happens to her in therapy.

SEX-ROLE ANALYSIS IS EMPLOYED AS A TREATMENT TECHNIQUE. The purpose of sex-role analysis is to expose covert expectations of oneself and others and to increase awareness of cultural expectations. With heightened awareness, cultural and introjected expectations can more easily be circumvented if that is the desire of the client. Nonsexist therapists may also use sex-role analysis as a therapy technique with women (Stevens, 1971); however, the use of sex-role analysis is always a central focus in feminist therapy (Brodsky, 1975; Elias, 1975). (This technique will be discussed later in this chapter.) An important ingredient of sex-role analysis is the generation of behavioral alternatives (see Table 3-II under "Feminist Sex-role Analysis as a Therapeutic Technique," this chapter.) Since feminist therapists specialize in the treatment of women, they are usually aware of more behavioral alternatives for women than nonsexist therapists.

IT IS NOT SUFFICIENT MERELY TO ENCOURAGE WOMEN TO DEVELOP THEMSELVES. THEY MUST ALSO BE GIVEN SUFFICIENT PERSONAL SUPPORT AND HELP IN ANALYZING EMOTIONAL AND SOCIAL BARRIERS TO THEIR GOALS. Encouraging women to develop their human potential without using a feminist analysis of the psychosocial milieu may be unhelpful and damaging to women's self-esteem. There are realistic barriers in the social structure to achievement and personhood for women. If unrecog-

---

*We wish to credit Dorothy Stewart with contributing this paragraph on the discussion of autonomy for women. (Eds.)

nized, these barriers may lead women to label themselves inadequate or personal failures. Also, women may experience internal blocks to their growth and achievement generated from conflicting social responses in their transition to role-free behaviors; sometimes women get punished for behavior inconsistent with the stereotypic feminine role and sometimes they get encouraged and rewarded.

WOMEN ARE TAUGHT HOW TO USE STRAIGHT COMMUNICATION AND HOW TO DROP COVERT, MANIPULATIVE BEHAVIOR. Covert, manipulative behavior is so typical of women that it frequently has been assumed to be innate. It is one of the things about women which men complain of most ("Never trust a woman.") and it is one of the things about women which puzzles men most ("What does a woman want?" or "I'll never understand women."). That manipulative behavior is not innate to women is clear when an analogy is made to minority group members. Clearly, the shuffling feet, the obsequiousness, the syrupy sweetness and the manipulative style are behaviors used by people who feel powerless (see Ch. 1).

The most useful technique for teaching women how to behave in nonmanipulative ways is assertion training. Many people, including women, erroneously confuse assertion with aggression, or fear an assertive woman will not be feminine. Both fears are unfounded. An assertive woman is one who is straightforward about both her negative and positive responses. None of her responses is at another person's expense. We have observed few techniques which have as much potency in increasing a woman's self-esteem and restoring her feeling of personal integrity as assertion training (see Jakubowski, Ch. 8).

WOMEN ARE TAUGHT WHEN TO USE STRAIGHT COMMUNICATION. When women learn assertive behavior, they are so enthusiastic that they may become almost "religious" in its use and feel guilty when they slip back into old manipulative ways. However, they should realize that *never* being manipulative would be viable if women had equal power with every person they encountered, or if they had equal power in society, or even if every person they dealt with had friendly intentions. Since these conditions do not exist, women who are indiscriminately assertive are taking great risks. Assertion may be viewed as uppity and sometimes misinterpreted as hostile aggression. The general guideline given women is that when they are dealing with people who are unfriendly and have power over them, they should be cautious.

WOMEN SHOULD HAVE THE MEANS OR THE SKILLS TO BE FINANCIALLY INDEPENDENT. A woman does not put herself in a position to need a man in order to survive economically. Not doing so insures that if she is living with a man, she is living with him because she chooses to, not because she has no other financial means to survive. She either has or acquires the skills to support herself financially, though she may or may not actually be financially independent. If a woman chooses to live without financial independence, then she is encouraged to negotiate a lifestyle that avoids penalizing her for not actively pursuing her occupation.

THE THERAPIST USUALLY TAKES WHAT THE CLIENT SAYS AT FACE VALUE. The therapist seldom offers interpretations. There are no interpretations of resistance. When the client's stated goals and behavior are incongruent, the therapist simply points this out to the client. The therapist does *not* interpret its meaning. S/he may ask for the client's own interpretation.

THE THERAPIST CONFRONTS CONTRADICTORY BEHAVIOR. If the client's behavior is contradictory or self-defeating and she does not come to this insight by herself, the therapist may share her/his opinion in behavioral terms about what s/he thinks is happening but it is offered as her/his perception, and not as a pronouncement of "what is really going on."

THE THERAPIST ASSUMES THAT THE CLIENT IS HER OWN BEST EXPERT ON HERSELF. If the client does not understand or disagrees with the therapist's explanation of what is happening in her life, she is encouraged to dispute the therapist's formulations rather than to defer to "authority." A woman's sense of her own experience is the standard against which she and the therapist measure the validity of all other information. This may be the first opportunity many women have had to disagree with an "authority" and so this strategy is politically and therapeutically important.

THE CLIENT IS GIVEN THE TOOLS TO BE HER OWN THERAPIST. The therapist uses plain language, no jargon or complicated abstractions. Though this requires more verbal skill and a better understanding of theory by the therapist, it is possible to translate psychological "wisdom" into the client's language. In addition, if she is interested, the client is directed to books which enable her to become her own technical expert (she is already her own personal expert). The books described in Chapter 18 are useful for this purpose. Techniques for feminist therapy which are listed at the end of this chapter also may be helpful to her. Homework or other procedures which the client can do on her own further develop the client's skill as her own therapist. The client develops her own skills by helping to write a homework contract rather than by being told what to do by a therapist.

DIAGNOSTIC TESTING IS NOT ORDINARILY USED. Testing puts the therapist in an expert position with the client. Having a client spend long hours taking tests and then giving her an evasive interpretation under the assumption that the therapist knows more about the client than she knows about herself are both means by which therapists mystify women clients and gain power over them.

Many feminist therapists, including the authors, reject the clinical use of tests altogether, especially objective personality tests. Vocational, intelligence, and projective tests should only be used with an awareness of their inherent biases. Some therapists, however, would argue that there are a few well-defined occasions when a feminist therapist could use diagnostic testing. For example, testing might be used at the request of the client for her direct benefit. However, caution is required even in this situation because the client may expect more from tests than they can provide. The therapist must educate the client regarding the limitations of tests whenever they are used.*

IF A CLIENT IS GIVEN TESTS, SHE IS ENTITLED TO THE RESULTS. The test results are hers and she has a right to the information. If the client does not know she has this right, the therapist should initiate the examination of the results with her.

THE CLIENT HAS ACCESS TO READING WHATEVER IS IN HER CHART, ESPECIALLY MATERIAL BEING SHARED WITH OTHER AGENCIES OR PROFESSIONALS. She may even be encouraged to participate in writing her own progress report.†

THE THERAPIST DOES NOT USE DIAGNOSTIC LABELS.‡ Diagnostic categories have notoriously low reliability. Diagnoses frequently reflect political and social power (Hollingshead & Redlich, 1958; Cannon & Redick, 1973) and have been a major instrument in the oppression of women. Therefore, if diagnostic categories are used, they must be used cautiously. Categories tend to label the person and often implicitly reduce respect for her.

A more therapeutically useful technique than diagnostic categories is conceptualization of the client's behavior through behavioral analysis. Behavioral analysis has the advantage of focusing on both the client's strengths and weaknesses, rather than concentrating on the weaknesses only, as diagnostic categories tend to do. Effective therapy requires building the client's strengths, not just eliminating her weaknesses. Furthermore, diagnostic categories describe deficit behaviors as if they were *traits*§ rather than *states*.§ In contrast, behavioral analysis specifies *when* a behavioral deficit may occur. Stating *when* a behavior may occur corrects the error of assuming that a behavioral deficit is an inherent quality of a person's character. This is not only more accurate but also more reassuring for the client.

FEMINIST THERAPY WITH WOMEN IS DONE MOST EFFECTIVELY IN

*Space does not permit an adequate discussion of this issue which is traditionally important to the training and professional service of psychologists. The authors hope to deal more completely with the issue of testing in a book on feminist therapy now in progress.

†We wish to acknowledge the contribution of J. S. Berman for this strategy (Eds.).

‡The use of diagnostic categories, like testing, is a complex issue on which feminist therapists are not in agreement. Space does not permit elaboration. As with testing, this topic will be more completely dealt with in the book the editors are writing on feminist therapy.

§A *trait* is behavior which remains stable across different situations; a *state* is behavior which changes from situation to situation (Mischel, 1968).

GROUPS. A group setting dilutes the power of the therapist. It provides an opportunity for women to learn to trust and relate closely to other women, perhaps for the first time in their lives. It is helpful for women to learn that they can receive support and protection from women as well as men and to learn to recognize women who can be relied upon for support.

In times of stress or crisis, women in groups learn to *seek* and to accept support and encouragement from other group members. Group support provides an alternate model to the traditional one which encourages focusing all dependency needs upon just one other person (usually a male).

In groups, women learn that they have many problems in common with other women. By comparing the commonalities, they are able to determine which of their problems are their personal responsibility, and which are culturally or situationally produced (see Ch. 16, Brodsky). By being present while other women are working through common problems, each woman gets closer to her own solution. In addition, a group setting provides models of new behavior from which to choose. Women have formerly lacked models because of their isolation from one another and because they have only been exposed to limited, stereotypic solutions. In groups, a variety of models are available.

In a group setting, women can more efficiently learn social interaction skills than they could in private therapy. These skills enable them to perform socially more effectively. Learning is carried beyond the group therapy session as well. Women in female therapy groups almost always relate to each other outside of group. Social activities with each other help to generalize their new therapeutic skills and attitudes about themselves and other women.

ENGAGING IN SOCIAL ACTION IS AN ESSENTIAL PROFESSIONAL RESPONSIBILITY OF THERAPISTS (see Adams and Durham, Ch. 22). Since the focus of feminist therapy is upon the cultural and social oppression of women, it would be inconsistent and shortsighted, indeed, for therapists to focus all their energies upon the treatment of individuals. To do so would make them, to use an old adage, guilty of treating the symptom (the client), rather than the disease (society). Therapists must take social action.

It is appropriate and may often be necessary for the therapist to be an advocate on behalf of a client. Especially in offices where individuals without such bureaucratic legal tender as title and prestige are not taken seriously, therapists can intervene on behalf of clients for speedy results.

CLIENTS ARE ENCOURAGED TO ENGAGE IN SOCIAL ACTION ON THEIR OWN BEHALF (see Gluckstern, Ch. 23). Successful social action can give clients the therapeutic experience of being effective, powerful people, capable of making some changes in the system. By encouraging the client toward social action, the therapist should be careful not to set up a client for failure. In order that a client be successful and that the results of her efforts be therapeutic, it is best that her first attempt be with small but valid issues.

FEMINIST THERAPY AS A RECIPROCAL INFLUENCE MODEL

In Chapter 2 we discussed a number of social-influence techniques which therapists use to change the behavior of clients. All of them were a variation of unilateral control. But, we also described an alternate model to unilateral control; that was Argyris' (1975) reciprocal-influence model (Model 2). Argyris' reciprocal-influence model provides a more ethical mode of influence than unilateral control (Model 1) because it provides safeguards against the misuse of influence (see Ch. 2).

Like Bandura (1974), we believe that the most reliable safeguard against manipulative control by therapists, however well-intended, resides in reciprocal consequences. We believe that feminist therapy makes an important contribution to the profession because it details strategies which provide reciprocal consequences to the therapist and the client. This is not true of psychotherapies generally. Table 3-I illustrates the parallels between Argyris' reciprocal-influence model (Model 2) and feminist-therapy strategies.

FEMINIST SEX-ROLE ANALYSIS AS A THERAPEUTIC TECHNIQUE

One of the major tools of feminist therapy is sex-role analysis (Brodsky, 1975). Traditional therapy often stagnates at the level of examining what is wrong with a client's behavior and never gets to the level of facilitating alternative directions. Table 3-II presents an analysis of the costs and benefits of fulfilling the feminine role, in contrast to the costs and benefits of fulfilling feminist values. Implied in feminist values are alternative behaviors.

A therapist uses sex-role analysis simply by bringing to the client's attention whenever relevant, unconscious sex-role expectations. (See Wyckoff, Ch. 20, "Radical Psychiatry for Women," for examples of sex-role analysis using a Transactional Analysis Model.) As women remedy the sex-role constrictions in their behavior, they discover strengths in themselves that they either had been unaware of or had regarded negatively. These strengths provide an important therapeutic base for pursuing rational and rewarding behavioral alternatives.

Sex-role analysis is also a useful means of lessening feelings of

TABLE 3 - I

PARALLELS BETWEEN ARGYRIS' RECIPROCAL INFLUENCE MODEL*
AND FEMINIST THERAPY STRATEGIES

*See Ch. 2 for a discussion of Argyris' (1975) Model

Reciprocal Influence Model	*Feminist Therapy Strategies*
I. Articulateness and advocacy of one's goals and values	Strategy 1. Before therapy begins, therapists have an obligation to clients to specify their values, especially those values regarding women's roles.
II. Invite others to confront one's views in order to alter them, based on the most complete and valid information possible.	Strategy 12. The therapist assumes that the client is her own best expert on herself. If the client disagrees with the therapist, she is encouraged to dispute her/his formulations rather than to defer to "authority".
III. Obtain the maximum contribution of each person involved in order to assure the widest possible exploration of views.	Strategy 18. Feminist therapy with women is done most effectively in groups.
IV. Share power with anyone who has competence and who is relevant in deciding or implementing the actions.	Strategy 2. Whenever possible, the personal power between the client and the therapist approaches equality.

	Strategy 4.	Before therapy begins the client and the therapist enter into a contract specifying the behavior the client wants to change.
	Strategy 13.	The client is given the tools to be her own therapist.
V. Do not make decisions for others.	**Strategy 3.**	Women are encouraged to be autonomous people.
	Strategy 4.	See IV above.
	Strategy 12.	See II above.
VI. Do not compete with others or use one-upmanship ploys for the purpose of self-gratification.	**Strategy 2.**	See IV above.
	Strategy 7.	Women are taught how to use straight communication and how to drop covert, manipulative behavior.
VII. If new concepts are created, the meaning given them by the creator and the inference processes used to develop them are open to scrutiny by those who expect to use them.	**Strategy 13.**	See IV above.

	Strategy 15. If a client is given tests, she is entitled to the results.
	Strategy 16. The client has access to reading whatever is in her chart, especially material being shared with other agencies or professionals.
VIII. Evaluations and attributions are minimized.	**Strategy 10.** The therapist usually takes what the client says at face value.
	Strategy 12. See II above.
	Strategy 14. Diagnostic testing is not ordinarily used.
	Strategy 17. The therapist does not use diagnostic labels.
IX. If evaluations and attributions are used, they are coupled with observable behavior that led to their formulation.	**Strategy 11.** The therapist confronts contradictory behavior. The therapist shares her/his opinion in behavioral terms. It is offered as her/his perception and not as a pronouncement of "what is really going on".
	Strategy 15. See VII above.
	Strategy 16. See VII above.
X. If evaluations and attributions are used, they are presented in such a way as to encourage open and constructive confrontation.	**Strategy 11.** See IX above.

TABLE 3 - II

A COMPARATIVE ANALYSIS OF SOME COSTS AND BENEFITS OF TRADITIONAL AND FEMINIST VALUES

Traditional Feminine Values Embodied in Cultural Female Role*	Benefits to Women* (for which there are no guarantees)	Costs to Women*
Reliance on a Male provider for sustenance and status	Economic security Less pressure to achieve	Subordination to men Less autonomy than men Lack of training and skills
Living through others and for others (men and children)	Emotional Security Ready-made solution for meaning and purpose of life. Development of positive feminine qualities of nurturance, warmth, sympathy, etc.	Loss of personal identity Emotional dependency Resentment from others who no longer need care Depression and bewilderment if there is no one left to care for
Ban on assertion, aggression and power strivings	Being taken care of and protected by men Being shielded from the anxiety of competition and risk-taking	Feelings of powerlessness Dependency on fair play from others No opportunity to develop confidence and determination
Emphasis on physical beauty and erotic qualities	Covert personal power over men	Development of narcissism Self-indulgence Crisis in aging Constricted personal development Frequent feelings of inferiority stimulated by unrealistic stereotypic standards of beauty and sexuality

*Adapted from Suzanne Keller: The female role: Constants and change. In Franks, Violet and Burtle, Vasanti (Eds.): *Women in Therapy: New Psychotherapies for a Changing Society*. New York, Burner/Mazel, 1974.

Alternative Feminist Values	Benefits to Women (which are self-guaranteed)	Costs to Women
Psychological and economic autonomy Having the skills to provide for oneself even if choosing not to do so	Possessing own social and professional status Development of own competencies and skills Not dependent on the benevolence of men	Pressure to achieve Physical illnesses due to competitive stress
Self-determination Control over one's own life	Development of own fully-functioning identity Choosing one's own life-style to fulfill closeness and intimacy needs Wide range of alternative life-styles from which to select Freedom to give to others by choice rather than by expectation Attendance to one's own needs before the needs of others Having more to give to others since more of one's own needs are met	Requirement of existential self-confrontation regarding meaning and value of one's own life Anxiety and "guilt" caused by old programming to devote oneself to others
Development of a full range of interpersonal skills and personal power	Greater satisfaction from personal and professional relationships A sense of control over one's own life Self-respect	Incurring risk of overt rejection from men Removal of the option to rely on others for protection
Pride in having a healthy strong body Emphasis on natural appearance	The experience of being centered and satisfied during sexual and physical activity	Loss of covert sexual power over men because sex is no longer used for manipulation and because traditional standards of beauty are no longer followed.

discouragement and depression sometimes experienced in the initial stages of therapy. This analysis shifts some of the responsibility for women's failure to act in ways they want to act from themselves to environmental constrictions. Traditional women locate a large portion of their personal dynamics within the fulfillment their sex-role. For them, sex-role analysis is a means of looking at their deficit behavior without losing as much self-esteem as they would if deficits were discussed in the context of personal inadequacy only — as with the traditional model of therapy. For a nontraditional woman, sex-role analysis explains why her behavior is unacceptable to others. Freed of defensive self-doubt, she can feel powerful and able to make necessary changes in her life.

While sex-role analysis conveys to a woman that it is not her fault that she is in her situation, it does convey that she is responsible for changing her situation. (See Feminist Therapy Value No. 4.) Personal autonomy is a very important feminist value. Constant protection from others is not feasible. Many therapists may worry that a client, who accepts a sex-role analysis of social conditions and, therefore, does not assume total responsibility for her predicament, will make no efforts in her own behalf. We have never found this to be so. On the contrary, the occasions in which women appear most unwilling to make efforts to improve their condition are when they are unwilling to accept the assumptions of feminist therapy and therefore a sex-role analysis. Instead they continue playing the blaming game: "If It Weren't for Him." (These games usually focus on how someone else prevents a woman from changing her own life.)

ISSUES

While it is not feasible to cover all therapeutic issues related to feminist therapy, we will deal with a few of those issues most commonly raised whenever we discuss feminist therapy with other feminist therapists: (1) Who can do feminist therapy? (2) Should male therapists treat women; if so, under what conditions? and (3) Are male therapists ever preferable to female therapists?

Who Can Do Feminist Therapy?

Therapists should not call themselves feminist therapists if they are not feminists. Feminists believe that skill, expertise, and a commitment to a feminist philosophy are more important credentials than formal degrees and titles. (This attitude is consistent with the egalitarian philosophy of feminism.) Therefore, having a professional degree is not a sufficient qualification nor is believing that women and men should be equal. Commitment to the principles of feminism is suspect if a therapist does not apply feminist principles to her/his personal as well as her/his professional life. Any therapist, female or male, is not qualified to treat women if s/he does not read the literature by women concerned with feminist issues and the subtle oppressions women experience. In addition, a therapist is not qualified to treat women unless s/he has participated in a consciousness-raising group.

Should Male Therapists Treat Women?

There is an advantage which male therapists, regardless of their skill, cannot offer to female clients. Only female therapists can serve as role models for female clients. This is very important because a tremendous amount of learning occurs through role models (Bandura, 1969).

Should men ever treat women? Some feminists, e.g. Chesler, 1972, take the position that men should not, both because of their inability to serve as role models and because of the built-in power differences between women and men in our society. We disagree with that extreme position. In our opinion, nonsexist and feminist men, who are knowledgeable about women's problems are qualified to treat women (see Brodsky, Ch. 16). Indeed, they would be *more* appropriate than a female therapist who is sexist in her approach to therapy. Some female clients are adamant about having a male therapist due either to antipathy toward females or internalized opinions of women's inferiority (Lazarus, 1974). If this is the case, treatment by a male therapist would be best.

When Men Should Not Treat Women

1. A man should not do therapy with an all-female group. Such a situation would be counter-productive to the goals of feminist therapy. It would produce a situation in which women are once more exposed to the role model of a powerful male to whom they are subservient. This situation reinforces old dependency conditioning and makes it difficult for women to learn to look to themselves for their own answers. It also sets up precisely the situation which women traditionally have learned is the only appropriate one in which to compete — competition for male attention resulting in alienation from each other as sources of support. Unless women learn competition in other areas is acceptable and that competition for male attention is self-defeating, they will not be able to form close emotional ties with other women, one of the essential ingredients

for feminist therapy (see Schultz, Ch. 19).

2. Men who have vestiges of guilt about the enforced subservience of women or who have rescue fantasies about women should not do therapy with dependent women whose husbands mistreat them. In such a situation, almost any therapist would wish that a woman had the courage to leave; such a male therapist, however, may feel so strongly that, unintentionally, he may direct her toward leaving without taking the time to first build up her self-sufficiency. A client's lack of self-sufficiency may be masked in therapy with a supportive male therapist because neither may realize that she has simply replaced the husband upon whom she was dependent with her male therapist. If she divorces, she will have great difficulty leaving therapy unless she first marries again.

3. Men should not do therapy with women who are hostile to men. Although the usual practice would be to assign such women to a male therapist in order to help them work through their hostility, that is surely the long way around. Such women are not likely to have much trust in male therapists at the beginning of therapy, when the work is the most difficult. It would be much better for a male-hostile woman to work with a female therapist and then, when the client felt she was ready, either introduce a male cotherapist or put the client in a mixed-sex group. Preparation for the change in the therapy arrangement can be facilitated by role-play and homework assignments toward new constructive ways to relate to men already in the client's life.

4. Men should not do therapy with women who relate to men primarily in a seductive manner. These women should be referred to a female therapist. Such women try appealing to male therapists sexually because that is the way they have learned to cope with men. However, it should be remembered that women have been socially conditioned to be pleasing to men and may have no intention to seduce the therapist, even though their behavior is often interpreted as seductive. The concern and interest of the therapist also may be interpreted by the client as sexual interest. These situations are avoided if the therapist is female.

Women who are extremely seductive, who would be labeled "blatant hysterics," often have tremendous dependency needs and have discovered no other way to deal with these needs.* For those women, seeing a male therapist would contribute no new learning to their methods of coping. A seductive woman usually has poor relationships with other women. A female therapist can provide such women with a model of a nurturant, but strong female from whom they can learn more adaptive coping mechanisms. Learning new places to receive support and new ways to relate to others (particularly women) will be facilitated in a feminist —

---

*Joy Kenworthy, personal communication, 1975.

therapy group. When these women develop close relationships with other women and increase their self-esteem, they no longer need resort to seductiveness in order to feel safe and powerful. When they arrive at this stage, participation in a mixed-sex group would be helpful to them in developing new ways of relating to men.

It is our opinion that the roles of lover and therapist should never be confused. Even when the justification is altruistic, sexual involvement of a therapist with a client is indefensible. The usual safeguards in the therapy setting that protect both the therapist and the client are lacking when the two people become sexually intimate. We do not think that analysis of sexual transference or countertransference is always essential to good therapy, though we do agree with Freudians that when these phenomena are dealt with in therapy, they should be handled verbally rather than acted out.

Perhaps the most important objection we have to the sexual involvement between therapist and client is to the political implication behind the involvement. The message conveyed by this behavior in a therapeutic setting is that a woman's sexual responsiveness is paramount to her emotional adjustment. This message from a therapist is particularly debilitating to a woman because our culture already defines a woman in terms of her sexuality at the expense of other aspects of her humanity. The therapist should be countering society's definition, not reinforcing it. We believe that how therapists and clients relate to each other after the therapy contract is terminated is a private matter between two consenting adults and not a professional concern. People should be able to do what they want, but they should not be able to call everything they do "therapy."

When It Would Be Preferable for Men Not to Treat Women

1. It would be best if men did not do therapy with women in the crisis of divorce. Women go through stages of grief after divorce, just as survivors of the dying go through stages of grief. During one of the stages a woman feels that she is a failure as a marriage partner, is unattractive to men, and is very frightened at the thought of being alone. This is a time in a woman's life when she is tremendously vulnerable to intense transference feelings. It may seem to be a great comfort to her to be able to ease her feelings of loss by replacing her husband with a new man, her therapist: warm, supportive, and interested in her. It may be so comforting that she would not be motivated to move ahead psychologically and become a strong, autonomous, adult person. She would remain as society conditioned her and as her therapist found her: dependent and getting all

her good feelings about herself from the attentions of a man. When her fantasies about her therapist are not realized, she might try to replace him with another man, the result would be that she learns nothing from the experience and grief of divorce; she only begins another round of looking for her life by looking for a man.

2. It would be best if men did not do therapy with extremely dependent, inhibited women who equate femininity with passivity and docility. These women would profit more from a female therapist who can model assertiveness and strength in the context of positive feminine qualities (see Ch. 8).

THERAPY TECHNIQUES

The following is a summary of psychotherapeutic techniques which are compatible with feminist therapy.

Cognitive Level

The purpose of these techniques is to raise consciousness regarding sex-role socialization and to modify belief systems that prevent women from breaking out of traditional patterns.

Bibliotherapy
Cognitive reprogramming
Consciousness-raising groups
Rational emotive therapy
Sex-role analysis
Sex-role scripting (from transactional analysis)
Women's studies

Emotional Level

The purpose of these techniques is to remove emotional blocks (guilt, anxiety, anger, fear) that prevent women from modifying traditional sex-role behaviors.

Bioenergetics
Creative fantasy
Gestalt exercises
Implosion
Psychodrama
Role Play
Systematic desensitization

Behavioral Level

The purpose of these techniques is to master skills for being more effective and competent in one's environment and to develop responsibility for overcoming feelings of helplessness and passivity.

Assertion training
Behavioral rehearsal (role play)
Contracts and homework assignments
Social and political action

Interpersonal Level

The purpose of these techniques is to improve interpersonal communication and interpersonal skills.

Communications training
Egalitarian relationship counseling (for couples)
Transactional analysis

Physical Level

The purpose of these techniques is to aid women to regain and improve physical power and strength, to overcome feelings of helplessness and passivity, and to increase positive body image.

Bioenergetics
Dancing
Karate
Physical fitness
Sports

CONCLUSIONS

The ideas about feminist therapy expressed represent our thinking to date. We do not consider them inviolate or the final word on the subject. Our thinking on feminist therapy is continually being revised as we exchange ideas with others engaged in feminist therapy and as we gain more experience with this new model.

We hope the values and strategies we have outlined will stimulate the critical thinking of others. The editors welcome dialogues, comments, and criticisms from other feminist therapists with the hope that conceptualizations of feminist therapy will be expanded, refined and enriched.

REFERENCES

Agel, Jerome (Ed.): *The Radical Therapist*. New York, Ballantine Books, 1971.

Argyris, Chris: Dangers in applying results from experimental social psychology. *American Psychologist, 30*:469, 1975.

Bandura, Albert: Behavior theory and the models of man. *American Psychologist, 29*:859, 1974.

Bandura, Albert: *Principles of Behavior Modification*. New York, Holt, Rinehart & Winston, 1969.

Bart, Pauline B.: Sexism and social science: from the gilded cage to the iron cage. *Know, Inc., 80*:10.

Brodsky, Annette M.: Is there a feminist therapy? Paper presented at a symposium, Issues in Feminist Therapy, Southeastern Psychological Association, Atlanta, March 1975.

Brodsky, Annette, Holroyd, Jean, Payton, Carolyn, Rubinstein, Eli, Rosenkrantz, Paul, Sherman, Julia, and Zell, Freyda: Report of the task force on sex bias and sex-role stereotyping in psychotherapeutic practice. *American Psychologist, 30*:1169, 1975.

Broverman, Inge K., Broverman, Donald M., Rosenkrantz, Paul S. and Vogel, Susan R.: Sex-role stereotypes and clinical judgments of mental health. *Journal of Consulting and Clinical Psychology, 34*:1, 1970.

Cannon, M. and Redick, R.: Differential utilization of psychiatric facilities by men and women — United States. Statistical Note 81. Washington, D.C., Survey and Reports Section, Biometry Branch, NIMH, 1973.

Chesler, Phyllis: *Women and Madness*. New York, Doubleday, 1972.

Deckard, Barbara S.: *The Women's Movement: Political, Socioeconomic, and Psychological Issues*. New York, Harper & Row, 1975.

Elias, Marilyn: Sisterhood therapy. *Human Behavior, 4*:56, April, 1975.

Erikson, Erik H.: Inner and outer space: reflections on womanhood. In Lifton, Robert Jay (Ed.): *The Woman in America*. Boston, Beacon, 1967.

Hollingshead, August B. and Redlich, Fredrick: *Social Class and Mental Illness*. New York, Wiley, 1958.

Jourard, Sidney: Lethal aspects of the male role. In *The Transparent Self*. Princeton, Van Nostrand, 1964.

Kaye, Harvey E.: *Male Survival*. New York, Grosset & Dunlap, 1974.

Lazarus, Arnold A.: Women in behavior therapy. In Franks, Violet and Burtle, Vasanti (Eds.): *Women in Therapy*. New York, Brunner/Mazel, 1974.

Mischel, Walter: *Personality and Assessment*. New York, Wiley, 1968.

Polk, Barbara B.: Male power and the women's movement. *Journal of Applied Behavioral Psychology, 10*:410, 1974.

Simon, Sidney B., Howe, Leland W., and Kirschenbaum, Howard: *Values Clarification: A Handbook of Practical Strategies for Teachers and Students*. New York, Hart, 1972.

Stevens, Barbara: The psychotherapists and women's liberation. *Social Work, 7*:12, 1971.

Chapter 4

COMPARATIVE CASE ANALYSES OF SEXIST AND FEMINIST THERAPIES

IN this chapter we will analyse two case histories: one taken from the literature and one taken from the files of one of the authors (D.K.C.). We will begin with the published case history.

"THE INTRACTABLE FEMALE PATIENT"

The published case history appeared in the *American Journal of Psychiatry, 129*:1, July 1972, under the title, "The Intractable Female Patient." It was written by H. Houck, M.D., Medical Director of the Institute of Living in Hartford, Connecticut.*

In using the phrase, "intractable female patient," Dr. Houck referred to a category of female patients with similar syndromes, histories, and courses of "illness." "Intractable," according to Houck, means that the patient is not easily governed, managed or controlled. The "illness" exhibited by these women is, therefore, difficult to relieve or cure. This intractability which leads to hospitalization actually appears long before the hospitalization is necessary. Although these patients may have a variety of diagnoses, Houck classifies them all under the category of *borderline syndrome* described by Grinker.†

The patient's presenting problems include anxiety and depression; chronic depression, characterized by anhedonia, is the most prominent feature. However, the patient may not describe herself as depressed, even though she looks and acts unhappy.

---

*We asked Dr. Houck's permission to publish his case history verbatim in this book; however, after we sent him material outlining the chapter in which his article would appear, he rescinded permission. He stated reasons were that our treatment would distort what he intended to say and that he did not wish to be placed, by implication, in either a profeminist or an antifeminist position. The reader will, therefore, have to rely on our summary of Dr. Houck's analysis. We recommend that the reader obtain Dr. Houck's original paper, both to form her/his own opinion of the case and to experience the full impact of Dr. Houck's approach.

†The borderline is a syndrome characteristic of arrested development of ego-functions. Some of the symptoms noted are: anger as the main affect, a deficiency in affectional relationships, depressive loneliness, and the apparent absence of self-identity. Although the borderline syndrome appears to be a confusing combination of psychotic, neurotic, and character disturbances with many normal elements, the process itself has a considerable degree of internal consistency and stability and is not merely a response to situational stress (Grinker, Werble, & Drye, 1968).

> Although they are often attractive, most of these women are socially awkward, sexually naive, and inhibited (p. 27) ... She is immature, anxious, and angry, usually aloof and contemptuous of other women, and demanding and suspicious of men (p. 28).

The early history of the patient reveals poor family relationships. Her mother was probably cold, aloof and dominating; her father, passive and withdrawn. Her husband "tends to be like the father: passive, variably indulent, and easily dominated" (p. 27). Sexual adjustment of the patient and her husband has always been poor. Child-rearing appears to be the stress that precipitated her hospitalization.

Soon after hospitalization the patient shows remarkable improvement. Houck attributes the improvement to secondary gains obtained by the patient in the form of relief from the demands of home and family. Labelling herself as "sick" legitimizes the patient's escaping from her life's responsibilities.

The hospital therapist, particularly a young resident, will immediately judge the patient as an excellent candidate for psychotherapy because, as Houck describes her, she is

> young, intelligent, articulate, psychiatrically sophisticated, well motivated ... She is, in short, exactly the kind of patient with whom the young resident in particular hopes to work (p. 27).

The resident and the patient quickly generate a lot of relevant case history material. The initial treatment plan includes intensive psychotherapy and, secondarily, some tranquilizing medicine. The patient rapidly develops a dependence on the therapist. Auspiciously, the therapist interprets this as transference.

Soon after therapy begins, a treatment crisis arises. The patient's depression and anxiety return without any apparent precipitating cause. Reassurances from the therapist and increases in medication merely exacerbate the problem. On the other hand, firm limits and control by the therapist lead to improvement. The patient's hostility diminishes, she becomes penitent, and improves. The young therapist may misinterpret this crisis and recovery as a turning point in therapy; however, similar crises continue to occur. The patient uses considerable guile and cunning to undercut the therapist's authority. She appears to derive pleasure from her ability to control therapy by producing a stalemate. In the face of repeated discouragement, the therapist, who is committed to psychotherapy, refuses to recognize that the patient is not making progress.

In spite of lack of progress, the husband seldom questions the hospital regarding treatment. He is actually more comfortable with his wife out of the home and he is, as noted above, a very passive person. In cases in which the husband does intervene by removing his wife from the hospital or by threatening divorce, the wife, faced with external conditions over which she has no control, may actually improve. Houck attributes improvement in this instance to the efficacy of environmental manipulation over intensive psychotherapy for this type of patient.

In contrast to the young therapist's treatment, Houck recommends short hospital stays without intensive psychotherapy and without encouragement of childlike dependence or regressive behavior.

> The patient's hospital stay must be comparatively brief, her therapy supportive and aggressively reality oriented, and her attention firmly fixed on home, family, and adult obligations ... The pressure throughout the whole of the hospital milieu moves ever toward control, maturity, and independence (p. 30).

In addition, Houck suggests that the therapist concentrate his effort on the husband to assist him in modifying

> lifelong attitudes of passivity and diffidence and to assume a posture of strength and resolution — especially toward his wife (p. 30).

The patient will, of course, be ambivalent about the personality changes occurring in her husband and she will use the ploys to test and undermine his dominance and control similar to those she used with her therapist.

She will not be happy to leave the hospital and return to the home; family stress may result in a return to the hospital. Again, the duration of hospitalization must be limited at the onset. Eventually it may be necessary to block hospitalization as an avenue of escaping her duties as wife and mother. Houck claims that the patient will not make progress until she exerts great pressures on the husband, testing him to take control:

> She will test him to the limit, but if he passes the test she is reassured and comforted. She will keep trying, but she is often aware, at last, that she really hopes she will not win (p. 31).

Comparative Case Analysis of "The Intractable Female Patient"

In the following comparative case analysis, Houck's conception of the problem, his values as a therapist and his approach to treatment will be contrasted with those of feminist therapists. Naturally, we cannot speak for all feminist therapists; thus the ideas expressed in the right-hand column represent our own views as feminist therapists. The concepts listed in the left-hand column represent our understanding or interpretation of what Dr. Houck has said in his article; we also assume full responsibility for that interpretation.

Dr. Houck's Therapy	**Feminist Therapy**
Conception of the Problem	*Conception of the Problem*

Terms such as "illness" and "disease" are used in describing the patient.

All the problems described in the paper are of a behavioral nature. The patient has "problems in living" (Szasz, 1971).

"Intractable" means that the patient is obstinate toward change and is not easily dominated. She has a strong will and she is not willing to be governed. In a woman these traits are evidence of pathology.

If the patient were male, such traits would be considered evidence of a well-integrated ego. Feminist therapists consider such traits to be healthy for *people*.

Her principal symptoms include depression and anhedonia.

If the patient is suffering from chronic depression, it seems that she is not sufficiently intractable for her own survival. Her intractability could be interpreted as a positive sign that she is fighting against being submerged as an individual.

The patient does not describe herself as depressed; however, she looks and acts depressed.

If the patient is depressed without awareness, she is out of touch with herself and her feelings; she may be attempting to suppress aspects of herself that are even more unacceptable to others than her present behavior.

The patient is hospitalized because she refuses to meet her adult responsibilities to her home and family.

The patient is hospitalized because of the failure of the traditional feminine sex role. As Bernard (1971) noted: "In truth, being a housewife makes women sick (1971, p. 53)." Since the patient and others in her environment (including her therapists) think that performing the fem-

Dr. Houck's Therapy	Feminist Therapy
	inine role is the only acceptable behavior for a woman, one of the patient's few alternatives is to "go crazy."
Soon after hospitalization the patient improved remarkably. This suggests that her hospitalization is providing her with secondary gains in the form of escaping from her home and family. Thus, her behavior is viewed from a moral perspective (shirking her responsibilities).	The patient has indeed escapped from the intolerable life situation — one that produced considerable stress for her. We view her behavior diagnostically, rather than morally, giving us clues to the nature of her conflict.
The patient's mother is described as cold, aloof, and domineering. Her father is described as passive and withdrawn. Her husband is also described as "passive, variably indulgent and easily dominated." In presenting these descriptions of significant others in the patient's environment, Houck implies that the root of her difficulties is a lack of adequate sex-role models.	We agree that the patient may be having difficulty in adapting to the traditional feminine sex-role. We also believe that the patient's important people, as described, would not provide effective role models for anyone, male *or* female.
The patient is described as attractive but "socially awkward, sexually naive and inhibited."	Houck's description fits the traditional female in our society. Appearance, sociability and sexuality are the dimensions on which women are judged. Other dimensions are assumed to be essentially irrelevant.
The patient is described as "young, intelligent, articulate, psychiatrically sophisticated and well-motivated." She is mistak-	The patient fits Goldstein's (1972) description of the ideal patient: YAVIS (young, attractive, verbal, intelligent, sophisticated).

Dr. Houck's Therapy	Feminist Therapy
enly viewed as an ideal candidate for intensive psychotherapy.	This description suggests that she not only is an ideal patient but also has considerable personal strengths to draw upon in spite of the pathonomic diagnostic labels she receives from psychiatrists.
The patient is described as immature. **Note:** "Immature" is a vague term which is not defined in the text. We assume from the context that Houck means the patient does not have an adequate (traditional) sex-role identification, i.e. she does not do her housework or take care of her children. She also has the audacity to challenge the therapist's authority.	According to our diagnostic formulation the patient does not have an adequate sense of her own personhood, even though she dares to struggle to define herself in the face of strong social and therapist disapproval.
Houck also describes the patient as contemptuous of women and suspicious of men.	In our culture women are trained in these behaviors and in turn are labelled pathological by therapists for exhibiting them.
The patient allegedly yearns for affection and dominance.	Wanting affection seems to us a normal human desire. Wanting to be dominated is the interpretation of a male psychiatrist based upon beliefs concerning appropriate behavior for a woman. We agree that the patient exhibits conflict over the issue of dominance, vacillating between dependency and attempts to assert herself. A basic theme that emerges in this case is one of control: whether the patient will be allowed to decide the course of her life or whether others (therapist and husband) will direct her life.

Dr. Houck's Therapy	Feminist Therapy

Houck insists that the core of the patient's syndrome is anger.

We agree, but view her anger as appropriate and healthy. Using sex-role analysis, a feminist therapist could assist the patient in articulating the basis of her anger and channeling it in constructive ways.

The sexual adjustment of this patient is difficult and unsatisfying.

Why attribute the sexual difficulties solely to the patient? Masters and Johnson (1970) attribute 50 per cent of any sexual problem to the wife and 50 per cent to the husband. Since we know that the interpersonal relationship between this couple is unsatisfactory, we would be surprised if they reported a satisfactory sexual relationship. Bardwick (1973) observed that the "normal" woman usually engages in coitus not to gratify her own genital sexuality but to satisfy her male partner's needs and to secure his love. Reduced to using sex as barter for affection, this woman, along with many other women, does not derive physical pleasure from sex.

* * *

Treatment Goals

Treatment Goals

Therapy is to be reality oriented; i.e. the patient should be encouraged to assume her adult obligations of housework and motherhood. In sum, the patient should achieve an adequate feminine identity.

The focus of treatment should

Therapy will include sex-role analysis. The therapist will show the woman how the traditional role expectations for women are related to her present conflicts. She will be encouraged to neutralize the effect of other's expectations upon her to decide what

Dr. Houck's Therapy

be toward independence and maturity.

Note: These words are operationally defined by Houck. He implies that an independent, mature woman carries out her adult obligations as stated above.

The husband should be helped to become dominant in the relationship and to control his wife who should be submissive and dependent in the relationship.

Feminist Therapy

she wants for herself, and to take charge of her life to attain her goals.

Feminists would not disagree with the goals of independence and maturity, but would define them in a different way. "Independence" implies that a woman has achieved a separate personhood, i.e. she has a sense of identity beyond that of wife, mother, and daughter. She also should have the means to be economically independent if she so chooses. "Maturity" means that she takes responsibility for the direction of her life and is capable of working in a persistant fashion toward achieving her goals.

Feminists oppose the traditional heterosexual relationship model of male dominance and female submission. Healthy relationships are based on equality between the persons involved. A basic inconsistency in the feminine role is that women are expected to be competent and strong, *except* when they are relating to men. The wife cannot achieve independence and maturity if significant males (therapists and husband) are consistently blocking and punishing her self-assertive responses. Both the husband and wife described in this case history would probably benefit from assertion training to learn how to assert their needs in an appropriate manner (see Ch. 8

Dr. Houck's Therapy	Feminist Therapy

and Ch. 9 for a description of assertion training for women).

*   *   *

Style of Treatment

Authoritarian. The therapist is expected to be in control of the patient who is ideally cooperative and docile. The therapist sets the goals of treatment and uses his influence over the patient and her environment to see that his goals are achieved. The therapist is cautioned by Houck to set limits and to exert firm control.

Style of Treatment

Egalitarian. The therapist and woman client will enter into a therapy contract agreeing on the goals of treatment. Feminist therapists assume that a woman can accurately report her own reality. If the therapist observes discrepancies in a woman's behavior or between her behaviors and therapy goals s/he will point out these discrepancies as the therapist's perception, not as reality.

*   *   *

Recommended Treatment Approach.

Environmental manipulation. Limited stays in the hospital, training the husband to be more dominant in the relationship, and blocking future hospitalizations in order to prevent the patient from escaping her responsibilities as a wife and mother are the treatment recommendations.

The patient's attempts to control and manipulate the therapist are to be avoided.
Note: This suggests suspicion and mistrust of her motives.

Recommended Treatment Approach

Environmental analysis including sex-role analysis. This recommended approach would neutralize the patient's feeling "crazy." Any environmental changes that she decides to make after careful examination of the consequences, including divorce or reconciliation with husband, are respected by the therapist.

The therapist and woman enter into a treatment contract which includes mutually agreed on goals and ways of achieving them. This reduces the possibility of manipulation by either party.

Dr. Houck's Therapy	Feminist Therapy
Houck opposes intensive individual psychotherapy. Presumably individual therapy will prolong treatment and collude with the patient's attempts to evade her responsibilities to her husband and children.	Feminist therapists prefer to work in group therapy. A group of women who have faced similar problems provide support and confirmation of the patient's reality. A group will not allow her to evade her responsibilities to herself. The therapeutic contract and feedback from the group will prevent the therapist or the woman from prolonging treatment.

* * *

Implied Values	*Explicit Values*
Acceptance of marriage as the only acceptable life-style for women.	Traditional marriage based on the dominance-submission model is oppressive to women; healthy relationships are based on equality. Many life-styles are acceptable for women.
A woman can be fulfilled only as a wife and mother.	Unless a woman is fulfilled as a person she cannot be fulfilled as a wife and mother (Seidenberg, Ch. 7).
A woman's mental health depends on her being submissive and having a dominant husband.	A woman's mental health depends on her having personal power — being effective in controlling her own life.

SARA: A CASE HISTORY

We would like to now consider another case history. This one was taken from the files of one of the authors (D.K.C.). The client, Sara, was a thirty-year-old, married woman with two adopted children. Her husband was a thirty-three-year-old computer programmer with a large firm. Their oldest child was an eleven-year-old male, diagnosed hyperkinetic, brain-damaged and emotionally disturbed. Their youngest child was female, three-year-old and normal. The client, Sara, had an apartment in a community where she attended a university. Wednesdays and weekends she commuted forty miles to her husband's home. Her daughter lived with her during the week and her son lived with her husband. Sara initially came in for vocational counseling and testing. Her major department had lost its federal funding and was being dissolved and so she needed another major.

When Sara requested her appointment, she asked to see a female therapist. During our intake interview her manner appeared to be somewhat constricted and I sensed that she was regarding me suspiciously. At that time I was at a loss as to the reason for this behavior. Sara did not indicate an interest in personal counseling and since she seemed reluctant to disclose much information about herself, I responded to her as a straight-forward vocational-education case. I was a little uneasy doing so. Because of her suspicious regard for me, I wondered about other concerns or misapprehensions with which she may have been struggling.

Sara took the Strong Vocational Interest Inventory (SVII) and we arranged for the interpretation the following week. During the second interview, Sara again seemed guarded and reluctant to do any exploration, and so we commenced with interpreting the SVII. The results of the test suggested that Sara had intellectual and verbal interests, that she would enjoy being helpful to others, and that she would be comfortable in a position of power and authority.

Sara's behavior first became unguarded when I told her that she had interests in common with people in positions of power and authority. When I conveyed that information to her, she appeared uncertain, looked down at the floor for a moment, and then looked up and asked if I thought that was all right. I did not at that time understand the significance of her concern. I therefore simply answered, "Of course, why not?" With that she appeared relieved and considerably more relaxed for the remainder of the interview. As we had not concluded the test interpretation at the end of the hour, we arranged for another appointment the following week.

During our third interview we completed the interpretation of the SVII. During this interview Sara no longer appeared to regard me with suspicion. She shared with me her sensitivity to appearing nonfeminine; that is, as strong and powerful and effective. She then described her experience at a mental inpatient facility where her son had been hospitalized. During the course of treatment for her son, she and her husband were in family therapy with her son's therapists, a psychiatrist and a social worker (both males). She said that during the therapy sessions she felt like a "rabbit being attacked by a wolf pack" (her words). She said that it was during family therapy that she began to view her power, effectiveness and strength as pathological.

During this third interview Sara also reported to me the response of her son's therapists when she told them of her intention to file for divorce. She said both men became very, very angry and said that divorcing her husband and breaking up the family would absolutely undermine any therapeutic gains that had been made with her son in the past year. They further stated that if she acted upon her intention to seek divorce, they would encourage her husband to contest the divorce and to seek custody of both children. They both said they would testify against her in court, and that the testimony would be so damaging that no judge would give her custody. Both men told her that at that time they considered her to be unstable and emotionally immature. They said they did not believe she would be able to raise children alone and, therefore, in the event her husband was not awarded custody, they would recommend removal of her daughter. They said that the judge would probably place both children in other adoptive homes. Sara reported that her husband, who was present, did not challenge their proposed course of action, even though that action would also adversely affect him.

In recounting the session she appeared terrified at the prospect of losing the children. I questioned the counselor's ability to carry out that threat, but she seemed convinced because it had been necessary to assign custody of her son to the state in order for him to receive hospitalization and because both children were adopted.

While puzzled by her description of the behavior of her former therapists, I did not question her further because I was reluctant to engage in a negative discussion about colleagues. I was somewhat disbelieving; however, except for her initial suspiciousness which had disappeared after the second interview, Sara seemed to be a reliable person. I, therefore, resolved to hold in abeyance either my belief or disbelief in Sara's story.

It was during this session that Sara asked if she could receive personal counseling in addition to vocational counseling. It was also during this session that she requested that I make no notes. This request was in reaction to the constant note-taking by her son's therapists of information which she later found being used against her.

Her commitment to personal counseling was ambivalent, even though she felt she needed it. Her ambivalence was due to her fear that seeking counseling might strengthen her son's therapists ability to substantiate her being "emotionally unstable" and an unfit mother. She believed that strengthening their case would surely result in the loss of her children if she were to divorce her husband. Sara felt strongly that she could not emotionally sustain the loss of her daughter; her feelings toward her son were mixed. She was concerned about his well-being but believed that in his present state, a structured residential treatment was preferable to an unstructured home environment. (Released from the state hospital, the son was living with Sara's husband and was creating problems which her husband was not effectively handling.).

When the two therapists threatened the removal of her children, Sara had dropped any idea of divorcing at that time. Instead, she began living in her own apartment near the university and commuting home on Wednesdays and the weekends. She said she still did eventually intend to get a divorce and that she would really like to do so as soon as possible.

In order for her to estimate what the two therapists might testify against her in a custody action, she asked for my help to determine the degree of pathology they believed she possessed. She wanted me to request a confidential report from them about her. I was reluctant to do that because it seemed like colluding with a client against colleagues. I resolved my conflict by reasoning that Sara did have a great deal of disruptive anxiety about this matter and that examining the report was, perhaps, the most direct way to resolve the anxiety. Consequently, I agreed to her request.

As this was the end of the semester, I suggested that she should make an appointment for the beginning of the next semester. However, she said she felt so anxious about the content of the psychiatric report that she did not wish to wait that long, and instead wished to make an extra trip to the university during Christmas vacation.

During our fourth session, I conveyed part of the contents of her former therapists' report to Sara. I did not feel it ethical to permit her to read it and so I paraphrased selected portions to her. When I paraphrased a part that indicated Sara appeared to the former therapists to be rejecting her son, James, she collapsed with body-rendering sobs. It was some time before she was quiet enough to speak. She then described five years of being isolated at home with a hyperkinetic, emotionally disturbed child. Neighbors rejected her son and would not permit him to visit. Church people rejected him and eased her and her husband out of the church. Friends rejected him and dropped her and her husband as friends. Everyone who rejected her son rejected her as well for having such a son. She said her husband appeared indifferent to the problem and that his passivity had increased during the years. He fell into the practice of being sick on weekends, lying in bed all day Saturday and Sunday and escaping to work during the week. Thus, he offered her no help. On the contrary, he formed an alliance with her son, supporting him against Sara when she attempted to impose discipline. For example, periodically their son would become angry with Sara and threaten to poison her food and kill her. The child would then put chemicals in her drinking water and needles in her food. When she became angry, her husband would say that she was overreacting because their son had told her what he was going to do.

I asked how Sara and her husband came to adopt such a troubled child. Sara explained that she and her husband had had James in their homes as a foster child when he was three-and-one-half years old. Before that time he had been rejected by both parents (divorced) and four sets of foster parents. He had apparently been badly treated in the foster homes because of his erratic and occasionally bizarre behavior. Because of the child's past history and age, his next placement would have been the state institution for the mentally retarded. Out of love and compassion, Sara and her husband adopted James.

My treatment goal for Sara was that her anxiety be reduced so that she could get on with the business of finishing school. I decided that her external dilemmas with her son and her husband should be held in abeyance until she had achieved some financial and personal independence. She would then be in a position to make decisions regarding the external dilemmas based on her own reasons and not in response to the demands of other people or to environmental stress.

In addition to the external threats of losing her children and a troubled marriage, I believed that Sara's anxiety stemmed mainly from her questioning her own stability. Her father was diagnosed as schizophrenic after WWII, but he had maintained himself well outside of institutions. Her son's therapists had spent a lot of time talking to Sara about her father and his effect on her. In contrast to her fear that she was truly immature and emotionally unstable, I believed that Sara was a very stable person: she had a great deal of ego strength and good coping skills. I believed her main problems were not internally generated but external: having to sustain a tremendous amount of environmental stress. I took a gamble on my clinical judgment and suggested that she take a MMPI as an objective indication of the degree of her health or sickness. Since believing that she was sick did not appear to be a part of her defense system, I thought such an illustration would be sufficient to convince her of her basic psychological integrity.

During our next interview I interpreted the results of her MMPI to her. The results indicated that her stability was easily within the normal range (with no T-score above 60). I told her that this profile was the most stable I had seen among a client population and that, in fact, it was probably lower than my own during the time when I was under the stress of graduate school. She was so thrilled that she asked for a copy of it to pin on her bedroom wall for reinforcement. I gave her a copy and she left the interview absolutely floating.

At our next interview Sara appeared very upset. She said that her husband accused her of being a lesbian, then she burst into tears. (I have since found this to be a common accusation of husbands who appear threatened by their wives' interest in feminism and closeness to other women.) She recounted the situation; she had not accepted her husband's sexual advances for the past several weeks. She feared being with him alone so had invited a girlfriend to stay the night. Her main fear of the accusation from her husband was that he would share his belief with her family. His telling her family posed a threat to her because she wanted their support if she divorced. She feared this would convince them to take his side in a divorce contest. She also feared that it posed a threat for the custody of her daughter. By the following week her husband had resolved his anger and had withdrawn his accusations.

I continued seeing Sara weekly for about three months. Her relationship with her husband, though tenuous, was stable and school was going well. I, therefore, suggested that we cut back on our sessions. When I suggested this, she said she would like to do something about her weight problem, which neither of us had mentioned up to that point. She was approximately one hundred and twenty pounds overweight. She said that weight had been a problem for a number of years. We initiated several approaches: nutrition, exercise and behavioral control. Later we added self-hypnosis. Her main interest in losing weight appeared to be wanting to feel better and to be more healthy and physically strong. She had visions of teaching her daughter to mountain climb.

We worked almost exclusively on the weight problem for about a month and were doing well. Then some time at the end of April, Sara came in very upset. She had a lot on her mind and because of anxiety had begun to overeat. She was depressed about her grades: she worked hard but seemed unable to get more than B's and C's in her courses and that was a worry since she wanted to go to graduate school. Also, her husband was complaining about the cost of maintaining Sara and their daughter in separate housing. She felt guilty about taking the money but she thought it was the only way she could get her degree. She also felt the money was due after performing household responsibilities for ten years with no compensation other than room, board and a limited wardrobe.

In addition, even though James was getting worse, her husband was unwilling to put him in a residential home. Sara had concluded that she could not live with her husband because of their son's unmanageable behavior. (Shortly before this time she had begun to feel stronger and more confident and her husband had appeared to try harder, so she had resolved to try to make the marriage work.) She was most disturbed by her son's behavior toward her daughter. Recently he had begun making overt sexual gestures toward the four-year-old. This alarmed Sara considerably, though apparently her husband was not concerned.

In processing her next anxiety we talked about her feelings about herself. She believed herself to be generally unworthy and felt that she had to earn or contribute ten times over anything she received in return. We concluded that this characteristic was probably a contributing factor in sustaining her husband's dependent behavior.

I saw Sara only sporadically over the summer and into the early fall. During that time she had continued to work on her weight and to work things out with her husband. She also continued her living arrangement at school, commuting home on the weekends to visit her husband and son. During the early fall she said that her husband was becoming quite passive again and she requested that he receive counseling. He was initially reluctant to participate but did eventually agree. Since Sara felt it was important that he see a female counselor, I arranged for him to see a woman on our staff. He saw her for approximately six sessions.

During midsemester, Sara was suddenly hospitalized for severe distolic hypertension. Her blood pressure had reached 205 over 120. She was placed on heavy medication (Aldomet®, Valium®, and Hydrodiuril®) with advice that this would be necessary for at least a year. Her doctors ordered her to avoid situations of stress. Sara concluded that the most severe stress on her at the present time was her reluctant participation in her marriage. She, therefore, finally determined to initiate divorce proceedings. Her husband's response was to threaten suicide. She believed the threat and it frightened her a great deal. The threat would have been effective, except that she now viewed the situation as either her life or his. She resolved that at least he had a choice and she did not, and that she must, therefore, continue with the divorce action. She did agree to marriage counseling prior to the final action in order to establish another therapeutic contact for her husband, should he wish to begin further counseling after the divorce.

The divorce action did not result in her husband taking his own life, nor did her two former therapists testify against her in court. Without the frequent trips to her husband's home, her blood pressure improved and she was able to decrease her medication. Decreasing her medication allowed her studying to become more effective and her outlook to improve considerably. I continued to see her on an informal, irregular basis through the next spring. Upon graduation she moved to a western state where she found employment in social work. Her daughter moved with her; her son did not.

She returned for a visit two years later and dropped by to see me. By this time James had been placed by her former husband in the state mental hospital. Her return visit was for the purpose of visiting James. Her repeated requests to the hospital for weekly or bimonthly telephone calls to her son (at her expense) had been denied by the medical administrator of the hospital. Her means of communicating with James for the previous nine months had been through her husband who had visitation privileges and by letter. However, Sara had been hesitant to write for fear that written communication with her son would not be private and that social workers and her former husband would read her letters and misconstrue her meaning.

Her trip was for the purpose of spending a chance three hours with her son. (Seeing him was not a certainty until the day before she was allowed to see him and James had not been informed that she wanted to see him.) She wanted James to know that she had not deserted him and that she was still concerned for his well-being. Through direct communication with him she hoped to ascertain his feelings about returning to his father's home after final release. If, however, he expressed a desire to live with her as he had previously, she planned to work for that end. While a decision was not made regarding James' final living situation, Sara did feel the visit was a success: She was able to convey her love and concern to James and her willingness to provide a home for him if that was his decision.

COMPARATIVE CASE ANALYSIS OF SARA

In the following comparative case analysis we will contrast Sara's former therapists' approach to treatment with the approach of feminist therapy. The statements expressed in the *Former Therapy* column are our interpretation. The statements are based on Sara's reports and on implications from the report about Sara. We assume full responsibility for that interpretation.

Former Therapy

Conception of the Problem

The former therapists' diagnosis was that Sara had deep-seated emotional problems, probably stemming from her relationship with her schizophrenic father. Evidence of her emotional problems included her strength in the relationship with her husband, her personal style of confidence and determination, and her career goal of a position of power and effectiveness. These emo-

Feminist Therapy

Conception of the Problem

The problem would have been perceived by feminist therapists as almost totally environmental. Sara's stability and ego control appeared very well integrated — amazingly so considering the amount of environmental stress with which she was living. Those characteristics which her former therapists perceived as pathological (confident personal style, determination, and professional

Former Therapy

tional problems resulted from a faulty perception of herself and a faulty perception of her role as a homemaker and a career woman.

Feminist Therapy

career goals) feminist therapists perceive as strengths.

Her perception of herself as a homemaker and a career woman appeared to be well-balanced. She was attending to both elements in her life. If there had been processing of the distribution of her energy between these roles, if possible, there would have been similar processing of her husband's distribution of energy between his roles as a wager-earner, father, and husband.

*   *   *

Treatment Goals

The treatment goals for family therapy are not directly comparable to individual therapy. Nevertheless, it is possible to illustrate contrasts in points of view.

The focus of therapy was on Sara's perception of herself, her role as a homemaker and a career woman. Based on the interaction between Sara and the therapists, treatment goals, (presumably) would have been achieved if Sara had moved back to her husband's home on a full-time basis and dropped back to being a part-time student. Of primary importance, of course, was that she process (submerge) her present dissatisfaction with her husband and stay married.

Treatment Goals

Even in family therapy a feminist therapist would not ask one of the parents to submerge his or her personal needs for the sake of keeping the family intact. This is often done, of course, in traditional therapy and it is usually the wife, rather than the husband who is asked to sacrifice. It is reasoned that since the husband provides the financial support, that his time and needs are less flexible than the wife's, whose apparent purpose, after all, is to care for the needs of others.

The treatment goal of feminist therapy is to encourage a woman to be as strong as she can be — at the very minimum, strong enough to take care of herself. My goal for Sara was simply to enable her to accept and affirm the

Former Therapy	**Feminist Therapy**

strength she already possessed.

* * *

Style of Treatment	*Style of Treatment*

Based on Sara's description, her therapy experience would be characterized as strongly authoritarian. Such a characterization is supported by the manner in which the therapist handled Sara's announcement that she intended to file for divorce. That interaction was outrageously authoritarian. It suggests anger on the part of the therapists and has elements of power struggle.

Feminist strategy emphasizes reciprocal influence. It is not, therefore, authoritarian; any semblance of a power struggle is avoided. If anger is felt toward a client, a feminist therapist would confront the client with her/his anger directly, taking personal responsibility for it.

* * *

Treatment Outcome	*Treatment Outcome*

Treatment outcome would be considered a dismal failure by Sara's traditional therapists. Sara continued with her studies, obtained a profession, divorced her husband, and her son, James, was returned, by her husband, to institutionalized care. This listing probably included almost everything the therapists were working to prevent.

Treatment would be considered an outstanding success by feminist therapists. When she entered therapy, Sara was suspicious, constricted, unsure of her stability and carrying tremendous environmental stress. Two years after treatment Sara was feeling strong and confident and, with one exception, had achieved all of her goals. She had obtained an academic degree, a satisfying profession, and a personal life of her own design. The unmet goal was a life for her son, James, which he would find secure and satisfying. However, with her recent achievements, she was feeling energetic

Former Therapy	Feminist Therapy
	and now was able to devote some attention to her son's happiness. That goal is still in process.

*   *   *

Implied Values	*Implied Values*
A woman should submerge her own needs for the sake of her family and children. For a woman not to do so creates suspicion that she may be an unfit mother.	Neither women nor people who may depend upon them can afford to have women submerge their own needs for the sake of others. Doing so is not only unjust, it is unwise. The result leaves the women with less ability to be supportive to others than if they were free to meet their own needs first.
A woman's place is in the home. Academic and career aspirations are properly curtailed in the event of any conflict.	A woman's (person's) place is wherever she is most happy and comfortable. For some women that happy place is in the home, for others it is not. Neither choice should impose a penalty in terms of limited personal growth or the critical regard of others.

Discussion

Sara's case was a very difficult one for me because I made three interventions which at that time I felt were therapeutic but which definitely went against the training I had received as a therapist. The first incident was my requesting the confidential report from Sara's former therapists. This request was for Sara's purpose and not mine. I would not have made the request for my own purpose, since I assumed that that treatment focused on the family constellation and not on Sara's personal growth. The second incident was my administering a personality test (MMPI) to Sara for the purpose of convincing her of her stability, rather than for my own need of diagnostic information. This would have been considered "gimmicky," shallow, and doomed to be ineffective by my nondirective, insight-oriented supervisors. The third incident was my giving her a copy of her MMPI profile to take home. This was a fairly extreme gesture since my training stressed that one only rarely showed a personality profile to a client. The possibility of a client's taking a profile home was never entertained.

When I was seeing Sara, I had not heard of such a thing as feminist therapy. It is interesting, therefore, that those interventions I made with Sara (and worried about) were all consistent with feminist therapeutic strategies. The first incident, by requesting the psychological report from her former therapists, would fall under Feminist Strategy No. 16, *The client has access to whatever is in her chart*, and Strategy No. 19, *Engaging in social action is an essential professional responsibility of the therapist*. Generally, a feminist therapist would be expected to take social action against repressive social institutions. In this case the repressive social institution was the institution of traditional psychotherapy. The second incident, administering the MMPI for Sara's purpose rather than my own, was an instance of Strategy No. 13, *The client is given the tools to be her own therapist*. Therapists' instruments should not be withheld from the clients, even at the discretion of therapists. Such a philosophy of withholding promotes control and elitism on the part of therapists. The third incident was my giving her a copy of her MMPI to take home. This was an instance of Strategy No. 15, *If a client is given tests, she is entitled to the results*. Since she produced the results and since the information is about her, she shares in the ownership.

In addition to the interventions I made, a situation which also made me uncomfortable was being asked to respond to Sara's report of her former treatment. I still would attempt not to discuss with clients their dissatisfaction with colleagues, however, I would now have much less trouble in believing that what the client reported had occurred. I am now aware of similar treatment occurrences with other women. (When strong women report an experience with traditional therapists, some of them also report difficulty with treatment and often end therapy feeling worse rather than better.) To have accepted Sara's report, rather than to question it as a possible symptom of pathology, is consistent with Feminist Strategy No. 10., *The therapist usually takes what the client says at face value,* and Strategy No. 12, *The therapist assumes that the client is her own best expert.*

At the time I was seeing Sara there was no such thing as feminist therapy and I was little acquainted with the feminist movement. During the following spring I was "drafted" to teach a women's studies course. This gave me knowledge of feminism; it was knowledge of feminism plus treating women in situations like Sara's which was responsible for my own personal and professional conversion to feminist therapy. I now use feminist strategies with no trepidation. Cases like Sara's are now not the most difficult for me, but the most easy. Strong, independent, assertive women like Sara respond quickly and easily to the values and strategies of feminist therapy.

REFERENCES

Bardwick, Judith M.: *Psychology of Women.* New York, Harper and Row, 1971.

Bernard, Jessie: *The Future of Marriage.* New York, Bantam, 1973.

Goldstein, Arnold: *Psychotherapeutic Attraction.* New York, Pergamon, 1971.

Grinker, Roy R., Sr., Werble, Beatrice, and Drye, Robert C.: *The Borderline Syndrome.* New York, Basic Books, 1968.

Houck, John H.: The intractable female patient. *American Journal of Psychiatry, 129*:27, 1972.

Masters, William H., and Johnson, Virginia E.: *Human Sexual Inadequacy.* Boston, Little, Brown, 1970.

Szasz, Thomas S.: *The Ethics of Psychoanalysis.* New York, Dell, 1965.

Section III

NONSEXIST APPROACHES TO PSYCHOTHERAPY FOR WOMEN

INTRODUCTION

A MAJOR value espoused by nonsexist therapists is equality of personal power between the sexes. The authors included in this section on nonsexist therapy demonstrate particular concern with the issue of promoting personal power for women. Shainess and Seidenberg, both psychoanalysts, are critical of current practices in psychotherapy which discourage women's strivings toward autonomy and self-mastery. Shainess' critique is primarily directed at individual psychotherapists and Seidenberg focuses on marriage counseling. Seidenberg is against *any* relationship (marriage) counseling. Even those readers who see this as an overreaction will be challenged by his thoughtful discernment of the documented abuses against women that take place in the name of marriage counseling and in the name of marriage itself. This section also contains a positive selection by Brien and Sheldon. They describe Gestalt therapy approaches to assist women in developing their personal power and in achieving full human potential.

In "The Equitable Treatment of Women in Psychoanalysis," Natalie Shainess criticizes therapists for their failure to provide therapy appropriate to the needs of female clients. She contends that the special problems of women in psychotherapy are either related to women's history of powerlessness or, in some instances, to simply being female. The false and contemptuous assumptions about women are reflected in therapists' value judgments about women's mental health and personality development and in the (mis)treatment women receive in mental hospitals at the hands of therapists.

Shainess charges that few therapists, due to their prejudices and personal needs, can understand the woman who takes steps to affirm her own authenticity. Concepts of self-worth and interpersonal mastery are important to women in the development of competence in many areas of their lives. This development is complicated by their guilt over self-assertion. Therapists need to assist women in developing constructive belief systems that affirm their rights as persons and in learning assertive skills (see Jakubowski, Ch. 9). Women in submissive positions fear risk-taking, yet risk-taking is essential to personality growth. Therapists must be alert to the subtle aggression women receive from men (often reflected in patterns of social interaction and linguistics) in order to help women

101

overcome guilt and anxiety rather than augmenting it.

Seidenberg's critique of marriage counseling, "Should this Marriage (Counseling) Be Saved?", is both an attack on the current practices of marriage counseling and on the institution of marriage itself. The structure of psychoanalysis (criticized by feminists for its hierarchical nature) is defended by Seidenberg, a psychoanalyst, for its emphasis on "privacy, confidentiality, and the autonomous strivings of the individual" which, in his opinion, practitioners in the field of marriage counseling have disregarded.

Seidenberg argues that persons, not marriages are worth saving. Marriage counseling implies a value judgement about marriage. He claims that "It is like learning about the choice of religion and atheism in the Vatican!" Therapists are often unaware of the oppressive nature of marriage (based on a dominance-submission model) for women. Women who complain to their therapists about their seemingly reasonable husbands risk being labelled paranoid or "sick." Therapists should consider that the problem may be in the institution itself. A benign master is still a slaveholder.

Since a woman gives up the rights of autonomy and choice in marriage, psychotherapy should be one place where she is not required to abdicate those rights. Psychoanalysis is designed to deal with individuals, not marriages, families, or communities. Seidenberg concedes that these relationships may be important to a woman, but her responsibilities to her family and her household cannot be well-served if she is not self-fulfilled. Her personal strivings, even if eccentric, should be the first concern of the therapist.

Married persons without internalized tools of operation or powers of persuasion have looked to others to perform managerial roles to make their mates behave. Traditionally, the clergy and the state performed these roles. Today psychotherapists and counselors have taken over this duty which involves religious, legal and psychological considerations. Innovations have been plentiful in this field where "everything works."

At the basis of marital problems is the question of human rights which are often not recognized. Marriage counseling is too often an unacknowledged adversary proceeding which lacks the legal safeguards of individual rights — due process, right to an advocate, etc. Therapists should follow the legal model and become advocates or agents for their clients, respecting the client's goals, privacy, and confidentiality. Although the intrusion of marriage counselors may provide some temporary stability in the relationship, Seidenberg maintains that the only ultimate solution to personal problems is to be found "in inner strength, understanding and communication between the inner and outer self, rather than attempts to change the other." He contends that the structure and rules governing the client and the therapist are of the greatest importance and can serve as a model of other relationships, including marriage.

Seidenberg's antimarriage counseling stance will undoubtedly appear unreasonable to those who practice in this field. However, his impassioned plea for therapists to make the needs and the rights of the individual client their primary concern and his analysis of the oppressive nature of marriage for women deserves the earnest consideration of all who practice psychotherapy. Relationships based on inequality between partners are truly not worth saving. Marriage counseling or any form of therapy that ignores the needs of individuals and elevates the importance of a relationship above the persons involved is not worth saving either.

In the last article in this section, "Gestalt Therapy for Women," Lois Brien and Cindy Sheldon point out that the phenomenological and expansionistic nature of Gestalt therapy does not support women (or men) in sexist roles. Gestalt therapists use experiments to aid women to get in touch with themselves and their bodies and to discover what they want for themselves and for others. Women are encouraged to overcome self-blame and take responsibility for their behavior and to work through introjected messages from significant others of what women should be. They are given support to accept their own uniqueness and to stop comparing themselves with other women in a competitive way. The authors acknowledge that the changes women are undergoing are often painful and that they may have adverse affects on their present relationships. However, this is necessary if, as in Gestalt therapy, "women are to grow into themselves."

Chapter 5

THE EQUITABLE THERAPY OF WOMEN IN PSYCHOANALYSIS*

Natatlie Shainess

*Love is not a profession
genteel or otherwise*

*Sex is not dentistry
the slick filling of aches and cavities ...*

*I am not a saint or a cripple,
I am not a wound, now I will see
whether I am a coward ....*
                    (Atwood, 1973).

THE history of discrimination against women sheds light on the roots of therapeutic prejudice today. Ancient law excluded women from social, legal and economic rights. In this country, in 1860, a Mrs. E. P. W. Packard was committed to Illinois State Hospital on her husband's petition. Under state commitment statutes of that time, married women and minors could be involuntarily committed at the request of a husband or guardian, without the evidentiary standard applicable in other cases (Brakel and Rock, 1971). After release three years later, Mrs. Packard campaigned for new commitment legislation. In lectures and books, she portrayed the horror of being wrongfully placed and committed to a mental institution. Through her efforts, Illinois enacted a "personal liberty bill", requiring a jury trial to determine commitment action. Such attitudes towards women rendered them children, made them vulnerable, and confirmed certain views men held about them.

Phyllis Chesler (1972) has written about the situation of women in mental hospitals today. While she has undoubtedly exaggerated, and, in a sense, denied the fact of genuine mental illness, what rings true is her insistence on the frequent mistreatment of women because of false and contemptuous assumptions (Shainess, 1973b). Furthermore, if anyone

---

*A portion of the material in this chapter appears in Shainess, Natalie: Fair treatment for the largest minority. In Goldman, G. D. & Milman, D. S. (Eds.): *Counseling and Psychotherapy with Minority Groups*. Springfield, Thomas, 1975.

should feel that the legal situation has changed to any noticeable degree, he/she has but to read Attorney Marguerite Rawalt's (1971) review of women's legal status today. In a paper titled "Women are Constitutional Outcasts" she stated that "the hidden truth about the U. S. Constitution is that it applies to men only." She points to the fact that the legal treatment of women as a separate class not only denies them rights, but also infantilizes them. The influence of legal codes upon value judgments is a very serious issue in the treatment of women since the codes influence concepts of gender identity, social and work roles, views of healthy and neurotic character, and development of personality.

The issues involved in treating "the largest minority group" are very complex because its members are a minority in terms of lack of power (not numbers) and because they are treated by a male majority. To complicate matters further, this minority is a house divided. Aside from those women who deny their disadvantaged status because of its special advantages, women have never been more at odds with themselves in their aspirations, vocational and professional goals, and sense of identity as women. They have diverse attitudes toward marriage, their social roles, sexual lives, maternal obligations, and the "style" of relationships with men.

WHAT IS GOOD THERAPY?

To discuss the question of therapy within the limits of a chapter is difficult, and requires focusing on specific areas. In general, therapy is good when it is *appropriate* to the person needing help. Good therapy requires a clear understanding of the undercurrents of the symptomatology or personality disorder, offers the most economic help in terms of energy, effort and money, and attempts to superimpose as little as possible from without. A minimum of drugs should be offered, electroshock is justified only in the rarest of circumstances (agitated and/or suicidal depression) (Shainess, 1971a, 1973c), and the ineptitude of a behavior therapy that deals only with symptoms rather than causes is dispensed with. The views of Frieda Fromm-Reichmann (1950) still apply: intensive therapy is that therapy, which, regardless of how frequent or how long, uses fundamental psychoanalytic principles of recognition of unconscious processes and of transference-countertransference expressions. In regard to women, good therapy incorporates one of the fundamental theories of Harry Stack Sullivan (1953): mastery leads to feelings of euphoria; conversely, impotence (call it passivity, ineptitude or other equivalents) leads to anxiety. Obviously, there is a feedback interaction in which these feelings then intensify the capacity for mastery or impotence.

The work and life of Virginia Woolf has come into renewed prominence recently. This author (Shainess, 1969) has previously suggested that Woolf's book (Woolf, 1928) was a vehicle for conveying that women could be as free, gifted, intellectual, and daring as men; while *A Room of One's Own* (Woolf, 1954) pleaded for truly equal educational opportunities for women on the same "grand" scale as for men's opportunities. But in relation to therapy, Woolf's voice, probably reflective of her own unsatisfied need in relation to men, spoke through the character of Rhoda, in *The Waves*:

> There is some check in the flow of my being; a deep stream presses on some obstacle; it jerks; it tugs; some knot in the centre resists. Oh, this is pain, this is anguish! I faint, I fail. Now my body thaws: I am unsealed, I am incandescent. Now the stream pours in a deep tide, fertilizing, opening the chute, forcing the tight-folded, flooding free. To whom shall I give all that now flows through me, from my warm, my porous body? I will gather my flowers and present them- Oh! to whom? (Woolf, 1955).

Woolf talks of many things — the agony of the creative process, then the feelings of its occurrence, and then its *reception*. Few men or women appreciate such an exceptional person who masters her fate. What psychotherapist appreciates or recognizes the woman who takes the necessary, sometimes unappealing (to the prejudiced observer) actions which stem from her own authenticity, *not* aggressivity? Understanding is a major task for the therapist. Educated as he or she may be (especially *he*) with a vision possibly blurred by the comfortable arrogance of the male university described in *A Room of One's Own* (Woolf, 1954) the therapist may also feel contemptuous of the impoverished, anxious woman. (And what is more annoying or anxiety-arousing in one person than the anxiety of another?) Even though educational institutions have changed to some extent since Woolf wrote, their long tradition of fostering such attitudes is secure.

Gordon Allport (1954), in talking about the nature of prejudice, cites an experiment in which children were asked to sort prejudiced statements into piles, representing degree of prejudice.

> It turned out that whatever a boy may have said against girls as a group was not judged to be prejudiced, for it is regarded as normal for an early adolescent to heap scorn on the opposite sex ... But when the children expressed animosity toward labor unions, social classes, races or nationalities, harsher judgments of prejudice were given.

Later, in describing the tolerant personality, he points out that such a person does not sharply distinguish between the roles of the sexes, nor agree that girls should only learn things that are useful around the house. Yet, the astonishing aspect of this thinker is that having given this brief lip service to manifestations of prejudice against women, he says nothing further about this *major* prejudice in our society and in the world. If a thinker concerned with prejudice is inattentive to that which sits *under his nose*, what can be inferred about therapists?

It must be clear by now that a major consideration in the treatment of women is the countertransference reactions, or as Sullivan (1953) put it, the *selective inattention* of male therapists. In female therapists, the problem is often more complicated — it is not just inattention, it is denial. The exceptional woman who has made a place for herself by using *male* power tactics is not likely to complicate her life by recognizing that others are underprivileged, especially when such recognition may threaten her personal life and marriage. The findings of Festinger (1957) apply here: A person confronted with data which refutes his/her prejudiced judgment, rationalizes the data to maintain the prejudice.

In a paper on counseling bias Schlossberg and Pietrofesa (1973) recognize prejudice as a serious problem, pointing out that "Since people-in-general hold strong beliefs about sex-appropriate behavior, we can assume that counselors also hold to these notions." By means of taped interviews they were able to study biased responses, among them the counselor-bias against women entering the "masculine" professions. Schlossberg and Pietrofesa advocate special programs for the reeducation of counselors against bias. Reeducation programs might include reading materials, special types of peer group interaction, and special supervisory work.

Whiteley (1973) also points to the problem of preconceptions marring the validity of "scientific" observation. She observed that the consciousness-raising groups of women and the new feminine self-consciousness were viewed by men as very threatening. This was confirmed to the writer at a recent meeting of psychoanalysts. A male analyst became enraged and challenged the statement of a speaker who, with her background as a geneticist had said that there is no sex differentiation of intelligence, and that male hormones are not the ultimate determinant of intelligence. The male analyst, in the presence of at least thirty female colleagues, shouted: "There is no sense in destroying institutions to admit the inferior."*

The concept of self- and interpersonal mastery as a crucial issue in the treatment and development of competence in other spheres, has been presented by psychologist Robert White (1973) of Harvard and by this author (Shainess, 1973a). A plea made by Anne Taylor Fleming is that she wants equal rights: professional, emotional and sexual. But she also wants the right to determine her direction, to refuse to be the *exact image*

---

*Reported in the *Chicago Tribune*, December 12, 1973.

*of a man.**

In a paper on "Facilitating the Growth of Women through Assertiveness Training," Jakubowski-Spector† (1973) observed that many women
find that their anxiety about producing interpersonal conflicts often prevents them from taking stances and expressing their true feelings and
beliefs. They become immobilized because of a conflict they see between
being strong, effective persons and being feminine. She correctly observed
the distinction between aggression and assertion, a distinction that few
analysts seem to be clear about when it comes to practical application.
She stated that

> ... assertive behavior is that type of interpersonal behavior in which a
> person stands up for her legitimate rights in such a way that the rights
> of others are not violated. Assertive behavior is an honest, direct and
> appropriate expression of one's feelings, beliefs and opinions. It com-
> municates respect for the other person, although not necessarily for that
> person's behavior (Jakubowski-Spector, 1973).

This is the key to many proper interpretations of a female patient's
behavior; women need help in becoming self-assertive in order to master
their interpersonal situations and their lives.

A case history is offered to underscore how problems of self-assertion
for women may exist at a very simple level. It illustrates that the woman
reared in traditional sex-role stereotypes, has daily choices to make which
are guilt ridden.

> A young married woman with a five-year-old-child did some writing
> in a special field. Ordinarily it took little time. She was eager to get back
> into things, and had a brochure of her background and experience
> printed, which she mailed out. To her surprise, it resulted in a good
> assignment for several months of work. She decided to do it at home,
> four days a week. Of course, her time devoted to her family was consider-
> ably curtailed. When a bedroom lamp broke, she hesitatingly asked her
> husband to take it in for repair on Saturday. He demurred because he
> did not feel it was *his* job. She thought she had better let it go. An
> excellent cook, she took to preparing simpler meals in order to conserve
> time. Her husband complained. A whole series of similar events oc-
> curred and her anxiety mounted. She began to question whether she
> should continue with the work. "I seem to recall that your husband was
> pleased when you told him of the job," I said. "Oh yes," she replied,
> "why, he has already decided how he would like to spend the money.
> I'm not sure I agree, but we'll see," she said. "He is sharing in your
> earnings?" "But of course!" "Well, if that is so, don't you think he
> should share in some of the extra effort that is required?" Her response
> to that was that she could see this, but was not sure she could *feel* it.

*Anne Taylor Fleming: "Up from Slavery — to What?" *Newsweek*, January 21, 1974.
†See Section IV, Assertion Training for Women.

Time, and further events, will clarify. But very simple assertion in an intimate relationship is one of the difficult areas for women who did not set out with an image of being autonomous.

The therapist must help a woman master her own life in her own way. Therapy must be more closely related to values than to libidinal conflicts.

To solve these problems, Jakubowski-Spector (1973) proposes group participation in workshops where certain problems are introduced, acted out and evaluated.

When the therapist using situations which are drawn from the client's life, carefully distinguishes among assertive, aggressive, and nonaggressive behavior, the client usually realizes quickly that she has an assertive problem ... In working with women, it is extremely important that these distinctions be carefully drawn.

She also talks of developing a belief-system in women to counteract irrational guilt. The significance of the belief-system in relation to the individual's interpersonal processes has been considered carefully by this author (Spiegel & Shainess, 1963) in relation to diagnosis, treatment, and psychodynamics. Taking a cue from Jakubowski-Spector's proposal, a workshop for therapists based upon the same principles could serve as a consciousness-raising process for them.

SIGNIFICANCE OF POWER AND LANGUAGE

Halleck, in *The Politics of Therapy* (1971), makes many cogent points about the power and the politics of psychotherapy. He stresses a cause of neurotic problems that psychoanalysis has been inclined to overlook in its deterministic approach:

A considerable amount of environmental stress is generated by *society's* (my italics) failure to satisfy the basic psychological needs of some of its members ... In such instances, the source of oppression can usually be traced *directly* to the selfishness, the apathy, or the malevolence of those in power.

His concern with the uses of power highlights another dimension of the problems of women. He has elsewhere noted the significance of power distribution in sexual relationships (Halleck, 1969). In considering the psychiatrist's social role, he observes that the psychiatrist must be a force for change rather than a force for the *status quo*, and so he emphasizes the political nature of psychiatric practice.

Robert Jay Lifton made similar observations in his discussion of *advocacy psychiatry*. In the introduction to *The Woman in America* (Lifton, 1965) he presents an imaginary dialogue between two characters, Inertia and Flux. In the dialogue, Lifton points to conscience-

salving *tolerance* which is really inertia hurtful to women, and he ends
with Flux's statement that "The only way for American women to be
women is to go on changing indefinitely." This book, his edition of a
Daedalus symposium on women which he moderated, was his advocacy
effort for women. Yet it stops short of Halleck's recognition of the
significance of power in relation to the patient's symptomatology, compared with the therapeutic intervention and societal forces.

It is but a step from this to what Alexandra Symonds (1973) has called
"the psychology of submission" which afflicts women, affecting their
sense of adequacy, and immobilizing them. As she indicates, it makes
them compliant and self-effacing, seeking only to satisfy their dependency needs. Thus, they fear isolation and autonomy. Symonds feels that
women are cast in a specific type of neurotic-dependent personality, and
adds that *confidence*, not just consciousness, must be raised. Women fear
the risk entailed in accepting the consequences of their own actions.

An example of the fear of such risk-taking would be the young woman
who,

> because of her impressive talents was promoted from her secretarial
> position into the lowest administrative position in a public relations
> firm — a small step overall and yet a major advancement for her person-
> ally. With the desire to prove herself and the fear of being inadequate,
> she initially worked like the proverbial beaver. Her capacity to grasp the
> essentials in any situation enabled her to do exceedingly well. Then
> trouble appeared: Decisions were left to her, and she was called on to
> express her views at conferences. Here, her fear of authority and of being
> considered wrong asserted itself. She became obsessed with doubt about
> almost everything she did at work; each decision became a weighty
> matter, frought with dire consequences. She had lost the protective col-
> oration of dependence and submission: Self-assertion and reliance on her
> own judgment became unbearably threatening. In her semidependent
> secretarial position relationship, she was safe. In the new independent
> position, danger seemed to lurk. This is the kind of conflictful situation
> which sometimes results in a regressive turn by the patient.

Symonds, in a paper titled: Phobias after Marriage: Woman's Declaration of Dependence (1971) (a title which tells it all), suggests how difficult
is the freeing of the self from a long-structured dependence, and how the
development of a phobia is symptomatic of the fear of becoming more
assertive. A series of articles have burgeoned on these therapeutic difficulties.*

Although the arrested growth process inevitably creates anxiety in
women, there is often greater anxiety in the possible consequences of self-

---

*Male psychiatrists — a help or harm to female patients? *Psychiatric News*, Sept. 5, 1973.

assertion, which carries with it the need to be self-critical and to internalize the superego. Yet risk-taking is necessary at every level, perhaps most in social life, where there is danger of offending others.

Patients have revealed several interesting situations which relate directly to this discussion. For a moment, let us consider a few.

A female graduate student in anthropology, who happens to be exceptionally beautiful, was invited to a department party. Two men came over and sat with her at once, but after an initial greeting, they began addressing their remarks to each other. Several other men came over, joined the group, and began conversing. She attempts to join the conversation and found it was impossible. Then she realized the men made eye contact with each other, but never looked at her. She began to feel "invisible," and extremely uncomfortable. At one point, she described herself as "bursting into the conversation," but found the opportunity did not return again. Finally, it happened that one after another of these men said they had been trying to give up smoking, but several opened a new pack of cigarettes. She asked one man: "Well, if you're trying to stop, why do you open a new pack? It's like *The Confessions of Zeno*."*
Asked about this, she related that every time Zeno thought of stopping smoking, he wrote down the date on something. Finally his books, his walls, his draperies were covered with dates. After "a queer look," a number of the men got up and walked away.

Now how shall this be interpreted? I would say that the men came over because she was very attractive, but because of her attractiveness, they made the assumption that she must have nothing to say. As a *good* budding anthropologist, she observed how she was being excluded, and in one fell swoop retaliated against them all, via *The Confessions of Zeno*. What should the therapist think about this? Was it aggression? My conclusion was that after being "put down" by being excluded, and after making several efforts to join in the discussion, the retaliation by her unconscious processes was self-assertive and justified. We discussed potentially more endearing ways to "join the boys" (intended!). However, I would not expect a woman to be an angel and would not characterize her behavior as aggressive when she has tried to cope in other ways first.

Social interaction, even on small scale, is very revealing of male-female patterns.

A couple married about two years came to consult me because their marriage was going very badly. It was obvious as they came into my office that they were both very angry. I asked them to tell me what the trouble seemed to be, and they sat there in stony silence. Finally, the husband said "Ladies first." His wife responded with "I have nothing to say." All kinds of inferences can be made from this brief interaction.

*Svevo, Italo: *The Confessions of Zeno*. New York, Random House, 1930.

The husband attempted a power tactic, in suggesting she speak first. She countered with an equal one. However, looked at in terms of social gender identity, the husband offered the conventional meaningless (but in this case fraught with meaning) facade of good manners toward a woman. And the wife responded by citing the male's attitude toward women: that they have nothing (worthwhile) to say.

Another example provides interesting material about sex and linguistics and, in addition, the therapist's interventions, which proved much more fruitful in this instance than simply letting the patient find her way:

A married woman of thirty came into treatment because she was extremely anxious about her four-year-old daughter who was extremely negativistic. The woman had a cool, distant, but not bad relationship with her husband. She described her father as a very demanding, authoritarian man who acted out his professional identity at home as well as at the college where he taught. Her mother was a *good little housewife* who cleaned, cooked, sewed all their clothes, and always agreed with her husband. The woman began to improve with treatment, but the greatest stimulant in that direction came when she reported a visit to her parents' home after they had visited Washington. While on vacation, her father had insisted on going to a topless restaurant. Her mother complained that she hadn't enjoyed it because "the food was not good." I asked, "What do you think the problem *really* was?" The woman was silent for a moment, and then started laughing. "Of course! My mother wouldn't dare say she hated to be forced to go to a topless restaurant! She often evades when she doesn't like what my father does — and so do I!" The woman had not missed the point that her mother couldn't assert herself against her husband because of their "unwritten law" that father is always right, and women are "unfeminine" if they challenge. This was the start of a very fruitful collaboration. The woman began to be more assertive herself.

On a later occasion this woman reported that she had been upset at a party:

Upon greeting her at the door, her host said, "My, you have nice legs; you can afford to uncover them. This is the first time I've seen you in a dress rather than slacks." She made no reply, but she felt upset. She did not quite see that two things were wrong: his unkind assumption that she must be covering up her legs because they were unshapely and his assumption that he had a perfect right, as a man, to comment upon her appearance. The discovery that her *host* was *aggressive*, and that she had a right to feel annoyed (not disturbed or anxious!) was comforting to her. During our collaboration, she began to think of appropriate responses.

Very recently she had a series of dreams that dealt with male aggression against her and her anger in response to the aggression. The dreams were a series of personal interactions with her host, her father, and her husband. The dreams were stimulated by another visit to the host's home. At his dinner table she had gotten into a conversation with another male guest over the title, *Ms.* He wondered why anyone would use it. She said it seemed unfair that a woman should have to reveal her marital status when a man doesn't have to. Her husband joined the conversation and attacked her. She was furious. Joining in also, the host's wife agreed that her own husband was a M.C.P. (male chauvinist pig). All ended amiably, but the woman remained furious with her husband. His attitudes did nothing to help their relationship. In fact, the more clearly she sorted out her own values and feelings, the more uncomfortable her marriage became.

The above examples may appear trivial. These are problems difficult for male analysts to comprehend. And yet, they are the warp and woof of sex-role stereotyping, and the subtle aggressions which women have had to endure — or felt they did — in bygone times. It is crucial for women to find ways to maintain a sense of personal integrity in social situations which are painful.

The following is another example of male aggression against a woman. Obviously, it was not understood by the therapist:

A woman in the midst of being divorced sought help after her husband suddenly revealed his affair with another woman he intended to marry. The patient was extremely distraught, and her husband agreed to pay for therapy. She found her psychiatrist quite helpful. When married, she was a wealthy woman, and paid his fee unquestioningly. However, with her divorce came a lower standard of living. She discussed the fee situation and what she might do about it with a friend, and was surprised to learn that the fee was much above the usual one in that area. Subsequently, she told her doctor that she wanted to continue treatment, but since she could not afford the fee she had been paying, and hoped he could reduce it. She had the misfortune — or fortune? — to add: "I hope you can reduce the fee, especially since your fee is somewhat high in comparison with others." His enraged response was: "What an aggressive woman you are!"

Obviously he was defending himself by attacking his patient, and by using the most common attack against her femininity. To resolve anxiety as a therapist by attacking the patient is hardly good therapy, no matter what the gender of the patient. However, in this situation, a woman therapist would not likely have resorted to such a statement.

What is important about all of these case illustrations is that they depend on subtle communication in which values placed upon them and the linguistics of the interaction are crucial. The therapist must have a kind of prescience, an ear keyed to hearing nuances of gender-related aggressions against women. He or she must be able to help the woman patient with the guilt feelings engendered by first efforts at resisting submissive action, and, when she does not have a support group, to help in the lonely effort at self-assertion.

Language is of crucial importance because ultimately it determines reality. Laffal (1965), in considering pathological and normal language says:

> There is good reason to believe that, like primitive men described by anthropologists, we are always organizing and reorganizing our experience in ways which highlight certain characteristics of this experience *at the expense of others* (my italics) and that, once such organizations of experience have been named and categorized in language, the name or category becomes a vital determinant of further experience.

He goes on to say that Cassierer's (1946) account of the power of names in metaphoric thought is sometimes reflected in the behavior of disturbed patients. The important point is that social agreements about the meaning of experience have done their share of harm to women, and the therapist must help women examine these in order to be more alert to the nature of what is said to them. Through the therapist's awareness of the nuances of what he or she hears, a "listening with the third ear" (Theodore Reik, 1949), the woman patient can find the courage to assert herself, in language and in action.

In the remainder of the paper I will briefly sum up some tenets relating to woman's sexual and reproductive role which *do* have unconscious psychic components, and which are the *only* psychologically related aspects to be equated with femininity. All else is simply *human* psychology which varies from person to person. For example, symptoms related to menstrual function are considered to be bioinstinctual by many analysts (Benedek, 1952, 1973). However, I found them to be a function of the mother-daughter relationship, the cultural milieu, and so, alterable (Shainess, 1962a, 1962b). The current generation, which is more peer-oriented, rarely suffers menstrual symptoms.

ABORTION

Since many analysts consider woman's response to abortion bioinstinctual, it is worth our attention here. Acceptance of the woman's right to have a wanted child permits her a degree of mastery and control over her own destiny (Shainess, 1966b, 1968, 1970, 1971b, 1972b). The mother-child tie, an enduring and unbreakable one whatever its nature, can only have strong positive elements where the child is wanted. Guilt and ambivalence in connection with abortion, seem to be disappearing now that societal attitudes have changed. Yet, among psychiatrists, there is a tendency to assume that guilt always accompanies abortion. In a fine research paper, "Making Abortion Consultation Therapeutic," Friedman (1973 reported the results of a study of over 400 women. The results would have been more useful if the investigator had not made assumptions of women's ambivalence about abortion. (This is not to deny occasional ambivalent feelings, often iatrogenically enhanced.)

There is no doubt that the longer a pregnancy continues before termination, the greater the endocrine changes, and, therefore, the greater the inference of body-loss which might lead to depression. Depression is possible even though the woman feels great relief and certainty that she did not desire the pregnancy. The suggestion that it is better to have the child and give it up for adoption can only be made by those (more likely to be men) who do not understand the significance of the bodily and psychological changes throughout pregnancy, and the nature of labor and delivery (Shainess, 1966a).

According to Friedman (1973) reported above, there is no proof that schizophrenia, suicidal ideation and postpartum psychosis are grounds for abortion, since women suffering these conditions have no greater difficulty than normal women in coping with a child. Yet postpartum psychosis is a condition stemming directly *from* the pregnancy and is direct evidence of the *threat* the pregnancy has posed (Shainess, 1966a). There is need for greater clarity among societal attitudes about abortion issues. A recent confirmation of this was an example reported in the *New York Times** of a paralyzed polio victim who, unable to adopt a child, decided to become pregnant in spite of repeated warnings from doctors not to do so. She observed that, interestingly, not one of the doctors who warned her against pregnancy suggested she should have an abortion.

SEXUAL ISSUES

It was good to hear Dr. Michael Carrera ask at a recent meeting†: "How does it feel to be a woman?" Of course, this question is relevant to the difficulties of conceptualizing feminine sexual experience. This is a big area with which to deal and only a few significant points will be considered here.

Sex therapists have overemphasized the point of women being "sexually repressed." Women cannot suddenly be "uninhibited" by a quick change of social attitude. Free sexual activity demands a *sense of self* and capacity for self-assertion which extends beyond new assertions of sexual equality. Sexual expression is a complicated matter, and sexual reponse a summation of many factors (Shainess, 1966). There are few women capable of instant, gratifying sexual involvement.

In summing up the issues included in her anthology, *Psychoanalysis*

---

*Polio Victim Disregards M.D.'s. *New York Times*, Nov. 25, 1973.
†Midwinter Meetings of the American Academy of Psychoanalysis, Dec. 6-9, 1973.

and Women, Jean Baker Miller states:

> Shainess has especially stressed the point that many of the so-called
> manifestations of 'free sex' have rapidly become attempts to remove sex
> from human communion, leading to increased degradation of women
> and isolation of men ... Shainess and Crain note that the attempt to
> keep love and sex separate has been the traditional operation of men in
> our culture. Recent advocates of sexual freedom for women often pre-
> scribe a corresponding course for them ... If women can move toward
> changing the context in which sex occurs, then they can perhaps free sex
> from its past bondage (for women) (Miller, 1973).

Sex, for the most part, must be learned in relation to a specific partner.
Perhaps it would be more accurate to say that there is a sexual dialogue
which must evolve. The significance of the distribution of power in a
sexual relationship has been considered by Halleck (1969); Seidenberg
(1972) has called attention to the nuances of coital play, not *fore-play* but
after-play, often an astonishing revelation of the nature of the relationship on either side. Seidenberg, perhaps, takes it a bit far in saying that
some intellectual women "get sex over with in order to then be able to
share the thinking of the man with whom they are involved" (Seidenberg,
1972). However, there is no doubt that men are frequently eager to share
bed and body, but not ideas, and particularly not intimacy. The model
presented by the film "Last Tango in Paris" is a shocker, but that model
is often more true than false.

In the past, and even in the present, it was assumed that sex was not
important to women. Married women were urged to be cooperative and
serve their husbands, regardless of how they felt. The need for honesty
and authenticity in sex and sexual relations which will lead to greater
satisfactions for both must be stressed in therapy. The development of
such openness is essential for mastery of a satisfying sexual life.

CONCLUSION

What are the special problems of women? The special problems of
their treatment? Basically, they are two-fold: those connected with *being*
female and second, those connected with women's long history of powerlessness and subservience. The lack of equitable treatment, especially at
the hands of those professing to love and care about them, has led to envy
of male privilege, but more often to great anxiety about self-assertion.
Women, living with (often arrogant) masters, have *identified with the
aggressor*. They have accepted the judgment of men and found themselves deserving of it. Sullivan's (1953) notion that the self is formed out
of the reflected appraisals of others certainly applies here. Women have
identified with the aggressor in other ways as well: Those who have

achieved exceptional success have nurtured a notion that they were different or more gifted than other women, thus failing to identify with and recognize the problems of vast numbers of women who may be equally gifted but less fortunate, or less skilled in hidden manipulative processes.

The days of ties to the land are gone, making the sexual division of labor obsolete. Gone also is the kind of devotion between a married couple that came from the struggle to survive. With change, the necessity for sex-role stereotypes has gone.

Again, the poetry of Louise Bogan speaks:

> **Women have no wilderness in them,**
> **they are provident instead.**
> **Content in the tight hot cell of their hearts**
> **to eat dusty bread (1954, p. 25).**

Of course, the very imagery she uses disproves her statement, as she well knows. Women may be provident, nurturant, conserving. But today they are daring to recognize that there *is* a wildness in them, that they will no longer eat *dusty* bread. The therapist whose intention is to be of help to women must recognize this, be truly empathic, imagining him or herself in the situation, and get away from the trite, unfeeling, routinized effort that has passed as therapy. Women need equal treatment to make their way on the rocky, risky, sometimes dangerous, but always exciting, independent road of life.

REFERENCES

Allport, Gordon W.: *The Nature of Prejudice*. Boston, Beacon Press, 1954.

Atwood, Margaret: Is/Not. *Aphra, 4*, Fall, 1973.

Benedek, Therese: *Psychosexual Functions in Women*. New York, Ronald Press, 1952.

Benedek, Therese: Psychoanalytic investigations. *Quadrangle*. New York, New York Times Book, 1973.

Bogan, Louise: *Collected Poems: 1923-1953*. New York, Noonday Press, 1954.

Brakel, Samuel J., and Rock, Ronald S. (Eds.): *The Mentally Disabled and the Law*, revised ed. Chicago, University of Chicago Press, 1971.

Cassirer, Ernst: *Language and Myth*. New York, Harper, 1946.

Chesler, Phyllis: *Women and Madness*. New York, Doubleday, 1972.

Festinger, Leon: *A Theory of Cognitive Dissonance*. Stanford, Stanford University Press, 1957.

Friedman, Cornelia M.: Making abortion consultation therapeutic. *American Journal of Psychiatry, 130*:1257, 1973.

Fromm-Reichmann, Frieda: *Principles of Intensive Psychotherapy*. Chicago, University of Chicago Press, 1950.

Halleck, Saymour L.: Sex and Power. *Medical Aspects of Human Sexuality, 3*, 1969.

Halleck, Saymour L.: *The Politics of Therapy*. New York, Science House, 1971.

Jakubowski-Spector, Patricia: Facilitating the growth of women through assertiveness training. *The Counseling Psychologist, 4*:75, 1973.

Laffal, Julius: *Pathological and Normal Language*. New York, Atherton Press, 1965.

Lifton, Robert J.: *The Woman in America*. Boston, Beacon Press, 1965.

Miller, Jean Baker: *Psychoanalysis and Women*. New York, Brunner-Mazel, 1973.

Rawalt, Marguerite: Women are constitutional outcasts. *The Woman Physician, 26*, Dec. 1971.

Reik, Theodore: *Listening with the Third Ear: The Inner Experiences of a Psychoanalyst*. New York, Farrar, Straus, 1949.

Schlossberg, Nancy K., and Pietrofesa, John: Perspectives on counseling bias: Implications for counselor education. *The Counseling Psychologist, 4*:44, 1973.

Seidenberg, Robert: Is sex without sexism possible? *Sexual Behavior*, Jan. 1972.

Shainess, Natalie: Psychiatric evaluation of premenstrual tension. *New York State Journal of Medicine, 62*:3573, 1962a.

Shainess, Natalie: A re-evaluation of some aspects of femininity through a study of menstruation. In Masserman, Jules H. (Ed.): *Science and Psychoanalysis, Vol V*. New York, Grune and Stratton, 1962b.

Shainess, Natalie: Psychological problems associated with motherhood. In Arieti, Silvano (Ed.): *American Handbook of Psychiatry, Vol. III*. New York, Basic Books, 1966a.

Shainess, Natalie: A re-assessment of feminine sexuality and erotic experience. In Masserman, Jules (Ed.): *Science and Psychoanalysis, Vol. X*. New York, Gruen and Stratton, 1966b.

Shainess, Natalie: Abortion: Social, psychiatric and psychoanalytic perspectives. *New York State Journal of Medicine, 68*:3070, 1968.

Shainess, Natalie: Images of woman: Past and present, overt and obscure. *American Journal of Psychotherapy, 23*:77, 1969.

Shainess, Natalie: Abortion is no man's business. *Psychology Today, 3*:18, 1970b.

Shainess, Natalie: Statement on drug advertising. Hearings before the U. S. Senate Committee on Small Business, Subcommittee on Monopoly: *Advertising and Proprietary Medicines, Part 2*. Washington, U. S. Gov't. Printing Office, 65-436 0, 1971. (a)

Shainess, Natalie: Testimony in "the women's case." In Schulder, D., and Kennedy, F.: *Abortion Rap*. New York, McGraw-Hill, 1971, p. 121. (b)

Shainess, Natalie: Abortion: Inalienable right. *New York State Journal of Medicine, 72*:1772, 1972.

Shainess, Natalie: Discussion of White's paper. *The Counseling Psychologist, 4*:41, 1973a.

Shainess, Natalie: Review: Women and madness. *American Journal of Psychotherapy, 27*:295, 1973b.

Shainess, Natalie: Women, drugs and well-being. *ADIT, 2*, Dec. 1973. (c)

Spiegel, Herbert and Shainess, Natalie: Operational spectrum of the psychotherapeutic process. *Archies of General Psychiatry, 9*:477, 1963.

Sullivan, Harry Stack: *The Collected Works of Harry Stack Sullivan*. New York, W. W. Norton, 1953.

Symonds, Alexandra: Phobias after marriage: Woman's declaration of dependence. *American Journal of Psychoanalysis, 31*:144, 1971.

Symonds, Alexandra: The liberated woman — healthy and neurotic. Paper presented at the meeting of the Association for the Advancement of Psychoanalysis, Oct. 24, 1973.

White, Robert W.: The concept of healthy personality: What do we really mean: *The Counseling Psychologist, 4*:3, 1973.

Whiteley, Rita M.: Women in groups. *The Counseling Psychologist, 4*:27, 1973.

Woolf, Virginia: *Orlando*. New York, Harcourt, Brace, 1928.

Woolf, Virginia: *A Room of One's Own.* London, Hogarth Press, 1954.
Woolf, Virginia: *The Waves.* London, Hogarth Press, 1955.

—— Chapter 6 ——

GESTALT THERAPY AND WOMEN

Lois Brien and Cynthia Sheldon

The average person of our time, believe it or not, lives only 5% to 15% of his potential at the highest ... So if you find out how you prevent yourself from growing, from using your potential, you have a way of increasing this, making life richer, making you more and more capable of mobilizing yourself (Perls, 1969).

A WOMAN who is aware of her internal process and how she prevents herself from growing is well on the road to being more alive. By expanding her repertoire of experience and feelings she cannot help but grow. The Gestalt therapist's efforts are directed toward moving the client to investigate her own phenomenology in innovative ways so that she may come to *her own* interesting and exciting discoveries. It is an ever new exploration, personally private to the individual, and devoid of cultural impositions. Largely because of this expansionistic viewpoint, we view Gestalt therapy as a nonsexist philosophy and approach to facilitating human growth. This approach allows "little girls" to become powerful and alive women with increased alternatives and possibly unlimited potential.

A short description of Gestalt therapy will illustrate its unique contributions to therapy for women. Gestalt therapy is a psychotherapeutic approach formulated by Fritz and Laura Perls in the middle 1940's and continually refined by them and their students. Its basic formulation is as follows: Life is a process of emerging figures out of the background composing one's existence. Through awareness, one comes in contact with and experiences the figure as a need. Awareness clarifies the need which leads to an action to get satisfaction or closure. The figure then subsides into the background and the emergence of the next figure begins. A simple example out of a day's activity is the desire for food which emerges into the foreground of awareness. After eating (closure of Gestalt) hunger subsides into the background making room for new figures to emerge.

Individuals frequently interrupt their natural organismic flow of experiences and actions. Such interruptions in functioning are produced in several ways: by blocking open expression (I am angry at you, but instead of expressing this, I smile and ask how you are); by maintaining poor perceptual contact (I look but I see only fuzzily, or I listen but hear with distortion), and by actual muscular repression (I tighten some area of my body and hold in my thoughts and feelings). The results of stopping the organismic flow in these ways are dramatic. Most psychiatric symptomatology comes from such stopping. Boredom, apathy, depression, confusion, physical tightness, and psychosomatic illnesses are all forms of being in a *stuck* place or an impasse.

Sandra, mother of four, is an example of someone in a *stuck* place. Beautiful yet thin, with hunched shoulders and a stooped posture, she suspected her husband of having an affair. She said nothing to him, thinking it was best not to know. Meanwhile, she began to look forty-five rather than her real age of thirty-five. Her aliveness was gone. She preferred to be vague and unclear about the reality of their relationship. It is likely that Sandra will continue to turn inward and be depressed or get physically ill. Many others have gotten *stuck* in these kinds of life-long impasses.

Gestalt therapy works to unblock such an organismic flow. The methods used to restore a normal ebb and flow are many and vary from one therapist to another. Typically, Gestalt therapists focus on how one is acting, not why. They are concerned with the here and now as opposed to thinking about the past or future, with actively experiencing instead of talking about, and with using tension as a springboard to action. They take clues from small units of behavior such as the tone of the voice or a choice of a word, increasing excitement, and muscular repression in the body. They encourage finishing unfinished situations, and integrating opposites or polarities. Most importantly, a Gestalt therapist focuses on *how* one stops one's organismic functioning.

The aim of Gestalt therapy is to develop more *intelligent* behavior. By becoming aware of *how* we block ourselves, we immediately become aware of alternatives; awareness of alternatives gives us a greater range of choices for action. In the above case, Sandra could learn how she depresses herself. Rather than remaining uncertain about the source of her depression, she could choose what to do about her unhappiness. She may decide to remain vague and depressed. She may choose to see her relationship with her husband more clearly, which may bring them closer together or may separate them. In any case, learning how she interferes with her own natural functioning will free her to move on if she wishes to do so.

The goals of Gestalt therapy are life-enhancing for men as well as for women. It applies to individual persons without gender designations. Gestalt interventions are designed to help the individual,

> ... make discoveries that reflect his (sic) her unique needs, her stylistic
> trademark. At that moment she stands on her own two feet; at that

moment she is self-actualizing and is doing quite nicely without the benevolent wisdom of therapist-guru. (Levitsky and Simkin, 1972)

Let us expand, now, on the uniqueness of Gestalt therapy for women. Because of the phenomenological nature of Gestalt therapy, it is difficult to support women (or men for that matter) in sexist roles. There is no *party line* about how women should be women, how men should be men, or how children should be children. Through experimentation, risk-taking and unblocking, women can develop their thinking and feeling apparatuses, thus increasing their repertoire of how *to be* in the world. Increased awareness leads to expanded feelings, energies, abilities and ultimately to increased personal power.

Sara, for example, who is married and the mother of one, realized the priorities she was living out: her family and child came first and her career as a computer analyst came second. She constantly told herself that she *should* put her own interests last. After discussing this with her husband, who was also locked into his role as provider, they decided to rearrange things. He stayed home to raise the children and to write and she got a job she loved which supported the family. Therapy helped her deal with her introjected traditional expectations and with relatives who tried to get her husband to go back to work and her to stay home with the child.

Another woman, Nancy, divorced and mother of two, decided after living alone with them for a year to let their father raise them while she went back to school to prepare for a law career. In Nancy's case she "gave up" her children, although she has visitation rights. Neither keeping the children nor being without them offered a satisfactory solution. The therapy helped her work through her guilt about abdicating her mother role. She continues to experience loss and sadness and at the same time her own development is continuing. So many women are stuck in rigid sex roles that have nothing to do with them personally. To risk acknowledging the thoughts and fantasies hidden even to oneself can open and expand one's limited being.

Women who come in for therapy usually have little awareness that they need anything more than symptom relief. A woman with a migraine wants medication. A woman beating her children wants something to help her stop her abusive behavior. A sexually blocked woman wants a cure for her uptight problems with men. In other words, these women believe that the problem is something wrong with them. "I'm a lousy wife, mother, sexual partner." Seldom does a woman go beyond her symptom and ask herself what she wants — from people she is close to, for her life. And if she does know what she wants, she often does not know how to get it.

In our society men know much more about what they want. They are raised to develop their creative and earning power through education and work. They ask themselves constantly what they want to do with their lives. Women, in contrast, are raised to look for a man! Seldom do they look at themselves as whole, creative persons. Rather, they see themselves fitting into a man's life and career. Our experience in working with many women is that they are out of touch with who they are and what they want from themselves and from others. Our initial task is to help them find this out.

At first a woman thinks only about what she wants from others. "I want my husband to be home more. I want him to take me out more. I want the children to stop bothering me." These are important wants to recognize, however, these are what she wants of others, not what she wants of herself. If she stops here, she gives to others her power for happiness. We go on, encouraging her to say what she wants from herself, "I want to be more loving, I want to feel more assertive . . . ." In Gestalt therapy it is important for women to get in touch with what they want from themselves as well as from others.

One depressed woman named Polly felt she was "sick." Home alone with the children all day, she was very lonely and isolated. Her husband wanted to be her only adult contact. As her depression continued, her ex therapist, and her husband felt she should be hospitalized. Gradually, she saw that she had been accepting her husband's idea of a suitable lifestyle for her. She realized two things she wanted: adult companionship and self-understanding. At this point, depressed, frightened, yet resolute, she came into Gestalt therapy.

Directing Polly away from focusing on what was *wrong* with her led her to open many new avenues. In addition to meeting new friends, she took a trip to India with an anthropology class and rekindled an old interest in flying planes. More important than these specific changes however, was her realization that her depression was the result of turning her energies inward. Laura Perls recently said in a workshop in San Francisco that "depression is the opposite of expression." This was certainly the case with Polly.

Naturally, losing vagueness and getting clear about what one wants can be risky. A woman may discover that what she wants she may not be able to get from those who are close to her, such as her husband and children. This can be very frightening. Often it feels safer to be vague, to be unclear, to live with symptoms or to try to change others. In Polly's case, her new interests and excitement have threatened her husband, and this, of course, jeopardizes their marriage.

Traditional clinical psychology and psychiatry have focused too much on what's *wrong* with people. The focus needs to be on what a woman's unique characteristics are, on what she wants. This attitude shift is basic. Everything takes on a new perspective when a woman asks, "AM I DOING WHAT I WANT WITH MY LIFE?"

SELF-RESPONSIBILITY

Taking responsibility for who one is at any given moment is a basic Gestalt tenet. There is a tendency among people to lay responsibility for who they are and what they do on others; parents, society, men. Fritz Perls said that "Freud grew up in an age of hysteria. We live in an age of paranoia." People often say that they are not to blame for their behavior because of an unhappy childhood. Of course, a person is influenced by her early environment, but as an adult she is responsible for dealing or not dealing with that influence. A blame framework stops and blocks movement. By turning the blame into responsibility there is direction for growth and change.

Since women are brought up to rely on and to give their power to men, they are willing to blame men for their shortcomings. For example, a woman may feel angry when she is in the presence of a man who constantly puts her down. She is responsible for her anger and he is responsible for his putdowns. If she takes responsibility for feeling angry, then she will find ways to deal with this feeling. She might talk to someone or learn to express her anger directly, or remove herself from the man's presence.

Mary blamed her husband for being distant with her. In therapy she realized that she was afraid to ask him to hold her. She would pull away from him telling him "I'll want too much." (This process is a version of "I'll never stop crying," or "If I begin to feel angry I might lose control.") During therapy she let herself be held by the therapist until she felt satisfied. The Gestalt was completed. This phenomenon surprised her. Now, as time goes on, she is able to ask her husband to hold her and to take from him the time she needs.

SELF-ESTEEM

Given that women frequently do not know what they want, do not take responsibility for themselves, or give their power to their men, to children, or to society, it is no wonder that low self-esteem is one of their chief characteristics. Frequently low self-esteem statements from women include: I don't give enough, I'm getting old, I'm stupid, I'm too fat, I'm too flat chested, I'm a lousy mother, I'm bitchy, I'm frigid, I complain too much, I don't have any interests. (One wonders how the bright ten-year-old girl who was ahead of her brothers academically and physically has been turned into such a self-denigrating human being!)

The Gestalt process recognizes that people *introject* rules for being in the world from parents, teachers, and other significant adults. Women continue to take in (swallow whole) how their men think women ought to be. These rules take the form of "shoulds" and "should nots": I should be supporting of my man, I shouldn't be bitchy, I should be warm and giving, I shouldn't be unresponsive. Since few people are able to live up to their shoulds, low self-esteem is a frequent consequence. Gestalt work makes women aware of their conditioning, encouraging them to keep those roles that fit and give up those that do not.

Jennifer had been taught that she should be pretty, pleasing and giving so that she could find a good man who would marry her. When both a husband and a lover left her for other women, she felt she was a failure. This feeling was reinforced by her mother. Now in therapy she is separating herself from her mother's expectations. However, she still vacillates from low esteem when she listens to her mother's messages to feeling good when she satisfies herself.

In combating low self-esteem, the Gestalt process encourages women like Jennifer to get in touch with their internal feelings and sensations — to literally check out their bodies to find out what feels right. The total organism participates in any experience, with messages coming from all the body parts. It is important to get all the information the organism has to offer. The *introjects,* which are often given too much attention, or shoulds are only one piece of data. Once all the news is in, the work proceeds to personally own the incongruencies. What truly *fits* is experienced throughout the entire body.

COMPETITION

Many women, feeling dissatisfied with themselves and needing reassurance, look for self-esteem by comparing themselves with one another in a competitive way. This is a major source of discomfort among many women we see in our practice. Even the attitude of professional people conveys the belief that competition among women is inevitable. Recently, when we recommended that a woman client see a female therapist, a female therapist present said she thought this was not a good idea since women are so competitive with one another. This attitude about and among women isolates them from one another. Our experience in leading women's groups for the last six years is that female competition is a superficial defense. When women learn that there are no real reasons for competition, the isolation among them vanishes and emotional contact is made. Women rejoice in discovering a bond they feel with one another.

Part of competition is comparison. Fritz Perls described the comparison process as the "fitting" game. When we get locked into seeing the world in categories, we try to "fit" all that we experience into the categories. Women spend hours of time and energy trying to fit themselves and others into various categories such as "glamour girl," "intellectual," or "supermother."

The fitting game sets the stage for getting into "I'm not OK and neither are you." It, like the blame game, restricts rather than expands. Our ability to experience, sense and feel is restricted when we put all of our energy into thinking such thoughts as: I'm better than she is, she is prettier than I am, she has more substance than I do. Soon we begin to feel like cans on the supermarket shelf. Our consciousness is in the realm of our "product"iveness. We are constantly comparing ourselves with others on the shelf. Some women pride themselves on their packaging and display effects, others pride themselves on their inner contents — all for the purpose of being saleable, chosen, or picked (usually by a man). However, the power goes to the buyer, not to the woman.

This consciousness of categories and competition implies that there is not enough of the important things to go around. It promotes the concept of scarcity. Scarcity of what? Men? Friends? Lovers? Money? Status? Since our culture is built on the notion of supply and demand, it feels dangerous to ignore the possibility that if every woman wants the same things, some women will lose out. However, if we adopt the opposite position to scarcity and think of ourselves as having an abundance of what is personally important, anxiety about measuring up diminishes. This concept of abundance can radically change the female consciousness of competition with and isolation from other women.

A few years ago, one of our clients had an experience that illustrates the difference between the "comparing" and the "abundance" positions. She spent a weekend with twenty women in a women's workshop. Initially she was apprehensive that she would feel competitive with everyone. Instead she saw each woman as beautiful in her own way — in her appearance, movement, expressiveness, ideas and interests. She realized she would not want to be like anyone else there, and she was able to appreciate herself and others for their differences.

This kind of experience can help a woman to enhance her own uniqueness rather than to try to fit into old, tight forms. Instead of wondering whether she is as good as another woman, she can ask herself such questions as: How might I experience that woman's world? What can I learn about myself by being with her? What is it like to be her? The Gestalt process encourages experiencing and appreciating differences. It conveys that there is plenty and more.

CONCLUSION

Our hope is that more women will honor their full potential and that as times passes, a respect and appreciation for their potential will occur. Thus, gamey, manipulative, symptom-filled, depressed, and powerless women will not have to remain in those states in order to have relationships with their lovers, their children, and society.

The Gestalt approach helps women enhance their self-esteem, discover their wants, take responsibility for themselves (not others), get out of the competitive mode and get into loving, supportive relationships with others. Gestalt contributes to creating a more fully alive, powerful and expansive person.

For women to take their power and run is frightening, but many women are no longer holding back. Old adages like "makes him feel like he's the boss," "don't outshine him," "be sure to stand and support him above everything else," no longer fit. Life-styles and attitudes of women are changing. Some are exploring lesbian relationships, and others are giving up their children. Gestalt therapy validates women who are moving into themselves. As women move into their full aliveness and internal power, old ways of being and old relationships suffer. The change is gradual and painful. Someone has said that we are the sacrificial generation. As individual figures and ground emerge and recede unfettered, allowing personal balance to come into focus, the old cultural homeostasis is being shattered. For many women this is a new and revolutionary place.

REFERENCES

Levitsky, Abraham and Simkin, James S.: Gestalt therapy. In Solomon, Lawrence and Berzon, Betty (Eds.): *New Perspectives in Encounter Groups.* San Francisco, Jossey-Bass, 1972.

Perls, Frederick S.: *Gestalt Therapy Verbatim.* Lafayette, Real People Press, 1969.

—— *Chapter 7* ——

SHOULD THIS MARRIAGE (COUNSELING) BE SAVED?*

ROBERT SEIDENBERG

People set out to remedy evils at the point where they appear; nobody pays any attention to their actual source and origin. This is why it is so difficult to give advice and have it heeded, especially by the general run of men, who are quite reasonable in everyday matters but seldom see beyond tomorrow.

Goethe

THE psychoanalytic tradition has been that one does not treat a marriage, or marital partners, but *persons*. A psychoanalyst may treat one person and not see the mate in treatment or even in consultation. This has led to a great deal of criticism of the analytic situation as being detrimental to marriage and family life. This type of criticism is consonant with the modern social welfare concept which looks beyond individualization to what is good for the family, the group, and the community. Perhaps sanctifying the individual, as psychoanalysis does, is an anachronistic ideal with a diminishing position in an era of mass action and communal enterprise. Psychoanalysis was quickly liquidated behind the Iron Curtain, where the nation's "truths" and goals preempt the individual's.

Psychoanalysis, in its classic form fiercely defends matters of privacy and confidentiality. This has engendered criticism of it as being some type of secret cult that demands of its practitioners and analysands a fealty, exclusiveness, and devotion, at the sacrifice of mate, children, and job (Giovacchini, 1955). This is patent nonsense, for in respecting the rights of the individual, psychoanalysis acts consonantly with the enlightenment that freed people from the tyranny of the horde and of Heaven. The basic proposition of psychoanalysis is that one is not owned by the external world and that one should not be enslaved by internalized irrationalities. Intimately involved in this liberation is the new imperative that a person make choices. The capability to make a choice, encom-

*Revised from "Marriage, Meaning, and Mittler," from a book by Robert Seidenberg, *Marriage in Life and Literature*. New York, Philosophical Library, 1970. Courtesy of Philosophical Library.

128

passing as it does freedom from internal and external shibboleths, should be the goal of psychoanalytic treatment. It is in the pursuit of this goal that psychoanalysis seeks the exclusion of all forces, good or bad, from the therapeutic relationship which might possibly interfere with the progress of choice-making (Szasz, 1965).

All the seemingly "crazy" rules of psychoanalysis serve to create this atmosphere. This is often done, paradoxically, even against the wishes of the analysand who, in perplexity, may want to relinquish to varying degrees the human rights of privacy, autonomy, and chance for choice. However, if these rights are meaningless, or if even the wish for them has been effectively extinguished, then psychoanalysis is not for the person any more than a democratic form of government is for Saudi Arabia at this time. When psychoanalysis is subject to external pressures and intrusions, it ceases to be psychoanalysis. By its very definition, psychoanalysis deals with the needs and/or anxieties of an individual, not of a marriage, or a family, or a community; although these are not necessarily antithetic, they may be. A woman may have important responsibilities to her husband, her children, and her household, but none of these can be well served if she is not self-fulfilled. Psychoanalysis does not aim at divisiveness, nor does it promote a secretive mode. It does sanctify privacy; without a secure modicum of privacy, there can be no identity. An individual is of many minds: she minds her husband, her children, her work. Without a mind of her own, there can be none of these other minds and mindings.

Psychoanalysis of one or both mates may be indicated and yet not be feasible. Usually what appears as problems of marriage are problems of individuals or problems of living, so that marriage counseling, like advice to the lovelorn, may be specious in theory and operation. Both the giving and receiving of "lovelorn" advice, as well as the application of gratuitous homilies, are weak balms. More than that, they are insulting to any but the simple-minded. My words may seem harsh and untrue, especially to many who have felt helped by professional marital advice. They may also sound extremely chauvinistic coming from a psychoanalyst who could easily be accused of promoting his own beliefs. However, the efficacy of psychoanalysis, even when formally applied, holds no guarantees. There are many disappointed participants who bitterly recall no help derived therefrom. Psychoanalysis as intervention can only do the best it can, limited in its results by the participation of the analysand, the skills of the analyst, and the intensity of the problem at hand. As treatment, it is not meant for all people or all seasons. It is, in fact, for reasons of economics and factors of intellection, in reach of a very few, just as a college education was in the past century.

The "social awareness" of the therapist is of utmost importance in helping a client toward understanding and action. Social awareness includes the sophistication of the therapist toward matters of forces in the culture and society which can be more consequential, helpful, or eroding than some legendary and perhaps mythical relationship at the age of five. The therapist must be at least relatively free from the prejudice that middle-class marriage and family life are the best and only way of living. S/he must be aware that a woman, for instance, may be the victim of persecution even with the most loving and "generous" husband. In such situations it really matters little that she happens to be married to a benign master. The marital situation itself may realistically cause her enslavement. To treat such a woman as a sick, paranoid person because she complains or is belligerent toward her husband's benign behavior is to miss the point. The therapist may be unaware, or may not want to be aware (he himself may be a slaveholder in his personal life) of the persecution because society has generally defined such inequities as "natural." Why is it that women more often institute divorce action? (Goode, 1956; Lasch, 1966)

It was the rare white Southerner who could ever feel that the Negro was persecuted. The roles of white and Negro were "natural" since they were always that way. It is entirely possible that the client may be ahead of the therapist in understanding the importance of human rights and dignity. In many instances the despair and disillusionment of clients are entirely justified. The lament that "the therapist just didn't understand me" can be all too true and not be a case of stubborn resistance which we hear about from self-righteous therapist clinical conferences.

Another instance of the need for awareness is the frustrating and corrosive effect of conformity on the male. The compulsion to compete, to win out, to get the top dollar has become a virtual hallmark of maleness. Many male therapists have proceeded in this fashion and feel this is the best and even the only way of life. To achieve, to get ahead, to dominate at home and at the office are prime virtues of middle-class morality. But is it good for everyone? In psychoanalysis, when confronted by a man who does not seem to want to get ahead, therapists often invoke the Oedipus complex as the main reason for this man's passivity in worldly affairs; he is fearful either of competing with or of overtaking his father. Even if such elements are present, they may be less consequential than honest appraisal and renunciation of conventional values for personal idealistic goals. The therapist must be aware of the possibility of such "honestly" derived goals which may not be consonant with the usual expectations of a marital partner. To hack away here at poor old Oedipus makes a mockery of true understanding. Therapists too often make the error of defining the client's condition as "sick and regressed" rather than seeing it as a valid attempt for freedom from the prejudices of parents, tradition, and society. It may prove to be the gravest error of psycho-analysis that it has called "neurosis" and "sickness" those attempts of young people to purge themselves of the demonolatry of their parents. It is unfortunately too often the case that the therapist attempts to cure the patient instead of healing her/himself.

In lieu of the understanding of the spectrum of operative forces both of the past and present, there are in our professions the disease of reduc-tionism and the cult of simplistic derivations. For instance, it is not unusual to find in psychoanalytic writings that the "character" of the male and the female is largely determined by the shape and direction of their bodies and sexual organs. To wit, the woman must forevermore be passive because her organ "receives" the penis. Is anatomy destiny? It unfortunately is, and may continue to be, unless we abandon our self-serving euphemisms and cant in favor of existential appraisals.

It may sound condescending and arrogant to ask for awareness in one's colleagues. But there are all too many amongst us who not only are "unaware" but take pride in their aloofness. They take the position of medieval monks, fearing that contact or knowledge of the temporal scene is contaminating. Some analysts indicate in their protocols of cases that the talk of patients about here-and-now events is "resistance" and non-consequential to the work of the analysis. They would prefer to work with the "internal disease" derived from eternal and static maladies of the soul without integrating these with the tensions of the age in which we live.

Yet the reader will rightly say that people have been helped throughout the ages by priests, wise men, good friends, and, in the present era, by social agencies. This observation is valid, but we are talking here of another dimension. People who seek and respond to this order of help would neither seek nor qualify for psychoanalysis. They generally want to be told how to behave or what are the expectations of them as mates. They also may want to justify their behavior and, at the same time, seek a moral judgment of that behavior or that of the mate.

There are innumerable people who need managers in marriage. Lacking responsibility and judgment even about the simplest matters, they seek out someone to tell them how much to spend on rent, whether beatings should be allowed, and how many times a week sexual inter-course is necessary. For the fights and arguments, an arbiter is needed to pass judgment on who is right, who is the aggressor, and who is the victim.

An intervention frequently sought is a scolding for an errant mate so that, with the authority of a psychiatrist or a social worker, the wife may be induced to take better care of the house. Or a wife wails, "Tell him he mustn't drink so much." Such appeals are like a child asking the adult supervisor to warn an adversary to be cooperative and play nicely. Admonition has always been the role of the clergy and often the judge and sometimes the attorney. They give the moral or legal warnings, and they may chastise and punish. It is the legitimate use of authority to bring about submission where internal control or judgment is inadequate.

Individuals with no adequate internalized tools of operation and bereft of powers of persuasion must look to others to make their mates and themselves behave. Is this managerial role a proper one for a psychiatrist, psychologist, or social worker? It is not psychotherapy in the sense of producing great insights or profound character changes, but nonetheless there can be some help in it. It is psychotherapy in the broad sense of the modern-day tendency to call nearly everything people do by themselves or together "therapy." Some people indeed do look upon life itself as a basic disease, and everything they do as part of the treatment. Everyone today seems to be philosophically therapy-minded. Hobbies, relationships, and careers are identified as therapies. Almost no one does things now because s/he likes to; s/he does them because they are "good therapy." Perhaps the world is one big mental hospital, as some of our cynics would have it. Certainly our diseases are multiplying faster than are doctors to care for them. Idiosyncrasies, quirks, and extremisms are not diseases whose bearers are to be placed in isolation wards.

Since marriage traditionally has been connected with religion, it is quite natural for the clergy to play a major role in marital problems. Religions have imposed the principal regulations and moralities governing conduct in marriage; the religionists thereby become the arbiters of an overwhelming number of issues. The clergyman may be able to counsel and advise whether certain behavior does or does not violate the moral code to which the marital partners have already committed themselves. For people who live by edicts of external authority, the force of approval or condemnation by such an authority has a regulating effect and may curb errant behavior. The dread of alienation from one's church or, even worse, the threat of losing the chance of a benevolent hereafter, may serve to keep many in line. This helps and it may change conduct; but is it psychotherapy?

The other institution with which marriage is inextricably involved is the law. Marriage must be performed in either a religious or a civil manner, usually in both. Along with religious edicts, the state governs the conjugal state with an iron fist. It insists on a minimal age for participants, requires blood examinations, and in some areas regulates the union of races. It is, therefore, no surprise that judges and lawyers are frequently called upon for advice. Here civil authority is depended upon to settle conflicts of interest or misunderstandings about prohibitions, liberties, rights, and responsibilities. Has one been victimized or has one stepped beyond the pale of the law in one's behavior? Of her/his attorney the mate may ask, "Am I within my legal rights?" Or, "What are my responsibilities in this matter and what are my mate's?" The punitive arm of the law can be invoked when personal power or influence fails. Let the judge or lawyer threaten with the possible consequences. Perhaps six months in jail is the lesson that is needed. The law is vital intrusion into the marital state — present at the onset and called upon thereafter as an aid. Can this be psychotherapy too?

Marriage counseling was once solely the prerogative of the clergy. With the intrusion of the state into marital matters, the situation became more complex, necessitating both spiritual and temporal information. With the advent of psychological knowledge, a new dimension was added; thus the modern marriage counselor combines, with varying degrees of success, all three roles — spiritual, legal, and psychological. This worldly knowledge, plus his personal skills in "handling" people, may enable him to act as a mediator of current issues involving rights, duties, and responsibilities, both moral and legal.

Today there exists a buyer's market in the choice of therapies. Excluding the physical therapies, from psychosurgery to tranquilizers which make no pretense of intellection, marital partners who seek help through understanding can visit the clergy, attorneys, social workers, psychologists, psychiatrists, psychoanalysts, and others who set themselves up exclusively as marriage counselors. This is a listing of professionals apart from friends, relatives, police, or even neighbors who are often called upon to intervene. Not to be discounted are the columnists of our newspapers and other media who also diagnose, prescribe, and refer. And, apparently the buyer needs no caveat because most reports and "scientific" communications regarding results indicate successes from all interventions. As Thomas Szasz has wryly observed: "In this field, everything works" (Szasz, 1961).

Symptomatic of the advent of mass society and social engineering is the appearance of a myriad of group enterprises and team effort. It seems now that no possible combination of therapists and clients has been overlooked; but the nature of "progress" being what it is, there will be more. Without engaging in an exhaustive explication and critique of each, some of these will be presented.

That everything "works" in psychiatry finds confirmation in the approach of Markowitz. His is "Analytic Group Psychotherapy of Married Couples by a Therapist Couple." Male and female therapists together either act as substitute parents or act as the good example for their misguided clients. Markowitz (1968) feels "most encouraged by our therapeutic approach" proving the "efficacy of heterosexual therapists working as a pair." However, the idea of providing a "mother" and a "father" as a therapeutic experience lacks a subtlety of approach that must be offensive to self-respecting adults. Nevertheless with the diversity of needs that exist in this world, such an arrangement might be acceptable to some persons. But do the purported benefits outweigh what must be a humiliation in the procedure? Or, are we to accept this degradation as therapeutic? Can one become mature by being treated as a child?

There is "married couples group psychotherapy" directed toward couples whose main problem is their marital relationship, especially when the partners are relatively effective in other sectors of life and personality. The group herein described consisted of four couples, two cotherapists and a silent recorder. The sessions continued for twenty months. It was reported that most of the objections and obstacles predicted by nonorthodox therapists are readily overcome. Furthermore, "the group process seems particularly effective for clarifying distorted communications, for helping couples to clarify ambiguous marital roles, and to resolve neurotic behavior primarily involving the marital relationship. Most significant is the fact that the symbiosis is dissipated and the partners become individuals who live real, rather than defensive, roles in their marriage" (Gottlieb and Pattison, 1966).

Another approach to airing marital disharmony is "collaborative therapy." Here each partner is treated by different therapists, who sometimes communicated with each other at intervals, either to "maintain the marriage" or, "for the purpose of facilitating therapeutic changes in their patients." This is also known as "stereoscopic technique," to indicate that psychiatry is up-to-date (Martin and Bird, 1953). The psychiatrists meet individually with the partners and thereafter consult with one another, "of necessity" comparing notes on the therapeutic problems of their couples. The conferences of the therapists, it was pointed out, are held not only with the full knowledge and consent of the marital partners, but also at the insistence of particular partners who want all possible help. Emergencies such as possible suicide, homicide, and desertion require "management."

What is accomplished? We learn that the regular review of the situation helps the partners recognize reality distortions. It also helps the therapists recognize the complementary neuroses that exist between the partners, that "both drew them together and pushed them apart." Another advantage, one of the greatest it is claimed, is that the stereoscopic technique affords the psychiatrists the opportunity of ending "transference-countertransference duels" by having different psychiatrists work with members of the same family. In other words, it is a supervisory check on the therapeutic situation.

The stereoscopic technique is psychoanalytically conventional in that it reconstructs even the earliest infant-mother relationships. It is deemed by its inventors as an effective instrument and a "welcome addition to our therapeutic armamentarium." One advocate of this method relates that many techniques can achieve the same thing; there are "many ways to skin a cat" (Martin, 1965).

For others, there is "concurrent psychoanalytic therapy." Here both partners are treated separately but concurrently by the same therapist. The purported advantages here are four. This combined technique extends hope for the restoration of the marital relationship. Emotional support for both members also becomes immediately operative. Thirdly, the therapist gains a multidimensional view of the marriage transaction; a "triadic communication system" is established so that knowledge of both past events and current conflicts can be gained in minimal time. And, since each partner knows that the other is also reporting, possibly on the same marital problem, there may be more "accurate" reporting by each. The fourth advantage, it is stated, is the "triangular transference." Feelings are directed toward the therapist and also toward the other patient, the mate. This allegedly might be an aid in the full explication of the oedipal constellation.

Patients are "directed" to report their dreams and as part of the therapeutic effect they agree not to discuss the contents of their respective interviews. These are the only stated demands of the therapist. This treatment, although using some conventional psychoanalytic techniques, is alien to most analysts because, the authors tell us, "a great majority are biased by their one-to-one patient orientations." It may be pure coincidence that a chief advocate and promoter of this triadic, judicially structured therapy is named Doctor Solomon (Solomon and Greene, 1965).

Another opportunity for the distressed couple is "conjoint marital therapy." Both partners are seen together by the same therapist or by cotherapists, one male and one female. This arrangement is for married couples without children. With children, all are brought in and the "family therapeutic approach" is instituted (Satir, 1964). Emphasis is placed on the opportunity to communicate which this setup allegedly provides. We are told that "this experience can serve as an ego-enhancing corrective and eventually reflects in clearer, more specific, and more direct communication between husband and wife" (Satir, 1965). This therapy's advocate, Alger, is amongst a growing number of therapists who have confused 'disease' and 'treatment'.

> Psychoanalysis, which was born at the turn of the century, and therefore originally reflected the more mechanistic thinking of that era, conceived of the individual as a closed type of system, and understood neurotic symptoms as resultants from the disturbed equilibrium of an inner economy of instinctual forces. Interpersonal, sociocultural, and communicational theories have all emphasized the point that an indi-

vidual cannot be understood apart from his relationships with other
human beings. (For these reasons, Alger contends) . . . psychoanalysts in
increasing numbers are openly using the techniques of conjoint therapy
of marital partners, as well as other methods which include the marital
partner in the therapy plan. Conjoint therapy: concurrent therapy in
which each spouse is seen by the same or by a different analyst, but not
together; and combined therapy, in which conjoint and individual concurrent sessions are both arranged, are all variations which take into
account in a direct way the fact that the primary patient is a member of a
family and that his behavior, whether or not to be labeled neurotic,
cannot be understood in isolation from other people (Rosenbaum and
Alger, 1968).

The logical fault in Alger's statement is that his sound observation,
about the patient not living in a vacuum and the interpersonal relations,
sociocultural considerations, etc., does not lead inevitably to the conclusion the only or best way to be of help to a person is in a "social" or
family type therapy — any more than a violinist should be given group
or "conjoint" lessons because s/he is destined to play in a symphony
orchestra. To my knowledge no one condemns individual and private
instructions in that area. The shortcomings of this analogy notwith-
standing, the private, confidential, one-to-one therapy which psychoanalysis provides does in no way exclude an understanding of either
interpersonal relations or sociocultural considerations. It may actually
increase understanding of these crucial factors by the distancing that the
private contract facilitates, distancing that we generally recognize of
prime importance in the learning process. Distancing allows for a modicum of a reflection needed for insight and decision-making. Although
we have been told that families who pray together stay together, there is
no surety that this is also true of "therapizing" together. Sometimes
therapy of this "social" nature may compound the crime in that the
principal problem is likely to be too much togetherness, too much community, too little privacy with too much intrusion into each other's lives.

Lastly, treating both partners together or alternately burdens the treat-
ment with an implicit value judgment about the marriage and marriage.
It is like learning about the choice between religion and atheism in the
Vatican! (Rosenbaum and Alger, 1968)

The above is but a partial list of the available therapies. Finally, to
leave no stone unturned, there is serious use of "individual, concurrent
and conjoint sessions as a 'combined approach'." This treatment, a combination of the best of all those mentioned above, "is based on a plan of
active support, including environmental manipulation; complementary
goals; clarification of role expectations and enactments; redirection of
intrapsychic and interpersonal energies; and evocation of 'healthier

communication' '' (Greene, Broadhurst, and Lustig, 1965).

Psychiatry obviously can never be accused of lack of zeal and inventiveness. And, as already indicated and confirmed by each "scientific" study, "everything works." Who can resist the doctor's prescription? Who cares if the doctor's prescription makes no mention of individual aspirations, the rights of privacy and confidentiality, the hypocrisy inherent in the role of judge-therapist, or the total blockage of meaningful communication which an "adversary-structured" situation, such as conjoint therapy, really is? Courts of law for centuries have clearly recognized the principle that the accused should not be asked to testify against her/himself. In marital problems each is the accused. In all these "social therapies" the inherent judiciary nature of their operations is never mentioned. Without the protection of basic rules of evidence, can one expect more than a modicum of disingenuousness on the part of the accused? We shudder at the image of a kangaroo court in modern society and yet they may be operating at full steam in the most unsuspected and most respectable places. We must not forget the kangaroo courts "work"; the accused is found innocent or guilty and is sentenced. What is missing, of course, are the rules of procedure and evidence that guarantee basic human rights *even if the accused her/himself may not be aware of them.*

"All the world loves a lover" is a lovely but inaccurate popular quotation. The sight or knowledge of people deeply in love and trustful of each other seems to stimulate the desire of some to split them apart. Perhaps such a desire is some inherent human capriciousness. It may be the work of misanthropes who, unable to find suitable mates themselves, cannot tolerate the happiness of others. Or it may be a lingering hostility from the oedipal stage of development, where the impotent youngster is overwhelmed with frustration at the closeness of his parents; divisiveness is his hobbyhorse thereafter in life.

A third force may be the needed, often self-created frustration and stimulus to carry one to the next stage of development; to counteract that tranquility which encourages stagnation and involution. In the modern idiom, it is needed for one's creative identity, in the sense of testing oneself in the cauldron of doubt, destruction, and dismay. Only in such a position can one concretely learn one's true mettle. It was Shakespeare who also wrote, "Sweet are the uses of adversity." Love is, then, never enough of a test for the developing human being any more than the caliber of a race horse can be fully known on a dry track. A basic characteristic of human mentality is that it is problem-seeking: if people do not have any problems, they will manufacture them. It seems that mental growth and general maturation depend on finding and attempting to solve problems. If a person cannot manufacture them in reality, s/he will do so in phantasy.

A third force brought to bear on a problem, whether analyst, friend, clergyman, social worker, or attorney, must be at best a temporary expedient. The ideal to be achieved by outside help is not a third leg for a stool (although often this is the most that can be achieved) but ultimately inner strength, the growth of the inner person. Familiarity with the inner self should be the chief strength of a person in matters of troubled relationships. Hopefully one can transcend some personal miseries through understanding.

The passion of love always carries with it expectations that for the most part are destined for disillusioning frustration. When the other person does not fill all the vacancies of one's soul, abject bitterness and hatred may result. The solution in most instances can only be the accretion of inner tissues to call upon when the outside fails, as it generally does. In the jargon of the trade, we can say that the fruits of affinity can never be known until there is identity. It is wonderful to love and be loved, to protect and be protected, but none of these is possible until or unless one is able to be alone. And it is impossible to be alone unless there is a firm, ongoing communication with an inner self. Stripped of its mystical trappings, Soul can be called the chief sustaining force of life. Soul is a reservoir of ideals, convictions, memories of pleasure and pain, of sustaining objects of the past and present, of associations with the world of people and things, and of proofs of achievement and worthiness. Hopefully, one has access to such an internal entity — and, most importantly, open communication with it. Psychoanalysis has as a chief goal the establishment of full communication between the outer and inner self. It is only here that ultimate reassurance and consolation will be found.

When people with marital problems come for help, they are rarely interested in the "inner being." The wife is more involved with the outer man who is reducing her to a state of impotent rage. After a battle, the urgent need is to get the wounds dressed and to justify the war. "Treatment" in these instances consists of a series of "white papers" issued by the aggrieved party attempting to justify the behavior which is "defensively" derived. Kubie's words can be readily confirmed by every psychoanalyst. "Psychoanalysis in marriages which are already on the rocks almost always encounters one particular complication. Individuals usually come not to get well, but to prove to a spouse that they are well; not to find out where they are wrong, but to prove they are right (Kubie, 1956).

For example, the husband comes to treatment because it is the thing to do, but it is hard to see how treating him is going to change "her obnoxious behavior," which is the cause of all the trouble. Then the inventory of oppressions begins, with the only area of self-doubt being, "I wonder in what state of irrationality I was to have married her." All of his grievances are reasonable; he is right. Yet he would have put up with all of them if only she had brought the fulfillment that no outsider can provide. He must face the humiliation that the promises of love alone are no substitutes for inner strength. If he is lucky enough to be able to see beyond his wife, he will gradually get down to the work of self-accretion, insead of self-justification, for preparation to live in a world which never lacks injustice, corruption, and chaos. The ultimate reunion with the self, which understanding brings, helps both to defend against these three and to rail against them more effectively.

Central to marital problems, after the pettiness is stripped away, is the awkward issue of human rights, such as self-fulfillment, autonomy, and privacy, as well as expectations of compassion, sharing, and mutuality. Marriages frequently land "on the rocks" because there is an assumption of one or both partners that the marital union somehow abrogates these rights, as if the holy writs give license to strip the other of what is generally held dear and sacred. Loving someone appears to some as the opportunity to overwhelm, to entrap, and to enslave. Love becomes a strange and puzzling experience indeed if, in its name, almost any indignity and intrusion of rights can be perpetuated (Blood and Wolfe, 1960). Bruno Bettelheim told us that love is not enough. It is nothing and less than nothing if it is not inextricably bound to a sense of justice. Love without justice is a yoke, which more often than not, not only enslaves but strangulates the human spirit. The sense of justice in human relationships is the consequential contribution of Martin Buber in his "I and thou" concept. Before him, love seemed the solitary requirement.

Because the issue of human rights in its variegated, subtle expressions is of paramount importance, the structure of therapy and its sensitivity to this issue takes on great meaning. Therapy, it would seem, should be a corrective paradigm in that it should respect with utmost care matters of goals, privacy, and confidentiality, as well as highly individualistic, even eccentric, aspirations. It seems appropriate and reasonable that the therapist be the client's exclusive agent, distinguished from the mate, children, relatives, and other therapists.

Therapies which downgrade and denigrate by design or accident the importance of individual worth and aspirations enhance neither self-esteem nor personal hope. A person must, in T. S. Eliot's idiom, seek his/her own salvation with diligence before s/he can save another, a family, or a marriage. Does this type of individual "attention" promote megalomania and selfishness? Isn't it the traditional job of therapy to shrink heads rather than expand them? No danger. The erosions of the human spirit are usually so immense that the restoration of human dignity and feelings of heightened self-worth can only be salutary. No marriage should ever be held of more importance than its participants. Persons, not marriages, are worth saving. It is the grand hypocrisy of our morality that we have attempted to sanctify and glorify a compact often irrespective of the plight of the human beings involved. Every lawyer knows that no compact or contract is ever worth more than the signatories. We will someday learn that this verity applies to vital human relations also.

Andrew S. Watson (1968) a psychiatrist and attorney, urges psychoanalysts to involve themselves in the problems found in the law of the family — domestic relations law — and to assist the legal profession in understanding human behavior. That this would be most rewarding for all concerned, we can wholeheartedly concur. However, I would suggest that psychoanalysis has already profited and can enhance itself further by the example of the law tradition especially in regard to the client-advocate relationship. Psychoanalysis has imitated the legal model, and in my judgment, psychiatry in general would do well to study it. When the attorney is the advocate of the client he therein acknowledges an adversary situation that inevitably develops in marriage either "on the rocks" or otherwise.

It follows then quite logically (and ethically) that an attorney does not speak privately to the mate of the client. It follows that the attorney does not reveal to the mate personal data gathered in confidence. It follows then that the attorney does not sit in judgment of the pair as to who is right and who is wrong or who is mature and who childish. Her/His role is that of agent or advocate of the client and s/he behaves as such under penalty of malpractice. Who would advocate changing this set of rules? Psychoanalysis, to its credit, felt that these rules should be applied to its own work. This basic structure of the psychoanalytic situation is not derived from the "mechanistic thinking of a past era" as some like to claim, but from the advocacy tradition which our law colleagues taught us. Knowledge of worldly sociocultural forces as well as the interpersonal ones have not impelled lawyers to stray from their basic rules for dealing with a client.

The problem of therapy involves ties and bonds to the past. These ties often remain to influence, often detrimentally, the new affinities the mature life demands. This is a lesson each generation must learn.

Freeing oneself does not mean forgetting family traditions, as some existentialists would have us believe possible. Both the forces of the sequence of generations and the reality rooted in love and work make us what we are. In our forging of an identity, we may modify this reality a little. This "little" may be more than enough. As Horace said to Sestius: "All of life is only a little, no long-term plans are allowed."

In summary, everything works in the "helping" professions and therefore all types of interventions are tried, rationalized, and established as "therapies." Since all claim good results and none can be placed under "scientific" scrutiny, the observer, as well as the client, must use moral criteria to make critical judgments as to their value. It is herein suggested that the structure of the therapy and the rules governing the behavior of therapist and client are of central importance. For the manner in which therapist and client conduct themselves can be the crucial and significant educative experience for other relationships. In terms of modern idiom, the medium is also the message. A therapeutic relationship, in which human rights are scrupulously honored as well as disciplined inhibition of exploitative and coercive instincts, is a salutary model that will be remembered for other relationships including marriage. Unfortunately, this model for human interaction is too often ignored by the "new", but really *old*, breed of interventionists.

In terms of humanistic tradition the structure of psychoanalytic therapy scores high. The innovators with their disregard for privacy, confidentiality, and the autonomous strivings of the individual appear to run counter to this tradition. There may be a legitimate role for the "mediator" in modern society, but is he a therapist?

REFERENCES

Alger, Ian: Joint sessions: psychoanalytic variations applications and indications. In Rosenbaum, Salo, and Alger, Ian (Eds.): *The Marriage Relationship, Psychoanalytic Perspectives.* New York, Basic Books, 1968, Chapter 18, pp. 251-65.

Blood, Robert O., and Wolfe, Donald M.: *Husbands and Wives, the Dynamics of Married Living.* New York, Free Press, 1960, pp. 221-235.

Giovacchini, Peter L.: The clinical approach. In Greene, Bernard L. (Ed.): *The Psychotherapies of Marital Discord.* New York, Free Press, 1965, pp. 39-81.

Goode, William J.: *Women in Divorce.* New York, Free Press, 1956, pp. 131-54.

Gottlieb, Anthony, and Pattison, E. Mansell: Married couples, group psychotherapy. *Arch of Gen Psychiat., 14*:143, 1966.

Greene, Bernard L., Broadhurst, Betty P., and Lustig, Noel: Treatment of marital disharmony: the use of individual, concurrent, and conjoint sessions in a 'combined approach'. In Greene, Bernard L. (Ed.): *The Psychotherapies of Marital Discord.* New York, Free Press, 1965, pp. 135-151.

Kubie, Lawrence S.: Psychoanalysis and marriage. In Eisenstein, Victor W. (Eds.): *Neurotic Interaction in Marriage.* New York, Basic Books, 1956, p. 38.

Lasch, Christopher: Divorce American style. *New York Review of Books, 6*:3, 1966.

Markowitz, Max: Analytic group psychotherapy of marital couples by a therapist couple. In Rosenbaum, Salo, and Alger, Ian (Eds.): *The Marriage Relationship, Psychoanalytic Perspectives.* New York, Basic Books, 1968.

Martin, Peter A., and Bird, H. Waldo: An approach to the psychotherapy of marriage partners, the stereoscopic technique. *Psychiat, 16*:123-7, 1953.

Martin, Peter A.: Treatment of marital disharmony by collaborative therapy. In Greene, Bernard L. (Ed.): *The Psychotherapies of Marital Discord.* New York, Free Press,

1965, pp. 83-101.

Rosenbaum, Salo, and Alger, Ian (Eds.): *The Marriage Relationship, Psychoanalytic Perspectives*. New York, Basic Books, 1968.

Satir, Virginia M.: Conjoint marital therapy. In Greene, Bernard L. (Ed.): *The Psychotherapies of Marital Discord*. New York, Free Press, 1965, pp. 121-33.

Solomon, Alfred P., and Greene, Bernard L.: Concurrent psychoanalytic therapy in marital disharmony. In Greene, Bernard L. (Ed.): *The Psychotherapies of Marital Discord*. New York, Free Press, 1965, pp. 103-17.

Szasz, Thomas S.: *The Ethics of Psychoanalysis, The Theory and Method of Autonomous Psychotherapy*. New York, Basic Books, 1965, pp. 11-28.

Szasz, Thomas S.: Recent letters to the editor. *New York Times Book Review*, 1961.

Watson, Andrew S.: *Psychiatry for Lawyers*. New York, International Universities Press, 1968.

Section IV

ASSERTION TRAINING FOR WOMEN

INTRODUCTION

THE two papers by Jakubowski in this section are sufficiently comprehensive to serve as a manual for assertion training, one of the most useful clinical techniques for working with women in psychotherapy. According to Jakubowski an important aspect of mental health involves the belief by individuals that they can make an effective impact on their environment; i.e. that they are not helpless victims and that their behavior can affect other persons in constructive ways. The opposite belief and resulting feelings of helplessness produce psychological problems. Jakubowski defines assertion as standing up for one's own rights without trampling on the rights of others. Assertion is contrasted with aggression, standing up for one's own rights in ways that violate the rights of others, and with nonaggression, permitting one's rights to be violated.

Assertion training is particularly important for women since women are typically socialized and rewarded for being nonassertive and are punished not only for being aggressive but also for being assertive. Women need to learn that they can be strong and effective and still remain sensitive and empathetic to others. Acting nonassertively causes women to lose in many ways: a sense of their own individual identity; contact with their own desires, feelings, self-esteem, and power; and the trust of others. In place of open, direct statements of their desires and feelings, women may resort to unsatisfying practices such as hidden-bargains, tears, or, when all else fails, sudden bursts of aggression.

Clinical problems of women which Jakubowski feels can be appropriately treated by assertion training include neurotic depressions, dating problems, job-related problems, child abuse, communication difficulties in couple counseling, psychosomatic problems, drug or alcohol dependency, agoraphobia and other irrational fears.

Jakubowski's second paper is concerned mainly with assertion-training techniques, rather than rationale or theory. She outlines assertion-training procedures for all-women groups consisting of six to ten members, meeting six to ten weeks for weekly two-hour sessions. Although both male and female facilitators can provide the necessary information on assertiveness, a female facilitator has added advantages. She can serve as a model who is both feminine and assertive. She can be someone in whom the women can confide more easily, and she will probably evoke less game-playing from members.

Assertion training involves replacing irrational belief systems with belief systems that support individual rights, the internalization of truthful self-sentences and the practice of assertive responses. To accomplish these ends, Jakubowski employs strategies and rationale drawn from behavior theory, rational-emotive therapy, gestalt therapy, bioenergetics, and transactional analysis. She delineates a four-phase program for training with overlapping phases. The four phases are as follows:

Phase I: Teaching discrimination between assertive, aggressive and nonassertive behaviors, developing motivation for change, and heightening awareness of one's own behavior patterns.

Phase II: Recognizing one's current belief system and how it interferes with assertive behavior, and making necessary changes in one's belief system to support assertiveness.

Phase III: Identifying psychological obstacles which prevent one from acting on the new beliefs and reducing or removing any obstacles.

Phase IV: Developing assertion skills through active practice methods including role plays, behavior rehearsals, modeling, and videotape feedback.

Because of the current active phase of the women's rights movement, we are in an era of extreme popularity for assertion training. In this crowded field, Jakubowski's approach stands out for its attention to differential diagnosis and for its comprehensive systematic application.

—— *Chapter 8* ——

ASSERTIVE BEHAVIOR AND CLINICAL PROBLEMS OF WOMEN

PATRICIA ANN JAKUBOWSKI*

As therapists we all have an implicit, if not explicit, model of emotional health which guides our therapy. Although it is beyond the scope of this article to present a full theory of emotional health, I believe that one aspect is central: *Emotionally healthy, fully functioning people believe that they can make an effective impact on the people in their environment. They do not feel that they are helpless victims of life's events or of other people's demands. Instead they feel in charge of themselves because they believe that they can engage in direct behavior which will affect other people in constructive ways.* White (1973) stresses the importance of a similar concept, interpersonal competence, for healthy functioning.

When people do not feel that their behavior can make an impact on others — in other words, when they do not feel interpersonally effective — their resulting feelings of anger, helplessness, and hurt may evolve into a wide variety of psychological problems. Although a person needs many skills to be interpersonally effective, one essential skill is the ability to be assertive.

I will examine some factors which hinder women from acting assertively and then I will discuss the relationship of nonassertive behavior to various psychological problems. Before dealing with these objectives, I will briefly define assertion, aggression, and nonassertion, since these terms are often misunderstood.

Assertion involves standing up for one's basic interpersonal rights in such a way that the rights of another person are not violated in the process. It is a direct, honest, and appropriate expression of one's thoughts, feelings, and beliefs. In contrast, *aggression* involves standing up for one's rights in such a way that the rights of the other person are violated. It is an attempt to dominate, humiliate, or put the other person down. *Nonassertion* is failing to stand up for one's rights and, consequently, permitting one's rights to be violated by others. It is failing to express one's honest thoughts, feelings, or beliefs, or expressing these in such an anxious, diffident way that permits the other person to disregard them (Jakubowski-Spector, 1973).

---

*Formerly cited as Patricia Jakubowski-Spector.

NONASSERTIVE BEHAVIOR

In our culture, women who act nonassertively — placing other people's needs above their own, waiting for others to take the initiative, withholding their own opinions in deference to other people — are generally viewed as engaging in desirable feminine behavior. Broverman's research (Broverman, Vogel, Broverman, Clarkson, and Rosenkrantz, 1972) reveals that the mental health prescription for female behavior is to be dependent, subjective, passive, noncompetitive, illogical, gentle, tactful, and sensitive to the feelings of others. Both men *and* women of diverse ages, religions, marital statuses, and educational levels not only expect women to act in these ways, but they also see these behaviors as being desirable for women. This stereotype increases the likelihood that women who engage in unhealthy, nonassertive behavior will be reinforced for exhibiting these "appropriate" feminine behaviors.

Although assertion is a healthy human behavior which is equally appropriate for either sex, the female stereotype suggests that women are more likely than men to be punished for acting assertively. Since assertion is almost invariably confused with aggression and aggression is viewed as a stereotypic male behavior, when women are assertive they may risk being thought of as "masculine" or as acting inappropriately. Because the stereotypic male is aggressive, independent, objective, dominant, active, competitive, logical and direct (Broverman et al., 1972), it is easier for men to be assertive since their assertion is congruent with the male sex-role stereotype. It is harder for women to be assertive since their assertion runs counter to both the female sex-role stereotype and their prior sex-role socialization.

As part of their sex-role socialization, women receive certain kinds of messages which overemphasize their responsibilities to other people. These messages are often perceived by them as dictates; if they fail to act in these prescribed ways, they feel they are unworthy and bad. Table 8-I shows those socialization "dictates" which are particularly likely to inhibit women's assertion.

Since these messages imply that the person is not entitled to have certain basic human rights, women who internalize these messages are likely to feel that it is wrong to be assertive. To help a client become more assertive, a therapist usually needs to do more than merely exhort or encourage her to act more assertively. The therapist may need to change the client's belief system by supplying more accurate and healthy messages which emphasize her rights and which place her responsibilities to other people in a more realistic context.

All females are exposed to sex-role stereotypes and sex-role

TABLE 8 - I

HOW SOCIALIZATION MESSAGES MAY NEGATIVELY AFFECT ASSERTION

Socialization Message	Effect on Rights	Effect on Assertive Behavior	Healthy Message
Think of others first; give to others even if you're hurting. Don't be selfish.	I have no right to place my needs above those of other people.	When I have a conflict with someone else, I will give in and satisfy the other person's needs and forget about my own.	To be selfish means that a person always places her/his needs above other people's. This is undesirable human behavior. All healthy people have needs and strive to fulfill these as much as possible. Your needs are as important as other people's. When there is a conflict over need satisfaction, compromise is a useful way to handle the conflict.
Be modest and humble. Don't act superior to other people.	I have no right to do anything which would imply that I am better than other people.	I will discount my accomplishments and any compliments I receive. When I'm in a meeting, I will encourage other people's contributions and keep silent about my own. When I have an opinion which is different than someone else's, I won't express it; who am I to say that my opinion is better than another's.	It is undesirable to build yourself up at the expense of another person. However, you have as much a right as other people to show your abilities and take pride in yourself. It is healthy to enjoy one's accomplishments.

| Be understanding and overlook trivial irritations. Don't be a bitch and complain. | I have no right to express anger or even to feel anger. | When I'm in a line and someone cuts in front of me, I will say nothing. I will not tell my boyfriend that I don't like his constantly interrupting me when I speak. | It is undesirable to deliberately nit pick. However, life is made up of trivial incidents and it is normal to be occasionally irritated by seemingly small events. You have a right to your angry feelings, and if you express them at the time they occur, your feelings won't build up and explode. It is important, however, to express your anger assertively rather than aggressively. |
| Help other people. Don't be demanding. | I have no right to make requests of other people. | I will not ask my friend to reciprocate babysitting favors. I will not ask for a pay increase from my employer. | It is undesirable to incessantly make demands on others. You do have a right to ask someone else to change their behavior if their behavior affects your life in a concrete way. A request is not the same as a demand. However, if your rights are being violated and your requests for a change are being ignored, you have a right to make demands. |

Be sensitive to other people's feelings.	I have no right to do anything which might hurt someone else's feelings or deflate someone else's ego.	I will not say what I really think or feel because that might hurt someone else.	It is undesirable to deliberately try to hurt others. However, it is impossible as well as undesirable to try to govern your life so as to *never* hurt *anyone*. You have a right to express your thoughts and feelings even if someone else's feelings occasionally get hurt. To do otherwise would result in your being phoney and in denying other people an opportunity to learn how to handle their own feelings. Remember that some people get hurt because they're unreasonably sensitive and others use their hurt to manipulate you. If you accidently hurt someone else, you can generally repair the damage.
Don't hurt other people.		I will inhibit my spontaneity so that I don't impulsively say something that would accidently hurt someone else.	

socialization; however, these cultural influences do not constrict all women's assertion to the same degree: (1) Families vary in the degree to which they accept these cultural expectations and in how they implement them; and (2) unique peer and educational experiences either help or further hinder a woman's ability to act assertively; and (3) individual temperament and abilities interact with cultural expectations of nonassertion.

An individual woman's unique family experiences can hinder her ability to act assertively in a number of ways. For example, a woman is even more likely to act nonassertively if she comes from a family where the following beliefs are inculcated: "You can't fight City Hall." "Children should be seen and not heard." "Fighting never gets you anywhere." "If you're not sure that you're 100% right, don't say anything at all." In yet other families, as the following example shows, a woman may have had repeated childhood experiences in which she was punished for expressing her honest opinions.

> As a teenager, Diane had several intense encounters with her father about religion. Even when Diane expressed her honest opinions politely, her father became outraged for days. Diane's mother would cry and beg Diane to apologize to her father and say that she was wrong, so that family peace could be restored. Feeling powerless to handle the situation, Diane always apologized, though she felt deeply angry and hurt. As a result Diane learned that it was best to keep her opinions to herself. Later as an adult she had great difficulty in defending her opinions logically, and she avoided situations in which she would have to express them.

In some families children repeatedly observe their parents acting nonassertively and learn vicariously that this is the only way to handle unpleasant situations (Bandura, 1969). A child who observes the interaction in the following example may learn that "You can't directly tell someone else what your own needs are," and that "It's dangerous to ask others for favors."

> The grandparents have called again saying that they would like to do something with the family this Sunday. Dad responds, "Oh sure we'd love to have you come with us to the picnic. Don't worry at all about it." As soon as he hangs up the phone, he starts complaining, "Oh my aching back! Don't they realize that we need some time to be alone!"

Thus far I have discussed nonassertion in terms of factors that hinder women from using their assertive skills; that is, they may not believe that they have the right to be assertive, or they may have had experiences which cause them to be afraid to act assertively. Another reason why women act nonassertively is because they simply have not acquired the needed assertive skills. For example, a woman may feel that she has a right to refuse a sexual invitation from an attractive date, but she may simply not have learned how she can do this in a tactful but effective way.

Regardless of the reason why women act nonassertively, when they do so, they may lose a sense of their own individual identity (Katz, 1971). This may occur when a woman becomes so accustomed to being attuned to other people's needs and preferences that she loses contact with her own desires. Another way a woman may lose contact with herself and her own genuine, spontaneous feelings is when she has taught herself to suppress her feelings as a way of avoiding conflict with others.

Even if a woman is nonassertive in only a few types of situations, she is likely to feel some loss of self-confidence and self-esteem and growing anger, hurt, and powerlessness. Other people may withdraw from her and distrust her because they feel that she is not being honest and genuine with them; they may feel guilty for taking advantage of her and/or they may lose respect for her as a person (Alberti & Emmons, 1974).

When a nonassertive woman does try to get her needs satisfied she may resort to indirect manipulation, such as the *hidden-bargain*. In this type of manipulation, instead of directly asking for what she needs or wants, the woman assumes that if she gives up some of her rights by not asserting herself, and acts in a way to please the other person, the other person is duty-bound to engage in a particular behavior which she wants. The classic example of this type of *hidden-bargain* manipulation is the woman who, instead of directly asking for a raise, works excessively hard in the expectation that her extra work will force her employer to increase her salary without her having to ask for it. Since these bargains are not verbalized, the other persons are unaware that the bargains exist and thus they typically do not keep their part of the deal. As a consequence, people who frequently engage in hidden-bargain behavior typically feel angry and victimized (Jakubowski-Spector, 1973a).

Other forms of manipulation in attempts to get one's needs met are using tears. Unfortunately, the very success of these methods further decreases the likelihood of learning how to be more honest and assertive in interactions with others.

People who are usually nonassertive will occasionally become aggressive; and, vice versa, people who are usually aggressive will sometimes become nonassertive. Nonassertion and aggression are actually flip sides of the same problem; in neither case can the person act assertively. In neither case, can the person establish a relationship in which both parties are equal.

AGGRESSIVE BEHAVIOR

When women are unable to act assertively and express their anger, irritation, or disappointment directly, they may resort to passive-aggression, or indirect aggression in the form of backbiting or candy-coated cattiness. That women have the reputation for engaging in these behaviors is an indication of the difficulty women have in acting assert-ively.

Direct aggression may occur after a long period of failing to act as-sertively. A woman accumulates hurt and angry feelings until she finally explodes in aggressive behavior. This type of aggression often occurs when the woman has assumed a self-effacing, martyr role in a relation-ship. Although this aggression may feel immediately cathartic, the woman may later feel guilty and disgusted with her aggressive outburst. Furthermore, it causes the recipient to feel angry, hurt, and vengeful.

When a woman expresses justifiable complaints in an explosive way, her complaints may not be taken seriously by the recipient who is likely to view the sudden stream of aggressive complaints as due to the emo-tional nature of women. In extreme cases, the woman may be viewed as mad (Chesler, 1972).

Direct aggression may occur when, in the course of acting assertively, the woman becomes afraid that she can not maintain her assertion and that she may back down. She becomes aggressive in order to prevent herself from acting nonassertively.

Short bursts of direct aggression may occur when a woman feels like she has hit a brick wall and that there is no other way to get through to the other person. When her aggression fails to produce a change in the other person's behavior, a woman may cry because she feels overwhelmed by her anger and her inability to change the other person. The other person often mistakenly views this instance of crying as manipulation.

Lastly, women may act aggressively because they both lack assertive skills and believe that they will be respected by others only when they are aggressive. In this case, the woman's aggression may be highly satisfying to her because it makes her feel powerful; she experiences few direct negative reactions from others, who usually withdraw from her and criti-cize her behind her back instead of to her face. However, as Alberti and Emmons (1974) have so cogently noted, the price that is paid for such aggressive behavior is that relationships are damaged and the joys that come from closeness are sacrificed. In contrast, assertive behavior can also make a person feel powerful but will generally result in changing other people's behavior without the hard feelings that are typically associated with aggression.

ASSERTIVE BEHAVIOR

Assertive behavior conveys respect for oneself and an appropriate re-spect, not deference, towards the other person. The following case example illustrates the kind of respect that is involved in assertive behavior.

> A woman was desperately trying to get a flight to Kansas City to see her mother who was sick in the hospital. Weather conditions were bad and the lines were long. Having been rejected from three standby flights, she again found herself in the middle of a long line for the fourth and last flight to Kansas City. This time she approached a man who was standing near the beginning of the line and said, pointing to her place, "Would you mind exchanging places with me? I ordinarily wouldn't ask, but it's extremely important that I get to Kansas City tonight." The man nodded yes, and as it turned out, both of them were able to get on the flight.
>
> When I asked the woman what her reaction would have been if the man had refused, she replied, "It would have been OK. I hoped he would say yes, but after all he was there first. He'd have had a right to turn me down."
>
> The woman respected herself enough to ask for the favor while at the same time she respected the man's right to refuse; had he refused, she would not have thought that he was selfish and insensitive, nor would she have felt that she had been a fool to ask.

In the above example, the assertion involved taking the initiative and making a request. Assertion may also involve a simple affirmation of one's rights. For example, when a woman is at a counter waiting to be served and the clerk mistakenly starts to take someone else's order before hers, the woman may simply affirm her right to be served by saying firmly, but not coldly, "I believe I was here first."

At other times, assertion may involve expressing one's anger or irritation. An angry assertion involves owning one's feelings, describing how the other person's behavior concretely effects one's life or feelings, and requesting or demanding that the other person change his/her behavior. In contrast, in an angry aggession there is an attempt to make the other person feel responsible for having caused one's bad feelings. In the following example, notice how "you" statements are used in the angry aggression and how "I" statements are used in the angry assertion.*

> "You make me so mad I could scream! Are you deaf or are you just trying to get my dander up today! If you know what's good for you, boy, you'll turn the stereo volume down and you'll keep it down!"
>
> "Johnny, I'm really getting irritated! I don't know if you realize it, but your stereo is so loud that I can't talk on the phone without shouting. Turn the volume down and let's keep it down ... OK, that's much better now."

According to Wolpe (1973) and others, another type of assertion is

---

*The concept of "I" versus "you" messages is based on Gordon's (1970) work.

positive or soft assertion which involves appropriate expressions of affection and tenderness, such as "I like you," "I enjoy talking to you," "I'm glad that I invited you to come for dinner," "You've been a big help to me."

Assertion is a social skill which in some situations may be made more effective if it is combined with other social skills such as empathy, confrontation, and contracting.

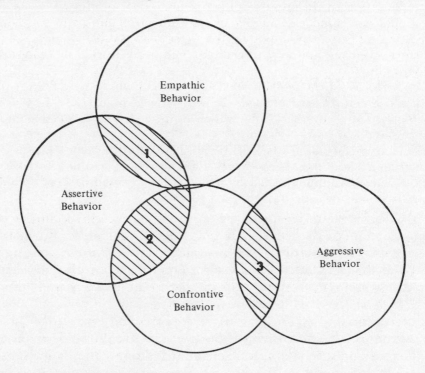

1. Empathic Assertion
2. Assertive Confrontation
3. Aggressive Confrontation

Figure 8-1. How assertive behavior relates to other social behaviors. (Modified from Jakubowski-Spector, 1973.)

High quality assertive behavior involves an empathic component in which the woman first acknowledges the other person's feelings or situation and then continues to make the assertive statement. For example, "I know that you give me advice because you don't want me to get hurt by mistakes I might make; but, at this point in my life, I need to learn how to make my own decisions and rely on myself, even if I do make some mistakes. I appreciate the help you've given me in the past and you can help me now by not giving me advice." Empathic assertions are particularly important for women since this behavior enables them to maintain the satisfying, positive part of their stereotypic feminine role behavior, sensitivity, while eliminating the destructive aspects of compliance, deference, and submission. Empathic assertions are particularly useful when the relationship with the other person is important, when one wants to reduce the chances that the other person will become defensive or feel hurt, or when one simply wants to convey understanding and still be assertive.

When people's words are discrepant with their actions, an assertive confrontation would be appropriate. For example, when an employer has promised a raise but has failed to give it, a woman may assertively confront the employer and say:

> I understood from our last talk that I would receive a raise in three months. I've been working here for four months and I haven't received my raise yet. I believe that my work has been satisfactory. Unless there is some problem that I'm not aware of, I would appreciate your taking whatever steps are necessary to have the raise included in my next paycheck."

Here the woman noted the discrepancy in a nonevaluative way and then stated what she would like to see happen regarding her raise.

Women who lack assertive skills may carry out their confrontation in an aggressive manner. An example of an aggressive confrontation is: "Listen, you're supposed to give me a raise after three months of work. This is the fourth month now ... and still no raise! What's going on here!" Here the woman tried to overpower her employer and ended on a note of insinuation.

Assertion may also involve developing a mutually acceptable contract which would specify what each person will do for the other. Since space limitations prohibit a detailed description of contracting procedures, interested readers are referred to Jakubowski-Spector (1974) and Homme (1969). A brief example will show how assertion and contracting may be used in a conflict situation.

> A graduate professor often continued evening class ten minutes or more beyond the normal class period. Although many students were irked by this behavior, one student was assertive and approached the professor after class one evening.
>
> *Student*: "I recognize that sometimes we get so involved in the discussion that you may not realize that the class is running overtime. I'd appreciate your ending the class on time because I have several commitments which I need to keep immediately after this class."
>
> *Professor*: "I don't really think that I've been late so often."
>
> *Student*: "I guess that you haven't noticed but the last three classes have been ten or fifteen minutes late. Is there any way I could help you

end it on time?"

   Professor: "As a matter of fact there is. I'm often so interested in the class that I don't look at my watch. It'd help me if you'd raise your hand five minutes before the end of the class period. If I don't stop in five minutes, signal me again."

   Student: "I'd be happy to do that."

In this example the student's assertion involved some recognition of the professor's situation, a clear request which indicated what effect the professor's behavior had upon her life, and an offer to help overcome whatever obstacle was preventing the professor from acting as she requested. The contract which evolved was a simple agreement in which the student would remind the professor about the time in exchange for the professor's ending the class promptly.

   When women act more assertively, they feel an increased sense of self-confidence and self-respect and generally find that other people respect them more. Their assertion provides more authentic and satisfying ways of relating to other people. In addition, Dempewolff's research* suggests that women's self-concepts may also significantly improve as a result of their learning to act more assertively.

   In the following section various psychological problems will be discussed which may be related to a client's failure to assert herself. Since clients rarely conceptualize their problems in terms of assertion, it is primarily the therapist's responsibility to make this clinical assessment. In discussing each of these clinical problems I have clarified the conditions under which assertive training would be an appropriate treatment strategy.

CLINICAL PROBLEMS

Depression: Experimental Analog Data

   Depression is probably the most common client problem. Although there are many theories of depression, Seligman's (1973) is particularly compelling and has the most implications for women and assertion. His theory is that laboratory observations of the cause, cure, and prevention of the laboratory-induced "learned helplessness" phenomenon (Seligman & Maier, 1967) can be applied to *reactive depression* or what Wolpe (1971) has called *neurotic depression.*

   According to the research of Seligman and his associates (Seligman, Maier & Solomon, 1971; Thorton & Jacobs, 1971), an organism learns to be helpless when it is repeatedly exposed to stress conditions in which no

---

*Dempewolff, Judy: *Personal Communication.* University of Delaware, 1974.

behavior in which the organism engages reduces the stress. When the organism is later placed in a different stress situation where it could act to eliminate the stress, it fails to do so and instead undereats, does not fight back when attacked, exhibits sexual disturbances, and has decreased norepinephrine levels in its brain.*

Seligman (1973) theorizes that clinical depression, like learned helplessness, occurs when individuals are unable to control important events in their lives.

Laboratory-induced learned helplessness is reversed when the organism is compelled to engage in behavior which enables it to escape the shock (Seligman, 1969; Seligman, Maier, & Greer, 1968). Depression may be similarly cured through therapeutic strategies which are designed to get the clients moving and acting on their environment. The therapeutic goal would be to demonstrate to depressed clients that their behavior can affect others and that they are not helpless and controlled by external events and other people.

Organisms who have had prior experiences in mastering stress do not become helpless when they later experience inescapable stress situations. This finding has implications for prevention: Seligman (1973) theorizes that people who have had extensive experiences in mastering their environment and have developed a wide repertoire of coping responses may be less vulnerable to neurotic depression.

Seligman's theory, based on his experiments, has at least four important implications for women's depression, and assertion: *First*, it helps to explain why women are more likely than men to become depressed. Women are usually socialized to be more passive, dependent, and nonassertive than men; this means that they are more likely than men to learn to depend on other people to take care of them. This, in effect, denies women an opportunity and a need to acquire a wide repertoire of coping skills. Furthermore, women are more likely than men to be told that there are certain situations which they cannot handle; women may avoid these situations and never learn how to master them. *Second*, the theory suggests that when a woman's failure to act assertively has made her feel powerless and subsequently depressed, assertion training would be a useful treatment for the depression.

Third, Seligman's (1973) theory puts women's feeling of fatalism into perspective. It helps to explain why it is so difficult to convince generally nonassertive individuals that it is both desirable and possible to act

---

*. . . Many people have associated lowered norepinephrine levels with clinical depression. The tricyclic antidepressants are known to definitely enhance the action of injected epinephrine and norepinephrine at peripheral sympathetic receptor sites; whether or not the tricyclic antidepressants actually release endogenous stores of epinephrine and norephinephrine is still unknown (Goodman & Gilman, 1970, p. 188).

assertively. If they learned directly or vicariously that they could not positively affect other people or their environment, then when they are in a new stress situation where they could be effectively assertive, they are likely to react with learned helplessness — rejecting the notions that assertion could be effective or that they could act assertively. It is common for them to simply say: "I couldn't do that (perform an assertive behavior) because it's *not me* to act that way!" Finally, the theory suggests that assertive training could be a preventative to depression. People who know that they can assertively handle a situation feel in control of themselves and feel that they are governing their own lives and that they are not victims of other people's expectations or demands.

Depression: Case Study Data

Various case studies have been reported which provide suggestive evidence that assertive training can be helpful in treating depression: Bean (1970), Cameron (1951), Katz (1971), Lazarus and Serber (1968), Piaget and Lazarus (1969), Stevenson and Wolpe (1960, case #3), and Wolpe (1958, case #2).

Depression: Clinical Examples

Newly Married Blues

Upon getting married any couple faces a certain period of adjustment during which their personal habits and preferences become synchronized into some mutually satisfying pattern. In some marital relationships the wife becomes depressed during this adjustment period.

Assertion training could be used to treat this depression when the following conditions are present: *One,* the wife feels that she must place her husband's needs and preferences above her own in order to be a good wife. She need not be sacrificing important preferences. As a matter of fact, she is usually sacrificing minor preferences, for example, giving up the side of the bed that she slept on before her marriage or changing her normal sleeping times to fit his pattern. Objectively, minor changes may acquire major significance when they represent a loss of some part of her own identity or a feeling of loss of power. In the early stages of marriage, particularly, a woman may be vulnerable to some identity loss if part of her identity has been attached to her birth name or to a loss of power if she must get her new husband's signature in order to keep her credit cards. *Two,* she resents making sacrifices, but feels guilty about feeling resentful. *Three,* she is afraid that if she were assertive the resulting conflict would be destructive to her marriage, but fears that if she is nonassertive that she will be submerged by her husband's personality. When these conflicts are seen as insurmountable, depression results and assertion training is needed.

Super Mom Syndrome

Bart (1971) has cogently noted that super moms often become depressed in middle age. In their youth they were extremely active — rushing to cart their children to dancing and music lessons, participating in community affairs, giving parties for their friends and their husband's business associates. When the children left, so did the energy and vitality. Assertion training would be appropriate when depression is caused by having expended so much energy in caring for other people that a woman has neglected her own development and needs and does not feel she has the right to care for herself.

Midlife Depression

This depression may occur in the woman's life when her husband is preoccupied with his work. He may be worrying about whether he still has time to make the dreams of his youth come true, or struggling with the knowledge that he will never be as successful as he had hoped, or striving to keep success (Sheehy, 1974). The woman is worried about what she's going to do with the rest of her life when the children are grown and is questioning her ability to change and to satisfy her new, emerging needs.

For those women who are searching for new directions in their lives but who do not know how to be constructively assertive with husbands and friends about desires to go back to work or school or to fulfill long-neglected needs, assertion training would be highly recommended. Among the many assertive problems which this type of woman is likely to encounter are: Telling her husband of her new developmental needs which must have consideration, counteracting her husband's fears of her new development and his objections to her new assertiveness, being assertive in the work world, and accepting her own legitimate assertive rights.

Depression Due to Loss

A widow or divorcee depressed over the loss of her husband may feel overwhelmed by new responsibilities. If she has not learned how to deal with banks, tax accountants, and unsolicited advice from friends and children, assertion training would help to decrease her sense of vulnerability and inadequacy. It would also give her skills she will need to take care of herself.

Dating

Women who are unable to form meaningful relationships because they lack effective interpersonal skills or who avoid getting emotionally close to a man fearing they would be completely dominated by him, are in need of assertion training. Some common areas in which these women need to develop assertive skills are initiating or limiting sex, asking for consideration or tenderness, expressing opinions different from their dates', initiating and refusing invitations, and expressing their own preferences for dating activities. Assertion training also would be appropriate when a woman feels that she can keep her boyfriend only by sacrificing her integrity and allowing her personal rights to be violated or when she is unable to ask for a more firm commitment in the relationship.

Job-Related Problems

Assertion training would be appropriate for a variety of work problems: being unjustly criticized, being the target of unwarranted backbiting and sexist remarks, receiving a discriminative salary, being unable to get her ideas accepted in meetings, being automatically rejected for higher positions merely because she is a woman. When the woman does not have effective assertive skills, she is likely to feel that no matter what she does there is no way that she can make a positive impact on the people in her work environment. For case studies giving examples of assertion training for work situations see Geisinger (1969), Wolpe (1958, case #1), Wolpe and Lazarus (1966, case #2).

Child Abuse

Assertion training may be a useful adjunct to therapy when a mother ricochets between nonassertive and aggressive behavior with her child — nonassertively denying her own needs by sacrificing herself for her child and when she is drained, aggressively overreacting to her feelings of helplessness and inadequacy that are triggered when the child cries or is disobedient and seems to be demanding yet more of her.

In such cases, a mother will need help in learning how to accept and assert her own needs, and how to express constructively her anger and disappointment with her child. She may also need training in assertion with her own parents and husband who may be highly critical of her and who, therefore, contribute to her feelings of inadequacy.

Couple Counseling

Therapists would generally agree that couples who fight aggressively or who pathologically avoid conflict would benefit from both learning how to express their requests and irritations assertively and how to listen with empathy. However, an accurate diagnosis of the situation is also needed, for example, when a wife has assertively told her husband that she is irritated about his repeatedly coming home late from work, her assertion will be for naught if her husband cannot assertively tell his employer that he is overworked and needs some additional help! If the therapist does not help the husband to realize that he has an assertive problem, she is apt to interpret his coming home late as an indication that he loves his job more than he loves her and that he is a thoughtless person. Assertion training may be used for two purposes in couple counseling: to establish a more healthy communication pattern between the partners and to help the partners change those nonassertive or aggressive behaviors which contribute to the marital conflict.

Fensterheim (1972) reports a case study in which he has successfully used assertive training for marital problems and provides a relatively clear description of his procedures.

Psychosomatic Problems

When the psychosomatic problems are caused or exacerbated by tension, assertion training may be useful if the situations that arouse the anxiety and tension are ones in which the woman fails to assert herself and instead inhibits her spontaneous reactions and suppresses her feelings of hurt, anger, or humiliation. There is some suggestive case study evidence that under these circumstances, assertion training in combination with other procedures, such as relaxation training, can benefit tension headaches (Dengrove, 1968), a variety of chronic dermatological problems (Seitz, 1953), some cases of asthma (Gardner, 1968; Wolpe and Lazarus, 1966, case # 3), and abdominal spasm (Lazarus, 1965).

Drug or Alcohol Dependence

Assertion training could be used with clients who are dependent on drugs or alcohol when these are used primarily (1) to escape from conflict situations with other people who overpower them, (2) to indirectly express hurt and anger towards significant others, or (3) to disinhibit themselves so that they may be able to say things that they would ordinarily have been too afraid to express. In addition, assertion procedures would be appropriate with clients who have overcome their dependence problem but who still have trouble refusing drugs or alcohol. Salter (1949) has reported success with problems of alcoholism (pp. 200-201) and drug addiction (pp. 213-214). (Also see Schultz, Ch. 19).

Agoraphobia and Irrational Fears

Agoraphobia appears to be mainly a woman's problem. According to Fodor (1973), the majority of agoraphobes are women. Typical agoraphobes are married women whose phobias peak after approximately five years of marriage. While these women may appear to be self-sufficient and independent before marriage (Symonds, 1973), after marriage they become, gradually or suddenly, extremely afraid to be alone or to leave home. While nonassertion may not be the cause of this phobia, there is some suggestive case study evidence that assertion training in combination with other procedures may help to reduce it (Lazarus, 1966).

Rimm (1973) has some case study data which suggests that his *covert assertion* procedure may be helpful in reducing irrational fears. In this procedure the client is taught how to stop her obsessive thoughts and make forceful and assertive statements when she is in the actual phobic situation.

Aggressive Problems

Although assertion training procedures are most often used for problems of nonassertion, these procedures also show promise for modifying aggressive behavior (Gittleman, 1965; McNamara, 1970; Rimm, Hill, Brown, and Stuart, 1974; Rimm, Keyson, and Hunziker, 1971 cited in Rimm & Masters, 1974; Sarason, 1968; Sarason and Ganzer, 1973; Wallace, Teigen, Liberman, and Baker, 1973). Rimm and Masters (1974) and Kaufmann and Wagner (1972) describe some special methods that therapists could use in working with aggressive problems.

CONCLUSION

Healthy, fully functioning people feel that they can make an effective impact on their environment; they engage in assertive behavior which makes them feel in charge of themselves and which affects other people in constructive ways.

Women's sex-role socialization decreases the likelihood that women will act assertively. When women are nonassertive, they usually feel a loss of personal power and self-esteem and an increased sense of anger and hurt. Various psychological problems may be caused or exacerbated by women's failure to act assertively. This view is supported by the clinical case study literature which suggests that assertion training is of help for a wide variety of psychological problems. Some of these problems were briefly discussed and the conditions under which assertion training would be an appropriate therapeutic strategy were presented.

I encourage therapists to help women achieve more fulfilling lives and reclaim their basic human rights by using procedures which will free them to develop assertion skills. Women need to learn that they can be *strong* and *effective*, as well as sensitive.

REFERENCES

Alberti, Robert E., and Emmons, Michael L.: *Your Perfect Right: A Guide to Assertive Behavior*, 2nd ed. San Luis Obispo, Impact, 1974.

Bandura, Albert: *Principles of Behavior Modification*. New York, Holt, Rinehart & Winston, 1969.

Bart, Pauline: Depression in middle-aged women. In Gornick, Vivian, and Moran, Barbara (Eds.): *Women in Sexist Society: Studies in Power and Powerlessness*. New York, Basic Books, 1971.

Bean, Kenneth L.: Desensitization, behavior rehearsal, then reality: A preliminary report on a new procedure. *Behavior Therapy*, *1*:542, 1970.

Broverman, Inge K., Vogel, Susan Raymond, Broverman, David M., Clarkson, Frank E., and Rosenkrantz, Paul S.: Sex-role stereotypes: A current appraisal. *Journal of Social Issues*, *28*:59, 1972.

Cameron, D. Even: The conversion of passivity into normal self-assertion. *American Journal of Psychiatry*, *108*:98, 1951.

Chesler, P.: *Women and Madness*. Garden City, Doubleday, 1972.

Dengrove, Edward: Behavior therapy of headache. *Journal of the American Society of Psychosomatic Dentistry and Medicine*, *15*:30, 1968.

Fensterheim, Herbert: Assertive methods and marital problems. In Rubin, R. D., Fensterheim, H., Henderson, J. D., and Ullmann, L. P. (Eds.): *Advances in Behavior Therapy*. New York, Academic Press, 1972.

Fodor, Iris Goldstein: Women's phobias. Presentation given at the Association for the Advancement of Behavior Therapy, Miami, Florida, December, 1973.

Gardner, James E.: A blending of behavior therapy techniques in an approach to an asthmatic child. *Psychotherapy: Theory, Research and Practice*, *5*:46, 1968.

Geisinger, David L.: Controlling sexual and interpersonal anxieties. In Krumboltz, John D., and Thoresen, Carl E. (Eds.): *Behavioral Counseling: Cases and Techniques*. New York, Holt, Rinehart, & Winston, 1969.

Gittleman, Martin: Behavior rehearsal as a technique in child treatment. *Journal of Child Psychology and Psychiatry*, *6*:251, 1965.

Goodman, Lewis S., and Gilman, A. (Eds.): *The Pharmacological Basis of Therapeutics*, 4th ed. London, MacMillan, 1970.

Gordon, Thomas: *Parent Effectiveness Training*. New York, Wyden, 1970.

Homme, Lloyd, with Csanyi, Attila, Gonzales, Mary Ann, and Rechs, James: *How to Use Contingency Contracting in the Classroom*. Champaign, Research Press, 1969.

Jakubowski-Spector, Patricia: Facilitating the growth of women through assertive training. *The Counseling Psychologist*, *4*:75, 1973.

Jakubowski-Spector, Patricia: Behavior modification for school personnel. *Focus on Guidance, 6*:1, 1974.

Katz, Ronald: Case conference: Rapid development of activity in a case of chronic passivity. *Journal of Behavior Therapy and Experimental Psychiatry, 2*:187, 1971.

Kaufmann, Leon M., and Wagner, Bernard R.: Barb: A systematic treatment technology for temper control disorders. *Behavior Therapy, 3*:84, 1972.

Lazarus, Arnold A.: Behavior therapy, incomplete treatment, and symptom substitution. *The Journal of Nervous and Mental Disease, 140*:180, 1965.

Lazarus, Arnold A.: Broad-spectrum behavior therapy and the treatment of agoraphobia. *Behavior Research and Therapy, 4*:95, 1966.

Lazarus, Arnold A., and Serber, M.: Is systematic desensitization being misapplied? *Psychological Reports, 23*:215, 1968.

McNamara, John Regis: The broad based application of social learning theory to treat aggression in a preschool child. *Journal of Clinical Psychology, 81*:199, 1970.

Piaget, Gerald W., and Lazarus, Arnold A.: The use of rehearsal-desensitization. *Psychotherapy: Theory, Research and Practice, 6*:264, 1969.

Rimm, David C.: Thought stopping and covert assertion in the treatment of phobias. *Journal of Consulting and Clinical Psychology, 41*:466, 1973.

Rimm, David C., Hill, George A., Brown, Nancy N., and Stuart, James E.: Group-assertive training in treatment of expression of inappropriate anger. *Psychological Reports, 34*:791, 1974.

Rimm, David C., Keyson, M., and Hunziker, J.: Group assertive training in the treatment of anti-social aggression. Unpublished manuscript. Arizona State University, 1971.

Rimm, David C., and Masters, James C.: Assertive training. *Behavior Therapy: Techniques and Empirical Findings*. New York, Academic Press, 1974.

Salter, Andrew: *Conditioned Reflex Therapy*. New York, Creative Age, 1949.

Sarason, Irwin G.: Verbal learning, modeling, and juvenile delinquency. *American Psychologist, 23*:254, 1968.

Sarason, Irwin G., and Ganzer, Victor, J.: Modeling and group discussion in the rehabilitation of juvenile delinquents. *Journal of Counseling Psychology, 20*:442, 1973.

Seitz, Philip F. Durham: Dynamically-oriented brief psychotherapy: Psychocutaneous exoriation syndrome. *Psychosomatic Medicine, 15*:200, 1953.

Seligman, Martin E. P.: For helplessness: Can we immunize the weak. *Psychology Today, 6*:42, 1969.

Seligman, Martin E. P.: Fall into helplessness. *Psychology Today, 6*:43, 1973.

Seligman, Martin E. P., and Maier, Steven F.: Failure to escape traumatic shock. *Journal of Experimental Psychology, 74*:1, 1967.

Seligman, Martin E. P., Maier, Steven F., and Geer, James H.: Alleviation of learned helplessness in the dog. *Journal of Abnormal Psychology, 73*:256, 1968.

Seligman, Martin E. P., Maier, Steven F., and Solomon, R. L.: Unpredictable and uncontrollable aversive events. In Brush, Robert (Ed.): *Aversive Conditioning and Learning*. New York, Academic Press, 1971.

Sheehy, Gale: Catch-30 and other predictable crises of growing up adult. *New York*, February, *18*:30, 1974.

Stevenson, Ian, and Wolpe, Joseph: Recovery from sexual deviation through overcoming non-sexual neurotic responses. *American Journal of Psychology, 116*:737, 1960.

Symonds, Alexandra: Phobias after marriage: Women's declaration of dependence. In Miller, Jean Baker (Ed.): *Psychoanalysis and Women*. New York, Penguin, 1973.

Thornton, James W., and Jacobs, Paul D.: Learned helplessness in human subjects. *Journal of Experimental Psychology, 87*:367, 1971.

Wallace, Charles J., Teigen, James R., Liberman, Robert P., and Baker, Val: Destructive behavior treated by contingency contracts and assertive training: A case study. *Journal of Behavior Therapy and Experimental Psychiatry, 4*:273, 1973.

White, Robert W.: The concept of healthy personality: What do we really mean? *The Counseling Psychologist, 4*:3, 1973.

Wolpe, Joseph *Psychotherapy by Reciprocal Inhibition.* Stanford, Stanford University Press, 1958.

Wolpe, Joseph: Neurotic depression: Experimental analog, clinical syndromes and treatment. *American Journal of Psychotherapy, 25*:362, 1971.

Wolpe, Joseph: *The Practice of Behavior Therapy.* New York, Pergamon Press, 1973.

Wolpe, Joseph, and Lazarus, Arnold A.: *Behavior Therapy Techniques.* New York, Pergamon Press, 1966.

—— *Chapter 9* ——

SELF-ASSERTION TRAINING
PROCEDURES FOR WOMEN

PATRICIA ANN JAKUBOWSKI*

SALTER (1949), Wolpe (1958, 1973), and Lazarus (Wolpe & Lazarus, 1966; Lazarus, 1971) developed assertion training many years ago; only recently have other therapists begun to refine their work. This article will present my approach to assertion training which extends the work of these founders and incorporates procedures which are taken from behavior therapy, rational-emotive therapy, gestalt therapy, bioenergetics, and transactional analysis.

In my work with adult assertion training, I work mainly with groups. These groups are composed of six to ten women who meet six to ten weeks for two-hour sessions. While many therapists prefer groups composed of both males and females (both sexes typically have assertion issues with each other), the Brumage and Willis (1974) research suggests that an all-female group may be more effective than a male-female group. Their study compared the effectiveness of single-sex groups, mixed-sex groups, and single-sex groups which later added opposite-sex members. Although all groups were satisfied with their experience and all made positive changes on the Rathus (1973b) Assertiveness Schedule, the single-sex groups made substantially greater gains while the mixed-sex groups made the least gains. Leaders of the single-sex groups reported that their members were more relaxed and more quickly disclosed assertion problems involving the opposite sex. These findings suggest that, optimally, therapists work either with all-female assertion training groups or with all-female groups which later add males. In a males-added group the number of sessions should be extended, and exercises which specifically deal with building trust and self-disclosure vis-à-vis the opposite sex should be used to establish group cohesiveness and an open work climate.

While a male therapist can provide male permission for a woman to act assertively, a female therapist may have several advantages: (1) a female therapist can be a model of a woman who is both feminine and assertive; (2) female members may more easily confide in a female therapist than in a male; and (3) female members may be less likely to enter into game-playing to please a female therapist. On the other hand, Friedman's

---

*Formerly cited as Patricia Jakubowski-Spector.

(1971) research suggests that a critical variable in assertion training is supplying information on how one can act assertively; therefore, it is possible that the therapist's ability to provide this information is more important than the therapist's sex.

In this article, references to assertion-training groups assume an all-female membership, and statements regarding the therapist's function refer to female facilitators.

A FOUR-PHASE ASSERTION TRAINING PROGRAM

A complete assertion-training program is one which involves four basic components: (1) helping clients to distinguish among assertive, aggressive, and nonassertive behavior; motivating clients to become more assertive; and increasing client awareness of their own behavior; (2) helping clients to identify and accept their interpersonal rights and to develop a belief system which will support their assertive behavior; (3) reducing or removing psychological obstacles which prevent clients from acquiring or using their assertive skills; and (4) developing assertive skills through active practice methods (Jakubowski-Spector, 1973a). Viewing assertion training in terms of these four components can help therapists to design programs which meet the specific needs of their clients and to evaluate client progress in the program.

Characteristics of the client population will dictate the extent to which the therapist will work with each of the four components. In some cases, it may be appropriate to use only one or two of the four components. For example, women who possess assertive skills but who are inhibited from acting assertively, may only need to have their consciousness raised about their right to act assertively. This program would give the women permission to use the assertive skills they have already acquired.

The four components of a complete assertion program are dealt with in somewhat sequential phases. Table 9-I indicates how these phases may overlap in a ten-session assertion-training program with college women. The X's indicate those sessions where the phase activity is likely to be especially important. While the group as a whole may proceed in the manner described in this table, individual members may progress at a different rate depending on the nature and severity of their problems.

Phase I: Developing Discrimination, Motivation, and Awareness

In this phase the therapist's objective is to help the members to form discriminations, to develop motivation to change, and to become more aware of their own behavior patterns.

TABLE 9 - I

SAMPLE FOUR-PHASE ASSERTION TRAINING
PROGRAM WITH COLLEGE WOMEN

Phase	Objectives	1	2	3	4	5	6	7	8	9	10
		Training Sessions (Weeks)									
I	Developing Discriminations	X	X	X							
	Developing Motivation to Change	X	X	X	X						
	Developing Awareness		X	X	X						
II	Developing Personal Belief Systems	X	X	X	X	X					
III	Reducing Psychological Obstacles			X	X	X	X	X	X		
IV	Developing Assertion/Skills			X	X	X	X	X	X	X	X

Teaching Discriminations of Behavior

Helping women to distinguish among assertive, aggressive, and non-assertive behavior is very important. Unless these distinctions are very clear, women may confuse assertion and aggression, and fear that assertion training will cause them to lose their femininity. Therapists may differentiate these behaviors through a talk* which covers the following basic points:

1. Defining assertion
2. Distinguishing between respect and deference
3. Describing the effects of assertion upon oneself and others
4. Defining and describing the different types of assertive behavior:
   a. Simple assertion
   b. Angry assertion
   c. Soft assertion
   d. Empathic assertion
   e. Confrontive assertion
5. Defining and describing aggression and the conditions under

---

*Points one through ten were fully discussed in the previous chapter, "Assertive Behavior and Clinical Problems of Women."

which it occurs:
  a. A result of pent-up feelings and failing to act assertively
  b. A way of preventing oneself from acting nonassertively
  c. A reaction to failing to make an impact on another person
  d. A result of believing that being aggressive is the only way one will be respected
6. Describing the effect that aggression has on oneself and others
7. Defining nonassertion
8. Describing the socialization messages which inhibit women from acting assertively
9. Describing the hidden bargain
10. Describing the effect that nonassertion has on oneself and others
11. Describing the anxious nonverbal behaviors which often accompany nonassertive behavior, i.e. smiling when angry
12. Describing how nonassertion involves sending double messages, e.g. when a woman says she does not mind cosponsoring a baby shower when in fact her uncomfortable body language shows that she does mind.

After the talk the therapist can demonstrate an assertive, aggressive, and nonassertive way of handling a situation, e.g. asking a male to stop his condescending remarks. This is followed by an assertion discrimination exercise which is introduced with this statement:

> We're going to listen to a series of statements on the tape recorder. Some of the statements will be assertive, some will be aggressive, and some will be nonassertive. As we listen to each statement, I'd like each of you to make an independent decision as to whether the statement is assertive, aggressive, or nonassertive. Afterwards, I'll ask each of you in turn to tell us what your private decision was. Don't go by majority rule in making up your mind.
>
> I'm particularly interested in those who see the statement differently from the rest of the group because this'll give me a chance to clear up whatever confusion may exist about these different behaviors. This is very important because so far we've been talking about these behaviors in the abstract; when we get down to discussing real situations, it's not always so easy to make the differentiations.

Table 9-II presents the script of an assertion discrimination audio tape (developed with Janice Van Buren) which can then be played. The situational contexts are verbally described by the therapist. As shown in Table 9-II, the assertive, aggressive, and nonassertive statements are intermixed on the tape. By using this exercise the therapist can clarify misunderstandings about the concepts.

Group members often confuse assertion with aggression when the issue involves anger and hurting the other person's feelings. Many women

TABLE 9 - II

ASSERTION DISCRIMINATION TAPE

Situational Context	Statement	Type
An acquaintance has asked to borrow your car for the evening.	Are you crazy! I don't lend my car to anyone!	Aggressive
A coworker has asked you to exchange vacation times with her.	I hope that you won't be disappointed, but I don't want to exchange vacation dates.	Assertive
A gas attendent has neglected certain services.	Will you please clean the windows and check the oil?	Assertive
You believe a clerk has overcharged you.	Can't you add? Or are you just stupid? You've overcharged me a dollar!	Aggressive
You'd like to end a telephone conversation with a friend.	I'm terribly sorry but my supper's burning, and I have to get off the phone. I hope you don't mind.	Nonassertive
An acquaintance has asked to borrow your car for the evening.	I'd really like to help you out, but I feel uncomfortable loaning my car.	Assertive
You're angry with someone at home who has consistently neglected to take out the trash.	Why can't you remember to take out the trash! Do you think you've got servants around here?	Aggressive
A coworker has asked to borrow your car for the evening	I don't know . . . well, it's not worth getting into a fuss about it. You can borrow it, but I should warn you that I've been having trouble with the brakes.	Nonassertive
You believe a clerk has overcharged you.	There seems to be a mistake on my bill. Would you double check it?	Assertive
You'd like to end a telephone conversation with a friend.	I'd like to talk longer, but I've got things to do. Talk to you later.	Assertive
A coworkers has asked you to exchange vacation times with her.	I don't know . . . Well . . . let me check with my husband. It's really not up to me, you know.	Nonassertive

believe that any statement which hurts feelings must automatically be aggressive. This is not surprising. Most women are socialized to believe that, in order to be good women, they must always be sensitive to the feelings of others, i.e. to be sure that other people are not hurt. However, when a woman is so unreasonably careful of others, she cannot or does not have to assume responsibility for her own feelings. *Taking care of others* also gives a woman the opportunity to blame others, e.g. her boyfriend for how she feels.

Assertion and nonassertion are also confused by clients. The more aggressive members of the group may misidentify an empathic assertive response as nonassertive because they perceive any show of consideration as weak. In dealing with this issue the therapist can present Rimm and Masters' (1974) concepts of the minimal effective response and escalation. According to Rimm and Masters, it is usually more appropriate to start with an assertive statement that can ordinarily accomplish the client's goal with a minimum of effort and a small likelihood of negative consequences. This minimal response is often one which is considerate or empathic. If this minimal assertion is ignored or not taken seriously, the woman is not at a loss since she has the alternative of escalating her assertion, making it increasingly firm and decreasingly empathic. The basic point is that the considerable power in assertive behavior does not have to be fully used all the time in order for a woman to be perceived as powerful. The following example illustrates escalation of a minimal effective assertion. The speaker is in a bar with a girlfriend, and a man repeatedly offers to buy them drinks.

Woman: "That's very nice of you to offer, but we came here to catch up on some news. Thanks, anyway!"

Woman: "No, thank you. We really would rather talk just to each other."

Woman: "This is the third and last time I am going to tell you that we don't want your company. Please leave!"

If the man had not left but instead had become irrationally persistent, the women would have either resorted to calling the manager or would have left the bar. Under some conditions, it is assertive to leave a situation!

Assertion and nonassertion may also be confused when group members are unsure whether it is necessary for a woman to offer an explanation for her behavior, e.g. explaining why she is refusing a request. A helpful guideline is that if a woman *wants* to give a brief explanation for her behavior, she certainly can do so, but profuse explanations and self-demeaning apologies are unwarranted and nonassertive.

Developing Motivation to Change

In the early training sessions, some clients' motivation to change need not be overwhelmingly strong; it is usually enough if they are willing to engage in the group assertion exercises and small homework assignments that the therapist suggests. Motivation can be developed by pointing out how a client's nonassertive or aggressive behavior has negative consequences for her life. Motivation may also be increased through the use of bibliotherapy. Clients who are primarily nonassertive may read Salter's (1949) chapter on the "Inhibitory Personality" while those who are primarily aggressive may read Bach and Wyden's (1968) *The Intimate Enemy*. In later sessions as the clients' assertion efforts meet with success outside the group, they usually become spontaneously more committed to changing their behavior.* The activities in the remaining phases also increase willingness to risk acting assertively.

Becoming Aware of One's Behavior

In order to change, group members must become aware of their assertive, aggressive, and nonassertive behaviors. There are at least three ways in which a therapist can help clients to increase their awareness: therapist comments, homework assignments or assertion logs, and questionnaires.

The therapist may help the members to become more aware of their behavior by commenting on the women's assertive, aggressive, and nonassertive behaviors in the group: "Are you aware that when you talk to someone in the group you do not look at that person?" "Did you notice that when you complimented Kay for refusing to babysit for her daughter you stated the compliment in such a way that you cut yourself down in the process?" "Do you realize that just before you ask a question or make a comment in this group, you apologize for taking up our time?" Video-feedback may also be used to supplement the therapist's comments and to increase the members' awareness.

A commonly used *Phase I* homework assignment is to have the group members observe their behavior during the week and describe their assertive, aggressive, and nonassertive experiences to the group. When clients write a daily assertion log of how they handled interpersonal situations in which they could have acted assertively, they note what they said and felt in the situation, the outcome, and, if relevant, what prevented them from acting assertively. There is some evidence that their noting how anxious they are about acting assertively may in itself reduce

---

*If the group is composed of many women who are not likely to become spontaneously motivated to change, the therapist will need to develop additional procedures for this phase.

the anxiety (Roszell, 1971). Some types of assertion logs can also be used to evaluate the assertion program's effectiveness (Hedquist & Weinhold, 1970).

Finally, feedback from questionnaires can be useful in inducing client awareness of behaviors and in addition may provide some measure of program effectiveness. Therapists who work with noncollege clients may use the Wolpe-Lazarus (1966) Assertiveness Questionnaire or the Alberti and Emmons (1974) Assertiveness Inventory. College clients may use the College Self-Expression Scale (Galassi, Delo, Galassi, and Bastien, 1974), the Rathus (1973b) Assertiveness Scale, or the Conflict Resolution Inventory (McFall & Lillesand, 1971). The relative merits of these scales are examined in Lacks and Jakubowski-Spector (1975).

Phase II: Developing a Personal Belief System

The basic goal of this phase is to help women to identify and to accept emotionally their basic interpersonal rights, and to develop a belief system which will support their behavior so that they can: (1) continue to believe in their right to act assertively even when they are unjustly criticized for their assertive behavior, (2) counteract any irrational guilt that may later occur as a result of having asserted themselves, (3) be proud of their assertion even if no one else is pleased, and (4) be likely to assert themselves in appropriate situations (Jakubowski-Spector, 1973b).

To help women to identify their basic human rights, therapists may use the film, *Assertive Training for Women* (Jakubowski-Spector, Pearlman, & Coburn, 1973), which shows short interpersonal scenes which call for an assertive response by the viewer. The film stimulates a discussion of the kinds of rights that women have in each of the scenes. The following list is a small sample of some of these basic human rights (additional rights may be found in Pearlman, Coburn, & Jakubowski-Spector, 1973):

- Right to refuse requests without having to feel guilty or selfish
- Right to feel and express anger
- Right to feel and express a healthy competitiveness and achievement drive
- Right to strive for self-actualization through whatever ethical channels one's talents and interests find natural
- Right to use one's judgment in deciding which needs are the most important for one to meet
- Right to make mistakes
- Right to have one's opinions given the same respect and consideration that other people's opinions are given
- Right to ask for affection and help

- Right to be treated as a capable human adult and not to be patronized
- Right to have one's needs be as important as the needs of other people
- Right to be independent

In each case the right entails a responsibility, for example, the right to have our opinions accorded the same respect as other people's opinions are given has the attendant responsibility of thinking through one's opinions, being open to the possibility that one's opinions are in some error, and to not dump one's opinions on other people. The stressing of the responsibilities inherent in these rights is particularly important when the clients have aggressive problems.

In the process of identifying and discussing these interpersonal rights, the therapist uses the group discussion to present the basic tenets of an assertion philosophy (Table 9-III).

TABLE 9 - III

THE BASIC TENETS OF AN ASSERTIVE PHILOSOPHY

1. By standing up for our rights we show we respect ourselves and achieve respect from other people.
2. By trying to govern our lives so as to never hurt anyone, we end up hurting ourselves and other people.
3. Sacrificing our rights usually results in destroying relationships or preventing new ones from forming.
4. Not letting others know how we feel and what we think is a form of selfishness.
5. Sacrificing our rights usually results in training other people to mistreat us.
6. If we don't tell other people how their behavior negatively effects us, we are denying them an opportunity to change their behavior.
7. We can decide what's important for us; we do not have to suffer from the *tyranny of the should and should not.*
8. When we do what we think is right for us, we feel better about ourselves and have more authentic and satisfying relationships with others.
9. We all have a natural right to courtesy and respect.
10. We all have a right to express ourselves as long as we don't violate the rights of others.
11. There is more to be gained from life by being free and able to stand up for ourselves and from honoring the same rights of other people.
12. When we are assertive everyone involved usually benefits.

Women can be helped to accept these rights and develop an assertion philosophy when they learn how to question the socialization messages which have in effect denied them their rights. In addition, the following probes, which are based in transactional analysis, are often helpful: "What in your background caused you to believe that you don't have these rights?" "Tell me how it is that you permit others to have these rights but you deny them for yourself?" "Can you give yourself permission to accept these rights?" "How do you go about making yourself believe you don't have these rights?"

The group process itself can also help the members to identify and accept their rights. In the course of discussing Alberti and Emmons' (1974) *Your Perfect Right,* those group members who feel assured about some of these rights can often provide a persuasive rationale for the other members, as illustrated in the following example:

> A coworker of mine wants to talk to me so much I can't get my work done. I believe I have a right to tell her that I can't chat with her right then. It's my life and my time, and I have a right to use them as I see fit. I'm not putting her down by not always talking with her, but I would be violating my own self if I said nothing and just got irritated. I used to think that it was best to just act disinterested when she got into coffee-klatching, but now I say, "Marge, I'd love to talk with you, but right now I've got to get these work orders processed. Let's talk when I'm done." Actually, this way I am not only more honest with her, but our time together is more pleasant, too!

When a woman intellectually realizes that she is entitled to a certain human right but finds that she cannot emotionally accept this right, a therapist may need to use therapeutic procedures (such as gestalt techniques) which are more emotionally involving. The following two case examples illustrate how these may be used:

> A twenty-five-year-old woman felt that she had no right to refuse to help other people once she discerned that they were in need of some help. Her acceptance of herself was highly contingent on others: "I am only acceptable to live if I try to fulfill other people's needs." Despite these deep feelings, she stated that she would like to feel comfortable enough to accept the right to have her needs be as important as other people's.
>
> Using the empty chair technique (Perls, 1969) the client placed the part of her that wanted to accept the right in one chair and the part of her that rejected the right in another chair. She started the internal dialogue from the side that needed the greatest strengthening. From the sidelines I gave her occasional prompts such as "Tell her that you have a right to live too."
>
> While this procedure did not result in an immediate emotional acceptance of the right to refuse requests and to have her own needs satisfied, she did become significantly more comfortable with such ideas.

In another case, a female graduate student did not believe that she had "the right to have rights." According to her, if she and another person had the same right and a conflict of rights resulted, this would mean that she was not entitled to the right for "it was not right to have conflict." Upon being asked where this message came from the client immediately described how her parents bitterly quarrelled. When it was pointed out that she was equating conflict with destruction and that as a child her parents' conflict had been overwhelming, but that as an adult she could act in ways that could produce nondestructive conflict, she cried.

While the woman could not yet give herself permission to produce conflict, she was able to accept the existential proposition that she had the right to make choices in life and to stand up for these choices even if these choices differed from those of other people.

Phase III: Reducing Psychological Obstacles

The therapist's objective in this phase is to help group members to reduce or to remove the psychological obstacles which prevent them from acquiring or using their assertive skills. Women's typical blocks to acting assertively include anxieties and fears about hurting the feelings of others, being embarrassed, disliked, or retaliated against, and expressing anger. While women may also be anxious about expressing affection, this obstacle is more common with men.

There are several methods such as rational-emotive procedures, relaxation training, systematic desensitization, bioenergetics, and behavioral procedures that the therapist can use to deal with these obstacles.

Rational-emotive procedures (Ellis, 1973, Goodman & Maultsby, 1974) are particularly useful in assertive training. As shown in Table 9-IV, the

TABLE 9 - IV

SAMPLE HOMEWORK OF A CLIENT SELF-ANALYSIS

Situation: I'd like to tell the man who cuts in front of me that he should go to where the line forms, but I'm afraid he and the other people will think I'm petty.

Irrational Beliefs	*Challenges*
I can't stand being thought of as petty.	I'm fooling myself when I say that I can't stand it. The fact that I'm alive shows that I have survived and can stand other people's negative thoughts about me.

A few people may think I'm petty, but it is likely that most people will be pleased that I spoke up. The few people who think I'm petty are probably thinking that they wouldn't speak up if they were in my position. But I'm not them. What may be right for them is not always what's right for me to do. If I knew them better, I probably wouldn't do or approve of a lot of things they do.

Even if all the people thought I was petty and wrong in asserting myself that would not necessarily mean I was wrong. Furthermore, even if I did make a mistake, everyone—including me—is entitled to make mistakes. It's impossible to avoid making some mistakes; and when I do make a mistake it is not a catastrophe, and I don't have to make myself feel bad.

I may think that I'm being petty, but something that is small is not necessarily petty. By keeping silent, I'm rewarding the other person for mistreating me. If I don't want to be mistreated, it's my responsibility and right to speak up.

therapist may assign and check homework in which the clients practice analyzing and challenging their irrational beliefs associated with assertion. In the illustration the client is dealing with one of several irrational beliefs.

Relaxation training involves teaching the client how she can reduce her anxiety by relaxing various muscle groups. Relaxation training may be used to reduce anxieties which occur when a woman's assertion breaks family injunctions or internalized sanctions; it may also be used to reduce anticipatory anxiety which occurs when a woman knows that there is an impending situation in which she needs to be assertive, e.g. to tell her parents that she's decided to not have children. For the research supporting this technique see Jakubowski-Spector (1971, 1974); for a description of the relaxation exercises see Wolpe and Lazarus (1966, Appendix 4) or Bernstein and Borkovec (1974).

When the client's anxiety about assertion is high, her imagery ability good, and specific anxiety-producing situations can be identified, systematic desensitization is an effective technique (Paul, 1969) which may be used to provide the client with a method of dealing with her anxiety (Goldfried, 1971). While she is relaxed, the client visualizes a series of successively more anxiety-producing situations in which she is acting assertively, e.g. telling her father that she does not want him to buy such expensive gifts for her children, assertively expressing her anger. Examples of assertion desensitization hierarchies may be found in Rimm and Masters (1974).

The fear that expressing anger will destroy relationships is an obstacle which often inhibits women from acting assertively. In reality, it is unexpressed — rather than expressed — anger which ultimately destroys relationships. As Claudeen Cline-Naffziger has so cogently noted: "Destruction of the other or of the self occurs when anger is unspoken hostility, distancing coldness, satirical, humorless teasing, or plain ordinary put-downs" (1974, p. 55). Women need to learn that they have a responsibility to themselves and others to experience their normal human anger and to decide how they will share these feelings with the people who have provoked them. When women fail to deal with their anger and simply suppress these feelings, their ability to express warmth, tenderness, and affection decrease as well.

Bioenergetics (Lowen, 1958) exercises may be used as a first step toward disinhibiting the fears of expressing anger and increasing the awareness of feelings of self-power and the ability to express these firmly and even angrily. One such bioenergetics exercise involves instructing two women to place their arms against each other's shoulders and push. One of the partners declares, "Yes, you will!" while the other responds, "No, I won't!" In this exercise women can experience their power and learn that they can be firm in their demands or refusals. When women do this exercise with a male they learn that they can nondestructively exert their full power against a man. Therapists who are interested in learning about other bioenergetics exercises are referred to Palmer (1973).

Behavioral-shaping exercises may also be used to help women learn how to experience and assertively express their angry feelings. In one such exercise for very anxious clients, the therapist warns the woman that the therapist will (gently) push her until she says, "Stop that!" or words to that effect. When the woman begins to get in touch with her irritation, she is instructed to give herself counter messages which reduce the anxiety, such as "Saying stop won't destroy" or "I have a right not to be pushed around." I have found such counter messages to be extremely important. When the woman is afraid to express her anger *because* her underlying belief is that her anger will destroy, this automatic internal message must be raised to awareness and then countered with an opposite message, e.g. "Saying stop won't destroy." Therapists need to help each client identify their own idiosyncratic anxiety-producing messages and to develop counter messages which are uniquely effective for the individual client.

When the woman does express her irritation, the therapist immediately stops and praises her — even if her irritation is expressed very timidly. In future sessions the therapist gradually asks for increasing expressions of firmness and irritation as the woman is pushed and each time the woman is instructed to practice thinking the counter messages while she expresses her irritations.

Phase IV: Developing Assertive Skills Through Active Practice Methods

In this phase, the therapist uses behavior rehearsal and modeling procedures to help women to acquire and to use assertive skills. Behavior rehearsal (Lazarus, 1966) refers to those kinds of role-play procedures in which clients practice behaviors that are to become part of their skills repertoire. These role-plays are intended to develop skills rather than insight or catharsis which is usually the goal of psychodrama or gestalt role-plays. The experimental literature in general indicates that behavior rehearsal can be effective (Friedman, 1971; Lawrence, 1970; Lazarus, 1966; Loo, 1971; McFall & Lillesand, 1971; McFall & Marston, 1970; McFall & Twentyman, 1973).

Literature also indicates that modeling can be an effective procedure in assertion training (Eisler, Hersen, & Miller, 1973; Freiberg, 1974; Goldstein, Martens, Hubben, VanBelle, Schaaf, Wiersma, & Goedhart, 1973; Hersen, Eisler, Miller, Johnson, & Pinkston, 1973; Rathus, 1973a). In the modeling procedure the particular assertive behaviors to be learned by the group members are demonstrated by a model (Bandura, 1969). The therapist and group members may act as live models, or models may be presented on film, typescript, video or audiotape.

In assertion training groups, behavior rehearsal and modeling procedures are usually combined. The sessions in this phase tend to fall into one of three basic patterns: spontaneous role-play sessions, exercise-oriented sessions, and theme-oriented sessions.

Spontaneous Role-Play Sessions

One of the most common patterns is an unstructured one in which role-plays are conducted which deal with whatever problems the group members are experiencing at the time. The following example illustrates my approach to behavior rehearsal which includes explicit coaching of a client's self-talk instructions* in addition to the usual modeling and rehearsal components. In this role-play, the client, a twenty-five-old woman, is trying to tell her aggressive roommate, Diane, to stop criticizing her clothing. (The client's attire is neat although casual.)

Therapist (as Diane): "Don't tell me you're out dressed like that!"
Client: "Uhmm."
Therapist (as Diane): "I'd think you'd at least have the decency to be embarrassed!"
Client: "Don't you think this outfit is nice?"
Therapist (as Diane): "Definitely not! You look sloppy."
Client: (clears throat) "Well . . . after all Dan and I are just going to the movies."

In the discussion following this role-play, I emphasized the need to be firm, but not hostile, in responding to Diane's aggression. In the next role-play, I modeled an assertive way of handling the situation, while the client played the role of her roommate.

Client (as Diane): "Are you really going to wear that outfit again! Please tell me I'm wrong!"
Therapist (as client): "Diane, I'd like to get something cleared up. I don't push my choice of clothes on you, and I don't criticize your clothes even if they aren't my taste. I'd appreciate the same consideration back (firmly but evenly). How about it (lightly)?"
Client (as Diane): "Well, all I've got to say is that either you don't care about your appearance — or your boyfriend doesn't care much about

---

*There is evidence that modeling may be made more powerful when it is combined with specific coaching instructions (Hersen et al., 1973). Client self-talk has been found to be particularly important in helping clients to learn how to control their own behavior, e.g. Meichenbaum, 1973; Thoresen & Mahoney, 1974.

you (starts to walk away).''

Therapist (as client): (following her) "I'm not asking you to change your opinions about my clothes, but I am asking you to stop putting your opinions on me. I don't try to make you dress the way I do, and I think it's only fair that you don't try to do that to me . . . Do you think I'm asking too much?''

Client (as Diane): (huffily) "Well, if that's the way you want it.''

Therapist (as client): "Yes, it is. Thanks, Diane.''

In discussing the modeled assertion, I emphasized that the client could feel effective rather than defeated when Diane begrudgingly agreed to her request. It was pointed out that aggressive people usually do not let others know directly, i.e. by apologizing, that something has made an impact on them; instead, they show they have been affected in less obvious ways such as suddenly being at a loss for words or by begrudgingly agreeing. The client was coached on how to convince an aggressive person that she is serious and won't acquiesce under pressure. She also was asked to keep these thoughts in mind when she was self-assertive: (1) be firm, but not cold; (2) be persistent — repeat the request when it is ignored; and (3) emphasize the essential fairness of the request. Finally, the client was instructed to remind herself that she had a right to ask her roommate to change her behavior. In the following role play, the client was instructed to use this self-talk as she practiced the modeled assertion. I, role-playing as Diane, had just criticized the client's clothing.

Client: "I keep telling you that I like my clothes the way they are — (*pauses and then completely stops*).''

Therapist: "Let's stop here. What messages were you giving yourself just then?''

Client; "What I'm saying to myself gets overwhelmed by what I want to say to her. (Pause) I want to say, 'Don't! Don't! Don't do that to me!' ''

Therapist: "Does the whole sentence go, *'Don't do that to me because* I can't take it?' ''

Client: "Yes (softly) . . .''

Therapist: "Where did that message come from?''

Client: (laughing) "That's *the* message of my childhood. It's always been 'You're not as strong as the other kids. You play so hard you'll wear yourself out. If you don't watch it, you're going to collapse. You aren't the type that — (voice breaks) — that can take it.' ''

Therapist: "A very strong message that part of you believes and. . . .''

Client: "I struggle with it all of the time (crying).''

Therapist: "What kind of information do you have about yourself that tells you that the message is a lie?''

Client: "Well, my life shows that's a lie." *(She describes specific times when she handles stress and other times, due to poor self-pacing, she did occasionally get exhausted.)*

Therapist: "The part of the message that says you can wear yourself out is true — you do need to pace yourself — but the part that says you can't handle stress is a lie . . . Can you say four times, 'I *can* handle myself under stress?' " *(Slowly and deliberately, the client repeated the self-affirming statement, taking a deep breath prior to the second repetition. She was then asked how she felt during the exercise.)*

Client: "First off, I couldn't say anything. I choked up — I wanted to say, 'Pat, I can't say that!' but I thought I can say it — I don't have to ask Pat for permission. And then I thought that one of the things that contributes to my tension is not stopping and learning to take a breath and so I did that! Each time I got a little more relaxed. And on the fourth time I really felt proud of myself!"

Therapist: "I could feel you growing with it! Now, let's try that again, and I'll give you some opposition this time!"

Each time the client repeated the self-affirming statement, the therapist opposed it. The purpose of this exercise was two-fold: (1) to give the client practice in self-affirmation under stress and (2) to enable the therapist to assess the client's strength. The client was instructed to practice the self-affirming talk whenever she became anxious while acting assertively. When the client again practiced the assertion in the succeeding role-play, her performance was substantially improved. The role-plays were repeated until her anxiety level was greatly reduced.

This behavior rehearsal procedure may be either used with an individual client as was illustrated above or may be modified to involve other group members who are asked to provide the modeling and/or to portray the other party in the role-play, while the therapist supervises and intercedes at critical points.

In these spontaneous role-play sessions, the therapist may also use behavior rehearsal procedures to strengthen the nonverbal components of assertion. As Serber (1972) has so cogently noted, the impact of verbal assertion may be seriously weakened when the accompanying nonverbal behaviors are deficient. He has identified six nonverbal and paralinguistic behaviors which are associated with effective assertion: loudness of voice, fluency of spoken words, eye contact, facial expression, body expression, and speaking distance from the other person. The importance of these nonverbal behaviors is beginning to be demonstrated through research (Eisler, Miller, & Hersen, 1973).

To help clients strengthen their nonverbal assertive behaviors, Laws and Serber (1973) developed a video modeling-rehearsing-shaping procedure which is extremely helpful, albeit time consuming. Their procedure involves the following steps: (1) client gives a short sample of her behavior on videotape; (2) therapist identifies the one nonverbal behavior which is the most deficient of the six and the client views the behavior on the video; (3) therapist models the appropriate behavior for the client; (4) client practices the modeled behavior on videotape; (5) therapist identifies and reinforces the improved behavior shown on the video and specifies any deficiency; (6) steps 2 through 5 are repeated until the target behavior is perfected; (7) client is alerted that the therapist will make it harder for her to be assertive, i.e. the therapist will act hurt, ignore, or aggressively attack her assertion; and (8) the next most deficient behavior is identified and the procedure is repeated, with the client finally practicing integrating the two behaviors which have been identified thus far before moving on to a third deficient behavior. The following example of this procedure was supplied by Janice Van Buren.

Therapist: "Mary, you indicated before that you'd like to be able to express your anger in certain situations. I'd like you to think of a recent situation where you were unable to assertively express your anger."

Mary: "The other day a friend was supposed to pick me up to go grocery shopping, but he didn't show up and he never did call. I talked with him later but never did tell him what I really thought about what happened."

Therapist: "Okay, now when I turn on the videotape, I'd like you to show me what you did when you talked to him and how you said it to him."

Mary: "You know, why didn't you call me? I was waiting on you." *(Mary's eyes drift away and are focused on the floor as she speaks.)*

Therapist: "When we look at the videotape replay, notice how your eyes drift away as you make the statement." *(Videotape is viewed.)* "I'm going to show you a way that you might handle the situation with your eyes. Notice how I keep eye contact and look serious but not hostile. 'Hey, I waited for you and you didn't come yesterday! What happened?' Now look straight at me and using your own words ask your friend what happened."

Mary: "Hey, what happened to you? I was waiting on you and you didn't show up." *(Mary keeps good eye contact but starts smiling.)*

Therapist: "Now, when we look at the videotape you'll see that your eye contact is much better. It was right on! Near the end, notice how you smiled when you became more firm." *(Steps 3 through 5 are repeated until Mary is able to maintain eye contact without smiling.)*

Therapist: "You're doing very well. Now let's see what happens when, as your friend, I respond back and try to evade you."

Mary: "What happened to you? I was waiting on you yesterday!"

Therapist (as friend): "What do you mean?"

Mary: "We were supposed to go out yesterday."

Therapist (as friend): "Well, I didn't think that was for sure."

Mary: "You said you'd pick me up at two o'clock."

Therapist (as friend): "I don't think that was definite, Mary."

Mary: "Well . . . what did you do yesterday?" *(Mary's eyes drop at this point. Mary continues practicing until she is finally able to express her irritation and maintain nonverbal firmness.)*

Spontaneous role-play sessions have the advantage of enabling the therapist to work in a flexible, in-depth way with clients who need much individualized treatment. However, in-depth focusing on a few clients can mean that the remaining group members receive little attention during the session and may have trouble meaningfully relating that client's problem to their own. The therapist will need to consciously develop group cohesiveness and ways of linking client problems together to offset this disadvantage.

Exercise-Oriented Sessions

When the assertion-training group members have fairly similar assertion problems, exercise-oriented sessions are useful. In this highly structured approach a set pattern of group assertion exercises are used in each session. The exercise usually begins with the therapist describing a situation in which assertion would be appropriate and modeling assertive ways of handling the situation, after which the group members individually, in dyads, or in triads practice the modeled responses and receive feedback. The usual homework assignment for the week is to perform the assertive behavior which was practiced in the group. Therapists who are interested in a description of some exercises should consult Rimm and Masters (1974); also, Judith Zeiger (1973) has developed excellent modeling tapes with exercises and has experimentally established the effectiveness of her videotapes.

The following group exercise developed by the author illustrates how group exercises may be used.

Sexist and Condescending Remarks Exercise

STEP 1. The therapist describes the situation:

You are at a party. On your way to the kitchen you see two men laughing uproariously. As you pass them, one of the men suddenly grabs your arm and still laughing asks you if you've heard the latest thing a well-known politician had to say about women. Without waiting for your reply he says: "It's okay to have a woman Vice-President of the United States if she will still remember to come home and cook the supper!" He looks at you expectantly, awaiting your reply. Assuming you wish to respond, what can you say? Here are some possible assertions: "Are you suggesting a Vice-President should be as concerned about cooking as the affairs of state?" "Well, to tell you the truth, I don't think it's funny." "I think it's about time women are given a chance to show that they can do something besides cook!"

STEP 2.

The group discusses these modeled responses and what would inhibit them from so responding, how such assertions may or may not differ in a work environment as opposed to a party, with a friend instead of an employer, with a woman instead of a man, when it is more appropriate to ignore rather than respond to the condescending remark when humor can be a part of assertion, i.e. when one likes, rather than dislikes, the other person, and when raising the other person's consciousness.

STEP 3.

The group members form two lines of five women. The first woman is instructed to stand in front of the person at the top of the line and to assertively respond to a sexist or condescending remark which is made. (This remark can be the same discussed by the therapist or it can be taken from the woman's personal experience.) Following a critique of her response by the group, she continues this exercise with the second member and her performance again receives feedback. The last two members of the line are instructed to each negatively respond to the woman's assertion when she approaches each of them in turn. They are to continue with their negative response — not taking her assertion seriously, trying to induce guilt, reacting indignantly — until the woman's assertion convinces them to stop or her assertion begins to falter.

STEP 4.

The woman at the top of the line turns to the person next to her and continues the exercise. Each member in turn has the opportunity to practice being assertive and receiving feedback after each assertion with four other members. In addition, all the members have an opportunity to vicariously learn a wide variety of different ways to handle sexist or condescending remarks.

Larry Kiel's (1973) Assertive Game represents another type of group exercise. A member of the group is given a stack of cards on which are printed various situations to be role-played, such as defending one's stand on the Equal Rights Amendment to an acquaintance. The woman takes the top card and role plays the situation with the member to her immediate right. Afterwards, the group votes (*Yes* or *No*) on whether the members played the scene realistically, whether the woman's assertion was appropriate, and whether the woman's nonverbal behaviors were congruent with her verbal assertion. Members who vote negatively are asked to demonstrate more assertive ways of handling the same situation. In this event, additional voting points are awarded for both the group member who modeled the assertion and for the woman who chose to redo her original role-play. The voting points may be tallied on a large scoreboard on which members advance so many squares for their points. The therapist may occasionally instruct the members to demonstrate how not to act, i.e. to act in such a way that other people would not take one's opinions seriously on the Equal Rights Amendment. This breaks group tension and creates a lively atmosphere (Seabourne, undated).

Exercise-oriented sessions are far more structured than spontaneous role-play sessions and have the advantage of (1) each member being actively involved in acquiring specific assertive skills each week and (2) creating a task-oriented environment where members can easily relate to each other and measure their progress from week to week. On the negative side, such sessions offer limited opportunity for an in-depth focusing on idiosyncratic client problems. (This disadvantage can be reduced by having the members act out situations which are unique to them, after they have practiced the modeled assertive responses in the standard group exercises.) A second disadvantage to exercise-oriented sessions is that they usually require some common assertive problems among the group members and where such commonality is limited the group exercises may result in being somewhat superficial.

Theme-Oriented Sessions

Theme-oriented sessions are moderately structured and combine some of the advantages of both spontaneous role-play sessions and exercise-oriented sessions. Each session has one or two themes which are general enough to apply to all the group members, regardless of their diversity. Examples of such themes are being in relationships where one is always doing favors for other people, being in situations where one is patronized and intimidated by a busy professional, being treated like a child by others, etc. Vignettes from the film *Assertive Training for Women* (Jakubowski-Spector, Pearlman, & Coburn, 1973) may be used to set the theme for each session. In the process of discussing the theme as it relates to each individual group member's life, spontaneous clinical role-plays may be conducted or if appropriate, group exercises may be used. Thus, this approach has great flexibility.

Which of the three basic patterns discussed is the most appropriate will depend on the kind and severity of the clients' problems, the commonality present in the group, and the leader's preference for structure. It is hoped that at some point in the future, research will provide more specific recommendations.

SUMMARY

This article introduced a four-phase assertion training program for women.

The phases of this model are (1) helping clients to distinguish among assertive, aggressive, and nonassertive behavior and motivating clients to become more assertive; (2) helping clients to identify and accept their interpersonal rights and to develop a belief system which will support their assertive behavior; (3) reducing or removing psychological obstacles which prevent women from acquiring or using their assertive skills; and (4) developing assertion skills through active practice methods, such as behavior rehearsal and modeling.

The goals for each phase and therapeutic procedures which could be used to obtain these goals were discussed. These therapeutic strategies were drawn from behavior therapy, rational emotive therapy, gestalt therapy, bioenergetics, and transactional analysis.

REFERENCES

Alberti, Robert E., and Emmons, Michael L.: *Your Perfect Right: A Guide to Assertive Behavior*, 2nd ed. San Luis Obispo, Impact, 1974.

Bach, George, and Wyden, Peter: *The Intimate Enemy*. New York, Avon, 1968.

Bandura, Albert: *Principles of Behavior Modification*. New York, Holt, Rinehart and Winston, 1969.

Bernstein, Douglas A., and Borkovec, Thomas D.: *Progressive Relaxation Training*. Champaign, Research Press, 1974.

Brumage, M. E., and Willis, M. H.: How three variables influence the outcome of group assertive training. Paper presented at the American Personnel and Guidance Association Convention, New Orleans, April, 1974.

Cline-Naffziger, Claudeen: Women's lives and frustration, oppression, and anger: Some alternatives. *Journal of Counseling Psychology, 21*:51, 1974.

Eisler, Richard M., Hersen, Michel, and Miller, Peter M.: Effects of modeling on components of assertive behavior. *Journal of Behavior Therapy and Experimental Psychiatry, 4*:1, 1973.

Eisler, Richard M., Miller, Peter M., and Hersen, Michel: Components of assertive behavior. *Journal of Clinical Psychology, 29*:295, 1973.

Ellis, Albert: *Humanistic Psychotherapy: The Rational-emotive Approach*. New York, Julian Press, 1973.

Freiberg, Patricia: *An Introduction to Assertive Training Procedures for Women*. Washington, D.C., American Personnel and Guidance Association, 1973.

Freiberg, Patricia: Modeling and assertive training: The effect of sex and status of model on female college students. Doctoral Dissertation, University of Maryland, 1974.

Friedman, Philip H.: The effects of modeling and role-playing on assertive behavior. In Rubin, R.; Fensterheim, H.; Lazarus, A.; and Franks, C. (Eds.): *Advances in Behavior Therapy*. New York, Academic Press, 1971, pp. 149-169.

Galassi, John P., DeLo, James S., Galassi, Merna D., and Bastien, Sheila: The college self-expression scale: A measure of assertiveness. *Behavior Therapy, 5*:165, 1974.

Goldfried, Marvin R.: Systematic desensitization as training in self-control. *Journal of Consulting and Clinical Psychology, 37*:228, 1971.

Goldstein, Arnold P., Martens, Jan; Hubben, J., Van Belle, Harry A., Scaaf, Wim, Wiersma, Hans; and Goedhart, Arnold: The use of modeling to increase independent behavior. *Behavior Research and Therapy, 11*:31, 1973.

Goodman, David, and Maultsby, Maxie, C., Jr.: *Emotional Well-being through Rational Behavior Training*. Springfield, Thomas, 1974.

Hedquist, Francis J., and Weinhold, Barry K.: Behavioral group counseling with socially anxious and unassertive college students. *Journal of Counseling Psychology, 17*:237, 1970.

Hersen, Michel, Eisler, Richard M., Miller, Peter M., Johnson, Miriam B., and Pinkston, Susan G.: Effects of practice, instructions and modeling on components of assertive behavior. *Behavior Research and Therapy, 11*:443, 1973.

Jakubowski-Spector, Patricia: An overview of the behavioral approach. In Beck, E. E. (Ed.): *Philosophical Guidelines for Counseling*. Dubuque, Brown, 1971.

Jakubowski-Spector, Patricia: Facilitating the growth of women through assertive training. *The Counseling Psychologist, 4*:75, 1973.

Jakubowski-Spector, Patricia: Behavior modification for school personnel. *Focus on Guidance, 6*:1, 1974.

Jakubowski-Spector, Patricia, Perlman, Joan, and Coburn, Karen: *Assertive Training for Women: A Stimulus Film*. Washington, D.C., American Personnel and Guidance Association, 1973.

Kiel, Larry: The assertive game. Paper presented at the St. Louis Chapter of the Association for the Advancement of Behavior Therapy, Washington University, St. Louis, November, 1973.

Lacks, Patricia B., and Jakubowski-Spector, Patricia: *A Critical Examination of the Assertion Training Literature*. Unpublished manuscript. St. Louis, 1975.

Lawrence, Philip S.: The assessment and modification of assertive behavior. Doctoral Dissertation, Arizona State University, 1970.

Laws, D. Richard, and Serber, Michael: Measurement and evaluation of assertive training with sexual offenders. In Hosford, Ray E., and Moss, Scott (Eds.): *The Crumbling Walls: Treatment and Counseling of the Youthful Offender*. Champaign, University of Illinois Press, 1973.

Lazarus, Arnold: Behavior rehearsal vs. non-directive therapy vs. advice in effecting behavior change. *Behavior Research and Therapy, 4*:209, 1966.

Lazarus, Arnold: *Behavior Therapy and Beyond*. New York, McGraw-Hill, 1971.

Loo, Russell M. Y.: The effects of projected consequences and overt behavior rehearsal on assertive behavior. Doctoral Dissertation, University of Illinois, 1971.

Lowen, Alexander: *Physical Dynamics of Character Structure*. New York, Grune & Stratton, 1958.

McFall, Richard M. and Lillesand, Diane B.: Behavior rehearsal with modeling and coaching in assertion training. *Journal of Abnormal Psychology, 77*:313, 1971.

McFall, Richard M., and Marston, Albert R.: An experimental investigation of behavior rehearsal in assertive training. *Journal of Abnormal Psychology, 76*:295, 1970.

McFall, Richard M., and Twentyman, Craig Y.: Four experiments on the relative contributions of rehearsal, modeling, and coaching to assertion training. *Journal of Abnormal Psychology, 81*:199, 1973.

Meichenbaum, Donald H.: Cognitive factors in behavior modification: Modifying what clients say to themselves. In Rubin, Richard R., Brady, J. Paul, and Henderson, John D. (Eds.): *Advances in Behavior Therapy.* New York, Academic Press, 1973, vol. IV, pp. 21-36.

Palmer, Robert D.: Desensitization of the fear of expressing one's own inhibited aggression: Bioenergetic assertive techniques for behavior therapists. In Rubin, Richard R.: Brady, J. Paul, and Henderson, John D. (Eds.): *Advances in Behavior Therapy.* New York, Academic Press, 1973, vol. IV, pp. 241-254.

Paul, Gordon L.: Outcome of systematic desensitization. In Franks, Cyril M. (Ed.): *Behavior Therapy: Appraisal and Status.* New York, McGraw-Hill, 1969, pp. 105-159.

Pearlman, Joan, Coburn, Karen, and Jakubowski-Spector, Patricia: *A Leader's Guide to Assertive Training for Women: A Stimulus Film.* Washington, D.C., American Personnel and Guidance Association, 1973.

Perls, Frederick S.: *Gestalt Therapy Verbatim.* Lafayette, Real People Press, 1969.

Rathus, Spencer A.: Instigation of assertive behavior through video-tape-mediated assertive models and directed practice. *Behavior Research and Therapy, 11*:57, 1973a.

Rathus, Spencer A.: A 30-item schedule for assessing assertive behavior. *Behavior Therapy, 4*:398, 1973b.

Rimm, David C., and Masters, John C.: *Behavior Therapy: Techniques and Empirical Findings.* New York, Academic Press, 1974.

Roszell, Byron L.: Pretraining, awareness, and behavioral group approaches to assertive behavior training. Doctoral Dissertation, University of Minnesota. Minneapolis, University Microfilms, 1971, No. 72-378.

Salter, Andrew: *Conditioned Reflex Therapy.* New York, Capricorn, 1949.

Seabourne, B.: Role training. Unpublished and undated paper. St. Louis.

Serber, Michael: Teaching the nonverbal components of assertive training. *Journal of Behavior Therapy and Experimental Psychiatry, 3*:179, 1972.

Thoresen, Carl E., and Mahoney, Michael J.: *Behavioral Self-control.* New York, Holt, Rinehart and Winston, 1974.

Wolpe, Joseph: *Practice of Behavior Therapy.* New York, Pergamon Press, 1958.

Wolpe, Joseph: *Practice of Behavior Therapy.* 2nd ed. New York, Pergamon Press, 1973.

Wolpe, Joseph, and Lazarus, Arnold: *Behavior Therapy Techniques.* New York, Pergamon Press, 1966.

Zeiger, Judith A. H.: The effects of video-taped modeling and behavior rehearsal through group training on assertive behavior. Doctoral Dissertation, University of Colorado, 1973.

Section V

CAREER COUNSELING AS THERAPY FOR WOMEN

INTRODUCTION

IT is unusual to find papers on vocational and career counseling in a book primarily concerned with psychotherapy. However, career development and financial independence are directly related to psychotherapy because the economic subordination of women has been one of the major means by which women have been kept powerless and dependent.

Because women have not been expected to provide for themselves through their own efforts in the labor market, almost all theories of vocational development are theories about men. Since women's vocational development is not identical with that of men, therapists must educate themselves about women's vocational needs. This education needs to include an awareness of career-choice development and the difficulties women face after they enter career fields, especially fields which are currently male-dominated.

These chapters in this section are written expressly for the educational needs of therapists to help them start to correct the years of neglect of developmental vocational theories and counseling techniques for women. In "Career Counseling for Women", Lenore Harmon presents an original alternative to conceptualizing and facilitating women's vocational development. In "A Nonsexist Approach to Vocational Counseling" Cindy Rice Dewey describes an instrument and technique especially useful for counseling women because it avoids the male-culture bias inherent in all published vocational counseling instruments. In the third chapter, Theodora Wells draws upon her own extensive experience as a professional woman and as a consultant to business, not only to outline the problems women face once they enter a career field, but also to encourage therapists to be aware of their own biases.

In the first article, Lenore Harmon identifies the important task in career counseling with women as helping them to take control of their lives and maximize their potential choices. Women coming to counseling without a strong sense of identity are not ready to choose work which will express their identity or explore their potential for competence and self-actualization. However, it is wrong to assume that someone other than the client knows the "right" goals for her. The therapist can help best by enabling the client to separate what is an appropriate goal for her *now* from what goal is *possible* for her in the future.

Developmental approaches accurately reflect current career development but do not exhaust the possibilities: Homemaking is emphasized for virtually all women but life-span job-market participation is not; single-track careers for men are emphasized but interrupted or double-track careers (homemaking and outside work) are not.

Established theories of career choices range along a continuum from sociological, external, to psychological, internal, factors. While most career choices made by either sex mix the two extremes, women as a group rely more than men on external influences. (Counselor bias likely contributes to this phenomenon.) "Choice" theories indicate that women choose within the cultural norms in order to avoid conflict, which means that their career choices are more influenced by external than internal motivation. However, internal motivations are more satisfying than external motivations. Vocational counseling will not be helpful to women until it deals productively with the conflicts in women's lives which restrict them to externally motivated choices.

Motivations for working differ widely; Maslow's hierarchy of needs is useful in understanding these motivations. From low to high, Maslow's hierarchy is physiological, safety, belongingness and love, esteem, and self-actualization needs. Physiological needs for men are usually met through their own public market labor and for women through association with someone else who labors in the public market. Women can, and some do, take care of their own physiological needs but they are not expected to. Opportunities for them are limited, and they are taught to believe that they cannot take care of their own needs directly. When women do take care of the two lower level needs for themselves, the physiological and safety needs, they suffer emotionally from not meeting the needs of the top three levels. However, many dare not risk the security of safety in order to improve their position; thus they are fixed at a lower level.

Men are esteemed for their successes, women often are not, especially in atypical areas. Also, many women have to compromise self-esteem in order to achieve love and esteem from others. Since self-esteem must be achieved before self-actualization can be obtained, and since behaviors leading to self-esteem may cut a woman off from meeting love and belongingness needs, conflict is clear. Except in cases of deprived people, career counseling usually focuses on planning to meet the upper two levels of the hierarchy — self-esteem and self-actualization; however, this focus is useless for women until they have resolved the conflict of achievement and self-esteem versus belonging and esteem from others. Since the barrier to a higher level most frequently encountered by men is their need to support dependents, altering vocational sex-role behavior, though painful, will be freeing to both men and women.

To remedy some of the problems of fixation at a low level of need satisfaction, Harmon makes the following recommendations: (1) determine which level of Maslow's hierarchy the client is at and how she got there; (2) develop her most immediately valuable skills for temporary income and security (with an older woman this step may include personal counseling to change her self-image); (3) change the idea that career counseling for women has been satisfied when subsistance needs are met; and (4) become aware of the conflicts involved in meeting higher-level needs. Counselors must help clients clarify personal values and recognize that values and decisions may change with time. Career decisions are not once-in-a-lifetime events.

Harmon also recommends that bias in this area be confronted — counselors' attitudes and professional materials often reflect sex-role stereotyping of jobs and careers. The implied forced choice between marriage and career must be eliminated and the option to combine both must be explored with women *and* men.

Cindy Rice Dewey, author of *A Nonsexist Approach to Vocational Counseling*, claims that traditional vocational counseling has not been helpful to women and other minorities seeking entrance into occupations that have previously been denied them. For many reasons, vocational counseling for women is a complex process. It must deal with a woman's own internal barriers, not just the cultural blocks. Certainly it must continue no longer as two or three contacts using mechanical, test-oriented approaches and instruments which norms are appropriate only for Caucasion males. Dewey describes an alternative approach, the Nonsexist Vocational Card Sort (NSVCS) which she developed.

The NSVCS is a vocational counseling technique designed to involve clients "in the exploration of feelings, needs, fantasies, values, biases, reasons, life-style alternatives, fears, conflicts, and environmental pressures in relation to personal growth and the opportunities in work and leisure activities." The NSVCS is a structured interview technique which takes at least forty minutes and intimately involves the client in the entire process of generating her own results. Dewey states that the focus of the procedure is primarily upon uncovering the client's values toward herself and toward work and secondly, upon occupations. Specifically, the NSVCS allows the client to confront her internalized sex-role limitations and to work through her sex-role biases about occupations. Dewey considers the NSVCS one option for tapping the unique talents of a group whose personal and social potential is being wasted.

The same barriers which operate to keep women out of male-dominated career fields also prevent women from advancing in these fields. In "Up the Management Ladder," Theodora Wells observes that women today who are attempting to move into management face a constant energy drain from being treated as "lesser" persons because they are female. Double standards of mental health, double binds in achievement orientation, and pressure to conform to the stereotype feminine identity are examples of the kinds of pressures with which women must contend.

As more women attempt to move up the management ladder, therapists will be seeing more career women as clients. These women will be very different from the traditional women that therapists have been accustomed to treating. To adequately deal with career women who are experiencing difficulties related to their work, therapists will have to understand the norms, expectations, and attitudes toward women in various organizational climates. For example, in paternalistic organizations, deference is expected from women.

The current position of women is ambiguous because of the conflict between traditional sex-role orientation and the pressure for equal opportunities. This results in double messages and covert power moves from within the organization. Since covert messages are difficult to confront, covertness maintains the traditional power relationships. In addition, women are hindered by their sex-role conditioning which causes them to distrust their own feelings regarding achievement and to be fearful of competing with men. In contrast, men are facilitated by their sex-role conditioning, by the conflict-free investment of masculine identity in job success, and by their greater credibility in our male-oriented society.

Wells contends that the essential therapeutic climate is one in which the ideas, concepts, and values of the therapist promote the career woman's personal and professional interests. Therefore, therapists must become aware of how the nonconscious subleties in therapists' perceptions of sex roles and the socialization-caused conflicts within clients can collude to stunt clients' growth both as persons and as professionals. Therapists must continually engage in self-searching and self-sensing to determine if they are engaged in a nonconscious contest of values with clients. Wells suggests the *reversal method* (imagining the client of the opposite gender) as a useful way for therapists to determine their possible differential valuing of women and men. To assist therapists to get in touch with their nonconscious sex-difference values and biases, Wells provides a self-test at the beginning and end of her chapter.

——— *Chapter 10* ———

CAREER COUNSELING FOR WOMEN

LENORE W. HARMON

WORK can be a way for individuals to express their identity and to explore their potential for competence and self-actualization. Women, however, seem unable to make choices about work in their lives. They literally live out Erikson's observations, that, "Young women often ask whether they can *have an identity* before they know whom they will marry and for whom they will make a home" (Erikson, 1968, p. 283). The important task in career counseling with women is to help them to maximize their potential choice and control of their lives.

Counselors are not responsible for the attitudes their clients bring to the counseling relationship, but they are responsible for their own responses to those attitudes (Smith, 1972). Thus, when women come to counseling without a strong sense of identity as a context in which to make career choices, the counselor may react in one of two ways. The first would be to assume that the situation is "natural" and one must work within the limitations it presents. The second would be to assume that the situation is painful and must be changed. The first reaction is analogous to regarding the bound feet of nineteenth century Chinese women as natural and the second reaction is analogous to assuming that everything will be fine if the bindings are simply removed. Both kinds of assumptions are being used in counseling women today and both assume that someone other than the client knows the "right" set of goals for her, whether it is raising outstanding children or winning a Nobel prize.

It is important to separate what is *now* from what is *possible* in the future and to view each woman's individual level of accomplishment as a product of her own choices which are not strictly rational or permanent. (The term *rational,* as used here, means uninfluenced by emotion and does *not* imply an evaluation.) Despite the romanticized visions of the potential roles available to women today, no life style is without its negative aspects. Each person must make choices on the basis of her own evaluation of the rewards available in a given situation.

THEORIES OF CAREER DEVELOPMENT

How people make career choices is a fascinating subject. Several types of theories have been proposed. They vary along two dimensions important to a discussion of career counseling for women. The first dimension extends along a sociological-psychological continuum. Theories at the sociological end of the continuum ascribe major importance to external events; theories at the psychological end of the continuum ascribed major importance to internal events. Psathas' (1968) outline of factors important in a theory of occupational choice for women is highly sociological with major emphasis on marriage and parental variables. Ginzberg, Ginsburg, Axelrad and Herma (1951) present a more psychological approach with emphasis on internal events such as fantasies. Super's (1951, 1963) approach also rests on a psychological basis emphasizing that individuals seek to implement a self-concept in making career choices. Obviously, no career choices made by either sex are purely sociological or purely psychological.

Findings show that men are more independent than women in their cognitive approach to tasks involving spatial perception (Sherman, 1967). It is tempting to generalize from these findings about the way women make vocational choices. To counselors, women seem to be extremely alert to external forces in making decisions. However, this perception itself may be influenced both by counselors' biases and by differences in the way men and women clients learn to talk about their choice process. For *anyone* making a career choice, the balance between external demands and internal factors is potentially conflict-ridden and deserves considerable attention in the counseling process. However, the author's hunch is that women, as a group, do take more account of external influences in making career choices than men do.

A second dimension of theories of career development extends from an emphasis on the developmental choice process to an emphasis on typology and content. Super's work (1957, 1972), for instance, emphasizes the process of career development with lesser concern for the content of the choices themselves. His (1957) approach leads him to suggest different career patterns for men than for women. While men's working patterns are limited to four, he suggests seven for women, including stable homemaking, double-tract (women who are married and continuously employed) and interrupted (women who leave the world of work for homemaking, but return to it) patterns. Zytowski (1969), who attempts to understand the career development of women, emphasizes the homemaking role as an important aspect of their career development. It is interesting to note that no theorists, as yet, postulate homemaking or interrupted patterns for men. All assume a lifetime span of participation in the job market for men. Neither is the fact that most men fit Super's double-tract category highlighted. While present developmental approaches may reflect accurately the way we currently conceptualize career development, they do not exhaust the possibilities.

The formulation of Roe (1957, 1972) falls near the middle of the developmental-content continuum because it relates childhood experiences to specific eventual choices.

The approaches which stress typologies such as Holland's (1966, 1973), underscore content rather than process. These approaches show clearly that the content of women's choices differs from men's choices. Holland (1974) reviews evidence that young women and girls choose predominantly social and artistic occupations while boys and young men choose predominantly realistic (manual, mechanical, agricultural, electrical and technical) and investigative (scientific) occupations.

These findings do not indicate that all women choose social or artistic occupations nor that all men choose realistic or investigative occupations. They do suggest that women choose within the norm for their sex in order to avoid conflict.

INTERNAL VS. EXTERNAL FRAME OF REFERENCE

Career decisions must be made with considerable attention to the internal frame of reference because internal determinants are more ultimately satisfying than the external ones (Herzberg, 1966). Thus, psychological determinants would be more important to career counseling than sociological determinants. Developmental and typological theories also depend on the ability of the individual to implement personal preferences without overwhelming influence from the outside. However, Bernice Sandler (1974), a counselor by training, who is now Director of the Project on the Status and Education of Women, Association of American Colleges, has argued, "Unless women come to grips with the conflicts and difficulties that being female presents in our society, I suspect that women's view of work will continue to be shaped primarily by externally caused factors. Traditional counseling, unless it deals with the contradictions of a woman's life, is not likely to have any great impact."*

MOTIVATION TO WORK

Vocational behavior would be easier to understand and explain if everyone worked for the same reason, but of course they do not. Industrial and management psychologists have noted the value of Maslow's hierarchy of needs in explaining the behavior of workers (Herzberg, 1966; Rush, 1969). However, neither Maslow nor those who have applied his theory to work have given much attention to how it might

---

*Sandler, Bernice, Personal Communication, 1974.

apply to women and their vocational behavior.

Briefly, Maslow postulates a hierarchical order of five types of needs: physiological needs, safety needs, belongingness and love needs, esteem needs, and self-actualization needs (Maslow, 1970). He believes that people do not become conscious of or attempt to gratify the higher-order needs (esteem and self-actualization) until the lower order needs (physiological and safety) are gratified. For example, to a hungry person, food is all important and she/he will do anything to get it, even if it means being cast away by peers or violating a personal sense of morality. The needs of belonging and self-esteem mean little in the face of all consuming hunger which is a physiological need. We can explore the general dimensions of Maslow's hierarchy of needs to explain vocational behavior in a way which will be useful for career counseling for women.

Social and cultural factors which are not under the control of the individual often determine whether the lowest level needs in the Maslow hierarchy — physiological, safety, and to some extent, love and belonging — are met. These gratifications are related to the sociological end of the sociological-psychological dimension running through career theories.

Most people in our society are not deprived of gratification of their physiological needs. However, it is interesting to analyze the mechanisms through which the physiological needs are met. For men, the usual means of gratification of physiological needs is through labor which produces either the needed food and water or the money to purchase them. For women, however, the usual means of gratification of physiological needs is through association with someone, husband or father, whose labor assures that her needs will be met. This is not to say that women do not work or that no woman has independently satisfied her physiological needs. But since the Industrial Revolution, the role of woman as housewife and mother has removed her from the world of work, at least in the view of society (Lewandowski, 1973).

When men have been unable to fulfill their own physiological needs independently it has been because of unforeseen natural and economic events or cultural values which systematically excluded some subgroups, such as Blacks and Catholics, from adequate opportunity. While no one would argue that women cannot independently assume responsibility for gratifying their physiological needs, most women have grown up in a world where they were not expected to do so and where, in fact, the opportunities for them to do so were limited compared to the opportunities offered to men. Thus, counselors have observed that the typical American housewife does not believe she can independently gratify her own needs. Neither, apparently, do many of the young women who marry out of desperation for someone to *take care of me*, nor do their parents who breath a sigh of relief once the wedding ceremony is over.

The same type of sexual dichotomy applies to the needs for safety and security once physiological needs are adequately gratified. Men can usually insure that in a stable society, their needs will be met directly by their labor. In contrast a woman usually works in the home to please a man who provides her a safe environment. However the newspaper advice columns are full of letters from women who begin, "My husband is a good provider and my life looks ideal to an outsider but ..." That "but" is usually followed by "he doesn't love me," "he treats me like a child," or, "I am bored. There is no growth in my life." These complaints correspond to the three highest levels of needs in Maslow's hierarchy.

An interesting reaction occurs in the woman who is able to insure her own safety and security by direct labor. The low-level jobs which are available to a woman may gratify her needs for safety to a minimal extent but keep her from risking that stability in an attempt to reach a higher level of employment and potential gratification. At this level she is not deprived physiologically and feels fairly secure and safe. However, even though her work does not gain her much belongingness, love, or esteem, she does not attempt to improve her position because she cannot risk losing the security. The extent to which failure to fulfill love, esteem, and self-actualization needs are common for American women is an indication that there may be conditions in our society which contribute to fixation of women's gratification at the level of safety.

The woman who ventures beyond the home *and* the typical woman's job (secretary, nurse, or teacher) is risking the loss of whatever feelings of belongingness, love, and esteem she receives for filling the typical female role. While men are loved and esteemed more highly for their successes, women are not always loved for their successes, especially if their successes are atypical for women. Horner's work (1969, 1970, 1972) on the fear of success in women demonstrates the conflicts women face in their potential and actual achievement.

A woman may have to compromise her need for self-esteem in order to achieve her need for esteem from others. Most bright women can recall a time when they concealed their abilities in order to avoid losing the esteem of someone else. More recently some women have been able to express their anger at having made or being expected to make this type of compromise. For women, more than for men, there seems to be a conflict between the behaviors which would lead to self-esteem and esteem from others. This is not as apparent for the woman whose interests are traditional (for whatever reason) as for the woman whose interests are nontraditional.

Maslow postulates that needs for esteem must be gratified before needs for self-actualization can emerge. The needs for self-esteem and self-actualization are at the psychological end of the sociological-psychological continuum, although there are probably no behaviors which are purely self-determined. However, Maslow's hierarchy suggests that psychological needs emerge after the others are adequately gratified. He also implies that people who gratify their needs for self-actualization, i.e. have become what they can be, reach a higher level of existence than those who have not (Maslow, 1970). Most career counseling rests on the assumption that it is possible to meet the needs for self-esteem and self-actualization, at least partially, through good career planning and decisions. The process of helping people decide how to meet their physiological and safety needs is exciting only if they have been severely deprived! Then the problem is to find some source of income. Most career counselors specialize in helping people find work environments which will be satisfying and exciting in addition to providing daily bread. It would appear, then, that career counseling deals mainly with the gratification of higher-level psychological needs of the individual.

This author is not sure that most women are prepared for such career counseling. Only if a woman's physiological and safety needs have been met and she has resolved her conflicts of achievement and self-esteem versus belonging and the esteem of others, is she free to make career plans and decisions which will fulfill needs for self-actualization. One might add that not all men reach this level either, and one of the large factors in their failure is their responsibility for dependent women and children. Although it is not usually clear to those experiencing painful changes in the roles of women and men, it is apparent that the more that women are free to satisfy their needs directly, the freer men will be to gratify their needs.

When applied to vocational behavior and problems, Maslow's hierarchy of needs suggests that (1) basic needs are fulfilled differently by women and men, (2) there is more conflict involved for women than for men in meeting higher-level needs which keeps women at lower levels of gratification, and (3) most career counseling and many career development theories are aimed at the high-level gratifications as postulated by Maslow. One is left with the question posed by Sandler, "Are women ready for career counseling?"*

COUNSELING APPLICATIONS

In career counseling for women a process suggested by an analysis of Maslow's hierarchy of needs may overlap with counseling approaches which are not usually considered career counseling. Schlossberg (1972) suggests the importance of assessing the developmental stage of each

---

*Sandler, Bernice, Personal Communication, 1974.

woman client in relationship to Tiedman and O'Hara's (1963) decision-making stages. In addition, it is important to assess for each woman client which of Maslow's basic needs she is meeting and how she is meeting them.

First, a career counselor should determine at what level the client is on Maslow's hierarchy and how she got there. It is important that every woman, adolescent or middle-aged, be sure that she can independently meet her needs for food and security. The old idea of having a skill *to fall back on* is not outmoded. In counseling young women, it is important that they realize what personal freedom they can insure for themselves by developing the most immediately valuable of their skills. It is not necessary to spend a lifetime as a computer programmer or dental technician. These skills can be used as a means to provide income and independence to do whatever a person wants: study nuclear physics, write a novel, or be a housewife. For the middle-aged woman the problem is often to help her reevaluate what skills she now has which would allow her to meet her own personal needs. Years of dependence on someone else have often convinced the adult woman that she really is helpless. Only major changes in her attitude toward herself will allow her to use the skills she already possesses or to learn new ones. In either case, it is true that until a woman can meet the lower-level needs through work, she will never be free to confront her higher-level needs.

One thing is clear: Many of the jobs society offers to women (and minority group members) are subsistence-level jobs which will barely meet their physiological and safety needs, much less go beyond them. A recent article in the *Milwaukee Journal* (Dembski, 1974) told the story of a woman reporter who worked as a nurse's aid in a nursing home for two weeks. She earned about two dollars an hour, and found it dirty, back-breaking work. She wrote, "But what really helped was the knowledge that I would not have to spend the rest of my life working in a nursing home." At a job like that, a woman will earn a little over $4000 a year. Even a woman without dependents would have little left over to devote to education, hobbies, or recreation after food, shelter and taxes. Too often job training programs prepare women for precisely this level of work. No counselor should consider such subsistence-level jobs as any more than a temporary solution when lower order needs must be filled. They and their clients should be seeking better, more rewarding solutions to the clients' career problems.

Women who are sure of their abilities to meet their basic physiological and safety needs present a different set of counseling problems. They often feel conflict between fulfilling their own needs and fulfilling the needs of others who are sources of love and esteem. For instance, the president of a business firm could not understand why one of his women

employees was using irrational excuses to avoid promotion until he remembered that she also had declined her last pay increase to avoid
making more money than her husband. Working through that kind of
conflict, helping a woman to label the forces that make up her dilemma,
and accepting her decision as to what she wants to do are also a part of
career counseling. For a younger woman, the specter of such conflict
makes her avoid certain nontraditional careers. It is important that a
woman choose what she wants whether it is housewifery or surgery but
she cannot choose until she is aware of the conflict. It is a counselor's
responsibility to bring the conflict to her awareness. It is hard to imagine
any one meeting her needs for self-actualization in a career into which
she has been forced by a desire to meet the needs of someone else.

"What will make me happiest and allow me the most opportunities for
personal growth?" is the kind of problem faced by the client who is
attempting to satisfy needs for self-actualization. Such a question does
not emerge until other types of needs are adequately satisfied. Career
counselors are best prepared by their theories and measurement techniques to handle clients with that kind of problem. Unfortunately, few
woman clients are at that stage in their hierarchy of needs. As a result,
career counseling with women has been a hopeless task for which there
has been no training. Until career counselors began to assess the hierarchical level of needs of women and vary their techniques accordingly,
career counseling with them will be frustrating both for the client and the
counselor.

COUNSELOR BIAS

Counselors will not be prepared to work in this way with their women
clients until they assess their own biases toward women and careers.
Schlossberg and Pietrofesa (1973) summarize much of the data on counselor bias and leave no doubt that both men and women counselors are
biased by the sex of the client. Counselors must begin to look at most
careers and jobs as androgynous. It may help in overcoming old biases to
explore why individual counselors and society have labeled each career or
job as *masculine* or *feminine*. It may also be worthwhile to explore the
results of such labeling. Clearly the range of acceptable vocational behavior has been unnecessarily narrowed for both sexes. This situation is
both a cause and effect of the low economic status women suffer.

Counseling aids such as occupational information and testing materials which imply sexual stereotyping must be revised. The same biases
which shape counselor behavior were incorporated in producing these
products. These biases will be altered as the market demand changes.
However, that demand will not change without fundamentally restruc-

turing the way counselors view the world of work. An interesting example of this process as applied to testing materials can be traced by reading the resolution introduced to APGA by Schlossberg and Goodman (AMEG Commission, 1973) and the proceedings of the National Institute of Education's recent Conference on Sex Bias and Sex Fairness in Career Interest Inventories (Diamond, 1974). Revisions in interest inventories follow the vocal protest of counselors and clients.

A final important observation for counselors is that the marriage-career dichotomy is overemphasized. To imply a forced choice between the two suggests that women must choose between independence and the kind of dependence which forces them to use someone else's labor to satisfy their most basic needs. The dichotomy also ignores the fact that most men have both careers and families. The whole question of combining a career and family should be explored with clients of both sees. The counselor's job is to help the client to clarify personal values and to recognize that those values and the decisions based on them, may change in time under new circumstances. Many of the middle-aged women a counselor sees today were convinced at age twenty that they never wanted to be anything but a housewife. At age forty, they are confused and frightened by their dissatisfaction with the role they expected to be satisfying for a lifetime.

Counselors should, after all, be helping clients to prepare for a world of changes. The old myth that career decisions can be made once for a lifetime has outlived its usefulness. Women (and men, too) need counselors who expect them to outgrow today's needs and decisions, who will help them to accept their changing selves, and who will provide them with a model for future decision-making. Career counselors themselves should expect to experience considerable change in the theories, techniques and materials they use in response to the needs of their clients.

REFERENCES

Association for measurement and evaluation in guidance commission on sex bias in measurement. AMEG Commission report on sex bias in interest measurement. *Measurement and Evaluation in Guidance,* 6:171, 1973.

Dembski, Barbara: Little time to give love. *Milwaukee Journal,* part 1, p. 1, January 27, 1974.

Diamond, E. (Ed.): *Sex Bias and Sex Fairness in Career Interest Inventories.* Washington, D. C.: National Institute of Education, 1974, in press.

Erikson, Erik: *Identity: Youth and Crisis.* New York, Norton, 1968.

Ginzberg, Eli, Ginsburg, Sol. W., Axelrad, Sidney, and Herma, John L.: *Occupational Choice: An Approach to a General Theory.* New York, Columbia University Press, 1951.

Herzberg, Frederick: *Work and the Nature of Man.* Cleveland, World Publishing, 1966.

Holland, John L.: *The Psychology of Vocational Choice.* Waltham, Blaisdell, 1966.

Holland, John L.: *Making Vocational Choices: A Theory of Careers.* Englewood Cliffs,

Prentice-Hall, 1973.

Holland, John L.: *The Use and Evaluation of Interest Inventories and Simulations.* Center for Social Organization of Schools, Report No. 167, Baltimore, John Hopkins University, January, 1974.

Horner, Matina S.: Fail, Bright woman. *Psychology Today, 3:*36, 1969.

Horner, Matina S.: Femininity and successful achievement: A basic inconsistency. In Walker, E. L. (Ed.): *Feminine Personality and Conflict.* Belmont, Brooks/Cole, 1970.

Horner, Matina S.: Toward an understanding of achievement-related conflicts in women. *Journal of Social Issues, 28:*157, 1972.

Lewandowski, C. M.: The evolving power of women in western society. Unpublished master's thesis, University of Wisconsin-Milwaukee, 1973.

Maslow, Abraham H.: *Motivation and Personality,* 2nd ed. New York, Harper & Row, 1970.

Psathas, George: Toward a theory of occupational choice for women. *Sociology and Social Research, 52:*253, 1968.

Roe, Anne: Early determinants of vocational choice. *Journal of Counseling Psychology, 4:*212, 1957.

Roe, Anne: Perspectives in vocational development. In Whiteley, J. M., and Resnikoff, A. (Eds.): *Perspectives on Vocational Development.* Washington, D. C., American Personnel and Guidance Association, 61-82, 1972.

Rush, Harold M. F.: *Behavioral Science - Concepts and Management Application.* New York, National Industrial Conference Board, 1969.

Schlossberg, Nancy K.: A framework for counseling women. *Personnel and Guidance Journal 51:*137, 1972.

Schlossberg, Nancy K. and Pietrofesa, John J.: Perspectives on counseling bias: Implications for counselor education. *The Counseling Psychologist, 4:*44, 1973.

Sherman, Julia A.: Problems of Sex differences in space perception and aspects of intellectual functioning. *Psychological Review, 74:*290, 1967.

Smith, Joyce A.: For God's sake, what do these women want? *Personnel and Guidance Journal, 5:*133, 1972.

Super, Donald E.: Vocational adjustment: Implementing a self-concept. *Occupations, 30:*88, 1951.

Super, Donald E.: *The Psychology of Careers.* New York, Harper & Row, 1957.

Super, Donald E.: Self concepts in vocational development. In Super, Donald E., (Ed.): *Career Development: Self Concept Theory.* New York, CEEB Research Monograph No. 4, 1963.

Super, Donald E.: Vocational development theory: Persons, positions, and processes. In Whiteley, J. M. and Resnikoff, A. (Eds.): *Perspectives on Vocational Development.* Washington, D. C.: American Personnel and Guidance Association, 13-33, 1972.

Tiedeman, David V. and O'Hara, Robert P.: *Career Development: Choice and Adjustment.* New York, College Entrance Examination Board, 1968.

Zytowski, Donald G.: Toward a theory of career development for women. *Personnel and Guidance Journal, 47:*660, 1969.

── Chapter 11 ──

VOCATIONAL COUNSELING WITH WOMEN: A NONSEXIST TECHNIQUE*

CINDY RICE DEWEY

BEING a woman in our society has determined the expectations of one's future roles in life. Women's development has been limited, regardless of their intellect, physical or emotional capacities, personality or potential. The needs of society, tradition, and superstition have dictated the female sex role. Counselors involved in vocational counseling with women also have contributed to perpetuating a culture which has squandered female resources and suffocated human potential. We are now in the midst of rapid changes in the attitudes of women, men and minorities toward their prescribed roles. The main thrust of the woman's movement has been to point out that women are disadvantaged by social norms and institutional arrangements. More women want to participate at the level of their actual ability rather than at the level expected of their sex.

Counselors involved in vocational counseling with women and minorities are beginning to realize that changing the content of the old Strong Vocational Interest Blank will not change a woman's self-image nor facilitate her confronting the limits she has internalized. Vocational counseling with women must allow the women to understand personal barriers to career development as well as social and cultural ones which suffocate their potential.

Traditionally, the counseling profession has perpetuated society's occupational stereotypes and myths through counselor bias (Eyde, 1970) and the use of vocational inventories whose alternatives, norm groups, and scoring systems have not been updated to reflect the changes in attitudes toward sex roles and minority roles (Dewey, in press; Goldman, 1973; Warnath, 1971). This bias has been particularly oppressive for women and certainly restrictive for men. Yet, test authors and publishers feel it is unrealistic to expect them to update norms, content and scoring systems when there is an economic advantage in maintaining the *status quo*. They argue that random samples including a meaningful number of both sexes would be impossible to collect because certain occupations

*This is an expanded version of an article which appeared in the *Personnel and Guidance Journal*, 52(5), January 1975, pp. 311-315.

207

continue to be dominated by one sex. In sum, test authors are saying, "We can only deal with and report what was true in the past or is true now in the world of work." Getting off this merry-go-round is difficult because our current occupational realities reflect the sexism and racism of our culture. How can we change the realities using instruments which compare our women and minority clients with norm groups which are, by definition, quite unlike the clients we are counseling? Vocational counselors must be aware that the concept of norm groups is inherently conservative and past-oriented and serves as a barrier to change by discouraging people from going where they would be different (Tittle, 1971).

THE NEED FOR CHANGE

At present many of our educational and counseling practices help perpetuate the systematic attrition of female potential. The counseling profession, along with the formal education system in America, occupies a position that gives it the power to change the psychological and social conditions of the American woman. Given the assumption that the control of population growth is a crucial problem for humanity, efforts need to be made to deemphasize the importance of having children as a natural part of a woman's role. We must also realize that people who are making career decisions today are in a different relationship to their environment and to society than people ever before.

We are witnessing the ruin of our environment in order to support a technological nation. The potential extermination of all humanity looms near. We have seen the disappearance of entire occupational groups in our lifetime; professionals and high-level technicians are losing their employment because of changes in national policies and other thousands are laid off as a sacrifice to government's desire to control inflation (Warnath, 1971). All this combined with sexism, racism, the shortage of energy and a population which demands an incredible degree of geographic mobility make career planning increasingly complex. The concept of vocational counseling as a few tests and a bit of guidance is certainly outdated. Nevertheless, the number of contacts per client in the typical counseling center averages slightly more than two, indicating that much educational and vocational counseling is still a form of the old trait-factor test interpretation process (Warnath, 1971). We have continued to treat the test interpretation process as a valid form of vocational counseling.

Traditional vocational counseling has been a process of grinding clients through a mechanical decision-making process, then using the business-industrial sorting process to match people with jobs. However, this process and the tests used by counselors have had relatively little impact on their clients and have affected vocational decision-making only to a very limited extent (Goldman, 1973). Counselors' traditional techniques are of little value except with Caucasion males. Considering that only half of our clients will end up in occupations remotely compatible with their test profiles (Campbell, 1974), even our best vocational test contributions do not seem very impressive (Goldman, 1973). As Warnath (1971) pointed out, it is only with an incredible leap of faith that one can tie test scores to a choice of a specific occupation three, five, or ten years in the future. Therefore, counselors who consider themselves agents of social change are now openly admitting that they are not willing to accept outdated traditional approaches to vocational counseling.

Cook and Stone (1973) found that women expect to make contributions to society, but planned to contribute through family, husband and community rather than through paid employment. Such an orientation does not take into consideration the statistics on divorce, desertion, death of spouse, the number of women with children to support on the welfare roles, the number of women stuck in "safe" but unfulfilling marriages, or the growing option of remaining single. Harmon (Ch. 10) suggested that the extent to which love, esteem and self-actualization needs are unfulfilled in many American women may be an index of the fixation of women's gratification at the level of safety in our society. Therefore, to meet the greater needs of women, career counselors must change the theories, techniques, and materials they use in vocational counseling.

WOMEN IN CONFLICT

Because of prior socialization to the traditional marriage and family role, girls and women tend to accept limited definitions of what they might be. Women are assigned work roles which are an extension of their sex role and as a group have avoided certain careers and high-level responsibilities. They continue to choose within the norm for their sex to avoid conflict.

Frequently, a woman is caught between the social, dependent roles she feels she should play and her conflicting need for developing and using her intelligence. When faced with the conflict between the feminine image and expressing their competencies or developing their interests, many women choose to adjust their behavior to an internalized sex-role stereotype. Thus, we have teachers, nurses, social workers and many other women in the labor force who have chosen careers which allow them to meet the demands of rigid sex roles while almost totally disregarding their own needs. In other words, the actual level of performance of many women does not reflect their true abilities (Horner, 1972). Their abilities, interests and intellects remain inhibited and unfulfilled. This lack of fulfillment does not occur without feelings of frustration, hostility.

resentment, bitterness, confusion and depression (Chesler, 1972). Women need to work through their feelings of competing with males and to deal with the anxieties emerging from choosing to oppose prevailing cultural expectations — the attitudes of family, spouse, parents, employers, and peers.

CAREER COUNSELING GOALS FOR WOMEN

Given the rapid changes taking place in our society, the overt and subtle sexism which still pervades most of the vocational interest inventories now available (Dewey, in press), and the fact that most vocational tests have had little impact on our clients, it would seem that counselors need to redefine their goals for vocational counseling for all their clients, but particularly for women.

Very basically, our goal should be to conserve human resources by humanizing our impact on our clients while giving special emphasis to the stifled potential of women and minorities. My goal for vocational counseling is to assist clients in learning how to use knowledge about themselves to make decisions. This enables them to cope creatively with an environment constantly in a state of flux, and to tolerate ambiguity in their lives.

In reality, lives are made up of a number of sequential short-range decisions made at various times (Goldman, 1972). Vocational counseling can be effective only to the extent that it can incorporate a client's current developmental priorities.

Vocational counseling should assist a woman to clarify her personal values while recognizing that the decisions based on them may change as she continues to grow. In the midst of the complex world with an unknown future, we need to help clients prepare for changes. Vocational counselors need to give primacy to the search for self while helping clients to accept their changing selves as well. Warnath (1971) points out that those counselors who are still dedicated to planning on the basis of current occupational literature and test information must do so "as if" the data will have relevance for the future. An encouraging trend in vocational counseling for women is the increased concern for techniques which recognize the unique needs of women and the barriers confronting them in their career development.

THE CRISES IN VOCATIONAL COUNSELING

Vocational counseling, as it has been traditionally practiced, is in crisis and appears to be close to obsolescence (Warnath, 1971). Within the counseling profession there is a growing acceptance of the fact that neither ethnic minorities nor women can be given adequate vocational counseling employing the usual methods and techniques. We are witnessing a shift in emphasis from the traditional test-interpretation approach to assisting clients to explore themselves in relation to their past and present environment, helping them to ask such questions as: What kind of person am I? What kind of relationships are important to me? What kind of life styles attract me? In what social or work environments do I feel most comfortable? These questions are more important than superficial ones related to fitting a client's tested characteristics to future occupations. No life style is without its negative aspects. Unless the vocational counseling process can also deal with the contradictions and conflicts in a client's life, it is not likely to have any great impact. It is a counselor's responsibility to bring a woman's conflicts into focus and help her to confront them.

THE NONSEXIST VOCATIONAL CARD SORT

As I have suggested, there is a need to revamp completely the approach to vocational counseling. The problem now is how to reach that goal. My work over the past three years in developing a technique called the Nonsexist Vocational Card Sort (NSVCS) provides one alternative (Dewey, 1974). The NSVCS stresses a client's involvement in the exploration of feelings, needs, fantasies, values, life style alternatives, fears, conflicts and environmental processes in relation to personal growth and the opportunities in work and leisure activities. A growing number of professionals involved in vocational counseling believe an emphasis on self-exploration makes more sense than the traditional stress on matching a person's characteristics which are of dubious predictive value anyway (Dewey, 1974; Goldman, 1973; Warnath, 1971; and Johnson, 1974). In fact, when a client takes a traditional paper and pencil interest inventory, most of the really significant information about a client is lost by the time of the test interpretation. While taking a test the client makes discriminations based on her* feelings, interests, values, and fears, but the client has little insight into how her answers relate to the computer test profile she's shown two weeks later.

The Nonsexist Vocational Card Sort procedure gives the client more responsibility in the vocational exploration process by initially setting the stage for her active participation. The counselor and client develop a partnership directed toward helping the client to organize and to clarify

---

*Since the focus of this book is on counseling with women, the female gender will be used in order to avoid the awkwardness of her/him, herself/himself. The technique is equally appropriate for use with men.

her feelings about herself and occupations, and to come up with some kind of meaningful summary. The summary is used to plan specific steps the client can take to gather more data or to ask other questions. The process of self-exploration in vocational decision-making allows the counselor and client to explore the conflicts and internalized limitations traditionally attributed to a client's sex or ethnic background.

USING THE NONSEXIST VOCATIONAL CARD SORT

Although it is impossible to derive any instrument or technique which is "nonsexist" using a language that is sexist, the Nonsexist Vocational Card Sort (NSVCS) provides a process-oriented tool which gives a greater range of vocational choices to both sexes. The same vocational alternatives are offered to men and women; the gender of the occupational titles has been neutralized, e.g. "salesman" has been changed to "salesperson," etc., and the process orientation of the technique allows the counselor and client to explore sex-role biases and internal conflicts as they emerge in the counseling session.

Format

The NSVCS was derived from a modified version of the Tyler Vocational Card Sort (Dolliver, 1967). Seventy-six occupational categories are printed on 3 x 5 cards and coded according to Holland's (1966, 1973) sex personality types so that some conclusions about the nature of a client's choices can be described. On the reverse side of each card is a summary of the primary job duties and responsibilities. The occupations included in the card sort were chosen as representative of a wide range of vocational values (See Table 11-I). Some occupations of the 1970's have been included such as "media specialist," "ecologist," and "skilled crafts person" of pottery, weaving, jewelry-making, etc.

Working With the Client

The card-sorting process begins with an explanation of the nature and purpose of the procedure. The process is described to the client as a means of helping her to organize her thinking and to talk about herself in relation to occupations. She is told that the counselor will record key words, values or themes which emerge during the card-sorting process, and that these will be used later in counseling with her. The counselor directs the activity noting the random comments that the client makes and exploring areas of concern to the client.

I have found that forming a partnership between the counselor and

OCCUPATIONS INCLUDED IN THE NSVCS
CLASSIFIED ACCORDING TO HOLLAND (1973)

REALISTIC-R

1. Engineer-i*
   nuclear
   chemical
   biomedical
   electrical
   industrial
   mechanical
   agricultural
   computer & information science
   mining & metal
   aerospace
   marine
   civil
   heating & air conditioning
2. Skilled Labor Trades-c
   carpenter
   plumber
   bricklayer
   roofer
   electrician
   mechanic
   housepainter
   T.V. repairperson
   welder
   machinist
3. Farmer
4. Military Enlisted-c
5. Barber/Hairdresser-sac
6. Sewing Machine Operator
7. Forester-i
8. Building Contractor
9. Military Officer
10. Printer-ic

INVESTIGATIVE-I

11. Biological Scientist
    biologist
    zoologist
    botanist
    microbiologist
12. Computer Programmer
13. Pharmacist-es
14. Mathematician-ra
15. Veterinarian-rs
16. Dentist-re
17. Medical Technologist
18. Radiologic Technologist
19. Physical Scientist
    physicist
    chemist
    astronomer
    geographer
    geologist
    meterologist
20. Agriculturalist
    plant scientist
    animal scientist
    plant pathologist
21. Physician-sa
22. Psychiatrist-sa
23. Economist-as

ARTISTIC-A

24. Author/Journalist/Reporter-se
25. Model-es
26. Interior Designer/Decorator-is
27. Skilled Crafts
    potter
    jeweler
    leather craftsperson
    weaver
    wood craftsperson
28. Musician-si
29. Artist-ir
30. Translator/Interpreter-se
31. Entertainer-es
32. Media Specialist
    broadcaster
    film maker
    mass communications expert
    producer
33. Architect-ir
34. Advertising Agent-es

SOCIAL-S

35. Social Scientist
    anthropologist-Iar
    psychologist-Isa
    social worker-ia
    rehabilitation counselor-ia
    guidance counselor-ea
36. School Superintendent-e
37. Librarian
38. Occupational Therapist
39. Clergyperson(minister, preacher, priest, rabbi, pastor, guru)
40. Nutritionist/Dietician
41. Nurse
42. Funeral Director-ec
43. Home Demonstration Agent
44. Director Community Organization-ec
45. Community Recreation Administrator-ce
46. Recreation Leader
47. Speech Pathologist-a
48. Teacher-ae
    elementary
    university
    junior college
    pre-school
    secondary
49. Executive Housekeeper-ce
50. Instrument Assembler-ce
51. Ecologist
52. County Agricultural Agent-ri
53. Physical Therapist
54. Personnel Director-ie
55. Dental Assistant-ai

ENTERPRISING-E

56. Manager
    small business-owner operator
    hotel & restaurant
    industrial manager
    retail sales
57. Salesperson-c
    real estate
    life insurance
    retail goods
    industrial
58. Garden Nursery Proprietor-re
59. Banker-c
60. President Mfg.-c
61. Lawyer-s
62. Purchasing Agent
63. Buyer-c
64. Art Dealer-cs
65. Florist-cs
66. Airline Steward/Stewardess-sa

CONVENTIONAL-C

67. Accountant-e
68. Bookkeeper-e
69. Office Worker
70. Bank Teller-r
71. Homemaker
72. Secretary
73. Police Officer-i
74. Production Efficiency Expert-is
75. Telephone Operator-se
76. Travel Agent-sc

*Lower case letters placed after occupational titles represent subclassifications made by Holland (1973).

client is facilitated by sitting on the floor of my office. This informal arrangement originally started because it was really the only space large enough to administer the card sort. I found that this arrangement also enhanced the climate of my vocational counseling sessions because clients tended to relax more than when we sat in chairs and I was perceived as less of an authority.

The materials involved in administering the NSVCS are: (1) the set of seventy-six 3 x 5 index cards of the NSVCS; (2) three "sorting" cards about 4 x 6, on one of which is written "Would Not Choose," on another "In Question," and on the third "Might Choose;" (3) note paper (plus carbon paper if you'd like to share the notes with your client).

Step (1). The client is asked to sort all of the NSVCS cards into one of the three sorting cards. I explain this procedure to the client as follows:

> The cards in the "Would Not Choose" pile represent those occupations that do not seem appropriate for a person like you or that really turn you off — let's say your aunt was a doctor and she really disgusts you, so you'd never want to be a doctor. In other words, any negative feelings you have about an occupation for whatever reasons sort into the "Would Not Choose" pile. Sort cards into the "In Question" pile for those occupations about which you are indifferent, in question, or uncertain about on the basis of your feelings right now. Try not to concentrate too many cards in this pile. Put cards in the "Might Choose" pile which have some specific appeal to you even if it's only a fantasy about how exciting it would be to be a musician or whatever.

Step (2). During the card-sorting process, the counselor can learn a great deal about how a client approaches a task: Does she tentatively place the cards? Does she stack them neatly or toss them into piles? How does she use the categories? Does she use her own experiences to assess herself or other's perceptions of her? Answers to these questions may be used as topics for discussion at another point in the session.

After the initial sort, all materials are put aside except the "Would Not Choose" pile. (I give her a chance to express negative feelings first. By starting here, we end the session with the positive "Might Choose" pile.) The counselor says:

> You have identified these as occupations you would not choose; now group those together which you have the same or similar reasons for not choosing. Say that you feel a sewing machine operator and an instrument assembler have minute and repetitious jobs; place these two cards in one group. Use as many groups as you feel you need, keeping the occupational titles visible this time, so that we can talk about each of them specifically. Also, in going over the occupations you've put in any category in the card sort feel free to juggle them from one pile to another if you want.

The cards that have been placed in these smaller groups are discussed one group at a time and the client is asked, "What were your reasons for grouping these together?" or "What is there about being a _____ that turns you off?" I find it helpful to reflect a client's negative statements back to her and to translate the negative statement into a more positive statement of the occupational value being communicated:

Client: I do not like doing work that is just a small part of some big finished product or project.

Counselor: It frustrates you to be in situations where you're required to focus on one minute part of a project. You're saying then, that it's important for you to be involved in the kind of work where you are closely involved with the whole process of the work goal.

The client's comments are recorded using key adjectives or phrases that can be written quickly as we are talking.

Step (3). The cards representing the "In Question" pile are considered next and the client is asked either to group them as above or to talk about them individually depending on how many cards are in this pile. Sometimes a client's statements about occupations in this group may suggest that some of them more appropriately belong in one of the other groups.

Step (4). The client is given instructions to sort the "Might Choose" group into piles in which the reasons for choosing them are similar. At the end of the grouping and discussion of the criteria for choosing each occupation, the client is asked to select and rank order the eight to ten occupations most preferred in the "Might Choose" pile. When a client ranks these occupations, she is implicitly ranking the importance of the values associated with them (Dolliver, 1967). At this point, the client is asked whether she feels she would like to add any areas of occupational interest to her hierarchy that may have been excluded from the seventy-six cards. If she mentions other occupations, I ask her about their relation to the vocations already in the hierarchy.

Using the notes jotted down during the sessions, the client and I summarize the things we have talked about. I find that in the random comments the client has described her self-perceptions while discussing her perceptions of certain occupations. The client should see that the NSVCS is a process technique and that she has generated her own results. The whole NSVCS process takes a minimum of forty minutes and continues as long as the counselor feels is appropriate for a particular client.

The focus of the whole procedure is, first, on the client's expressions of herself and her values and, second, on the specific occupations in the NSVCS. The emphasis is on self-exploration and the development of "personal competence" — the ability to "discover and evaluate where I

am in relation to the changing world of work and my changing environment and to feel the confidence to take the necessary risks to actualize my
goals" (Johnson, 1974). Experience has taught me the importance of
helping the client plan before leaving the office specific steps to follow in
order to gather more data about the areas to which she feels most attracted. Vocational resource material such as the *Dictionary of Occupational Titles*, and the *Occupational Outlook Handbook* may be useful,
but the client should be aware that many of these resources are still very
sexist in orientation. More meaningful sources of information are in-
dustry or professional magazines; *Saturday's Child* (Seed, 1973), an excellent book of female role models; and direct referrals to resource persons in
the field. Resource persons can share with a woman a realistic look at
what it is like to be in that field, what the most rewarding and challenging aspects are, and what the frustrations and "crud work" are like.

Using the NSVCS in counseling with women allows the internalized
sex-role limitations to be confronted and worked through along with the
sex-typed biases about occupations. Some case studies may better illustrate this point.

THREE CASE STUDIES

Esther, a forty-eight-year-old woman, described herself as a "wife of a
state politician" and "mother of three children." She was referred for
vocational counseling by the instructor of a course which focused on
women reentering the labor force after a lapse of time. She has a
bachelor's degree and had no pressing need for extra income, but she
complained of feeling empty inside. The counselor chose the NSVCS as
a means of exploring the "emptiness" Esther was experiencing. Esther's
reasons for grouping certain occupations into the different categories
frequently included some mention of her husband or children. When the
counselor brought this to her attention, Esther discussed the difficulty
she had thinking of herself as a person separate from her family. She felt
tremendous guilt at the thought of using family money to further her
education. At one point the counselor said, "I get the impression that
you have a hard time putting yourself first. It sounds like the way in
which you sacrificed for your husband's career was often at the expense
of your own needs for fulfillment." Esther agreed that her style as a
"self-sacrificing wife and mother" was no longer appropriate now that
her husband was successful in his career and her children were adolescents.

The counselor asked Esther to sort the cards again as if she were the
most important person in the family. The card sort looked completely
different this time. Esther came up with several vocational areas that she
wanted to explore further, one of them was management. The counselor

provided her with occupational literature, gave her the names of several contact persons in the community, and helped her practice by role-playing the confrontation with her family when she would announce she was going to graduate school and would have less time for many of the household maintenance tasks she had performed in the past.

* * * * *

Sharon was a twenty-nine-year-old woman who had given up her studies in Art Education during her junior year in college in order to start a family with her husband who was a graduate student in painting. Her sons were now seven and nine and her husband was an instructor in painting at the university. Recently, her husband had confronted her with his intention to move out because he found her to be an uninteresting and unchallenging person. She came for vocational counseling because of the desperate and helpless feeling that she might have to be on her own and support her two children. Sharon's vocational problem consisted of two parts: first, identifying the skills or resources that she could develop to meet her immediate needs for security, and, second, determining the direction she would want to seek for her long-run career fulfillment. Using the NSVCS and exploring a two-stage concept helped Sharon to alleviate some of her anxiety about needing to make plans right now for the rest of her life.

Because of her love of the outdoors and the freshness and creativity she found in children, Sharon was attracted toward a job in recreation. In order to meet her immediate needs for income and independence, she found a part-time job with a university research project. The job was observing the play of children on various kinds of equipment so she was allowed to bring along her own children. She also began taking courses in order to finish her degree in Art Education.

* * * * *

Another client was a twenty-three-year-old woman who was employed as a secretary even though she had a B.A. degree in psychology. Jackie was considering enrolling in graduate school as the only relief she could think of from the monotony of her $4000/year job. When Jackie was going through the card-sorting process, the counselor noted several emerging themes: "I am depressed and feel wasted and angry; I want to be involved in a kind of work which is socially relevant but do not want to work directly with people; I want to be able to express my creativity and to have the freedom to choose the direction I will go; while I want autonomy, I am really afraid of being in a leadership position with a lot of responsibility."

Since the counselor was familiar with this last fear — that of responsibility, she shared with the client the fact that many women find that they are afraid of responsibility and thereby lower their vocational aspirations. The discussion which followed dealt with how it was easy to accept the limits that women have internalized without ever testing the limits ourselves. The client disclosed an experience in adolescence which fit this theme. She had wanted to run for student government president in her high school but had been encouraged by her council advisor, her mother and female friends to seek the vice-presidency instead. She recalled other experiences in her life when she had her goals for herself that "others" had sabotaged by redirecting her toward a different goal. The counselor reflected Jackie's anger and resentment and pointed out how women are taught in many subtle ways that they function best in supportive, nurturing or secondary roles.

One field Jackie chose to explore further was parapsychology, a field which held both challenge and excitement for her. She had given up her interests in it in response to her parents' notions that it was a "weird field." Through the card-sorting experience, Jackie began to get some notion of how she could separate her own feelings, values, and experiences from those of her family and friends. She was able to begin the process of redirecting her energy toward fulfilling herself, rather than living out the female sex-role stereotype (Dewey, 1974).

VALIDITY AND RELIABILITY

Within the framework presented here, the Nonsexist Vocational Card Sort is a structured interview technique which deals mainly with a client's reasons, feelings, fantasies, biases, and needs for making choices about occupations. The concepts of validity and reliability have quite a different meaning in relation to an interview technique than to a vocational test. As Dolliver pointed out, "There is often low validity and reliability between an early counseling interview and a later one, since from early topics of discussion evolve new, more pertinent topics" (1967, p. 920). Bordin and Wilson (1953) suggested that reliability should be negatively valued in the process of counseling. In going through the NSVCS procedure, it is expected that the responses and choices of a typical vocational client would change. The NSVCS elicits "expressed interests" directly, by asking the client what she is interested in and by using a card-sorting technique. Expressed interests have been found to have predictive validity of "inventoried interests" (Dolliver, 1971). To meaningfully evaluate whether the NSVCS has validity, one would have to ask whether its use led more quickly than a vocational interest inventory or unstructured interview to the identification of vocationally relevant topics for further discussion. My experience and the experience of others using the NSVCS over the past three years is that it definitely does.

SUMMARY

In response to the sex-role stereotyping which pervades our culture and, more specifically, to our counseling approaches, the Nonsexist Vocational Card Sort provides an alternative approach to traditional vocational counseling at a time when vocational counseling is in crisis. Our traditional counseling tools are of little help in meeting the special needs of women and minorities who are seeking entrance to occupations that have heretofore been denied them. The NSVCS stresses the client's involvement in the exploration of self in relation to work as the primary goal of vocational counseling. The process illuminates the conflicts, self-doubts and strengths that need to be dealt with if our vocational counseling is to have any meaning in a world whose future is uncertain.

Most clients generate a wealth of personal data. The NSVCS frees counselors from having to attach clients to computer printouts in order to organize the data generated. It represents one alternative for counselors seeking new answers. We need many more creative options to help us tap the talents of women whose potential we are wasting.

REFERENCES

Bordin, Edward S., and Wilson, Earl H.: Change of interest as a function of shift in curricular orientation. *Educational and Psychological Measurement, 13*:297, 1953.

Campbell, David P.: *Strong Vocational Interest Blank Manual.* Stanford, Stanford University Press, 1974.

Chesler, Phyllis P.: *Women and Madness: When is a Woman Mad and Who Is It Who Decides?* Garden, City, Doubleday, 1972.

Cook, Barbara and Stone, Beverly (Eds.): Special topics in counseling. *Counseling Women, Series VII.* Guidance Monograph Series, Boston, Houghton Mifflin, 1973.

Dewey, Cindy Rice: Don't give another vocational test without giving it some thought. *Psychological and Vocational Counseling Center Monograph Series.* Gainesville, in press with University of Florida.

Dewey, Cindy Rice: Exploring interests: A non-sexist method. *Personnel & Guidance Journal, 52*:311, 1974.

Dolliver, Robert H.: An adaptation of the Tyler vocational card sort. *Personnel & Guidance Journal, 45*:916, 1967.

Dolliver, Robert H.: Strong vocational interest blank versus expressed vocational interests: A review. *Psychological Bulletin, 72*:95, 1971.

Eyde, Lorraine: Eliminating barriers to career development of women. *Personnel & Guidance Journal, 49*:24, 1970.

Goldman, L.: Test Information in Counseling: A Critical View. Proceedings of the 1973 Invitational Conference on Testing Problems. Princeton, Educational Testing Service, 1973, pp. 28-34.

Holland, John L.: *Making Vocational Choices: A Theory of Careers.* Englewood Cliffs, Prentice Hall, 1973.

Holland, John L.: *The Psychology of Vocational Choice*. Waltham, Blaisdele, 1966.

Horner, Matina: The motive to avoid success and changing aspirations of college women. In Bardwick, Judith M. (Ed.): *Readings on the Psychology of Women*. 1972, pp. 62-71.

Johnston, J.: Vocational inquiry that develops personal competence. Keynote address at the Innovations in Career Counseling Conference. Gainesville, Oct. 1974.

Seed, Suzanne (Ed.): *Saturday's Child: 36 Women Talk About Their Jobs*. Chicago, O'Hara, 1973.

Tittle, C. K.: Studies in psychological measurement: Sex differences, science and objectivity. Paper presented at the meeting of the Southeastern Psychological Association, Miami, Florida, 1971.

Warnath, Charles F.: *New Myths and Old Realities: College Counseling in Transition*. San Francisco, Jossey-Bass, 1971.

EDITOR'S NOTE: The Non-sexist Vocational Card Sort (NVCS) can be purchased by writing to Douglas Dewey, Route 4, Box 217, Gainesville, Florida 32601.

— *Chapter 12* —

UP THE MANAGEMENT LADDER*

Theodora Wells

Picture yourself in your office. You have just finished the second session with a woman who is having difficulty with a husband who takes her for granted, "runs around with other women," and generally treats her badly. She has come to you to try to get her husband to change. You have your own feelings about this objective for therapy. You also have some thoughts on the general approach you will use in working with her.

Now your next client has arrived. She is Ann Caldwell, keeping her first appointment which she made five days ago. She is reasonably attractive, dressed somewhat conservatively, casually groomed. She appears calm on the surface but smiles nervously and does not seem fully at ease. "Fairly common behavior for a first visit," you think. And from here the scene opens. . . .

You: (Giving full attention) What seems to be the situation, Ann?

Ann: (Talking fast in reporting tone) I'm feeling so discouraged and frustrated. I've been working long and hard to be promoted to the project manager on one of our contracts. Five days ago, when I called you, a man was promoted who has less education, less experience and who's always picking my brains. He's been making more money all along and he'll probably get more now. *(Getting excited, defensive)* I know damn well it's because I'm a woman. They think I can't manage the men even though I've been doing it for over eight months. *(More objectively)* My work's first-rate, I just saved 'em a pile of money on another project, and I took the management training they said I had to have. *(Complaining indignantly)* But it doesn't do any good. You know what my boss said when I asked him why he picked Tom?

You: (In a neutral tone) You confronted your boss then?

Ann: (Assertively) You bet I did. That promotion meant a lot to me. And you know what he said? He said, "I know you worked hard for that promotion but try to understand that we gotta have someone who can really make that project on schedule. We feel Tom can make the deadline because he's already got the confidence of the men." *(Can't have a woman boss, you know.)* Then he talks about Tom's wife having a baby about the same time this project is done and I'm supposed to *understand* that, being a woman!

Then he had the gall to say, *(mockingly)* "Now I want you to bury the hatchet and get in there and help Tom — you know, really support the team effort. And I can promise you when the next chance comes along, you'll have first crack at it."

(Angrily sarcastic) Now how's *that* for a first-rate fuckover. Earn the next promotion by "understanding yourself out" of this one. Be a nice girl. I don't get the job because *men* have a hangup about women bosses. And besides Tom's having a baby . . . isn't *that* the clincher! Never mind education, experience, proven performance. I'm dead-ended by a bunch of scared *men*. There's *gotta* be a way around it. It's so damn frustrating. You've gotta help me figure out what to do. . . .

You: *(Write down responses you think you would probably make; note tentative reactions to Ann and her situation and some notes on what ways you might go next with Ann. Please do this before continuing with the interview.)*

Now, let us assume that you acquire the following historical and background information during the next several sessions with Ann.

Age: Thirty-six

Marital Status: Married, two children, girl thirteen, boy, eleven.

Husband's Views: He is a skilled technician earning about $20 thousand a year. He thinks Ann should be home with the children. He does not approve of her ambitions, although he goes along with them somewhat by helping around the house some. He does not like having a live-in companion-sitter for the children. He feels he earns enough for the family.

Children's Views: They seem to get along well with Ann. They sometimes complain that she is gone too much and does not do enough with them. They say they're too old to have the sitter and wish Ann would be home so they would not have to have one.

Marital Relations: Ann is not well-satisfied sexually. Relations are too infrequent, the last time being about three weeks ago. Work and the children seem to get in the way, resulting in feeling "too tired" or "not in the mood." It is becoming a problem. Otherwise, the relationship seems generally adequate but with the continual low-key tension typical of two-career families.

Work History: Employed twelve years with breaks for childbirth and raising, two years the first time, three months the second. Started as computer programmer working on special projects requiring design innovation. Three promotions and regular salary increases. Ann's focus has been on professional/technical excellence. She also has had some assistant team-leader experience. She earns about eighteen thousand dollars a year.

Education: M.S. in Mathematics. Extension courses in computer sciences. Company courses in management development. Willing to study whatever it takes to get ahead in her profession.

Medical/Therapy History: Takes birth control pills, no side-effects. No other medication. This is her first individual experience with therapy but has been in some group experiences about which she has mixed feelings. Her career ambitions were questioned and she was told she intellectualized too much.

Given this history so far, take a few minutes to note down your responses to the following questions. This is important to do NOW as these notes will be used later in the chapter to compare with another case situation.

What objectives do you feel are important for you and Ann to work on? (Consider all aspects of her life, her view of it, your view of it, etc.) In what ways do your views differ from hers? What seems the best way to work on resolving Ann's job situation? How does this compare with your earlier notes (before you had this history) on what directions you go next?

YOU AS THERAPIST: YOUR VALUES AND VIEWS

You were invited to participate in the Ann Caldwell case, noting down your responses, as a way of working with some of your own values and views as a therapist. Many of you who choose to read this book may be more aware than others of potential double-standards in treating women and men and possible differences in criteria you may use in choosing your therapeutic directions. Many of you may be seriously concerned with becoming aware of these factors to increase your personal and professional excellence.

Regardless of whether you are a male or female therapist, it is likely that you carry sex-role values from your own upbringing which are reinforced by most contacts with our daily culture. Your professional training was almost certainly affected by beliefs held by your professors. Many of you may not have extensive contact with typical, large, work organizations, their values, and their climate so you may have overlooked the fact that the more career-committed a woman becomes, the more she steps out of traditional sex-role expectations. When she comes to you it is probably because she feels conflict over "stepping out of woman's place." Her view of herself and her effectiveness as a person will be profoundly affected by how "stepping out of role" is perceived and valued by her therapist, her husband and family, her supervisor, coworkers and subordinates, and the upper management of her company.

I suppose the reason a book such as this one has been written is that there is so much change occurring and so many questions and conflicts being raised and discussed that we need to take a good long look at the values we hold and may impose on others. Some of the comments made by therapists to women I have worked with highlight, for me at least, the urgent need to take these self-searching steps. I wonder if you also find that the following comments violate the integrity of the woman client:

"It sounds to me like you're denying yourself as a woman."

"It's clear you *really* want to be a man."

"You should try being more feminine."

"You should try being more masculine." (Yes, it happens!)

"What does your husband think about all this?"

"What do you want to be a women's libber for, anyway? You're attractive, smart and feminine."

"You really hate men, don't you?"

"We better work on your father-complex."

"Now that's irrational. Don't you see that you're getting in your own way by expecting others to change? What you have to do is . . ."

"Why do you want a career? Perhaps we better explore that."

The concern I have about such comments is with the authoritarian assumption that someone else, anyone else, is more qualified than the particular woman to define her feelings, her perceptions, her role, and her behavior. Implicit in all these statements is something like: "Just listen to me, little girl, and I'll tell you how to be. You don't really know how to live your life as a woman, so I'll tell you . . ." Perhaps this Father (Mother)-knows-best attitude goes with the role some therapists learned as appropriate for their professional role; perhaps it comes from being in a one-up position in relation to the client; perhaps it reflects unconscious sex-role expectations. Whatever the reason, it seems pervasive.

High-aspiring career women often get similar remarks in more potent versions, such as:

My first therapist was a woman. She gave me an MMPI . . . and it said I had very high ego strength which she said was a bad thing. I knew it's bad in the sense that . . . it's supposed to mean rigidity, but for a woman trying to do well . . . ego strength is important. My second therapist told me I was the coldest woman he had ever had the misfortune to meet, that I was castrating. His professional judgment was that I would never get into any kind of long relationship. He pitied any man that ever got involved with me. . . . (Chesler, 1972)

In the first instance, the therapist seems to consider ego strength as "bad" in itself, perhaps linking it to the Freudian definition that women have a "weak superego" and, by implication, have something wrong with them if it is strong (Marmor, 1968). The first therapist evaluated without reference to the reasons for the behavior. And, she *evaluated* . . . thus placing herself in the definer role. To me, that violates. In the second instance, the therapist appears to be saying more about himself and his ability to relate to a woman who, to him, appears cold. He has neglected to state the criteria or standard against which he is making the comparison "cold . . . castrating." Attacks of this kind are, to me, counterproductive and personally violating. Unfortunately, these are not isolated instances. Get any group of women together who have some awareness of these matters and listen to them share their horror stories.

We have not even touched on the sex-between-therapist-and-client issue yet. At a psychological conference a few years ago, a panel of all male "humanistic" therapists discussed the appropriateness of such sexual relationships. They decided that it is OK with a consenting adult and then debated whether or not to charge for the time in or out of the office. This is reverse prostitution under the label of professional license!

Now, clearly my values are coming through, so it is time to spell them out. The central question is "Is a woman a person?" The standard of personhood in our society is the male who is considered to be the "ideal" adult. I think this standard deserves questioning since many men who are primarily concerned with the male-role for personal identity are not "persons." These men include, of course, many supervisors, *husbands, and perhaps therapists of career women.*

In rejecting the belief that "male" is ideal, I offer the following definition of a person: One who assumes primary responsibility for her/his own emotional, intellectual, sexual, financial, spiritual and physical well-being, and is able to achieve most self-determined objectives adequately. Persons look to others for voluntary validation, emergency support and for temporary "leaning-on" as needed and offered. They also are available to meet others' needs by choice, not compulsory duty. Their self-worth is not a function of the approval of others, but is centered in self-approval with outside validation. Rejections can be handled selectively without severely undermining or demolishing one's sense of self-worth.

If we can agree on this definition in at least a general sense, it becomes evident that neither the male nor female role expectations in our society lend themselves to fully functioning personhood. The female role is especially person-lessening. Let's look at the general social context in which we function, a male-role-dominated one, in order to see how male-female relationships operate. We then can better understand how these expectations affect the woman with career-goals in an organizational context which reflects the values of the larger society.

THE PSYCHOLOGICAL CONSEQUENCES OF SEXUAL INEQUALITY

Miller and Mothner (1971) have summarized the psychological dynamics of inequality in one of the clearest statements I have seen. Briefly, here's what happens between the dominants and the subordinates who need each other.

Dominants

1. Actions of the dominant group tend to be destructive to the less powerful.
2. The dominant group usually puts down the subordinates, labeling them defective in various ways. Sometimes this derogation can seem to subtly elevate the subordinate.
3. The dominant group usually acts to halt any movement toward equality by the subordinates. It also "polices" against any changes toward rationality or greater humanity among its own members, e.g. men who "let their women" have more than their usual rights are subject to ridicule.
4. The dominants obscure the true nature of the relationship, the existence of inequality. They rationalize the situation by false explanations, such as inferiority.
5. By proffering one or more "acceptable" roles, the dominants attempt to deny other areas of development to the less powerful subordinates. These roles usually provide a "service" that the dominant group does not choose to, or cannot, do for itself. The functions they prefer to perform are closely guarded and closed off to the subordinates.
6. Since the dominants determine society's ethos, philosophy, morality, social theory and science, they legitamize the unequal relationship and incorporate it into all the guiding cultural concepts.
7. The dominants are the model for "normal" human relationships. It may then be "normal" for everyone to treat subordinates as described above.
8. The dominants are bound to suppress disruption of these relationships and to avoid open conflict that might bring into question the validity of the established *status quo* situation.

Subordinates

1. The less powerful group is primarily concerned with survival. Therefore, direct, honest reactions to destructive treatment are avoided. For women in our society, open action in their own self-interest can mean economic hardship, social ostracism, psychological isolation and even the diagnosis of personality disorder by some psychiatrists.
2. Subordinates resort to various disguised reactions to "put on" the dominant one while appearing to please him.
3. The subordinates may absorb some of the untruths created by the dominants, e.g. those women who believe they are less important than men. This is more likely to occur if there are few or no alternate concepts at hand.
4. Subordinate group members have experiences and perceptions that more accurately reflect the truth about themselves and the irrationality of their positions. Their own more truthful conceptions are bound to come into opposition with the mythology they have absorbed from the dominant group. Inner tensions are almost inevitable.
5. Despite the obstacles, subordinates always tend to move toward more free expression and action. There were always some women who spoke out. Most records of these actions are not preserved by the dominant culture, thus making it difficult for subordinates to find a supporting tradition and history.
6. Within the subordinate group, there is a tendency for some members to imitate the dominants and to treat their fellow subordinates just as destructively. Others may try to reverse the dominant/subordinate roles. This has been called the Queen Bee Syndrome (Staines, Tavris, and Jayaratne, 1974).
7. To the extent that subordinates move toward free expression, exposing the inequality and questioning the basis for its existence, they create open conflict.

ARE THE SEX-ROLES CHANGING?*

The psychological consequences described here are pervasive and institutionalized. There is typically a long time lag between a challenge of the established system and its eventual incorporation into conventional

---

*This section and the following one are adapted from Wells, Theodora: Psychology of Women, an invited chapter in Warmouth, Arthur and McWaters, Barry: *The Art and Science of Psychology: Humanistic Perspectives*. Monterey, Brooks/Cole, in press.

wisdom. Consequently, the so-called "sexual revolution" that we have been experiencing seems to me to be a sex-*act* revolution, not a sex-*role* revolution. So far, the message is the same: You *are* your sex and female is less. These attitudes pervade work organizations so that a woman seeking to move into management, a closed-off "male world," must contend with her identity as a person-who-is-woman at many turns. Dealing with these ambiguities causes a steady, perhaps nonconscious, energy-drain.

Considerable recent psychological research confirms how role expectations affect the self-concepts of women as well as the double-standard of mental health that people-helpers have absorbed. The Rosenkrantz research (Rosenkrantz, Vogel, Bee, Broverman, and Broverman, 1968) showed which traits are valued in men and which others are valued in women. All the competence and leadership traits were, as expected, valued when shown in men. These included traits such as "decisive, knows the way of the world, competitive." Twenty-nine traits were valued in men, only twelve in women, which included nice-girl and need-for-security traits such as "religious, quiet, concern for appearance." The researchers found that "women also hold negative values of their worth relative to men," the impact of which, they concluded, was "enormously powerful." These investigators (Broverman, Broverman, Clarkson, Rosenkrantz, and Vogel, 1970) also found the existence of a double-standard of mental health among male and female clinicians who were asked to describe mentally healthy adults, males and females. Healthy women are perceived as less healthy by adult standards.

Matina Horner (1970) found similar patterns in women's achievement motivations. The desire to achieve was curtailed by a "motive to avoid success" that seemed to be acquired early in life along with other sex-role expectations. High-achieving graduate women, she found, would not fully explore their intellectual potential when they had to compete, especially with men. Many changed their majors from "male fields," such as medicine and law, to more "feminine" majors, such as literature and the arts. This same dynamic often occurs in work environments. Women dependent on male approval participate in the double-bind of femininity which Horner describes: "If she fails, she is not living up to her own standards of performance; if she succeeds, she is not living up to the societal expectations about the female role." Another way of stating this is: If she succeeds she stands to lose the man (or her job-promotion); if she does not try, she shortchanges herself. This is society's femininity game: *You win by losing.*

As a result of this double-bind, Horner found that high-achieving women tended to disguise their abilities, not admit their successes and downgrade their strengths. They tended to believe that men were smarter than they, thus making it important to appear less smart with those men from whom they sought self-esteem.

In later research, fears of dislike or loss of femininity seem to occur only in those women oriented toward traditional wife-and-mother roles. Less traditional women were commonly also high achievers who see achievement as entirely appropriate for women (Alper, 1974). However, in my own work with women in management-development courses, I find traditional patterns creating conflicts within the growth and career goals of most women.

HOW THE MALE AND FEMALE ROLES NEED EACH OTHER

As Miller and Mothner noted, the dominants and subordinates need each other. (Also see Ch. 20, Wyckoff.) Added to this power relationship is a social value of competitiveness, of winning. In our society, to achieve is to win. In a male-dominated society, supports for achievement and winning are more amply provided for males than females. Society provides the vehicles for men to achieve their "appropriate" dominance and power positions over women. As noted above, if the woman succeeds, she stands to lose the man. But if the man succeeds, he stands to win the girl (so to speak). Put in a nutshell:

The masculinity game: You win by gaining power-over-others;
The femininity game: You win by losing power-over-self.

Of course, many women and men are not heavily committed to their sex-roles as primary sources of personal identity. However, the environments in which they work and live bring considerable pressure to conform to traditional patterns which are still the norm. Traditional women who have invested their personal identity in the wife-mother role may criticize another woman whose life-style seems to reject their own, and traditional men who get substantial identity from adhering to the male role will likely feel that the nontraditional, career-committed woman is questioning his manhood. In his eyes, she becomes the "castrating bitch."

Male and female roles intermesh and reinforce one another. One example of how the roles intermesh would be with self-esteem in the woman, and vulnerability in the man. The woman, adhering to role expectations, relocates some of her self-esteem in the man, who is expected to take care of and reinforce her self-esteem. In his role as a man, he takes total responsibility for decisions, and protects and provides for her. His self-esteem is enhanced by her relocation of self-esteem into his care. She "gives herself to him" if she loves him. On the job, this takes the form of looking to the authority figure, the *male*, for opinions, judgments, guidance, and his "greater intelligence." The man in authority has an investment in seeing himself in this light, whether or not it happens to be accurate. (Please keep in mind that these comments refer to people with role-based identities, not *all* men and women.)

The man, in his role, also relocates some of his self-esteem in her, by trusting her with some of his vulnerability, his "I-don't-knows," which he is not permitted to express in most other relationships. On the job this is frequently the relationship between a man and his secretary who serves in the confidante role appropriate to women. She is expected to nurture these vulnerable feelings and, when he's hurting, provide solace and sympathy.

Each one places a central source of personal identity in the others' hands, setting up a mutual dependency. The content for each sex is different, the process is similar. The dependency created by this socially-sanctioned and expected exchange also sets up a mutual control system. She has to go through him to gain access to her self-esteem, to maintain her sense of value. "Going through him" means that he can give or withhold approval, thereby controlling her choices or behavior. She learns that she has to get his approval to feel worthwhile.

He, on the other hand, has shared some vulnerabilities with her. In a personal relationship, his access to those feelings is through her. In a business relationship, he may not need access, but she has power over these feelings. If the woman wants to control him, perhaps to get him to give his approval to her, she can "hit him where it hurts" since she's the keeper of his vulnerabilities. The game plan for the battle-of-the-sexes unfolds.

This is only one example of complex mutually dependent role-exchanges in which someone is expected to give power over one's self to the other in the name of love or appropriate business/social behavior. When conflict develops, each has a means of manipulating the other.

This is not, however, as balanced as this example suggests. In a male-valuing society, where traditional educational and employment channels are developed by and for male achievement expectations, he has more access to external power sources than she. So she learns to give more of herself to him in hopes that he will use his larger power-access to her advantage also. She may learn that she has no right to direct power herself, so she must hope that she will gain through his payoffs. It's "betting on the come" . . . his.

The power relationship with the male dominant and the female subordinate has become accepted as "right." It serves the best interests of a society where men are the definers and decision-makers, and accounts for the nonleadership, service nature of most jobs women hold. To question these roles is high-risk for the woman. However, question them she must if she is not to participate in her own self-destruction. And question them she must if she is going to do something effective (beyond the scope of the home, that is) in this world. For this effort toward growth and increased effectiveness, she is often punished, sometimes severely.

The situation with Ann Caldwell is so common that it becomes painful. Many women train boss after boss without ever getting an opportunity to use their knowledge directly in that higher-level position. Promotion rates for women lag behind men and increasingly so the further up the management ladder one goes. Women typically can get to first-level management positions (sometimes euphemistically titled for government-reporting purposes) more easily due to the affirmative-action impetus. But moving upward from there is extremely slow and difficult, if it happens at all. Tokenism is the practice and there is no evidence of change in sight. Economic recession tends to reduce or cancel gains previously made as the male *status quo* tightens to protect their own. (Women are not the only ones affected. Nonwhite minority males as well as females are also in subordinate roles.)

In working with career women clients, it seems to me that the therapist needs to have a general feeling of some of the values, dynamics and games that tend to permeate large, work organizations so it is possible to keep separate what the client is personally responsible for and organizational factors with which she has to contend. The organizational climate is not the same for aspiring women as it is for men. To make any assumption that it is the same will distort the therapist's perception of her experience. Since most of us, consciously or not, filter some of what we hear through our own sets of assumptions, to be on the safe side the therapist should assume that what the career-woman client tells him/her is probably an understatement of the situation. The constant stream of double-messages such women typically receive can be "crazy-making." One important question to always ask is, "Who's crazy, the environment she's in, or the client?" Let's take a closer look at how some of these organizational factors operate. First, let's look at some basic climate descriptions, then let's review the overt/covert power dynamics between dominant/subordinate people in organizations.

THE ORGANIZATIONAL CLIMATE*

As one approach in describing the climates of work organizations, Rensis Likert (1967) has developed a convenient four-system model. Modified to reflect women's potential within these systems, these can be described as:

1. *Exploitative:* maximum *use* of people with minimum concern for

---

*Adapted from Loring, Rosalind, and Wells, Theodora: Managerial climate, Ch. 4. *Breakthrough: Women into Management.* New York, Van Nostrand Reinhold, 1972.

their needs.

2. *Paternalistic:* the top man ("Father") knows what's best for people, and keeps the prerogative to decide for them.
3. *Consultative:* people, both men and women, are encouraged to contribute to organizational goals and tend to be taken seriously as responsible adults. Decision-making is centrally-held but people near the function involved are consulted, with their expertise valued and used, as feasible.
4. *Egalitarian:* Both women and men have more influence through the use of their competence and creativity since decision-making is widely diffused, more coordinated than controlled at the top.

The exploitative and paternalistic climates are created by men (virtually no women are in top positions) who hold certain assumptions about what people are like. In varying degrees, they see people as motivated by the paycheck, as "clock-watchers," as having little personal involvement in organizational goals, and as needing to be pushed and pulled to do their jobs. People are expected to be passive and do what they are told (McGregor, 1960). Obedience and deference to authority is expected rather than leadership or problem-solving abilities. (There are, of course, many degrees and variabilities within which these values are expressed from day-to-day, as we shall see.)

In the other direction, moving toward the consultative and egalitarian climates, the norm-setters tend to operate from another set of assumptions about people's motivations. They are more likely to assume that people are self-motivated in a supportive climate, that they have personal goals that enhance organizational goals, that capacities for problem-solving and decision-making are widespread, and that satisfaction gained from reaching personal and organizational goals is a major motivational factor (McGregor, 1960). Power relationships are less steeped in hierarchial structures, sex-role expectations and formal authority systems. Capabilities of people, both men and women, are a stronger norm for career advancement. Women often have more opportunities to use their talents, education, and experience in such organizations, although they are still sorely limited.

According to Likert, most large, work organizations operate at the middle of system 2 (Likert, undated). In his research, Likert (1967) uses a descriptive instrument on which supervisors and managers record their perceptions of organizational factors. A short version of this is shown on Table 12-I. On the left are listed some of the variables that describe a climate. The shaded area, at 2½ on the continuum, describes the climate in which most people work. In this climate, women have intensive mixed-messages about their worth and value, and only token evidence

ORGANIZATIONAL PROFILE*

Company _____ Div/Dept _____ Date _____

As perceived by _____ ☐ Male ☐ Female/Job Title _____

Organizational variables	SYSTEM 1	SYSTEM 2	SYSTEM 3	SYSTEM 4	Item no.
LEADERSHIP					
How much confidence and trust is shown in subordinates?	Virtually none	Some	Substantial amount	A great deal	1
How free do they feel to talk to superiors about job?	Not very free	Somewhat free	Quite free	Very free	2
How often are subordinate's ideas sought and use constructively?	Seldom	Sometimes	Often	Very frequently	3
MOTIVATION					
Is predominant use made of 1 fear, 2 threats, 3 punishment, 4 rewards, 5 involvement?	1,2,3, occasionally 4	4, some 3	4, some 3 and 5	5, 4, based on group	4
Where is responsibility felt for achieving organization's goals?	Mostly at top	Top and middle	Fairly general	At all levels	5
How much cooperative teamwork exists?	Very little	Relatively little	Moderate amount	Great deal	6
COMMUNICATION					
What is the usual direction of information flow?	Downward	Mostly downward	Down and up	Down, up, and sideways	7
How is downward communication accepted?	With suspicion	Possibly with suspicion	With caution	With a receptive mind	8
How accurate is upward communication?	Usually inaccurate	Often inaccurate	Often accurate	Almost always accurate	9
How well do superiors know problems faced by subordinates?	Not very well	Rather well	Quite well	Very well	10

CHART 12 - I (continued)

| | Mostly at top | Policy at top, some delegation | Broad policy at top, more delegation | Throughout but well integrated | 11 |

At what level are decisions made?

| | Almost never | Occasionally consulted | Generally consulted | Fully involved | 12 |

Are subordinates involved in decisions related to their work?

| | Not very much | Relatively little | Some contribution | Substantial contribution | 13 |

What does decision-making process contribute to motivation?

DECISIONS

| | Orders issued | Orders, some comments invited | After discussion, by orders | By group action (except in crisis) | 14 |

How are organizational goals established?

| | Strong resistance | Moderate resistance | Some resistance at times | Little or none | 15 |

How much covert resistance to goals is present?

GOALS

| | Very highly at top | Quite highly at top | Moderate delegation to lower levels | Widely shared | 16 |

How concentrated are review and control functions?

| | Yes | Usually | Sometimes | No – same goals as formal | 17 |

Is there an informal organization resisting the formal one?

| | Policing, punishment | Reward and punishment | Reward some self-guidance | Self-guidance, problem-solving | 18 |

What are cost, productivity, and other control data used for?

CONTROL

1. On each of the 18 scales, place a mark (x) somewhere along the scale which you feel best describes how things happen in your work-unit now. Then draw a vertical line joining your marks into a profile of your unit.
2. Repeat, this time placing your marks (o) on the scale where you would want it to be for you to feel most productive. Draw a second profile, joining these marks.

*From *The Human Organization: Its Management and Value* by Rensis Likert. Copyright 1967. New York: McGraw-Hill Book Co., Inc. Used with permission of McGraw-Hill Book Company and Rensis Likert.

that substantial career advancement is possible.

THE OVERT/COVERT POWER DYNAMICS
IN A PATERNALISTIC SYSTEM*

Benevolence characterizes this management stance, kindliness dispensed with an expectation that "what they're doing for women" should be appreciated. If a woman does not feel grateful for gains she makes, many such managers may feel she "expects too much." Even though she receives less for her efforts than a man would, her complaints are often discounted with "We're doing all we can. You can't expect it to happen overnight." Inequality is glossed over.

Appropriate behavior in subordinates, especially women, is one of deference. This is consistent with the social stance generally practiced between men and women. Many male managers dislike working women who do not relate to them that way (Bass, Krussel & Alexander, 1971). Bass points out that male managers, in the main, have not had experience with women as *equals,* and until they do they are likely to continue to relate to women as inferiors and expect deference.

In addition to the traditional sex-role orientation held by many, if not most men, the organization and its managers and supervisors are now under pressure of threatened legal action from the government and sometimes from internal women's groups to comply with the law requiring nondifferential treatment for women. These pressures increase women's leverage in the organization's power system.

Pressures to change the *status quo* result in double messages: Overtly, we say we are good citizens who are democratic and want all our employees to have equal opportunities (those who are qualified, that is), but covertly we know that women, by nature, can't really handle a "man's job" (and therefore aren't qualified). Management's "giving in," complying, takes some power-over-others out of the hands of management. While the official stance has to be one of compliance, the resistance to distributing power invites lip service only, and thus, double messages. In such a climate, it is difficult to get a straight story since management may fear pressure which may show that their actions do not match their words. Their fear motivates the exercise of covert power based on sex (and race).

In Table 12-II the zig-zag line at the left is a profile of a double-message climate. For example, achievement of organizational goals is seen here as fairly widespread (item 5), but problems involved in reaching those goals are not recognized by upper-level people (item 10). In other

---

*Adapted from Wells, 1973.

CHART 12 - II

THE ORGANIZATIONAL CLIMATE*

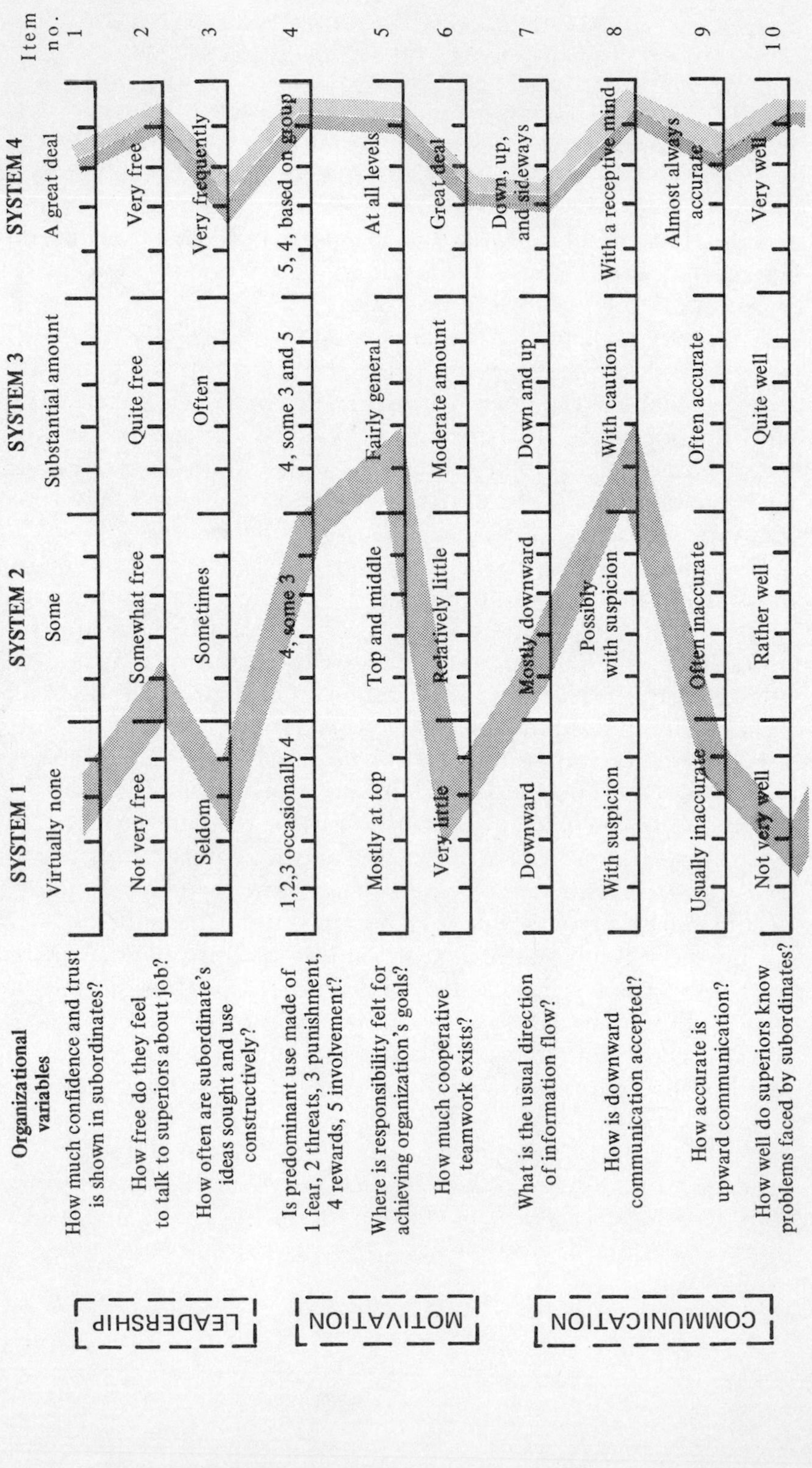

Organizational variables	SYSTEM 1	SYSTEM 2	SYSTEM 3	SYSTEM 4	Item no.
How much confidence and trust is shown in subordinates?	Virtually none	Some	Substantial amount	A great deal	1
How free do they feel to talk to superiors about job?	Not very free	Somewhat free	Quite free	Very free	2
How often are subordinate's ideas sought and use constructively?	Seldom	Sometimes	Often	Very frequently	3
Is predominant use made of 1 fear, 2 threats, 3 punishment, 4 rewards, 5 involvement?	1,2,3 occasionally 4	4, some 3	4, some 3 and 5	5, 4, based on group	4
Where is responsibility felt for achieving organization's goals?	Mostly at top	Top and middle	Fairly general	At all levels	5
How much cooperative teamwork exists?	Very little	Relatively little	Moderate amount	Great deal	6
What is the usual direction of information flow?	Downward	Mostly downward	Down and up	Down, up, and sideways	7
How is downward communication accepted?	With suspicion	Possibly with suspicion	With caution	With a receptive mind	8
How accurate is upward communication?	Usually inaccurate	Often inaccurate	Often accurate	Almost always accurate	9
How well do superiors know problems faced by subordinates?	Not very well	Rather well	Quite well	Very well	10

LEADERSHIP

MOTIVATION

COMMUNICATION

CHART 12 - II (continued)

DECISIONS	At what level are decisions made?	Mostly at top	Policy at top, some delegation	Broad policy at top, more delegation	Throughout but well integrated	11
	Are subordinates involved in decisions related to their work?	Almost never	Occasionally consulted	Generally consulted	Fully involved	12
	What does decision-making process contribute to motivation?	Not very much	Relatively little	Some contribution	Substantial contribution	13
GOALS	How are organizational goals established?	Orders issued	Orders, some comments invited	After discussion, by orders	By group action (except in crisis)	14
	How much covert resistance to goals is present?	Strong resistance	Moderate resistance	Some resistance at times	Little or none	15
CONTROL	How concentrated are review and control functions?	Very highly at top	Quite highly at top	Moderate delegation to lower levels	Widely shared	16
	Is there an informal organization resisting the formal one?	Yes	Usually	Sometimes	No – same goals as formal	17
	What are cost, productivity, and other control data used for?	Policing, punishment	Reward and punishment	Reward some self-guidance	Self-guidance, problem-solving	18

How I see it now

What I think would be most productive

*Courtesy of Rensis Likert and McGraw-Hill, Publisher.

words, "I'm held responsible, but do I get the needed backup to be able to perform well?" "Catch 22" situations are not uncommon in such climates. The profile to the right describes a common view of the type of climate in which people would feel most productive. Consistently, the more participative system is seen as more conducive to higher productivity.*

In the paternalistic system 2, the purpose is to *appear* to be complying with expected change while redistributing minimum power — a double message. Surface arrangements and overt messages are constructed in such a way that management is able to deny credibly that any covert discrimination is occurring. For example, management announces that change is occurring, points to the token woman executive just appointed and does little to change the work-roles of women down the line. No real change is made to get more women into more kinds of positions that lead upward. Superficial arrangements are made to look like there is equality and to establish credibility but not commitment. Then managers claim to be innocent of discrimination against women, effectively denying any covert inactivity which, in the above example, is inaction at the lower levels preparatory to women's advancement. Some even believe in their own innocence, which makes it more difficult to uncover duplicity.

Women who raise questions are assumed to be unreasonable, hypersensitive or unduly suspicious. They must take an aggressive position just to raise questions. These questions challenging authority are visible, conscious and intentional. Especially in the paternalistic climate, this is "not done." If it is, a manager's surface response is often kindly tolerance while the covert motive tightens toward punishment for misbehavior. They can point to their surface credibility to "prove" innocence; the woman usually has no overt "proof" and is thus placed in an off-balance, defensive position. She may already feel defensive because the system sends powerful subtle messages that she is worth less than men, so this can increase those factors which further lessen her credibility.

Double messages are the common methods of maintaining covert power. The more important the hidden message, or the greater the risks if exposure is achieved, the more elaborate is the system of smoke screens. If the maintenance of this power for Mr. Authority is important for either his self-concept or his position within the male power relationships or both, his motive to maintain covertness is strong. As long as he can convince women subordinates that his overt messages are true, that the covert situation is unlikely or nonexistent, or that there is nothing she can do anyway, her inaction or lack of success becomes silent assent.

---

*I often use the short form of this instrument in my work with women aspiring to managerial positions. This "ideal" view is very similar to Likert's findings, his subjects being mostly male supervisors and managers. It appears to be a nonsex-linked direction.

Many women may doubt their own perceptions since they are hard to prove. Many have long since learned, through deference, that "maybe the man is right;" such women do not trust their own perceptions and feelings fully. Even if they do trust their own judgment, the options for handling covert situations appear nonexistent, leaving a helpless feeling. Women typically have been socialized to compete against women for the attention of men, therefore, the option of getting together for action does not occur to many. If it does, they may feel uncomfortable, inappropriate or "unladylike." This subordinate socialization is very useful to the men in maintaining power over them.

Covert power can be used over women only as long as:

1. The authority person(s) have the cooperation of women, either through fear or deference;
2. The authority's credibility is not undermined by a woman questioner(s) who succeeds in sufficiently disturbing the surface appearances or shaking his credibility and exposing the genuine possibility of covert motives or activity;
3. Women do not have sufficient counterpower and visibility to reveal the covert discrimination without losing their credibility.

It is a battle for credibility with the odds favoring the man, since the organization tends to give him greater support by virtue of his sex and position (Rosen & Jerdee, 1974). This is further reenforced by the masculine identity many men get from their occupational roles played out in a competitive, win-lose climate. For some men, to "lose to a woman" is to "lose as a man." Castrated. When their male identity, genitally located, is at stake, many men will use their "natural" aggressiveness to "preserve their manhood." They can count on considerable support from other men with similar motives. This sex-identity energy powers the "male backlash" against women's efforts to gain equal access to advancement. Promotion represents masculine power to such men. As more women compete successfully on *objective* performance criteria, more men feel "the squeeze" on *subjective* masculine-identity criteria (Gallese, 1974).

Implications for the Therapist

What has this to do with you, the therapist? If you are a man, to what degree do some of these factors operate within you which can affect your perceptions of your career woman client? Her credibility is often what she is dealing with. Your perception of her credibility is often what you are making internal judgments about. Many women have been put in mental institutions because the credibility based on her reality of dealing with the covert messages did not match the therapist's reality of giving credibility to her overt messages.

When male values are the norm, messages sent by males have more credibility than those perceived by women. When males see themselves as the knowledgeable definers of women, they may have an investment in defining "how it *really* is." Done with a scientific aura of "professional judgment," considerable violation can be done to the woman who needs to step out of the female role to use her capabilities. If her male management tells her that her capabilities are wanted, yet feels threatened when she uses her skills well, they may be tempted to conclude that *she* has a personal problem. In fact, she faces an *inter*personal and *inter*organizational conflict which arises out of others' needs for her to be less capable.

Female therapists themselves may be in a double-bind, depending on conflicts between their socialization as women and the male-role values they have absorbed in professional training. To personally "make it" in a so-called male field has its own satisfactions stemming from acceptance as a professional, possibly a sense of being different from other women, possibly the power of successful achievement. Many subtle internal cross-currents can affect one's perception of the career woman's credibility. Even though female therapists may share some of the problems clients are dealing with. Therapists may not understand them if they feel they have not been discriminated against. It may be tempting to advise a female client, "If you just work as hard as I did, you can make it too. It is simply a matter of excellence, not favors" (Staines et al., 1974).

Male or female, the socialization process in each of us usually affects our perceptions of others. If we do not try to understand the subtleties in ourselves, it is possible to psychologically maim a woman just at the delicate, vulnerable stage of her growth toward becoming a more fully functioning person. If her frustration, her anger, her suspiciousness does not seem credible to therapists because they do not understand that she is responding to covert realities in her work life (or home life), it is possible to diagnose her urge toward growth as a dysfunctional abnormality. To me, the implications are frightening. And this is the last thing most professionals I know would want to perpetrate; it violates their values also.

Creating a Therapeutic Experience with the Career Woman Client*

How can the well-intentioned therapist avoid some of these traps? I would like to offer a number of ideas, concepts and values which, in combination, seem to me to provide a professional climate within which

---

*I am indebted to my feminist psychology colleagues for the codevelopment of many aspects of this section, especially Dr. Hannah Lerman (1974).

to serve the interests of the career woman client and the values of the conscientious professional. This list is in no way exhaustive, but these are some beginning indicators to which you, the therapist reader, may have many additional contributions. The therapist should show:

1. Willingness to relate to the career woman client (or any woman) as a credible, responsible adult.

2. Willingness to assume that she comes with a healthy urge for growth, rather than because she is "sick." Therapy goals should include acceptance and work on skills in perceiving and handling her ambitious, multiple-life situations.

3. Willingness to consider the possibilities that what she may have learned as a result of female socialization may be a vital area for "un-learning." Often this might be the goal of therapy, since the well-played female role fits certain diagnostic categories of mental illness, for example, hysterical personality.

4. Willingness to deeply listen, letting go of the "self-listening" typical of the male socialization. "Self-listening" involves listening to the first part of the client's presentation, preguessing the conclusion, then shifting to an internal dialogue of analysis, diagnosis and definition, so that when the client has finished, you have an interpretation ready. This is one version of the adversary, debate mode of thinking which many men learn in their competitive socialization (Farrell, 1974). Therapists should abandon this method.

5. Willingness to honor the client's life realities as valid as she sees them, trusting in her ability to sort out her own distortions as her thinking unfolds in a validating climate with you.

6. Willingness to provide that validating climate by examining and taking responsibility for your own ideas and values, including those which carry shades of sexist double standards. Being open, cleanly honest with the client about these subtle biases can be an avenue to contributing to mutual validation of different perceptions.

7. Willingness to see the client as a person trying to gain more power and control over herself and her interpersonal effectiveness, and a willingness to consider this appropriate for her as a person who is a woman. This is a growth orientation which the client may not yet have defined for herself. It is a direction *toward* a goal of her own, a direction *away* from an unwanted, confining goal that others have for her. Many women have learned that they should please others at any price, even if their personal goals (which they are not expected to have) take second place.

8. Willingness to see her as an individual coping with social and organizational contexts which often do, in fact, devalue her achievement and power needs. Also, a willingness to consider these needs as appro-

priate for a woman.

9. Willingness to provide a climate that does not encourage dependency. A careful look at one's beliefs in the transference process may be vital here. The manner in which transference dynamics are used can, in effect, generate considerable dependency which must then be overcome. It can be a subtle power-play that works against the objectives of the client, rather than with them. To automatically assume that dependency is an essential part of the therapeutic process contributes to unintentional violation of the client.

10. Willingness to take control of one's own power needs, including sexual fantasies, particularly in reference to male/female role expectations. If a male therapist conducts his therapy according to traditional role patterns, it may be difficult for him to see his own desire for the woman client to *need* his guidance. The therapeutic objectives, I feel, are ideally centered in helping the client help herself.

11. Willingness to support *her* choices for self-direction, even when these are at variance with one's own values or opinions. If she does not feel ready to make such choices or, as often happens, does not know how, a clear negotiation of the therapeutic goals is essential. The therapist's role might well be one of helping her learn how to generate options, how to assess them for her own benefit, and how to make choices that lead to her own self-enhancement.

12. Willingness to support the client's efforts at reclaiming those parts of her identity that she has learned to place in others, especially men, including aspects of her self-esteem, her personal strengths, goals, and desires. The therapist who triggers self-doubt because of role conflicts set up for career women by our society, simply contributes to the woman's subordinate socialization and impedes her growth as a person.

13. Willingness to consider wife and mother relationships as factors in the client's life to be balanced with work relationships. This is substantially different from roles which define a person. Instead, these are relationships among many which she, as a separate individual, seeks to balance in a way that meets her needs and ambitions in satisfying ways. Few people gain a sense of personal fulfillment by serving others' needs at the expense of their own. While many people, such as therapists, gain a sense of self-fulfillment through serving others, these same people may not realize that the female socialization process often insists on the requirement of serving others "at the expense of one's own needs."

14. The therapist's willingness to tell the client if and when she/he may not be of help because there is too great a gap in her/his own values and the client's to relate to her *without putting her down*. In our society where maleness is more valued than femaleness, the put-down is pervasive in the life experiences of most women. Many are not conscious of

this pervasiveness because it is so common. Having a put-down come from a socially sanctioned professional could reactivate past messages of worthlessness.

15. Willingness to abdicate the authority role, seeking to relate on a person-to-person basis. This lets the client practice relating to an authority, the therapist, who has licensed power, expert knowledge and experience. Many women (and men, too) have difficulty relating to authority persons without abdicating some of themselves. A career woman, to achieve her personal goals, must learn to "own" herself when dealing with male authority persons, especially in the conflict situations when she steps out of her subordinate role.

16. Willingness to negotiate the therapeutic contract in terms of goals, content, method and time. The *location of control* should remain in the hands of the client as part of the therapeutic process. If she vacillates in her ability or willingness to do this, this may be due to her uneven attempts to learn how to claim her right to make these decisions for herself. Most women have received repetitive messages by the waterdrop method that they are incapable of decision-making, or if they *are* capable of it there is something wrong with them. Validation of the client's right to function as a self-defining person is central to her growth.

17. Willingness to analyze the various aspects of the female and male role expectations to see the qualities as a cluster of socially defined expectations which contain variously valuable human traits which can be available to all human beings regardless of their anatomy. By differentiating the role from the person, we find that the role is not the person and the person is not the role. Only then can people make guilt-free choices among *all* the ways of being human and among all the strengths available for handling situations in self-enhancing ways. With these larger bases for personal identity, the traditional battle-of-the-sexes arranged by role expectations can go down the tubes. Instead, we can anticipate collaborative win-win relationships between men and women, *between men and men, between women and women.*

18. Willingness to entertain the idea that whatever the client is feeling at any time is OK for her to be feeling. Concurrently, the therapist should show willingness to trust that when she is uncomfortable enough with what she is feeling, she will select some alternative feelings that better serve her needs. This has far-reaching implications. It means that no feelings are good or bad, right or wrong, healthy or sick, positive or negative, rational or irrational. It means that *all* feelings are OK to have, that none are x-rated.

The context determines the appropriateness of *expression* of feelings, *not* the appropriateness of feelings themselves. This means that the therapist may be faced with feelings that she/he has long learned to consider as negative. Anger is a good example. Normal, healthy anger at being personally violated is rarely separated from the general evaluation that anger is negative. Many people have acquired quite a backlog of repressed anger in trying to become "mature persons in control of their emotions." It is the *backlog* of anger that can be destructive in human relationships or within one's self, not the anger itself. When that backlog is reduced and legitimacy accorded to *anger for* the right to self-dignity, then anger can be a vital energy which enhances self-worth and the work of others while not allowing interpersonal violation.

19. Willingness to examine the sources of one's own personal identity for whatever contribution it may make in helping or hindering the client's growth process. For example, many men fear the expression of *anger for* in women since it means that they will not be under the man's control. The fear is "If I can't control my woman, what kind of a man am I?" Those men who find substantial sources of personal identity in the male role are likely to find this fear within themselves. Until such men take responsibility for finding more valid bases for personal identity, they will continue to contribute to the denigration of women and, in the process, of themselves. If this fear unconsciously influences the relationship with a woman client, therapy will not be therapeutic for the client.

20. Willingness to think in terms of a partnership-in-growth between relative equals (not the authoritarian model of doctor/patient). Central themes of therapy for women with high achievement and/or power needs should include work on problem-solving skills and a self-chosen personal identity. These are among the energies needed to move up an organizational ladder.

A Method for Checking Out One's Self

The implications of the above suggestions are many and pervasive. They reach into the depths of personal philosophy, personal identity, and personal self-worth. If a contest emerges between therapist and woman client, if win-lose values become operational, the client is set up to lose. This is not therapeutic for her.

How is a therapist to know whether or not he or she is a nonconscious participant in a subtle contest? There are no simple answers. A continuing self-search and self-sensing is essential. However, one of the most powerful ways to get some quick clues to possible differential valuing of women and men with similar life goals is to imagine the woman client is a man. This helps reveal sex-linked views which are often obscured by "objective criteria."

If you would like to try one small check-out of yourself, let's go back to your office again. Your next client has arrived. He is Dan Caldwell keeping his first appointment which he made five days ago. He is reasonably good-looking, dressed somewhat conservatively, casually groomed. He appears calm on the surface but smiles nervously and does not seem fully at ease. "Fairly common behavior for a first visit," you think. And from here the scene opens. . . .

You: (Giving full attention) What seems to be the situation, Dan?

Dan: (Talking fast in reporting tone) I'm feeling frustrated as hell. I've been working long and hard to be promoted to the project manager on one of our contracts. Five days ago when I called you, a *woman* was promoted who has less education, less experience and who's always picking my brains. *(Getting excited, defensive)* She got the job because she's a *woman*, goddammit. And *that* I know because a friend of mine in Personnel told me it was an affirmative action deal. *(More objectively)* My work has been first-rate, I just saved 'em a pile of money on another project, and I took the management training they said I had to have. *(Complaining indignantly)* But it doesn't do any good. You gotta be black or female these days to get anywhere. Do you know what my boss said to me when I asked him why he picked Jane?

You: (In a neutral tone) You confronted your boss then?

Dan: (Assertively) You bet I did. That promotion meant a lot to me. And you know what he said? He says, "I know you've worked hard for that promotion but try to understand that we gotta have someone to keep us out of trouble with the government. At least Jane's qualified and can probably cut it OK." He tells me, "It's a worse risk right now to be hit up for so-called discrimination than to be a little late on the delivery date."

Then he had the gall to say, *(mockingly)* "Now I want you to bury the hatchet and get in there and help Jane — you know, really support the team effort. And I can promise you when the next chance comes along, you'll have first crack at it."

(Angrily sarcastic) Now how's *that* for a first-rate fuckover. Earn the next promotion by "understanding yourself out" of this one. Be a nice guy. I don't get the job because *women* got a problem. I don't have anything to do with *that*. Talk about *reverse* discrimination! Never mind education, experience and performance. I'm dead-ended by some *broad*. There's *gotta* be a way around it. It's so damn frustrating. You gotta help me figure out what to do. . . .

You: (Write down responses you think you would probably make. No fair referring back to the beginning of the chapter! Make notes on your tentative reactions to Dan and his situation and some notes on what lines you may follow with Dan.)

Now let us assume that you acquire the following historical and background information during the next several sessions with Dan.

Age: Thirty-six

Marital Status: Married, two children, girl thirteen, boy eleven.

Wife's Views: She is a skilled technician earning about $15 thousand a year. She thinks that Dan should be around home more with the children. She does not approve of his ambitiousness and wants him to share in the responsibilities around the house. She does not like having a live-in companion-sitter for the children and would like to trade off working and staying home. She earns enough, she feels, for that to be a viable option.

Children's Views: They seem to get along well with Dan. They sometimes complain that he is gone too much and does not do enough with them. They say they are too old to have the sitter there and wish Dan would be home enough so they would not have to have her.

Marital Relations: Dan is not well-satisfied sexually. Relations are too infrequent, the last time being about three weeks ago. Work and the children seem to get in the way, resulting in feeling "too tired" or "not in the mood." It's becoming a problem. Otherwise the relationship seems generally adequate but with continual low-key tension typical of two-career families.

Work History: Employed twelve years with breaks for military service, two years the first time in Vietnam, three months the second time for reserve duty. Started as a computer programmer working on special projects requiring design innovation. Three promotions and regular salary increases. Dan's focus has been on professional/technical excellence and he also has some assistant team-leader experience. He earns about $18 thousand a year.

Education: M.S. in Mathematics. Extension courses in computer sciences. Company courses in management development. Willing to study whatever it takes to get ahead in his profession.

Medical/Therapy History: Takes little or no medication. This is his first individual experience with therapy but has been in some group experiences about which he has mixed feelings. He felt confronted about some of his defenses and was told he intellectualized too much.

Given this history so far, take a few minutes to note down your responses to the following questions.

What objectives do you feel are important for you and Dan to work on? (Consider all aspects of his life, his view of it, your view of it, etc.) In what ways do your views differ from his? What seems the best way to work on resolving Dan's job situation? How does this compare with your earlier notes (before you had his history) on what lines you will follow next?

Now that you have made your notes, check back to the beginning of the chapter and make your comparisons. As you note any differences between your notes about Ann and Dan, try to identify what assumptions or expectations you had made about Ann in her job situation and about Dan in his. Are the differences linked with your views of sex roles? Are they linked with behaviors or expectations that you might consider reasonable for a woman or a man to have toward their jobs?

What about possible differences in how you viewed the spouse's views, the children's views, the limited sexual satisfactions? What hypotheses do you have that you might pursue? Have you made any assumptions as to the ethnic background of either Ann or Dan? No information has been given about that. Do you mentally picture them as being of similar color or background as yourself?

You may find that you have had some different expectations and chosen some different directions for how you work with Ann or Dan. If this happened with you, you now have clues pointing to certain areas that could affect the quality of your listening to the client. The differences contribute to the selective listening resulting from our internal filter systems created by values and beliefs.

In my opinion, it is reasonable to expect that one would have differential perceptions in a society so heavily constructed along sex definitions. Few, if any, escape it. It is the nonconscious nature of it, the "doesn't everybody" syndrome of conventional wisdom which makes it difficult to perceive how sex-role values operate in one's self. Such views are difficult to "own" as part of one's self-concept. Without question, this is an uncomfortable process, especially if you share with me my view of myself as objective, humanistic, open-minded . . . all those good things. As much as I have worked with my own socialization on my road to becoming a person, I still find more subtle layers to unpeel. Worse, I still find some of the layers which I thought had been laid to rest cropping up when I am not looking, still needing to be consciously dealt with one more time.

On the other hand, I find that this never-ending process, sometimes painful but always rich, helps me become more internally centered in my self-integrity and externally authentic in my personal and professional relationships. I feel centered in myself, and centered in consciously chosen values which I can openly share. Others can reject me for my values yet I can still honor them in myself. *My values are me.* As I evolve my own self-definition, I find others accepting me on my terms. They seem to sense that I know who I am, that I am someone with whom they can interact.

When I do not allow me to violate myself, I find it easier to not allow others to violate me. In some circuitous way, others seem to value me and themselves while honoring our differences. When these differences are too great for comfort, we can accept going our separate ways while still respecting each other as persons. Agreement is not necessary; acceptance of our differences is.

I invite you to consider the many options and values which will contribute in some way to your learning and continued development. I have not found any magic pills around, although I have found many people looking for them. For me, the continuing dialogue, the searching exchange, the sense of communion which reveres *all* of life's energies, not only the sexual, can keep us connected along our mutual though separate paths toward our larger, multiple selves. As we move ahead in this wider sense of being human, we will be in a position to help others honor their own human needs, create supportive environments, and to respect the needs of others.

REFERENCES

Alper, Thelma G.: Achievement motivation in college women: A now-you-see-it-now-you-don't phenomenon. *American Psychologist, 29*:194, 1974.

Bass, Bernard M., Krusell, Judith, and Alexander, Ralph A.: Male managers' attitudes toward working women. *American Behavioral Scientist, 15*:221, 1971.

Broverman, Inge K., Broverman, Donald M., Clarkson, Frank E., Rosenkrantz, Paul S., and Vogel, Susan R.: Sex role stereotypes and clinical judgements of mental health. *Journal of Consulting and Clinical Psychology, 34*:1, 1970.

Chesler, Phyllis: *Woman & Madness.* Garden City, Doubleday, 1972, p. 256.

Farrell, Warren: *The Liberated Man, Beyond Masculinity: Freeing Men and Their Relationships with Women.* New York, Random House, 1974.

Gallese, Liz Roman: Up-the-ladder blues, white males complain they are now victims of job discrimination. *Wall Street Journal, 183*:1, 1974.

Horner, Matina: Femininity and successful achievement: A basic inconsistency. In Bardwick, Judith M., Douvan, E., Horner, Matina S., and Gutman, D. (Eds.): *Feminine Personality and Conflict.* Belmont, Brooks/Cole, 1970.

Lerman, Hannah: What happens in feminist therapy? Paper presented in symposium, *Feminist Therapy: In Search of a Theory,* American Psychological Association, New Orleans, 1974.

Likert, Rensis: *The Human Organization: Its Management and Value.* New York, McGraw-Hill, 1967.

Likert, Rensis: A conversation with Rensis Likert. *Organization Dynamics.* New York, AMACOM, undated booklet.

Loring, Rosalind and Wells, Theodora: *Breakthrough: Women into Management.* New York, Van Nostrand Reinhold, 1972.

Marmor, Judd: Changing patterns of femininity: psychoanalytic implications. In Rosenbaum, Salo and Alger, Ian (Eds.): *The Marriage Relationship.* New York, Basic Books, © 1968 by Society of Medical Psychoanalysts.

McGregor, Douglas: *The Human Side of Enterprise.* New York, McGraw-Hill, 1960.

Miller, Jean Baker and Mothner, Ira: Psychological consequences of sexual inequality. *American Journal of Orthopsychiatry, 41*:767, 1971.

Rosen, Benson and Jerdee, Thomas H.: Sex stereotyping in the executive suite. *Harvard Business Review, 52*:45, 1974.

Rosenkrantz, Paul S., Vogel, Susan R., Bee, Helen, Broverman, Inge K., and Broverman, Donald M.: Sex-role stereotypes and self-concepts in college students. *Journal of Consulting and Clinical Psychology, 32*:287, 1968.

Staines, Graham, Tavris, Carol, and Jayaratne, Toby Epstein: The queen bee syndrome. *Psychology Today, 1*:55, 1974.

Warmouth, Arthur and McWaters, Barry: *The Art and Science of Psychology: Humanistic Perspectives.* Monterey, Brooks/Cole, in press.

Wells, Theodora: The covert power of gender in organizations. *Journal of Contemporary Business, 2*:53, 1973.

Section VI

PSYCHOTHERAPY FOR LESBIANS

INTRODUCTION

THE two authors in this section write with the authority of self-identified lesbians. In addition, both have extensive practical experience in the mental health field. Escamilla-Mondanaro is a physician affiliated with the California School of Professional Psychology and medical director of the Adolescent and Young Adult Alcohol Program in San Francisco. Sang is a psychotherapist in private practice in New York City and is affiliated with the Homosexual Community Center of New York City. Neither paper is concerned with specific therapy techniques but rather provides consciousness-raising material designed to aid psychotherapists' understanding of the needs of lesbian women who seek psychotherapy. Both Escamilla-Mondanaro and Sang document common problems lesbian women bring to therapy which are related to their minority status. That the authors independently arrive at many of the same conclusions strengthens the validity of their observations and fills a significant gap in the psychotherapy literature of the treatment of women.

While neither author categorically rules out "straight therapists" doing therapy with lesbians, both agree that few "straight therapists" are qualified for the task. Mere acceptance or tolerance of alternative life-styles is insufficient to qualify therapists to work with lesbians. Therapists need to be knowledgeable concerning the lesbian subculture, the societal pressures lesbians face and the political significance of lesbianism. Even when "straight therapists" meet these qualifications, Sang points out that a lesbian therapist has the added advantage of serving as a role model to counteract negative self-images internalized by most lesbians. Each author has a unique viewpoint and emphasis which highlight the issues in different ways so that reading both papers enhances the reader's understanding of the issues more completely than would reading either paper alone.

In "Lesbians in Therapy," Josette Escamilla-Mondanaro contends that the conflicts that bring lesbians to therapy are generated by the pressures of being a lesbian in a heterosexual society rather than by their sexual relationships. Women must choose between societal abuse if they live openly as lesbians and the self-alienating experience of living a lie. Psychotherapists who want to understand lesbians must recognize that lesbianism is more than an alternate life style: *it is a political statement by women that they are defining themselves independently of men.*

Escamilla-Mondanaro believes that at the present time only lesbian therapists are qualified to treat other lesbians. The training received by psychotherapists has not prepared them to work with lesbians. She feels that lesbians are justified in their distrust of straight therapists because, at best, so-called liberal therapists profess tolerance of alternate life-styles but are unaware and insensitive to the struggles lesbians constantly face in society and to the political significance of lesbianism. At worst, unenlightened therapists view lesbians as "sick" persons who need to be cured.

The professional literature does not give an accurate picture of lesbians. The information about lesbians is either extrapolated from studies of male homosexuals or based on clinical studies of lesbians in psychotherapy. Therapists who want to be effective with lesbians must be willing to replace their ignorance and defensiveness with a desire to investigate the whole issue of lesbianism. The numerous myths surrounding lesbianism which must be confronted and destroyed include: (1) defining sexuality as reproduction rather than the expression of self and loving feelings; (2) defining women by their relationship to men and by what they do in bed; (3) defining lesbians as sick; and (4) defining lesbianism as the symptom of a sick society.

Escamilla-Mondararo discusses specific groups of lesbians which require special attention from therapists. These groups are adolescents, lesbian mothers, and lesbian couples (or families). An adolescent's lesbian desires are often dismissed by therapists as fantasies or merely a "stage" of development. Adolescents need validation of their feelings and a safe supportive environment in which to discuss these feelings, for example, at teenage rap groups sponsored by the feminist or lesbian community. Lesbian mothers are automatically considered unfit by the courts; these women need advocates from the mental health profession to support their rights to raise their children. Lesbian couples, like heterosexual couples, sometimes need couple therapy to help stabilize long-term relationships.

Sang's paper, "Psychotherapy with Lesbians: Some Observations and Tentative Generalizations," consists of selected observations based on eighty lesbian women seen by Sang in psychotherapy, either through the Homosexual Community Center in New York City or as private referrals. Her sample is not a representative group of homosexuals in general nor like those which have been studied by researchers.

Among the problems lesbians bring to therapy, Sang identifies the following eight areas which are consequences of having a minority-group status:

1. Lesbians who have been in a long-term relationship may not have

associated with other homosexual persons for fear of being labeled *gay*. When their relationship breaks up, they find themselves socially isolated.

2. A few women are confused about their sexual orientation.

3. Some women are afraid of their homosexual feelings and need someone with whom to "share their secret."

4. Some lesbian women who feel competent in many areas of their lives are often awkward and unsure of themselves in personal relationships because of having had few opportunities for early social and emotional experiences.

5. Some lesbian women make premature commitments to relationships because of having limited opportunities for experience with other lesbians.

6. Women may have unresolved guilt feelings about sex as a consequence of being punished for lesbian relationships in their teens.

7. Lesbians often fear losing their partners to a heterosexual relationship. Lesbians are more vulnerable than heterosexual women to rejection because of the limited number of available partners.

8. Lesbian women who feel they must hide their feelings because they fear societal reactions have difficulty being open and spontaneous.

Sang shares the impression of other investigators that many lesbians seek therapy. She points out three reasons why this happens:

1. People who are "different" may spend considerable time reflecting on their differences and, consequently, become more aware of other aspects of themselves they want to work on or change.

2. There are many social pressures on lesbians and few safety valves; thus, therapy may be the only place where they can share their problems.

3. Lesbians may need someone in authority to approve their sexual orientation. This need for validation should not be viewed negatively since the culture and psychotherapists sanction heterosexuality.

Sang believes that good therapy allows people to get in touch with their own feelings. Therapists who overtly or covertly disapprove of the lesbian client's sexual orientation will be destructive to her personal growth. Neither author views changing the sexual orientation of a lesbian to that of a heterosexual as a viable goal in therapy; such a therapeutic goal would reveal a bias against homosexuality.

Escamilla-Mondanaro contends that mental health institutions which profess to treat lesbians fairly must demonstrate good faith to the lesbian community by hiring lesbian therapists. In order that lesbian therapists be properly trained, academic departments should hire lesbian faculty.

Escamilla-Mondanaro, who identifies herself as a lesbian, concludes her paper by issuing a challenge to lesbian therapists to come out and risk societal reprisals in order to fight the oppression of lesbians.

—— *Chapter 13* ——

LESBIANS AND THERAPY

Josette Escamilla-Mondanaro

People fear most and understand least those human phenomenon in which they have little experience and no reliable knowledge to aid comprehension.

(Weltge, 1969)

THE validity of this statement is perhaps evidenced nowhere more clearly than in the issue of lesbianism. What scarce investigatory work one might find regarding homosexuality can usually be discounted on any one of several bases. First, research questions, summaries, and conclusions have, in the past, been based on this society's understanding and expectations of how people are supposed to function and adjust. Culturally prescribed sex role traits such as aggressiveness and independence for men, and passivity, dependence for women, have been viewed as innate, natural behavior. Heterosexuality has also been considered a natural absolute as opposed to a societal norm for which individuals in this society are trained and groomed. To this end, researchers have asked such biased questions as what goes wrong to cause homosexuality and what can be done to either prevent it or cure it (Weltge, 1969). Secondly, the questions have been stimulated by a small visible segment of the homosexual population. Often, information is gathered through therapists' files and/or interviews with individuals in a bar setting. These particular people may represent a group of individuals who have little to lose by disclosure of their homosexual identity. Thirdly, the main portion of written material regarding homosexuality actually deals with homosexual men and either entirely disregards lesbians, or erroneously extrapolates from the male data to include lesbians. The dearth of information regarding lesbians reflects, in part, this society's attitude of deeming women and their activities less valuable and thereby less worthy of investigation than men.

While there is a lack of unbiased information regarding lesbianism, there is no scarcity of ugly myths and cruel folklore. Even without reading the literature, people quickly assimilate this society's "line" on lesbians. Everyone believes that she or he knows what a lesbian is, and what detrimental home environment goes into the creation of a lesbian. In the fall of 1973, I taught a course entitled *Lesbianism* at San Francisco State University. Of the thirty women taking this course, by self-

256

definition, approximately one-third considered themselves lesbians, one-third believed that they were bisexual or uncommitted, and one-third stated they were "straight" (heterosexuals). In a very tedious and painful process, the women who identified themselves as heterosexual shared their "fantasies" concerning lesbianism. Lesbians were women who: were masculinized by some hormonal or anatomical deficiency; were ugly and therefore could not "get a man"; had been raped or brutalized by men and then rejected all men; were raised as boys by parents who really preferred boys. They believed that lesbians role-played, some (the majority) were "butch" and dressed up in men's clothing, and had very short hair cuts, that these women were attracted to feminine women who fit the sterotype of *woman* in this society. And last, the *masculine* woman was not a "real" woman, but the feminine woman who falls in love with the butch was a "real" woman.

The fallacious bases of these fantasies were slowly disclosed and dispelled through a continuous dialogue between the heterosexually identified women and the lesbians. What is really alarming is that the women who believe these fantasies were young women in their twenties living in San Francisco in 1973. This is a horrifying indication of the level of lesbian folklore permeating this society even at this date.

LIBERALISM IS NOT THE ANSWER

Historically, the church has considered homosexuals sinners, the law has termed particular homosexual activity as criminal, and the mental hygienists have viewed this behavior as deviant and pathological. As lesbians, we can find little comfort in the current liberal approach to homosexuality. The church has adopted a view that God loves all Her/His children, even the homosexuals. The liberal legal view sees society as sick and homosexuality as a symptom of this diseased political state. The understanding here is that if this society cleaned up its "act," people would not have to resort to homosexuality. This attitude ignores and discounts an individual's capacity to exercise personal preference. It also blatantly misses the political meaning behind women not supporting their oppressors, men, in this sexist society.

Mental hygienists appear to fall into two camps. One which states that if you cannot cure them, the least you can do is make them comfortable in their weird neurosis or sick behavior. The second group of therapists state and restate *ad nauseam,* "I don't care what you do in bed, that's your business." This last stance is particularly naive and potentially quite deleterious to the well-being of a client because it totally discounts her existence and her daily struggle in a society which constantly assumes she is heterosexual. This approach negates the price the individual must pay

when she is either open and subjecting herself to everyone's fantasy of
what it must mean to be a lesbian, or when she remains in the closet and
acts *as if* she were heterosexual. One therapist at the Center for Special
Problems, San Francisco, held this popular, *modern* therapeutic view
that it did not make any difference what her clients did in bed. During a
staff meeting where we were discussing the need to hire more lesbian
therapists, she proceeded to expose her true sentiments by stating that she
did not "want any bull dagger stomping around here." She said this
knowing that I am a lesbian, and at a center which proposes to be liberal
and accepting of individual choices of sexual life-style. It is rather apparent that the issues become more complex and subtle as *liberals* approach the topic of homosexuality from textbook absurdity and life-style
ignorance. We should not be overjoyed that any group of psychiatrists,
social workers, and psychologists have decided by *vote* that homosexuality is not necessarily pathological behavior. The absurdity of having to
lobby your local psychiatrist for a vote of sanity is quite apparent, not to
mention appalling. Lesbians, as well as other oppressed minorities, have
earned the right to distrust the keepers of mental health.

LESBIAN THERAPISTS

Any therapist, raised and trained in this society, who is not a lesbian
herself, is not equipped to work with lesbian clients in a therapeutic
setting. Even if a lesbian enters therapy for reasons other than her sexual
preference, she will be faced with the therapist's fears and fantasies of
lesbianism. Until *professionals* recognize that there is nothing in their
training which facilitates their working with lesbians, and as long as this
society discriminates against lesbians, lesbians should and will continue
to distrust "straight" mental health workers. Admitting ignorance and
replacing defensiveness with a willingness to explore the entire issue of
sexuality, are the first steps a heterosexual therapist must take if she
wants to work with lesbians.

BUT WE LEARNED ABOUT LESBIANS IN SCHOOL

At this time, many schools and clinics are including discussions of
sexuality in training programs. Unfortunately, most of these panel discussions turn the students or staff members into voyeurs observing the
freakish accounts of *other* individuals' sexuality. At Stanford Medical
School I was invited to speak about being a lesbian. I was on a panel
with one homosexual man, one prostitute and two couples who engaged
in swapping and swinging. A real voyeuristic orgy! I remember quite
painfully a similar situation where I was among the spectator audience in

a medical school sex education program. I prayed that someone would validate the existence of homosexuals and lesbians in our class instead of having us take notes with the implicit assumption that we were all heterosexuals. Now when I speak I demand that a heterosexual be included on the panel (and a celibate and bisexual, too!), and I attempt to include the audience in an exploration of their own sexuality.

Basic to discussions of sexuality are the issues of androgyny and sexism. A distinction must be made between *sexuality* as an extension of one's self, as an expression of warmth and closeness, as an intimate encounter, and *copulating* for reproduction. Indeed, it is the *natural order* of the human species for eggs and sperm to unite for reproduction. But one makes a rather long leap to say that the manner in which humans express warmth and closeness is also part of the *natural order*. As humans, we are obviously physiologically pansexual, capable of experiencing an entire spectrum of sexual feelings through masturbation, homosexuality, and heterosexuality. We are also capable of engaging in no sexual activity through celibacy. An individual may find any one or combination of these experiences *appropriate* for herself at any given time. As Kinsey wrote in 1953, "It is not so difficult to explain why a human animal does a particular thing sexually. It is more difficult to explain why each and every individual is not involved in every type of sexual activity" (Kinsey, Pomeroy, Martin, and Gebhard, 1953).

We must realize that the terms homosexuality and heterosexuality could only exist in a sexist society which judges the value and identity of a woman by what she does in bed. The difference between lesbians and "real" women is that "real" women are constantly subjected to the sexual advances of *men*. Once again, we are faced with women being defined by how they fit into the *male* view of the world.

Lesbianism is not a "bedroom issue." Recently magazines and television talk shows have attempted to titillate their audiences with glittery tales of jet set Hollywood bisexuality. Having a *physiological* capacity for ambisexuality and having sex with both men and women should not be confused with the political statement women are making when we consider ourselves lesbians. "The lesbian/feminist is the woman who defines herself independently of the man" (Johnston, 1973). To consider women worthy of our total emotional sexual commitments is to see ourselves as complete, whole individuals.

WHAT DO LESBIANS DO IN BED ANYWAY?

Equipped with a basic understanding of feminism, sexism, sex role stereotyping, and an exploration of her own sexuality, a therapist must then test her fantasies regarding lesbianism against reality. One of the finer research works published at this time studied the careers and life-styles of sixty-five lesbians in Philadelphia between 1964 and 1970 (Hedblom, 1972). According to this study: Lesbians demonstrate a high achievement pattern, sixty-four out of sixty-five respondents preferred stable relationships, 70 percent maintain a heterosexual front, 91 percent *never* sought therapy to be cured of their homosexuality, and 26 percent did seek out therapeutic assistance which did *not* pertain to their homosexuality. Smashing still another myth regarding lesbians, Hedblom (1972) found that 47 percent of these women played a passive but willing role and 53 percent played a dominant role during their *first* experience with another woman. The myth states that younger unsuspecting women are lured to the Isle of Lesbos by older more experienced women. This study demonstrates that "initial contacts are the result of a mutual willingness to explore homosexuality" (Hedblom, 1972). As for role playing (butch vs. *femme*), 18 percent of Hedblom's respondents considered themselves *femme*, while the majority played both roles interchangeably.

These responses appear to be dated, as women are finding it less meaningful to *role play*. Lesbians have, in the past, aped heterosexual society by dividing into polar opposites to justify attraction. With the support of feminism, we as women can see *role playing* as a hindrance to the expression and exploration of our total personalities.

Another study recently published found that:

> The majority of female homosexuals are mentally healthy and do not desire to be heterosexual. Female homosexuals have the same or lower incidence of psychiatric disturbances when compared to matched heterosexual controls. No significant difference in the prevalence of neurotic disorders exists between female homosexuals and heterosexuals ... It was found that lesbians do not have a higher incidence of depression, attempted suicide, or suicide such as was previously reported ... The results of the Adjective Check List tests in the study of lesbians ... revealed an overall normal pattern ... and found the only difference between female homosexuals and their respective controls was that the lesbian groups were "more self-confident" (Rosen, 1974).

SPECIAL GROUPS

A therapist should also acquaint herself with the attitudes and oppression of special groups such as the adolescent lesbian, the lesbian mother, and lesbian couples and families.

Adolescent Lesbians

Hedblom's (1972) study revealed that 14 percent of the respondents had their first homosexual physical experience before the age of ten, and 79 percent before the age of twenty. Twenty percent of the respondents had their first experience when they were between twenty and twenty-five years old. Adolescents who engage in exploration of homosexual feelings are oppressed on many levels. They are told that teenage homosexual fantasies and feelings are normal for their age, and that they will grow out of them. What an outrageous belief system to perpetuate when thousands upon thousands of adolescents do not grow out of these feelings, and, indeed, grow further into them. Teenagers are told that they will outgrow these feelings because they are *expected* to outgrow them to fit more easily into this society. Fear of society's punishment, fear of the stigmatized identity of *lesbian*, and fear of parental and peer rejection torture many adolescents.

Can you understand that the pain a woman experiences is not inherent in her lesbian relationship; the relationship itself is seen as beautiful and supportive. The sham, having to lie, the constant fear of disclosure followed by rejection, the alienation and feeling that no one understands comprise the source of pain. The teenager is truly alienated. She is torn between the myths society has taught her about lesbianism, and the reality of her own feelings and experiences. Older women have the *gay community*, dances and bars where they can begin to meet more women and discard societal myths. In her isolation and with the fragility of her adolescent self-identity, a younger woman experiences much anxiety. If therapists are not capable of working with lesbians, they are even less prepared to work with teenage lesbians.

Many teenagers are forced into *involuntary* therapy by their parents to be cured of their homosexuality. It is obvious that therapists are quite willing to undertake the responsibility for this ludicrous task.

The director of an adolescent clinic in San Francisco was asked about his approach to adolescent homosexuality. His answer, loud and clear, was, "Set them straight!" At another center which supposedly specialized in troubled adolescents, a young woman client spoke about her love for another woman. The staff psychiatrist and psychologists (all male) decided that this relationship was only fantasy and that the staff members should ignore her discussions and questions about homosexuality. Months later when they were informed by a woman on the staff that this teenager did have a sexual relationship with another woman, the psychiatrist then said that she should be encouraged to be heterosexual since she would incur much hostility and disapproval as a lesbian. These situations occurred in 1974.

Some therapists have explained to their teenage clients that homosexuality is not *bad* but that they should continue therapy to appease their parents. This collusion between the therapist and client not only brings a financial reward to the therapist, but continues to burden the already confused teenager with double messages.

Being aware of these traps, validating the individual's experience, and creating a safe place for teenagers to discuss their feelings will all help alleviate much anxiety. If you believe that people should not be lesbians because they would then have to incur society's wrath, you can begin by changing your own attitudes and not the teenager's. Gay and women's liberation have set up teen rap groups throughout the country. This type of consciousness raising for young women is valuable therapy. Therapists should be prepared to refer teenagers to such groups, and to suggest reading some of the newer books written by and for lesbians.

Lesbian Mothers

Lesbian mothers represent still another oppressed group. A common misconception concerning lesbians is that they are women who do not care to have children. Actually, one third of the members of the Daughters of Bilitis do have children (Abbott and Love, 1972). Debate is now being waged in the courts as to the fitness of a lesbian to be a parent. In Seattle, Sandy and Madeline won custody of their children, but were forced to establish separate residences. In Santa Cruz a lesbian maintained custody of her children only under the condition that her lover did not live there. Obviously, the courts have taken it upon themselves to decide, without evidence, that homosexuality is deleterious to children. One can not help but wonder when the atrocities against lesbians in this society will stop. Sandy and Madeline wrote a pamphlet, *Love Is for All* (Schuster, 1974), and produced a movie, *Sandy and Madeline's Family*, in an attempt to educate people. They are presently involved in yet another custody hearing for *flaunting* their relationship. Out of ignorance and with a complete lack of information, the courts decide that a lesbian family is detrimental to the child's well-being, and then the courts make sure that they and no one else will hear the true story by silencing the mothers. As the homosexual minister in Sandy and Maddy's movie said, "If a homosexual family is harmful to heterosexual children, then a heterosexual family must be harmful to homosexual children. I was raised in a heterosexual family, and a heterosexual society, and it never rubbed off on me."

Many lesbians who want to have children and do not want to marry artificially inseminate themselves or engage in intercourse with willing donors. Since most custody fights revolve around the husband, women who bear and raise children without husbands are not faced with the same harassment.

Lesbian mothers' unions are being established throughout the country to assist women in court battles and to support one another. These lesbians believe that the open, nonjudgmental, nonsexist environment of their homes, their political understanding, and the equal, nonoppressive nature of their relationships all help to create a nurturing warm atmosphere for children. It is obvious that with a rising divorce rate there are an increasing number of one-parent families. It is ludicrous to assume that a woman working and raising a child alone could necessarily offer a better environment than a woman who is able to share her responsibilities with another woman. If therapists were interested in working with lesbian mothers, they could begin by using whatever power they have to stop the courts from making custody decisions which are based entirely on a woman's sexual preference. As long as workers in mental health remain silent, the courts will continue to legislate in this area of human behavior.

Lesbian Couples

Lesbians tend to favor stable long-term relationships, and to this end couple therapy should be provided. The lesbians' commitment must be seen as equal to a heterosexual marriage-type relationship. When heterosexual couples are having sexual difficulties, a therapist would not suggest that the partners try out homosexual relationships. Conversely, when homosexual couples experience difficulties, they do not wish to be told that they should change their sexual orientation. More and more lesbians are finding it possible to have long-term commitments to women, to create the family atmosphere they desire and to carry on their vocational and political work. The strength of the lesbian commitment and the fulfillment women experience in these relationships should not be underestimated.

CONCLUSIONS

Lesbians bear the battle scars of their violent encounters with the keepers of mental health. Clearly, the lesbian has no proof that a therapist does not believe the sordid folklore surrounding the issue of homosexuality.

If therapists who are lesbians do not feel that they can be open about their sexual life-style at work, then we should conclude that this particular clinic is not suitable for lesbian clients. If lesbians who are students believe that disclosure of their sexual identity would jeopardize their chances for advancement, then this school is obviously not graduating therapists who would be capable of working with lesbians. If women who have power, the therapists, are oppressed, what hope is there for the less powerful individuals, the patients?

There is only one way for mental health centers and schools to demonstrate their *good faith* to the lesbian community, and that is to hire lesbian therapists and faculty.

Lesbian therapists must come out! "Everytime you keep your mouth shut you make life that much harder for every lesbian in this country. Our freedom is worth your losing your jobs and your friends" (Brown, 1972).

Lesbians can facilitate the hiring of lesbian therapists by sitting on the advisory boards to community mental health centers. The lesbian community must evaluate all services offered to lesbians, and advise women as to the sincerity and efficacy of these programs.

We, as lesbians, have already wasted much precious time hiding in our closets. Our anger must be turned outward to the society which taught us our first lesson: it is alright to hate and fight in the daylight, but we must love in the darkness. As Judy Grahn (Grahn & Sjoholm, 1974) wrote in her poem, "A Woman is Talking to Death"*

> Have you committed any indecent acts with women? Yes, many. I am guilty of allowing suicidal women to die before my eyes or in my ears or under my hands because I thought I could do nothing, I am guilty of leaving a prostitute who held a knife to my friend's throat to keep us from leaving, because we would not sleep with her, we thought she was old and fat and ugly; I am guilty of not loving her who needed me; I regret all the women I have not slept with or comforted, who pulled themselves away from me for lack of something I had not the courage to fight for, for us, our life, our planet, our city, our meat and potatoes, our love. These are indecent acts, lacking courage, lacking a certain fire behind the eyes, which is the symbol, the raised fist, the sharing of resources, the resistance that tells Death he will starve for lack of the fat of us, our extra. Yes I have committed acts of indecency with women and most of them were acts of omission. I regret them bitterly.

SUGGESTED READINGS

Brown, Rita M.: *Ruby Fruit Jungle*. Vermont, Daughters, Inc., 1973.
Isabell, Sharon: *Yesterdays Lessons*. Oakland, The Women's Press Collective, 1974.
Martin, Del, and Lyon, Phyllis: *Lesbian-Woman*. San Francisco, Glide Publications, 1972.
Miller, Isabel: *Patience and Sarah*. New York, McGraw Hill, 1972.

REFERENCES

Abbott, Sidney and Love, Barbara: *Sappho was a Right-on Woman*. New York, Stein and Day, 1972.

_____

*Reproduced by courtesy of Judy Grahn.

Brown, Rita M.: Take a lesbian to lunch. In Jay, Karls and Young, Allen (Eds.): *Out of the Closets: Voices of Gay Liberation*. New York, Douglas Book Corp., 1972.

Grahn, Judy, and Sjoholm, Karen: *A Woman is Talking to Death*. Oakland, The Women's Press Collective, 1974.

Hedblom, Jack H.: The female homosexual: Social and attitudinal dimensions. In McCaffrey, Joseph A. (Ed.): *The Homosexual Dialectic*. New Jersey, Prentice Hall, Inc., 1972.

Johnston, Jill: *Lesbian Nation: The Feminist Solution*. New York, Simon and Schuster, 1973.

Kinsey, Alfred C., Pomeroy, Wardell B., Martin, Clyde E., and Gebhard, Paul H.: *Sexual Behavior in the Human Female*. Philadelphia, Saunders, 1953.

Rosen, David H.: *Lesbianism: A Study of Female Homosexuality*. Springfield, Thomas, 1974.

Schuster, S. L.: *Love is For All*. Washington, Mountlake Terrace, P.O. Box 82, Schuster-Isaacson Family Productions, 1974.

Weltge, Ralph W. (Ed.): *The Same Sex: An Appraisal of Homosexuality*. Philadelphia, Pilgrim Press, 1969.

—— *Chapter 14* ——

PSYCHOTHERAPY WITH LESBIANS: SOME OBSERVATIONS AND TENATIVE GENERALIZATIONS*

BARBARA E. SANG

UNTIL recently lesbianism has been considered to be a pathological entity. The goal of psychotherapy for the lesbian was therefore to change her sexual orientation. Although evidence today points to the fact that lesbianism is a positive and viable life-style (Brown, 1975; Freedman, 1968; Oberstone, 1974; Rosen, 1974), there is as yet nothing in the psychotherapy literature that reflects this new perspective. Many lesbians who have been in therapy report feeling misunderstood and misinterpreted. Their therapists have little knowledge about the lesbian subculture and the societal pressures that must be coped with.

From my own experience working with lesbians in therapy, it became apparent that there was a need to describe and examine the unique forces that impinge on the lesbian in this society today. Only in this way can psychotherapy be relevant and meaningful to her.

I will present a brief description of the approximately eighty lesbian women whom I have seen for an initial intake interview or for psychotherapy over the past three years. These individuals were referred by the Homosexual Community Counseling Center† or by private sources. The women range in age from their early twenties to early fifties with a median age of twenty-nine. They are from varying socioeconomic, ethnic, and religious backgrounds. The population would, however, appear to be biased in two respects: (1) Most of the women are in the mental health profession or in the arts. Many have had graduate training and/or are multitalented; (2) The lesbian women seeking help come directly to a counseling center or to a therapist known to view homosexuality positively.

---

*Revised from a paper presented at the meeting of the American Psychological Association, New Orleans, September, 1974.

†The Homosexual Community Counseling Center (HCCC) located in New York City was founded in 1971 to meet the needs of homosexual men, women, and their families. It is staffed by professionally trained individuals who view homosexuality as a variety of sexual expression and not as a deviation or sickness.

It is of interest to note that few of the individuals in this group had involvement with the feminist or homophile movement before therapy. Since current researchers have almost exclusively relied on homophile groups for their subjects, the lesbians I will discuss may represent a different lesbian population from that described in the research literature. In contrast to a few recent studies which show lesbians to share specific negative characteristics, e.g. to come from broken homes or to have drinking problems (Wolff, 1971; Saghir and Robins, 1973), no consistent pattern is observable for the present group. If one salient characteristic does emerge, it is that almost all the lesbian women assumed from childhood that they would be economically self-supporting as adults. (In striving for autonomy and more meaningful interaction with her world, the lesbian brings to therapy the conflicts and problems directly related to her rejection of the stereotypical female role.

It is my impression that lesbians who enter therapy and counseling do so for reasons similar to those of heterosexual women. However, lesbians bring to therapy experiences which might only be heard or understood by therapists who have some familiarity with the lesbian subculture. As Nuehring, Fein, and Tyler (1974) have found, one of the major obstacles to satisfactory exchanges in counseling and therapy of gay college students was the professionals' lack of practical knowledge about homosexuality and homosexual life-styles. The following are some typical experiences or problems that lesbians bring to therapy as a consequence of their minority status. In many cases that which is experienced as a personal hang-up is often a natural reaction to societal oppression common to all lesbians. Feelings of doubt and inadequacy disappear on the part of the individual lesbian as her experiences are placed within the broader social context.

1. Some women have been in long-term lesbian relationships and yet do not interact with other homosexual persons for fear of being labeled "gay." At the point when such a relationship breaks up, there are no friends or acquaintances to whom the lesbian can go to unburden herself. Thus, professional help may be sought to work out a loss that might have been worked out with family or friends.

The lesbian who is isolated from other homosexual persons is frequently more anxious and depressed about not knowing how to make future social contacts than she is over the termination of the previous relationship. The fear of being alone and isolated is realistic in view of the fact that knowledge of where other lesbians meet has not been easily accessible. (In some areas, this picture is beginning to change.) An important part of counseling or therapy for this lesbian can be assisting her to overcome fears of other gays and learning options open for meeting people. The more the counselor or therapist is aware of the mores and styles within the homosexual subculture, the more effective she can be in helping the client make contact with the gay community and clarify what is happening to her.

The case of C. is an example of how the knowledgeable therapist can help her lesbian client.

> C. is a forty-five-year-old woman who ended a fifteen-year relationship with another woman one year ago. She came to therapy feeling depressed and discouraged over her felt social inadequacy. It quickly became apparent that C. was experiencing the usual pressures and stresses of being a single person after being part of a couple for many years. But, in addition, her feelings of inadequacy had much to do with the gay group she had accidentally found herself in. The only place that C. knew where to meet lesbians catered to women who were considerably younger than herself and who did not share her values. Unable to form meaningful relationships with these women, C. saw herself as inept and was equally critical of the younger lesbian women. The therapist suggested another lesbian group of similar age range to C. which proved to meet her needs.

2. A few women came for help because they were unclear about their sexuality. One woman, for example, felt physically attracted to men, but emotionally and physically attracted to women. In working with a woman, it is more important to help her get in touch with her own feelings and options than to get her to categorize or label herself. (The number of women with whom I have worked who expressed clear doubts about their sexual orientation were small, possibly because it took a certain amount of acceptance of homosexuality to make contact with a homosexual center.)

The case of Y. presents an example of a woman's confusion regarding her sexuality.

> Y. has had about equal sexual experience with men and women. Although she feels more turned on physically by men, she prefers the emotional intimacy that characterizes her relationships with women. Y. describes herself as less sexually active with women than she is with men. At one point in therapy, Y. began to question whether she might not be gay because she was more physical with men. As she explored her own needs, preferences and options, Y. found it senseless to spend energy finding the right label. For the present time Y. feels content to focus her involvement on women, although, she does not rule out the possibility of relating to men at some later time.

3. It is not uncommon for a woman to have had homosexual feelings for a good number of years and yet to be too threatened to deal with these feelings. Upon hearing about a counseling center for homosexual per-

sons, one woman hoped to share her "secret" for the first time.

> N. is a forty-two-year-old woman who has had a close friendship with a woman of the same age for the past ten years. They share the same job, go on vacations together, and visit one another on weekends. Although A. was willing to accept the intimacy and closeness of their relationship, she panicked at N.'s mention of the word "lesbianism." N. felt that she had to conceal her sexual feelings from A. so as not to lose her. She found herself, however, continually provoking fights and doing dramatic things as an expression of her discomfort. In therapy, N. was able to articulate her need for an open emotional and sexual relationship with a same-sex person. However, it took many months before she stopped being ashamed of having lesbian feelings. Because she shared many of the negative ideas about what lesbians were like, it took her many more months to be able to attend her first lesbian group.

4. Because of the stigma of homosexuality, many women are too frightened to enter lesbian relationships even though they know they are attracted to other women. It is not unusual to find women in their late twenties, thirties, or forties who are having their first gay relationship. Lesbian women who have had little prior experience in relationships often feel enraged and angry at themselves as they deal with the felt discrepancy between their everyday competence and their unsureness in relationships. When looked at within the context of the fact that our society does not allow homosexuals the opportunity to obtain early social and emotional experience, it is not surprising that a woman having her very first relationship later in life will be faced with feelings of inadequacy which she no longer feels in other areas. The following example illustrates this.

> L. had been a cheerful, outgoing person until high school when she abandoned all friendships and focused exclusively on her studies. In retrospect, L. recognized that she withdrew from people in order to avoid the heterosexual dating scene. It was not until her late twenties that L. had her first relationship with a woman. Having had little social experience, L. was easily taken in by a women who exploited her financially. After the relationship broke up, L. was lonely, but did not feel ready to meet other gay women because she felt too unsure of herself. When L. eventually did attend her first homophile meetings, she did not know how to make friends; she worried that she was misleading a person if she asked them out for a cup of coffee. As is the case with many lesbian women who have been socially cut off, it did not take L. too long before she developed her own style of relating comfortably to others. The tragedy is that she had to waste so many good years.

5. Whereas heterosexual women have the opportunity to experience many different people before they choose to make a commitment, the lesbian woman's options are frequently limited. She may find herself in a

permanent relationship with the first person she meets. Long-term plans
are often made before the couple has even had a chance to get to know
one another. Such premature commitments may be the result of a fear of
not knowing where to find other gay people. (The fear of isolation also
keeps lesbian women from breaking up relationships that are not working.)

An additional problem is that a woman who has made a series of
unsuccessful commitments often sees herself as a failure. It can be helpful
to point out to her that she has accepted the heterosexual success model
which is not necessarily applicable to her. T.'s experiences demonstrate
the former problem, limited opportunity for meeting others and premature commitment.

> T. is a twenty-seven-year-old woman from a small town in the South.
> She had just broken up a five-year relationship with a woman of similar
> age and with similar background. T. entered therapy because she had
> recently moved to New York City and felt shaky about her ability to
> meet and relate to people. In discussing her relationship to H., T. says it
> was her first. The women met in their junior year of college. Both were
> ecstatic to have found one another. Three months after the relationship
> began, T. and H. realized that they did not have enough in common to
> make a go of the relationship, so they agreed to see other people. How-
> ever, since T. and H. were not able to meet other gay persons, they
> would find reasons to justify their continued living together. The rela-
> tionship ended when T. decided to take an important position in the
> East.

6. A number of women begin to have lesbian relationships in their
teens. It is not uncommon for such women to be "found out," ridiculed
and punished for their behavior. These women may bring their guilt
about relating to their own sex to future relationships. Such a situation is
illustrated by the case of G.

> G. had been attracted to her own sex ever since she can remember. At
> the age of thirteen her parents accidentally caught her experimenting
> sexually with a close girl friend. The parents were extremely upset by
> this incident and would frequently ridicule their daughter about lesbi-
> anism. In college school authorities assessed that G. was having a les-
> bian affair with D. It was G. who was expelled for corrupting her friend.
> After completing her education in a different school, G. had a series of
> close emotional relationships with women who would not permit sexual
> contact. G. entered therapy at the point that she was having a mean-
> ingful relationship with an openly gay woman. G. could not understand
> why she felt uncomfortable with sexual contact. In looking over her
> experiences with sexuality it made sense to me that G. was "nonsexual"
> so she would not lose the persons she cared about.

7. Not infrequently, lesbians find themselves having a series of relationships with women who eventually leave them for heterosexual relationships. Although it may be argued that the possibility of rejection exists in all relationships, the point is that in their desire for closeness and in the absence of choices, lesbians embark upon contacts which are intrinsically more precarious. Because of this reality, lesbians are apt, in turn, to feel more vulnerable when entering a new relationship. This was J.'s experience.

> J. had never knowingly met a lesbian person. Over a period of years, she became involved intimately with three women in her community who never had had an experience with a woman. Each relationship lasted a few years, but in every one J. was left for a man. J. is presently involved with a self-acknowledged gay woman, but has fears that this woman might also "go straight."
>
> It is important for the therapist to validate J.'s reality, for example: "Based on your past, it is no wonder that you are worried now. You are not the only gay woman who has had this kind of experience. There is nothing wrong with you. If it had been possible for you to have met a wider range of self-identified lesbians, then you might have had a choice."
>
> A former therapist once told J. that she picks women who are not available because she does not really want to get involved. This interpretation puts all the blame on J. and fails to acknowledge how difficult it is for lesbians in some areas to know about the existence of other lesbians.

8. Being a homosexual in a "homosexphobic" world is bound to have its effect on the lesbian's personality. As one woman aptly stated it, "I have spent so much of my life making sure which of my feelings were acceptable and which were not, that now I am often unsure what it is *I* feel." Many lesbians learn to put on a "mask" so that their lesbianism will not be apparent when they have loving feelings toward other women. Some women spend so much energy trying not to give themselves away (monitoring their thoughts and feelings) that this interferes with their capacity to be open and spontaneous. The case of S. details some of such burdens.

> S. has a high executive position in which her success depends on appearing heterosexual. When relating to the women in her office, S. closely watches her facial gestures and degree of physical contact least she be suspected of being a lesbian. Through the years S. has trained herself to appear turned on to men and to talk about heterosexual dates. On those occasions that S. brings her lover to an office affair, one would hardly recognize that these two women knew each other; they relate in such a detached manner. (S.'s lover would feel personally rejected at such

events even though she understood the need for pretense.) S.'s need to be cautious about displays of feeling and affection extends to most public places. She must be discrete for fear that someone from work may be close by.

As the above observations illustrate, lesbians may bring special problems to a therapist. In a recent study on homosexuality (Saghir and Robins, 1973), it is stated that "the homosexual woman is not more neurotic or more psychotic, although she tends to seek psychotherapy more often." The authors offer the explanation that therapy is sought for depression after a relationship breaks up. I agree that a good number of lesbians seek out therapy, but I would like to offer some alternative reasons relating to why they do so:

1. Any person who is different from the "average" is likely to spend a good deal of time reflecting on why she is different. In having to account for why she is, the lesbian may become aware of other aspects of herself that she wants to explore or work on.

2. There are more social pressures on lesbians and fewer safety valves to deal with those problems. As previously indicated, until now, therapy may be the only place that an isolated lesbian can share her problems.

3. Some lesbians may look toward therapy as a way of having someone in authority approve of their orientation. (For some women, a consciousness-raising group, a homophile organization, or a gay peer may be more appropriate than therapy or counseling.) The need for the therapist's acceptance of one's lesbianism in the course of therapy should not be viewed negatively. Is not the acceptance of heterosexuality already implicit in the psychotherapeutic procedure? Women who cannot accept their homosexuality often want a therapist to force them to become heterosexual. Care must be taken by the therapist to allow these women to become who they are rather than who they think they should be. There are lesbian women who will subtly test their therapist's viewpoint on homosexuality before they reveal themselves. I have met several women who have had months of therapy and yet have not told their therapist of their lesbianism because they did not feel it was safe.

Good therapy involves helping a person get in touch with who she or he is whether this be in the area of sexual orientation, feelings, life-style, or values. Therapists who believe that their function is to change homosexuals into heterosexuals deprive the individual of choosing what is best for herself. Therapists who believe that homosexuality is pathological, but do not make their views explicit, can be just as destructive as those who openly claim that homosexuals are sick. One woman in training with a well-known psychoanalyst reports that her supervisor attributes all the homosexuals' problems to their orientation, though he says nothing about his own bias. Another woman is currently seeing a therapist whose views about homosexuality have not been articulated. Yet, each time she is having difficulty with her female lover, the therapist reminds her how much better her relationships are with men. But, the client pleads, her relationships with men are *different;* she is not emotionally involved.

For some therapists, lesbianism is not important to talk about because it is seen as a symptom of other underlying emotional problems: Once changes are made in other areas, the lesbianism will disappear. R. went to a therapist who had such an attitude toward lesbianism.

> She originally entered therapy because she was disturbed about her attraction to women. It was reassuring to hear that her homosexuality was merely a symptom which would disappear as she worked on her other problems. R. forced herself to date men and had continuous superficial relationships with them for ten years. Finally, at the age of thirty-five, she had her first meaningful relationship with a woman. She reentered therapy to explore parts of herself that had previously been excluded.

There are therapists who verbalize positive attitudes toward homosexuality and yet, unwittingly, betray a heterosexual bias. J. reports that her therapist tells her that "It's OK to be a lesbian, but you are not one." He offered as evidence to prove his point, her one sexual encounter with a male. This woman knows that she is both emotionally and sexually attracted to women and feels that the therapist is negating her reality. K. has observed that when she talks about her male lovers, her therapist is more attentive and asks more questions than when she talks about her female lovers.

P.'s therapist also betrays an underlying heterosexual bias. Her therapist says that she has no intention of forcing her to go straight if she wants to be a lesbian. At the same time, however, her therapist will not describe her views on homosexuality to P. because she does not see them as relevant to the "treatment." P. finds herself exploring relationships with men to make sure for the fifth time that she is not rejecting them prematurely. She feels angry at herself for not using therapy for the reason she entered it: to work on her relationships with women. In the course of therapy, P. began to get in touch with the fact that her therapist did indeed have negatively biased and stereotypical attitudes towards lesbianism. This made P. reluctant to discuss her female relationships. Although P. felt that she was getting something from her therapist, she questioned whether she might have made more progress with a therapist who had more positive feelings toward lesbianism.

These examples illustrate what a friend of mine recently pointed out to me: the double standard that exists between lesbian and straight women in therapy. Whereas lesbian women are encouraged to be bisexual so that they do not "exclude men," the heterosexual woman is not encouraged to be bisexual so that she does not "exclude women."

The women who seek out the services of the Homosexual Community Counseling Center want to assure themselves of a therapist who views lesbianism positively. However, most of these women are not simply looking for an atmosphere of acceptance. Rather, they want someone who understands the nuances of their life-style; they want someone who already knows their "world" so that it is not necessary to interpret and clarify continually. Knowing that a therapist has knowledge of the gay subculture or is involved in it may be an important, and as yet unexplored positive force in the therapeutic process. From my own experience, a trust or rapport is established which frees the individual to focus on other aspects of herself. There are other, often more subtle, changes that take place in an interaction between a gay therapist and client. If a therapist who is also a lesbian feels good about herself, her positive image may in itself make for changes in the client that might have otherwise only been brought about through many months of talk and direct communication. Although most of the lesbian women seeking the services of HCCC feel comfortable with their lesbianism, they nevertheless, have also internalized the negative stereotypes of their minority. A therapist who has struggled with the very same problems can validate her clients' struggles. Such a therapist may also be quick to confront the client when she is using the negative stereotypes to put herself down.

The question of whether a straight therapist is qualified to be a therapist for gay persons invariably comes up. I personally feel that a straight person who has given more than passing thought to the problems of the lesbian minority does have something to offer. However, even a therapist who feels positively about lesbianism, but who has little knowledge or awareness of what it means to be a lesbian, would be suitable only if other alternatives were not available. At this time, I feel that a lesbian in therapy has the most to gain from working with someone who closely shares her context.

REFERENCES

Brown, Laura: Investigating the Stereotypic Picture of Lesbians in the Clinical Literature. Paper presented at the American Psychological Association Convention, Chicago, 1975.

Freedman, Mark J.: Homosexuality among women and psychological adjustment. *Ladder, 12*:2, 1968.

Nuehring, Elane M., Fein, Sara Beck, and Tyler, Mary: The gay college student: Perspectives for mental health professionals. *The Counseling Psychologist, 4*:64, 1974.

Oberstone, Andrea: A Comparative Study of Psychological Adjustment and Aspects of

Life Style in Gay and Non-gay Women. Unpublished doctoral dissertation, California School of Professional Psychology, 1974.

Rosen, David: *Lesbianism, A Study of Female Homosexuality.* Springfield, Thomas, 1974.

Saghir, Marcel T., and Robins, Eli: *Male and Female Homosexuality.* Baltimore, Williams and Wilkins, 1973.

Wolff, Charlotte: *Love between Women.* New York, Harper and Row, 1971.

Section VII

FEMINISM AS THERAPY

INTRODUCTION

THE four papers in this section describe various procedures through which women are discovering feminist ideology and experiencing the personal changes which follow such a discovery. Actually, it would be more precise to say that women are discovering feminist *ideologies* because there are several points of view which have polarized in the women's movement (Deckard, 1975). The author of "Feminism as Therapy," Anica Vesel Mander, discusses the *cultural feminist** position and illustrates how cultural feminists redefine the past in terms of their present conceptions of women.

She stresses the healing aspects of feminism — turning self-doubt into anger which leads to the recovery of personal and political power by women. In contrast, the papers by Brodsky, Guzell, and Sanders and Stewart do not reflect a clear-cut ideological position. Annette Brodsky and Marie Celeste Guzell provide an objective account of some of the effects of feminism on women. In Brodsky's "Therapeutic Aspects of Consciousness-Raising Groups," she indicates that C-R groups are particularly beneficial for women with identity problems. In "Problems in Personal Changes in Women's Studies Courses," Guzell describes the positive changes as well as the anxiety and stress that exposure to feminism generates among some women. Sanders and Stewart, through the means of selected readings and the rationale of bibliotherapy, offer a feminist-therapy tool. All the papers in this section suggest that exposure to feminist ideology has effects on women similar to therapy, that is, the effects may be positive or negative.

In "Feminism as Therapy," Anica Vesel Mander draws material from the work of nine women who met in three-hour weekly sessions over a five-week period to explore the ways feminism had been a healing force in their lives. In these weekly sessions the women focused on topics which often emerge as common concerns whenever women come together to explore their feelings and personal experiences in consciousness-raising or feminist groups.

Mander describes feminism as dealing with both external and internal

---

*The cultural feminists, at their best, urge the creation of a culture based on female talent, productivity, and value — in the arts, in myth, in historical interpretation, in the evolution of a more humane lifestyle based on cooperation rather than male competitiveness (Rosenfelt, 1973).

rights which are inseparable and which unite self-exploration with action. So described, feminism is both an affirmation of internal power and a healing process for women. Mander also defines therapy as *healing,* not *helping.* Healing refers to recovering inner strength, becoming centered, and feeling whole, alive, and creative.

Feminism rejects the hierarchical model of traditional therapy. It redefines therapy for women by developing new tools and methods. Society's cultural norms and myths about women invalidate women's feelings and experiences. This creates self-alienation and self-doubt. For this reason, women who are attempting to change themselves and their lives need the support of other women. This is best provided by feminist groups. Groups can be in the form of collective, cooperative systems and operate both as a political tool and a therapeutic process. Only by supporting and learning from one another can women build a base of strength.

When women understand their oppression, they become angry at the way men have misused power — destroying the natural environment and creating oppressive societies. Although Mander acknowledges that anger appears unpleasant, unfeminine and, at times, immobilizes some women, she affirms that "it also needs to be viewed as an important organic healing device built right into our gut." Women must learn to express their anger against the world men have created, with this anger leading to positive, responsible action toward healing the ugly aspects of organized society. By getting in touch with their feelings, especially anger and self-doubt, women can release their personal power.

Another drain on women's personal power, in addition to repression of their anger, is repression of their sexuality. By daring to talk openly, learning from their own and other women's experiences, women are countering sexual repression and forming their own sexual values. This enables them, for the first time, to relate sexually to men in authentic terms, as active participants and as equals. Mander concludes that feminism "is an integration of various heretofore incompatible elements built on a collective base of thought-action-feeling." Through the integrative impact of feminism "women can learn to rejoin themselves and their society into a harmonious whole."

In "Therapeutic Aspects of Consciousness-Raising Groups," Annette M. Brodsky discusses a unique phenomenon of the 1960's women's movement — the C-R group whose dynamics foster personal changes and can help in the treatment of identity problems of women in therapy. In C-R groups, women share their personal experiences, give and receive support, and gain strength from the encouragement of other women. By sharing their experiences with others, women come to realize how they have been molded by society. C-R groups, then, serve a resocialization function.

To free oneself from very basic assumptions is a difficult process and requires a warm, supportive atmosphere created by other women going through the same process. Women discard female competitive interaction by putting the importance of men in perspective and in so doing, achieve closeness and intimacy with one another. A sense of trust and closeness based on common problems, easy intimacy with one another, and loyalty, all bind the group into a cohesive unit. Women give strength to one another in the difficult task of translating skills into action outside the group where women face much opposition for nontraditional behavior.

Since personal change is painful, the C-R group does not pressure any woman to change more than she herself desires. Personal changes in women are observed long after they leave their C-R group. Eventually a C-R group must turn to public action as a mechanism for personal change, otherwise the group will lose morale and stagnate.

Brodsky indicates that when women attempt to transcend the limited cultural definition of *feminine*, they must step outside the culturally assigned, stereotyped roles. Problems may then arise because, in violating social stereotypes, women risk conflicts over sex-role identity. C-R groups are more effective than therapy groups in helping women with identity conflicts because: (1) The group requires women to act as individuals rather than as passive conformists; (2) Women are exposed to female models who aid in learning new behaviors, e.g. assertiveness; and (3) When women work out their identities with other women first, they respond more productively to the sexist values of many men toward women and the suspicion and hostility of many women toward men.

C-R groups differ from therapy groups in several important ways: (1) They are not suitable for women in need of intensive psychotherapy or for women who are too defensive, too vulnerable, and too alienated from the group norms: (2) All-female groups are more empathic and less constrictive for women than mixed-sex groups due in part to the historic dominance-submission interaction patterns between males and females; (3) The environment rather than intrapsychic dynamics are assumed to be the cause of women's problems; (4) The content is topic-oriented rather than person-oriented; and (5) The basic therapeutic process is not self-disclosure and corrective emotional experiences but the identification of problems common to the participants and therefore to all women.

C-R groups have several important implications for therapy for women with identity problems. These include: (1) the identification of areas in which women need support; (2) the therapeutic effect of women taking personal and/or political action for themselves; and (3) the necessity of therapists' understanding women's problems in a sexist society. Therapists often suffer from sex-role biases and lack of understanding of women's problems. Rather than being therapeutic, treatment from such people can produce further conflicts and frustrations for women clients.

While acknowledging the importance of female role-models to psychotherapy for women, Brodsky does not agree with the extreme position taken by some feminists that only women should be therapists for other women; it is not practical to require that therapists always have the same experiences as their clients. However, it is important that therapists be nonsexist, that they be open about their own values about women with female clients, that they respect women's capacity to accurately report their own experiences, and that they remain informed about issues concerning women.

In "Problems in Personal Changes in Women's Study Courses," Marie Celeste Guzell describes the effect on women of Women's Studies (WS) courses. These courses grew out of the women's movement in much the same way as Black Studies courses grew out of the Black movement. The emotional and behavioral effect on women as described by Guzell, is in between the impact of regular college courses and C-R or feminist therapy groups. The benefits of WS courses to women are similar to those of C-R groups: learning to think for oneself, recognizing the commonality of women's problems, achieving insights into women's rights, and feeling the closeness of other women. The courses differ from C-R and women's therapy groups in the firmness of a contract for information, in the commitment to continue in the course, even if the going gets rough and often in the absence of group support and opportunity to process emotionally disturbing issues. Guzell characterizes these courses as *the creation of the need for therapy in a group of individuals operating in an essentially nontherapeutic environment.*

While many positive changes occur, the courses can also be stressful because exposure to feminism generates conflict about traditional sex-role behavior among some women and anger toward men in others. When this occurs without the kind of safeguards which are built into C-R or women's therapy groups, the generated stress may not get processed and the effect can be negative. Women who hold traditional values experience the most intense conflicts and, therefore, the most stress. Changes come about most readily when women are less traditional to begin with, when the community atmosphere is liberal in its values, and when support groups are available for continuing growth.

Guzell presents empirical research to document the problematic nature of some of the personal changes that occur in women taking a women's studies course. Some problems are fear and anxiety related to sex role analysis and awareness of passivity; anger, especially toward men which is released as consciousness is raised; and conflicts between the traditional view of femininity and the perceived direction of personal growth.

In order to make women's studies courses more therapeutic, Guzell makes a number of practical recommendations to instructors: (1) time students' exposure to explosive material; (2) prepare women students for the anxiety, anger and other negative emotions that these courses often evoke; (3) minimize guilt and potential anger in males, e.g. early in the course, correct misperceived goals of feminism, discuss the adverse effects of sexism on men, etc.; (4) avoid excessive stereotyping of men; (5) prohibit men from dominating class discussion in the traditional pattern; (6) teach *androgyny* as a model of a healthy personality in order to counteract fears about loss of "femininity"; (7) point out that sex roles and sexual potency are not casually connected; (8) emphasize political action as a channel for anger-stimulated energy; (9) generate a list of feminist psychological treatment and legal services to which students can be referred when necessary; (10) provide female students with suitable reading material to share with significant males to help them understand changes the women are undergoing; (11) provide small support groups which use group process techniques in which relevant personal material can be shared and anger can be processed; (12) provide assertion training opportunities to avoid a build-up of current anger and to more quickly close the gap between new ideas and old behavior.

"Feminist Bibliotherapy — Prescription for Change" is a selected and annotated bibliography by Jane Sanders and Dorothy Stewart. Typically, bibliotherapy provides fictional characters and situations with which persons can identify and experience catharsis. However, by design, the nature of this focus is cognitive and nonfictional. Increased awareness through cognitive information and insight often has an emotional component. This is especially true for feminist literature to which women often respond with increased feelings of self-respect and decreased feelings of alienation. While bibliotherapy does not require treatment in actual groups (although that would be a possibility), a kind of community of thought and feeling is formed through the written word by women's sharing their experiences and ideas.

Feminist bibliotherapy can be used in several ways. Its best use is as a supplement to therapy. It should not be used as a replacement. Its most important function is to enable a client to identify her main sources of socialization and environmental stress. This is essential for clients who either by choice or circumstance are engaged in rejecting old, constricting attitudes and values about women. A heightened consciousness is crucial to the process of feminist therapy.

The bibliographic materials have been grouped under four major headings: societal values, therapist values, client values, and future values. The emphasis on values is a reflection of the nature of feminist therapy — a philosophy rather than a set of techniques. In the section on societal values are included general areas of socialization that have had negative effects on women. Awareness of external influences is the first step for a woman engaged in the process of feminist therapy. The section on therapist values contains materials of use mainly to therapists rather than to clients. Included is evidence regarding the effect of therapists' private values on the process and outcome of therapy. Containing selections of typical client concerns, client values presents information about particular problems and differing life-styles for women. These items are basic to a feminist bibliotherapy library. The final section, future values, contains anthologies, bibliographies, and primary sources for additional readings. It covers positive options for women from assertive behavior to body work, and so concludes this chapter on an optimistic note.

REFERENCES

Deckard, Barbara: *The Women's Movement: Political, Socioeconomic, and Psychological Issues.* New York, Harper and Row, 1975.

Rosenfelt, Deborah: What Happened at Sacramento? *Women's Studies Newsletter.* Old Westbury, New York, the Feminist Press, 5:1, Fall, 1975.

—— *Chapter 15* ——

FEMINISM AS THERAPY

ANICA VESEL MANDER

Feminism is an affirmation, not a power-seeking ideology. It deals with power, but not the perverted kind of power we have learned to associate with the word through world politics. Rather, it deals with internal power, the kind that must not be suppressed, the kind that makes individuals strong and whole and active. We call it *affirmation*. In this way, feminism is functioning *as* therapy for women: It is a healing process. This chapter is based on the work done by nine women in a group setting during which we explored the ways in which feminism has done its healing on us. The quotes are taken directly from tape-recordings of the women in the group — Margot Briggs, Barbara Hazilla, Anica Vesel Mander, Mary Beth Noonan, Anna Ostrom, Susan Rannells, Barbara Shawcroft, Christy Shepard, and Ann Stutzman — which met for three hours a week over a five-week period, during which we agreed to focus on the following topics:

1. Feminism: definition
   Therapy: redefinition
2. Anger: outer-directed
   Self-doubt: inner-directed
3. Power: personal and political
   Repression: personal and societal
4. Taking Responsibility: past, present, future
5. Integrative session.

We read the following books:

Phyllis Chesler: *Women and Madness* (1972)
Sylvia Plath: *The Bell Jar* (1971)
Anne Kent Rush: *Getting Clear* (1973)
Monique Wittig: *Les Guerillères* (1971)

FEMINISM: DEFINITION

The healing powers of feminism. I know it inside of me, I feel it, I see it, I feel the energy and it is going to save the world. Feminism, for me, is a study of how women have integrated their feelings into their lives and actions, into their politics and how it's changing women and therefore changing society.

Feminism is a political term, political in women's sense of the word: It deals with our rights both in societal and in personal terms. Simultaneously feminism is about equal participation in the external, political decision-making process and personal, emotional, psychic development. These two areas of human rights, the external and the internal, like body and mind, cannot and must not be separated. That is one of the basic healing-teachings of feminism.

> In my mind, *feminist* is about the broadest term I can think of. I know that in a certain way it sounds limited: I don't think in terms of separating humankind into two species and putting the men on one island and the women on the other; what I think in the broad sense is that the planet has been in the hands of men for a long time and it has reached a dangerous point now and so I think it's time for us to do something for humanity, not just for women, so that means children and men and everybody.

Feminism, then, is about self-exploration and about action. It is about integrating the two.

THERAPY: REDEFINITION

Through feminism, therapy is being redefined — therapy for women at the very least. Not much is known about the female psyche because knowledge in the past has been organized along male principles. Traditional male terms are useful, but limited. Now women are developing tools to deal with our life situations, with our problems, with our sickness. We are also developing new methods for fulfilling our creative potential; we are developing new research techniques, reexamining history and mythology, dealing with our sex-roles, altering our image both on the inside and on the outside, and in a myriad other ways, discovering that there are alternatives to seeing the world the man's way. We, as women, are *seeing* differently.

One of the ways women have been getting in touch with their strength and their power is by developing noncompetitive ways of relating to each other. In small groups, women have been learning in the last few years how to decondition themselves from the separatism imposed upon them by rules of good behavior such as loyalty to their man or right to privacy — and from the competitiveness set up between women in the male marketplace where a woman's survival depends on her being selected in preference to another woman for the bed-kitchen or the store-office.

Now women are replacing this competitive way of relating to one another with collective, cooperative systems; instead of fighting one another we lend each other support and are thereby building a base of strength which, when translated into power-politics, is effecting important societal changes.

> I feel a constant urgency to keep on redefining my life...and everytime I get to a certain point, that makes it even more urgent to get beyond...I've also gotten to a point where my life can be more collective rather than just individual. So that's what I would like to do: get into the collective feeling of relating, of committing myself.

Group work is both a political tool and a therapeutic process in the feminist movement: Through women's groups, we have discovered our collective oppression and relieved ourselves of much of the self-blame that individual therapy instilled in us. Groups enable us to learn from other women how to deal with situations that are often almost identical. By sharing *private* information we have been able to take a second look at our natures, to define and discover what it really is to be a woman and to assume responsibility for our lives without leaning on authority figures who only further our dependence and contribute to our confusion.

> I feel like I spent all my life in isolation, so I know I can't use that anymore. I don't want that. Redefinition of therapy, for me, means I have to keep tapping the source of power in order to get that feeling of reinforcement, myself, I have to keep defining where I am at and clearing all the shit away.

Therapy in feminist terms, then, means healing, not helping. It means working in groups to pool information and building a base of strength. There are no experts, no authorities. There are no patients, there are no doctors. There are no labels. There are, instead, facilitators; there are organizers. There are clients, there are clues. Feminism does not exclude individual therapy, but it does say *no* to the traditional therapist-patient model. We, as women, work against hierarchical systems: The therapist is not the objective observer of our soul; she is another woman with intuitive and intellectual reactions to us which stem from her own personal sources which need to be acknowledged if any useful work is to be done. It is harmful for women to be treated as sick, weak, and isolated. We want to assume responsibility for our own lives and this can only be done if we are treated as adults by equals.

ANGER: OUTER-DIRECTED

What are some of the healing ways women have developed? A crucial area in this respect is bodywork: women are learning techniques for releasing pent-up energy and held-in emotion; we are also discovering ways of relating to each other nonverbally by overcoming the taboos against touching one another; we are learning about our bodies and how we relate to ourselves.

Another way women have found to heal each other and themselves is through the Consciousness-Raising Group. While the C-R group started among a small segment of the white student population, it has now crossed age and ethnic lines, spread to the suburbs and been written in *Redbook*. It has "caught on." Out of these experiences we have discovered that perhaps the single most therapeutic element that has come out of feminism is the anger that has been released. When Black men and women got in touch with their oppression in an active way, anger started pouring out. That was the beginning of the healing process in the sickness of racism. The same is happening to women. While anger is unattractive and "*un*feminine" and hard to take when it is directed at you and you are the boss or the husband, it also needs to be viewed as an important organic healing device, built right into our gut.

What is this anger all about? It is about the way men have been running the world. It is about the way they have been destroying the natural environment, about the way they have concentrated wealth and power in the hands of a few, with disregard for the natural rights of all other creatures. It is about the killing and the maiming and the general egomania that rules. This global kind of anger most often gets indirectly expressed to the man for not doing the dishes or not getting up in the middle of the night to take care of baby. It is legitimate anger and it needs to come out.

Anger can lead to action — positive, life-saving action. It need not, however, all come out at the individual man who is right there beside us. Domestic oppression exists and it must be eliminated. But we must remain clear about where the responsibilities lie so that we can effectively combat them. Once the connection between the dishes and nuclear power plants is made, there is no way to go back.*

The healing process has begun.

> I had a strange dream a few nights ago. I seemed to be on another planet — there was a feeling of another world. I was standing with three other women in darkness, and we were looking across this flat and empty space to where four men were sitting around a bonfire. I turned to the woman behind me and said: "Is it time?" She said: "Yes" and we started walking single file toward the bonfire. The men looked up, startled and said: "We didn't hear you coming." I said: "That's because

---

*The "connection" between dishes and nuclear power plants may be expressed in the following quotation by Rollo May:

The greater our alienation from nature — alienation's ultimate symbol being the atomic bomb and radiation — the closer we actually are to death ... and here the mother symbol enters; we speak of *mother* nature. It is not a far cry from experiencing the achievement of splitting of the atom as gaining power over the "eternal feminine". (May, 1974, pp. 106). (Eds.).

we have always been here." There was a feeling of tremendous power in the words and the men looked startled and sort of upset.

To achieve our personal and political goals we have discovered that anger is a necessary part of the process:

> You have all this shit that's accumulated inside of you and you really have to vomit it all out, there is no way to bypass that.

Yet, there are many among us who are having a great deal of trouble with this anger. There are those of us who are angry all the time and cannot get beyond it so that it immobilizes us. There are those of us who cannot get in touch with our anger and that immobilizes us, too. Probably those of us who have the greatest trouble with our anger are the women who have been most successfully conditioned to be "nice."

> You're not supposed to have the shit and you're certainly not supposed to vomit it. . . .

We as women have been conditioned not to express anger and, thereby, have been making ourselves ill, psychically and organically ill. "Female disorders," as they are called, often stem from repressed anger. Feminists are saying: "Get it out, be angry, allow yourself your rightful anger so that you can become whole and do some work."

> The way to deal with the "good girls" is to encourage them not to be so nice to you. . . .

How does this anger express itself? It may be directed against individual men. I still get angry if a man, while talking to me uses "he" or "his" or "mankind" as generic terms. How does he expect me to be able to relate to what he is saying if he is not including me as a member of the species? Or if somebody calls me a "girl;" a man my age never gets called "boy" anymore. . . . But behind these simple anger-responses lie more complicated socio-politico-historical responses which must not be underestimated. They contribute at least as much to a woman's anger as her own personal history.

Ever since the world turned from matriarchies to patriarchies, the balance and harmony necessary in the universe has been tilting so that it has now reached dangerous proportions.*

Women are passionately angry about this. Man — white, Western man, for the most part — has taken power over the social structures and let his ego run rampant. He has developed a technology capable of extermi-

---

*Although the concept of matriarchy is not well established historically, we accept it as a feminist myth. We use the term *myth* in the spirit expressed by Rollo May:

> I use the term "myth" not in its deteriorated popular sense of "falsehood," but in its historically accurate sense of a psychobiological pattern which gives meaning and direction to experiences. (May, 1974, pp. 106). (Eds.).

nating the whole human race and undermining the life of this planet. Children, in the meantime, are still dying of hunger. Politicians are still debating whether women have rights over their own bodies. Nonwhite men are being locked in prisons because they are saying *no* to white man's ways of doing things. Old people are locked in institutions because their consciousness is not technological. These are banal facts. We all know them and most of us have accepted them for a long time. We, as women, recognize that we sat by and did not stop this insanity; we also recognize that we, nonetheless, did not develop it. And so we are angry. This anger may be the most healing force operating in the world today. As it heals individuals, it can also heal societies.

SELF-DOUBT: INNER-DIRECTED

> I set myself up to function with my strength and I experience myself as weak and ineffectual, not being understood at all . . . I feel like rivers are washing against me . . . Self-doubt . . . I have grown so used to being ignored, to being a failure that that is the way I experience myself. I don't know how to say, "this is how it feels to be strong and to do something."

There is very little in organized society that validates our feelings and so, along with anger, we also experience self-doubt. Many blatant forms of sexism are still unrecognized by the society at large. As our grandmothers obtained the vote, we have obtained affirmative action programs. Inherent in both is the underlying assumption that laws can change attitudes. They can and do in the long run. Yet, in the short run, they act as appeasements. Every female alive knows what it is to be dismissed as a person, not taken seriously, disregarded, not counted, categorized. Little girls *giggle*, little girls *whine*, little girls are *weak*. It is not an accident. This is their self-image, based on self-doubt:

> You're being strong but you're feeling "It's just me being ineffectual again" and then you're surprised when they say, "Oh, you made so much sense" that you don't really acknowledge yourself; you don't even feel it.

There is very little approval around for what feminists are doing. We have discussed the support and nurturing we give each other; we, nonetheless, must recognize that most of the time we function in an alien society which looks upon feminists with derision or hostility. If we recognize the sociology of self-doubt, so to speak, we can turn it into a positive, useful tool in our healing process.

If we walk around the society we live in with our feminist consciousness, we are bound to run into obstacles which will make us question ourselves. How do we deal with this? The most effective way to deal with self-doubt is never to function alone, to always assure ourselves of the support of at least one other feminist. That is not always possible.

The other alternative is to be *prepared*. We must not push situations beyond our ability to handle them. And so we must be very cognizant of our reactions, of our changing attitudes, our monthly cycles, our moods. We must stay in touch with ourselves, not overtax or overextend ourselves. We are educating by raising consciousness and so we must be prepared and stay clear. We are not fighting, we are not penis-envying. We are in touch with a reality that cannot be disputed and we are putting others in touch with it as we go. We need not present facts in the right order. We are not arguing. And, if we are alone and do not have the support from our sisters, we must take care of ourselves and not expect too much. Good old self-doubt is there to remind us of that.

POWER: PERSONAL AND POLITICAL

Where do we go from anger and self-doubt? We go toward power; *power* in the feminist sense of the word. A lot of women stay away from that word because it has been so badly misused by men. It is a fine word, however, and needs to be reclaimed. It refers to a force we all have inside of us which, when released in health, exerts its benefits on others; it radiates throughout the world. When misused, as it has been by all the major political powers, it radiates destruction. This is why we must pay close attention to the way we use our power.

> I have been hearing the word power and I am really into that: I am just beginning to feel like the tip of the iceberg of the power I have and it feels so good. I just want to know more about it and I want to get more into it. I just feel so powerful lately . . . And the other word for me is fear, fear of the power, fear that there are going to be no men around to relate to with that kind of power.

Feminists have been discovering the relationship between personal power and external power. By coming in touch with our feelings we have released our energies so that they can be used to affect society:

> How much control do we really have over ourselves? My body functions are getting almost out of control, the more I open myself up. For instance when I am going through a period when I feel really open, my bladder is really open, it's almost as if I can lose control of my bladder and all these things are happening to my body, I feel myself holding back from it, I am not allowing it to go its full strength, but I am more open and my body is . . . I feel I am losing the kinds of controls that we are supposed to have . . . and it doesn't worry me . . . Another thing is that when you loosen up is when you get in touch with your own power

because all of a sudden you just see how things are working and therefore you realize that by making a change you can make them work better
and then you get in touch with your own power . . . I see so many things
that are not working. . . .

Through feminism women are saying: "We are full members of this
society and it is time that we assume our full role." Women want to move
on. Women *are* moving on. But we do not want to use power the way
men have misused power. We are trying instead to develop alternative
methods for expressing our power: without oppressing others, without
ripping anyone off, without being violent, by releasing our creativity, but
letting our energy flow freely.

It doesn't have to be antagonistic, that's a man's way of doing it. With
them it's like a football game: You always have to have an enemy.

As women do their work in groups together and as we discover our
strength, we are beginning to call this strength *power* and to make the
connections with our power and the power in organized society which are
being imposed upon us. As these connections are made, our realization
becomes clearer and clearer that what is happening out there does not
correspond with our sense of what power is or how it must be utilized so
that it not be misused and channeled into destructive acts. Through this
process individual healing is beginning to translate itself into societal
healing.

Women have a great deal of internal power, but they have very little
external power. Such statements as *women control the money in this
country* are totally misleading: Women spend money for running house-
holds, but the money comes from men. If the relationship between a man
and a woman is severed, the woman goes back to her original economic
position, which is, for the most part, a position of poverty. Florynce
Kennedy, founder of the Feminist Party, says there are no middle-class
women, because women are all poor. That is a very important statement.
White women are middle class only as long as they are *kept* by men
through marriage, job or otherwise. . . . They are middle class in attitudes, but they are poor in terms of economic control and political power.

How is feminism dealing with this inequity?

I have a feeling we're going to keep going back to the collective thing
because there isn't just one person that moves up on the level of consciousness but it's a group thing and it occurs in different places at the
same time. You can pick up pieces of pottery and you can see that there
was a time when groups of people in different places on the earth were
doing the same kind of form so that there must have been some level of
consciousness that was going on then. Maybe the level of consciousness
or the power that we are picking up has something to do with physics or

something. Most of this stuff we don't know anything about; we're just sort of guessing about it. Some people pick it up sooner than others.

When asked, "What are your goals?" we answer, "To cooperate." Instead of setting up specific political platforms, feminism is healing the society of its old ways first; alternatives will emerge organically once the process is healthy again:

> Yes, and I think to get into that collective thing is the only way to get into a total integration of yourself with the whole thing that's happening on the outside. We have to do it by stages. I really want to get into our connection with the universe because I've discovered I am not alone anymore. I didn't feel it for a long time and now I really feel it. Once you get a knowledge of being part of the whole collective scene, you're never alone; it's really a good feeling.
>
> What do you mean by "collective?"
>
> Using the word "we" instead of "I." And not to just be mentally aware of my connection with the whole macrocosm, but to feel it too . . . I think I get a great sense of strength and warmth and power because I am not just an isolated person. I am a tiny little thing that goes into making the whole thing work. I want to be really able to feel that and I also want to have some knowledge about the way it works.
>
> I am learning all the time how to function collectively because it is against all my training and against all my acquired information; not against my instincts, but my instincts are so buried that I can hardly get at them anymore . . .
>
> I think it is the basic question of survival now. I am really into that survival scene. It's the biggest, hardest, most complex problem in my life: to survive as an independent woman artist. And then right away it has to be collective because I am not here on this earth alone . . .

REPRESSION: PERSONAL AND SOCIETAL

We cannot explore power without exploring its polarity: repression-oppression. *Repression* is what happens to us inside, *oppression* is what is done to us by the outside to keep us from feeling-exerting our power both on the inside and on the outside. We have learned in working with each other that, in order to get in touch with our power, we must trace back to the particulars of our repression:

> The strongest foundation for my resentment toward my parents is that I feel myself holding back my potential as a human being . . . They gave me the word that I was supposed to hold back, and I accepted that word most of my life. I am just beginning to break out of that. Hold back, in every way, physical and mental; not do things as well as I can do them, not relate to people as well as I can relate to them, not have best friends when I was growing up, not win the race if I was running. *To hold*

back. I find myself holding back from people I really like. My mother would say to me "Why do you have to like that girl so much?" and she was my best friend!

We are looking back and focusing on the ways we were conditioned to be "feminine"; we are discovering that, while the individual histories vary a great deal in affective and sociological context, there is an underlying commonality of experience based on society's image of what women are and how they should behave. Discovering this common self-image has helped us put our personal histories in perspective and to lessen the weight of blame on our parents. We are learning how much of what we had assumed in the past to be our particular hang-up is a basic female hang-up imposed on us by our culture. Our parents were, for the most part, simply the carriers of the message; they did not invent the message.

In examining the phenomenon of repression we have found that it is useful to study sexual repression for it is a microcosm of our more generalized role-oppression. Sexual oppression has been used against women to keep us from exerting our power in society:

> My mother, who was also voicing the opinions of my father and everyone else, would say: "Don't touch, don't sexualize!" Essentially that was the message: "Don't express passion." When I started living my own life, I started questioning that and the more I questioned it, the more I couldn't follow what she had trained me so carefully to do but I also started thinking, and I am still thinking about what the message really was. She wasn't just saying "don't touch yourself," she was giving me some very profound message which reflected her view of society and from where she came from it was the only message she could possibly have given me. It's not the message I needed and it's not the message I can live by, but it was the message that had grown out of her experience as a woman in the second and third decade of this century. And so I feel it's crucial for me to catch the essence of that conditioning and to figure out what it means in political terms. That is the mechanism I use and then I can do something about it: The message, recorded in my body, goes through my head where it is put in historic perspective and then it is translated into political action, i.e. change.

> One of the messages I got from my mother is that I mustn't overstep her, to make her into a shadow. It would be so easy for me to do that. "Always play a secondary role to me," that was one of her strong messages.

> I think women do that with their children because they are so oppressed themselves that it is the only way that they can elevate themselves outside of their oppression, by oppressing somebody else.

As the three great enemies of feminism — patriarchy, monotheism and monogamy — began to be practiced in large portions of the world, women found it necessary to repress their sexuality. They had been made dependent on men to such a degree that they could not afford to give full vent to that power within them. For self-protection they had to control their sexuality and to use it as their most powerful weapon. The much-blamed mother was essentially training her daughter for survival.

With the advent of contraception came the possibility of choice. Contraception was probably the single most important development which led to the present feminist revolution since it freed women from the slavery of childbearing and rearing which patriarchal societal laws imposed on us. Under matriarchal systems children were not solely a woman's responsibility: They were, as they should be in any sane society, the communal responsibility and joy of all. Under present conditions, birth control is the only way that a woman can be in charge of her own life and at the same time give full expression to her sexuality if she chooses to do so with men.

From our mothers we got the double message that we must not develop our sexuality for our own pleasure and at the same time that we should develop it as our most valuable asset for manipulating men. Very few of us were ever given any real information on sexuality and our interest in it was fed on the one hand by male romanticism and on the other by Freudian, i.e. Judeo-Christian male, analyses of human sexuality. Since sexuality was the key to the competitive task of *catching a man*, we never shared our real feelings about it with other women. Now that women are telling each other the truth, another picture is arising.

All kinds of misconceptions about female sexuality are being rectified. As we talk with each other openly, we have discovered how similar our experiences are and how much lying there has been in the past. This reexamination of our nature is proceeding simultaneously on the collective and on the private level. Together we are talking to each other in groups, we are sharing skills with each other, reading each other's writings and some of us are learning about each other by making love to each other. Private exploration is being done through self-analysis, diaries, autobiographies, dream analysis, masturbation. We are learning from other women about ourselves. We are learning about ourselves from ourselves. As a result, our understanding of female sexuality is being drastically revised from the concept that had been taught us.

A new self-concept is emerging and we are taking better care of ourselves as a result. For the first time since patriarchy was imposed upon the world, we are relating to men sexually in authentic terms, from a postition of strength, as active participants and as responsible adults. As our self-concept slowly changes, our image in the world changes as well. In this area also, the healing process is operating concurrently inside and outside.

TAKING RESPONSIBILITY: PAST, PRESENT, FUTURE

As we reexamine world history and our own private histories we become more and more clear about our responsibilities: We, as women, let men take over the world in the past; we are responsible for having allowed that to happen. Through feminism we are rectifying that imbalance of power. Our parents oppressed us and now those of us who have children find ourselves oppressing them in turn. We can no longer just blame our parents; we must assume responsibility for this oppression. What happened in the past is still happening and unless we effect changes now, sexism will continue in the future.

As we look around us we see a society in crisis; as we look around the world we see a planet in danger. Economists and scientists analyze the situation, politicians attempt to deal with it, journalists report to us on their findings. What are we as women doing? What are our choices? There are those who say: "Why talk about us as women separately, aren't we all part of the same species, why not say what are we as people doing?" In an equitable world that would be true: there would be no separation of sexes, races or ages. But, as it is, each of those categories represent a social class in the hierarchy set up by white men on this planet. Women, when considered as a *class*, represent strength in numbers and weakness in political and economic power. This imbalance needs to be rectified, our power must represent our strength. This can be achieved only if we assume responsibility for our lives, for the lives of our children, mothers and fathers, and for the lives of other living species on this planet.

Choice is a key word in this process of taking responsibility for our lives, choice in the existential sense: If we recognize that by not engaging we have nonetheless made a choice — except that the choice is negative — then we might be willing to reconsider and change our choice to a positive action. What can we do? We do as much as we have inside of us and if we do it together we can build a base of collective strength which will multiply that creative energy.

Patriarchal systems have kept women in isolation: By separating us from each other, we have been prevented from using our active energy. To begin with, then, we must break out of this isolation and reach out to those women who are still maintained in such a way that they are serving a system that aggravates their situation as well as ours.

In order to break through the isolation we have to build a base of trust: trust in each other and trust in ourselves. The process is always the same: As we work on ourselves, we also work with each other so that we reach out as we reach in.

As women we already know a great deal about our inner lives and our perceptions of the inner lives of others are often very accurate; we do not, however, always trust those perceptions. One way to learn to trust them is to check them out. People usually like to know how others perceive them so as we tell others we can test our own perceptual mechanism. Another useful tool is to encourage others to give us feedback so that our self-image can be mirrored in the visions of others: In this way, we not only learn about trusting ourselves, but we also learn about trusting other women. We learn about trust and how it can be reinforced.

As our confidence builds from the inner sources we can begin to express what we have learned to the outside world. We must take care of ourselves and go at our own pace, not overtax ourselves, for only if we remain centered will we be able to project our strength. We must not measure ourselves against others or against imaginary yardsticks. If another woman is a better public speaker than we are, we do not need to do that because we can support her doing it; we can do something else. Or, we can do it at another time. If, on the other hand, we want to do something but we are scared, then we need to give each other a push:

> I think every time you come in contact with a basic feeling that you want to do something and you feel scared to do it and then you go ahead and do it anyway, *that* for me is getting in touch with what I really want and where I really want to be at and what I really need for myself and then managing to go through the fear and the reluctance to risk whatever is going to be risked and to try to do it. Every time that I am aware of that tension place, I am pushing myself past some kind of an obstacle.

What can we do? What are we capable of doing? These questions come up over and over again, like a refrain, in women's groups. We have found that there is a correspondence between what we like to do and what we can do. We need to pay attention to what we like because it is a clue to where our energy is centered. It is sufficient to make a mental note of what we like; our brain will store that information for later use when action is required or when we need to decide what action we are capable of undertaking.

As women move from individual to collective action, as we work together we are devising new working systems: There is no assigning of tasks, there is simply assuming responsibility for what needs to be done. Saying: "I'll do the poster," "I'll call the press," "I'll take care of the mailing" makes one choose what one can do and the very commitment to the task facilitates execution. We are now counteracting conditioned repression by assuming responsibility for our own lives, by contacting the power within us and finding ways of translating it into action, into power on the outside. The internal and external changes function concurrently in feminism.

INTEGRATION

Integration is a key word in feminism: It might be said that feminism is an integration of various heretofore incompatible elements built on a collective base of thought-feeling-action. Throughout this chapter we have seen how feminists are constantly working on integrating their inside world with the outside world. This work stems from a deep conviction that only by accomplishing this integration can society and individuals become whole again. This conviction is based on an intuitive as well as on a scientific understanding of the world: In the natural habitat, all elements are integrated and interrelated. Man has invented opposites like "good" and "evil" or "mind" and "body." Western man has found it necessary to classify knowledge and observations around principles that separate; feminism wants to rectify that error.

Feminism integrates the subjective and the objective, the rational and the intuitive, the mystical and the scientific, the abstract and the concrete aspects of the universe and considers them harmonious parts of a whole, rather than opposites of one another. We do not believe that there is such a thing as a "masculine" and a "feminine" side of human nature and that one is active and the other passive. Instead, we believe that active and passive are forces that function in harmony with one another and that they are totally interrelated, like the tides and the moon.

Our cycles teach us a great deal about ourselves; they have information to which we are now beginning to pay serious attention. We, as women, have always been aware of how our bodies and our mind-feelings are coordinated and integrated. It has been a strain to relate to the world of separation, to rationalism, to an ordering and classifying of systems that do not correspond to our perceptions of reality. Now we are validating our information and we are beginning to observe ourselves. The emphasis that rationalists have placed on the intellectual, the visible, the tangible has kept them from being tuned into the other equally important forces operating all around us. We do not mean to do away with the rational process, but we want to integrate it with the intuitive process.

Through feminism, then, we are working on reintegrating the various forces operating in the biosphere while, at the same time, working with each other and with ourselves to overcome the conditioned reflex to hold back, not to trust our impulses, not to overstep the boundaries set up *for* us, not *by* us:

> I keep getting a flash of that power and what it actually means to have that power where you can become just golden. I keep getting flashes of that. I feel like I am almost touching it with my fingertips, but I really have to do a lot of work to get to that place. I see it in me but there is a

feeling like I have to take another jump.

REFERENCES

Chesler, Phyllis: *Women & Madness*. New York, Doubleday, 1972.

May, Rollo: *Love and Will*. New York, Dell, 1974.

Plath, Sylvia: *The Bell Jar*. New York, Harper & Row, 1971.

Rush, Anne Kent: *Getting Clear: Body Work for Women*. New York, Random House, 1973.

Wittig, Monique: *Les Guerillères*. Translated from the French by David LeVay. New York, Viking Press, 1971.

—— Chapter 16 ——

THERAPEUTIC ASPECTS OF CONSCIOUSNESS-RAISING GROUPS*

Annette M. Brodsky

W ITH the reawakening of the feminist movement in the 1960's, women began to investigate what Friedan (1963) identified as the "problem that had no name," the boredom and disillusionment of middle-class housewives with prescribed roles that provide little opportunity for individual talents and needs beyond the roles of "kinder, kuche, and Kirche" (children, kitchen, and church). Later in the decade Bird (1968) discovered what women in the working world suspected but dared not voice aloud. She found that when a woman leaves the stereotyped roles, she fights a battle against subtle and blatant discrimination. The battle is a lonely one for those who must overcome the initial fears of loss of femininity, social disapproval, and disdain from men and women alike who resent her daring to compete in the male domain.

CONSCIOUSNESS-RAISING GROUPS

Consciousness-raising (C-R) groups grew out of the sense of restless constraint in housewives and the awareness noted by professional women of being different and alone. In an important contribution to the women's movement, C-R groups helped to develop the awareness among women that other women shared the same self-doubts. The present analysis focuses on the psychological impact of consciousness-raising, and its relationship to psychotherapy.

The small-group structure of the women's movement is ideally suited to the exploration of personal identity issues. The technique of heightening self-awareness by comparing personal experiences is as basic to the continuance and solidarity of the movement as any other tactic. Women find themselves eliciting and freely giving support to other group members who often are asserting themselves as individuals for the first time in their lives. They gain strength from members who confront others and they learn to ask for their own individual rights to adopt new roles and express new behaviors.

---

*Revision of: The consciousness-raising group as a model for therapy with women. *Psychotherapy: Theory, Research and Practice,* 10:24, 1973. Used with permission of the journal.

Women in C-R groups do not react in the traditional female interaction patterns commonly seen in all-female therapy groups. For example, ask a therapist about the interaction patterns of an all-female group of mothers, of patients, or of institutional groups. Typically, the women are described as catty, aggressive, competitive, and much tougher on each other for digressions, than they are toward men.

In their traditional roles, women have been isolated from each other and from events in the larger political and economic world beyond their narrowly confined psychological space. The C-R group offers a sense of closeness or intimacy with other women as opposed to the media-produced sense of competition and alienation. The development of the concept of sisterhood arises as a shared understanding of the unique problems of being a woman in a man's world.

There is evidence that all-women groups led by women produce greater levels of empathy than mixed-sex groups (Aries, 1974; Halas, 1973; Meador, Solomon, & Bowen, 1972). The crucial difference between all-women relationships and those with men as therapists or group members is, in my opinion, primarily that men must overcome too much of the male perspective (socialization) in order to be aware of the ramifications of the social issues concerning women. Also, many women do not trust their knowledge of the situation and are inhibited by men's presence. This is neither a condemnation of the men nor the women, but reflects that present level of consciousness in both sexes.

By education and training, women have been encouraged to be conformists and to be passive with men. In C-R groups women must act as individuals. They are encouraged to examine their uniqueness apart from their roles toward others, such as wife, mother, or secretary. In this atmosphere it appears easier for a woman to reveal taboo subjects and feelings, such as not liking to care for young children, wishing one had never married, feeling more intelligent than one's husband or boss, or being tired of boosting a man's self-esteem at the expense of her own. A woman who finds that her feelings are not abnormal, but common experiences of other women, may undergo an experience similar to religious conversion in the C-R group (Newton & Walton, 1971). Another important aspect of an all-women group is the exposure to appropriate female models. (This is discussed in greater detail below.)

The exclusion of men from C-R groups is often misunderstood (Whiteley, 1973). Most men, while sincere, do not realize the subtleties of the women's situations. Indeed, some men are feminists, but they are very few. Furthermore, feminism cannot always be determined by verbal report to that effect. Women's suspicion toward men being included in their groups is natural at this stage of the women's movement. In therapy assignments, I have seen this suspiciousness forced into confrontation by

a staff member insisting that a woman participate in a mixed group, or
see a male therapist. Conversely, I have seen suspicion reinforced by the
isolation of women (women's group, women's center, woman therapist,
woman physician, etc.) from men so that these women have not yet
learned to interact comfortably with men in any setting. It seems to me
that the women-to-women setting can eventually lead to the handling of
a woman-to-man setting. In training therapists, I do not believe in assigning "hysterical" women to male therapists to work out their intense
transference problems. A better solution is for the client to work out her
identity as a woman with a same-sex model, and later to deal with how
she can effectively relate to men in sexual and nonsexual ways.

In contrast with therapy groups, C-R groups start with the assumption
that the environment, rather than intrapsychic dynamics, plays a major
role in the difficulties of the individuals. The medical model of abnormal
behavior based on biological, innate causes is not acceptable to these
groups. They are struggling to redefine the very concepts that have assigned women to a helpless patient role, destined to behave in certain
ways as victims of their biological nature (Chesler, 1971; Weisstein, 1969).

The individual changes that women experience in the context of C-R
groups are quite different from the changes that they may have experienced in previous therapy. Occasionally the C-R group may serve as a
recovery from a sexist experience in therapy (Brodsky, Holroyd, Sherman,
Payton, Rosenkrantz, Rubenstein, & Zell, 1975). Some C-R groups actually are more therapeutic than therapy groups. The intensity of feelings
produced, the feeling of group support, the role modeling, and the empathy developed is often at such a level that therapeutic effects for the
members are better than effects from the individual therapy sessions in
which they are concurrently enrolled (Smith, 1975).

However, while C-R groups may be therapeutic, they are not therapy
groups. Therapy is deliberately designed to be a corrective experience; C-
R groups are not. Of course, women may have corrective experiences in
C-R groups. The primary goal of self-disclosure in C-R is not primarily
individual change but the identification of problems facing women in
a society that needs social reform. Thus, if a woman enters a C-R group
with great distortions about reality and poor coping skills with people,
but emerges with a more realistic view of the world and her potential
impact on it, she may well be said to have had a therapeutic experience in
the C-R group. On the other hand, a woman in the same group who
discovers the commonality of her own views and feels a sense of relief that
she has always been "normal", is now able to grow to a fuller potential,
uninhibited by previous reservations and low self-esteem. Her experience
is less a therapeutic one than a growth or self-actualizing one.

APPROPRIATE CANDIDATES FOR C-R GROUPS

C-R groups are topic-oriented rather than person-oriented. They are geared to women who want role fulfillment but who do not have major mental stumbling blocks. Perhaps the greatest distinction between C-R and therapy lies in the intensity of the need of the individual and the response that results from that experience; while techniques from C-R groups can be adapted to therapy with women, women who need intensive therapy cannot be served exclusively through the C-R experience. The rise of feminist therapy as a specialty area has partially resolved the referral concerns of C-R groups (Brodsky, 1975).

Some candidates may be deemed inappropriate for a C-R group if they appear too defensive about or too vulnerable to the issues, or if their position is so deviant from the group's values that alienation and lack of support might be an issue. Antifeminists are not converted to feminism by C-R groups. The feeling of discontent with the *status quo* of traditional female roles is a necessary beginning point to face the issues of the women's movement.

C-R GROUP DYNAMICS

A sense of trust in other women and a closeness based on common problems that arise from external sources as well as internal self-doubts, serves to bind C-R groups into continuing, relatively stable units. The attrition rate for the groups my colleagues and I have encountered as well as for those studied by Newton & Walton (1971) appears to be lower than those of typical voluntary therapy groups or sensitivity groups. Group members appear to move to an intimacy stage rapidly and to maintain a strong loyalty. Dropouts occur early, often due to a woman's conflict with a man who is threatened by changes in her dependency behavior.

The processes that occur in C-R groups are akin to assertion training, personal growth groups, achievement-oriented training and self-development groups. In assertion training, the key technique involves role models provided by other group members. Women as models are more convincing than male authoritarian leaders for whom the assertive role is a cultural expectation. Likewise, achievement needs are raised more readily in an all-woman group. In C-R groups as in Synanon, Recovery, Inc., or Alcoholics Anonymous, experienced members give strength to the neophyte.

I have seen faculty women return to long forgotten dissertations and take advanced courses, and housewives confront their husbands for more rights or domestic help. Others got divorces from marriages that were

security traps, and childless women stood up for their right to refuse to
have children simply because others thought they should.

Even with the empathy and support of the group, the process of translating skills discussed into action is a great hurdle, but, if accomplished,
is the greatest value of the C-R experience. Difficulty arises when women
try to transfer their new behaviors outside the group. In a fashion parallel
to the sensitivity group member who expects others outside the group to
respond as positively as the group, C-R group members often find that
the outside world has not changed to correspond to the group's level of
awareness. It is at this stage that women tend to become angry with their
employers, lovers, and old friends for continuing to act in chauvinistic,
stereotyped patterns. Because the women are behaving in new ways that
society usually does not condone, these women may be ignored, misunderstood, patronizingly laughed at, or subject to retaliatory confrontation. In frustration, the women may overreact and provoke just the
response they fear to get. For example, loud demands for better treatment
on the job by a previously meek woman may well meet with a backlash
response terminating her job. Frustration with the outside world often
leads to a period of depression, either in the individual or the group as a
whole. They feel that while they can become aware of their situation and
make individual changes, they cannot make much of an impact on the
outside world. There is little outside reinforcement to continue their
motivation. At this later stage, dropouts occur: the faculty woman gets
pregnant instead of completing her dissertation, the potential divorcee
decides that security is more important after all, the frustrated housewife
announces that "Joe thinks this group is making me unhappy and he
wants me to quit," or the graduate student cannot find time because she
is staying up nights typing her boyfriend's thesis.

If these regressive tendencies are weathered by the group, the most
crucial, and often the most effective, stage of the group experience develops. The women plan to actively alter their environments in a realistic
manner to make them more compatible with the developing growth
needs of the members. The direction of the group turns from personal,
individual solutions (except for occasional booster-shot sessions as the
need arises) to some sort of group action. Actions that groups may take
vary according to talents, age and needs. They might consist of organized
protests, political lobbying, educational programs, or missionary goals of
helping to organize other groups to expand the population of the enlightened. The C-R group works to give a sense of social as well as
personal worth to the members, and as a by-product, serves to help
modify an environment insensitive to the needs of growing population of
restless women.

In a four-year follow-up of women in one C-R group in an academic setting, further growth from the impact of the group can be seen even when the original benefit was doubtful. Thus, in reference to dropouts, it is interesting to discover what the women eventually resolved at a later period. The graduate student, whose attendance was inconsistent because of conflict with her husband over how the group was affecting her, completed her degree, readopted her maiden name, and now has a professional position. The woman who decided to get pregnant rather than to complete her long-delayed dissertation or to fight for her job (which was threatened because of her feminism) also made surprising changes. She divorced her husband, filed a suit against her employer for discrimination, completed her degree, and is now applying for a position commensurate with her abilities and aspirations. Another member of the group who did not raise personal concerns about her job is gaining status in that job and feels free of peer pressures of academic women to get pregnant. She is now raising a baby without sacrificing her career to her child.

The pressures on women's roles come from two directions: a pull to remain with traditional ties even when they are stultifying, and a pull to move onward, even when aspects of the traditional role seem desirable. The ideal C-R group raises the issues, the anger, the assertiveness, and offers group support for action. But it does not insist on actions, demean choices made, or become disheartened when a member's consciousness is lower than expected. Growth continues after the group disbands. The parallels to therapy are obvious. No one finishes therapy by attaining their ultimate goals. Therapy initiates a process of growth which must continue after the regular sessions terminate. The impact of a good or bad therapist may affect an individual years later. Investigations today into the negative impact of therapy on individuals, and in particular women, are being pursued (Brodsky et al., 1975).

TRANSFER OF C-R VALUES AND TECHNIQUES
TO INDIVIDUAL THERAPY

An implication of the above discussion is that the C-R groups of the women's movement are relevant for the treatment of identity problems of women in therapy. The following suggestions are possibilities for transferring the C-R group dynamics to individual therapy. First, in working with women on identity issues, therapists should be aware of the increasingly wide range of roles and personality traits for healthy functioning women (Maccoby, 1971). For example, assertion should not be interpreted as aggression because the behavior occurs in a female. Second, a good therapist should be aware of the reality of the female client's situation. Many factors are beyond the client's control. She cannot realistically expect to attain achievement comparable to a man's unless she has greater intellectual and/or motivational abilities. Discrimination does exist (Amundsen, 1971; Astin, 1969; Bernard, 1971; Bird, 1968; Epstein, 1970). Because of this discrimination, encouragement through training in assertion and independence, is of paramount importance counteracting the many years of discouragement through subtle, cultural mores. The therapist can serve as supporter and believer in the client's competence throughout the regressive, dropout stages and, in the face of individual frustrations, the therapist can also recognize the need for some direct and meaningful activity related to improving societal situations.

Working with women's C-R groups offers a number of insights to a therapist about the particular problems women face in trying to resolve the difficulties of living in a world that revolves around men's work. For example, those women who report patterns of intrusive male behavior often appear to be oversensitive to slights and minor brushoffs. C-R group experiences help women to confirm their reality of such slights, rather than denying their existence or passing them off as projections. A man can overlook such incidents as exceptional and not understand them as a frequent experience of women who are not taken seriously or accepted as thinking individuals.

For a woman, the experience is the rule rather than the exception (unless she is an exceptional woman). Her sensitivity to such slights comes out of an awareness of the situation, and a concomitant frustration in being unable to defend herself without appearing pompous, "uppity", or paranoid.

The accumulation of experiences of being interrupted in conversations and having opinions ignored can severely affect a woman's feelings of competence and self-worth. Her desire to be assertive, or to make an impact on the environment is continuously weakened by the lack of affirmation of herself by others.

There are therapists who maintain that women act insecure or inferior in order to get secondary gains from such postures (using feminine wiles); therefore, they consider the woman's verbalizations of a desire for independence or responsibility as not genuine. Therapists often do not understand that without role models or encouragement from the environment, these women have no real choice but to accept what they have been indoctrinated to believe about the capabilities of their sex. There are other major themes which some therapists are apt to misjudge or overlook when dealing with women clients. Unaware therapists still tend to consider marriage uncritically as a solution for women's problems without realizing that, as with men, divorce or no marriage may often present the best available alternative for the individual. When a woman proposes such a solution, the therapist may become more concerned with her nontraditional life-style than with her personal reasons for wanting such a life-style.

Some therapists, who have not been exposed to the issues that a C-R group might raise, automatically assume that a woman's career is secondary to her mate's career. The conflict over "having it both ways," by wanting a career and family is then seen as the wife's burden, not the husband's also. New patterns of division in household tasks and child care are no longer stigmas that should label individuals as deviant. Therapists have been guilty of producing iatrogenic disorders in women who felt comfortable with what they were doing until the therapist suggested that they were selfish and unreasonable, or pointed out how no one expected them to accomplish so much because they would be loved and accepted without this unrealistic drive to compete.

Perhaps related to the foregoing is the frustration women have experienced with therapists who can empathize readily with a man who is stifled by a clinging, nagging wife, but who interpret the same complaint from a woman as her being cold and unfeeling for not responding affectionately to her insecure, demanding husband. The crucial point in such misunderstandings is that many therapists have a double standard for men and women in mental health and adjustment (Broverman, Broverman, Clarkson, Rosenkrantz, & Vogel, 1970). Their attitudes restrict their capacity to allow their clients a free expression of the various available roles. Women, after all, have needs for self-esteem, independence, anger and aggression, just as men have needs for security, affection and the expression of fear and sorrow. While both need greater freedom in sex-role expression present, men have more diverse models in our society for the development of an adequate masculine role. For the most part women's models have been restricted to housewives or the narrow traditional feminine occupations (Block, 1973).

Perhaps the strongest message in the success of C-R groups is that women are capable of using other women as models. The identification of women with role models of their own sex has been largely limited to the traditional homemaker roles or the feminine occupations such as teaching and nursing. The acceptance of more varied roles and personality traits in women will help to integrate a larger portion of women into the "mentally healthy" categories.

Until more female role models are available, perhaps, as Chesler (1971) suggests, only women should be therapists for other women. On the other hand, if therapists must have had the same experiences as their clients in order to help them, we would be very restricted. In the long run, whatever the situation or therapeutic format (individual, all-women or mixed-sex group) it is crucial that the process not be sexist. No matter what the sex of the therapist, the values of the therapist about the role of women in society must be made explicit to the client so that she can make a choice about the goals of therapy before a therapeutic relationship is established.

Because male clinicians know women in their personal lives, they frequently assume that they know enough about women's conflicts to treat them. However, casual attention and personal relationships do not provide sufficient clinical data on which to base treatment. Many clinicians assume that women do not face different social conditions than men and, therefore, do not require *any* special treatment. Obviously, women do face a different world than men do; those different circumstances must be taken into consideration by the therapist.

The Freudians did assume that women were a special category, and required special attention. However, they also assumed that women could not be trusted to report feelings honestly. Like children and psychotics, women needed analysts to interpret their actions accurately. Today, C-R groups are not only demonstrating that women are capable of understanding their own motivations, but that Freudian theories of female development served to discourage women from seeking legitimate goals.

Every clinician must be aware that the training s/he has received, and/or is receiving, does not sufficiently prepare her/him to treat women with role conflicts. *Any* therapist who has not kept abreast of current theories and issues relating to women is treating them from a position of ignorance and should disqualify her/himself from treating women clients.

Studying C-R groups is one way to learn alternatives to sexism in therapy. Workshops about women, supervision by feminists, and consultation with women colleagues are some other initial steps therapists can take to learn to eliminate their sexism. Not all therapists can or want to be "feminist therapists", but *all* should aspire to be nonsexist.

REFERENCES

Amundsen, Karen: *The Silenced Majority: Women and American Democracy.* Englewood Cliffs, Prentice Hall, 1971.

Aries, Elizabeth: Interaction patterns and themes of male, female, and mixed groups. Paper presented at the American Psychological Association, New Orleans, August, 1974.

Astin, Helen: *The Woman Doctorate in America.* Hartford, Sage Foundation, 1969.

Bernard, Jesse: The paradox of the happy marriage. In Gornick, Vivian, and Moran, Barbara (Eds.): *Woman in Sexist Society: Studies in Power and Powerlessness.* New York, Basic Books, 1971.

Bird, Carolyn: *Born Female: The High Cost of Keeping Women Down.* New York, McKay, 1968.

Block, Jeanne H.: Conceptions of sex role: some cross-cultural and longitudinal perspective. *American Psychologist, 28*:6, 1973.

Brodsky, Annette M.: Is there a feminist therapy? Paper presented at the Southeastern Psychological Association Symposium, Atlanta, March, 1975.

Brodsky, Annette; Holroyd, Jean; Sherman, Julia; Payton, Caroline; Rosenkrantz, Paul; Rubenstein, Eli; and Zell, Freyda: Report of the task force on sex bias and sex role stereotyping in therapeutic practice. American Psychological Association, 1975.

Broverman, Inge K.; Broverman, Donald M.; Clarkson, Frank; Rosenkrantz, Paul; and Vogel, Sue R.: Sex-role stereotypes and clinical judgments of mental health. *Journal of Consulting Psychology, 34*:1, 1970.

Chesler, Phyllis: Patient and patriarch: Women in the psychotherapeutic relationship. In Gornick, Vivian, and Moran, Barbara (Eds.): *Woman in Sexist Society: Studies in Power and Powerlessness.* New York, Basic Books, 1971.

Epstein, Cynthia: *Woman's Place: Options and Limits in Professional Careers.* Berkeley, California Press, 1970.

Friedan, Betty: *The Feminine Mystique.* New York, Dell, 1963.

Halas, Celia: All-woman groups: A view from inside. *Personnel and Guidance Journal, 52*:91, 1973.

Maccoby, Eleanor: Sex differences and their implications for sex roles. Paper presented at the American Psychological Association, Washington, D.C., September, 1971.

Meador, Betty; Solomon, Evelyn; and Bowen, Marcia: Encounter groups for women only. In Solomon, Lawrence N.; and Belzon, Betty (Eds.): *New Perspectives on Encounter Groups.* New York, Jossey-Bass, 1972.

Newton, Esther; and Walton, Shirley: The personal is political: Consciousness-raising and personal change in the women's liberation movement. In Schoepf, B. (Ed.): Anthropologists Look at the Study of Women. Symposium presented at the American Psychological Association, November, 1971.

Smith, Alma D.: Consciousness raising groups: a viable alternative to therapy for women. Paper presented at the Southeastern Psychological Association, Atlanta, March, 1975.

Weisstein, Naomi: Kinder, kuche, kirche as scientific law: Psychology constructs the female. *Motive, 29*:6, 1969.

Whiteley, Rita M.: Women in groups. *The Counseling Psychologist, 4*:27, 1973.

—— *Chapter 17* ——

PROBLEMS OF PERSONAL CHANGE IN WOMEN'S STUDIES COURSES

Marie Celeste Guzell

M Y experiences in teaching women's studies (W. S.) courses have led me to believe that the responsibilities of the professor in such courses are far more extensive than for other courses. Instructors for traditional courses need not be concerned with Dewey's philosophy of educating the whole person, because the student leaves at home most of her "whole" person. This is not the case in women's studies courses. Interdisciplinary and egalitarian, these courses invite students to bring their "whole selves" to class — their personal and social concerns — whether or not the instructor desires it.

I believe that women's studies courses, like psychotherapy, have the potential to open people to change in meaningful ways. These changes can be either positive or negative, or both. Accordingly, this paper analyzes characteristics of women's studies courses, explores the kinds of changes that occur, and, finally, makes recommendations to women's studies instructors for promoting growth and avoiding stress and confusion in their students.

CHARACTERISTICS OF WOMEN'S STUDIES COURSES

A women's studies course lies somewhere between any college course and a consciousness-raising group, but it is not exactly either.

Differences From Other Courses

Beginning soon after ethnic studies and Black studies, women's studies developed out of the Women's Liberation Movement of the early sixties. The first courses were characterized by a militant break from established disciplines, and developers had to look to other disciplines and popular feminist literature for fresh, innovative approaches. In spite of a recent decline in militancy, women's studies courses are still dedicated implicitly (if not explicitly) to feminist goals of equality and human freedom. No matter how humanitarian other college courses may be, they simply do not pursue their goals with the same extensive commitment found in movement-born courses.

Who signs up for a women's studies course? This has changed. Earlier, women already directly involved in political liberation movements signed up. Now the typical student is a young man or women who, stimulated by the mass media, seeks to examine her/his own attitudes and confusions about sex roles and cultural expectations. The motivation of some of the students is exactly the same as it is for courses in psychology — "I took the course to learn more about myself." Herein lies student motivation for personality change!

Another characteristic is the open expression of antagonism between the sexes which frequently surfaces in a highly ambivalent manner. Hostility between the sexes in society is a fact. The women's studies classroom provides the focus and the forum for venting discontent between males and females.

Women's studies courses, then, differ from other academic courses in their history, goals, volatile subject matter, and student expectations. In these respects, such courses resemble consciousness-raising groups. In both, participants learn about sex-role oppressions and experience a very personal involvement. However, women's studies courses do differ from consciousness-raising groups.

Differences From Consciousness-raising and Therapy Groups

An advantage of women's studies courses over C-R and therapy groups is the rather firm contract for exposure to information. Any course involves a contract whereby the student exposes her/himself to learning for a limited number of weeks for course credits. After initial drops, students stay in the course whether or not they like it. This is not so for C-R or therapy groups in which participants may drop out when their interest wanes or when the going gets rough. The course contract increases the potential for change. Among reluctant participants, especially, the change potential is greater than for C-R or therapy groups.

The major differences between women's studies classes and C-R or therapy groups relate to the structure and process of groups in general. In comparison, some disadvantages of W.S. courses become apparent. Classes may be too large for persons to express themselves, especially about personal matters (which they very much need to do). In a sociological sense, the composition of the classroom is more of a collectivity than a group, more a secondary group than a primary group, more *gesellschaft* than *gemeinschaft*. In the formal class context, role prescriptions and restrictions make personal communications more difficult than in C-R or therapy groups. Personal concerns, once expressed, run the risk of being met with an unexpected attack from a peer, hostile indifference, bland disinterest with no follow-up comments, and, worst of all, no promise of confidentiality. As a large and loosely knit collectivity of "sometime" participants, a classroom suffers from the absence of processes operative in small groups. One cannot count on group pressures to curb obstructionistic maneuvers of some students, nor can one rely on group support for those who need help with a relevant course-related problem.

Finally, it should be remembered that in a W.S. course a voluminous amount of novel and disturbing information must be digested. The new information often conflicts with currently held beliefs and values, so that cognitive dissonance is the rule. One is fueling the fire in an environment where there is ordinarily precious little means to control the heat.

In summary, women's studies courses are unlike other college courses in that the subject matter and needs of students are similar to those of participants in C-R and therapy groups. However, they differ from the latter two in that principles of small-group processes are ordinarily not expected nor employed. One might characterize a women's studies class as *the creation of the need for therapy in a group of individuals operating in an essentially nontherapeutic environment.* The seed is planted, but the fertilizer supply is limited.

CHANGES IN STUDENTS IN WOMEN'S STUDIES COURSES

Change in women in W.S. courses varies considerably. Some do not change at all. Some experience minor attitudinal changes. A minority experience considerable psychological problems. Others may display wholesome personality change. Changes result not only from individual differences, but also from differences in the total feminist milieu in which the course takes place. Where women have recourse to additional women's studies courses, C-R groups, women's political organizations, an institution sympathetic to women's problems, and/or relationships with enlightened associates and friends, more extensive and positive personality changes are possible. On the other hand, when a conservative student from a conservative community takes only one W.S. course and there are no social supports in the town and campus community, then unresolved conflicts are more likely.

My own experiences have included teaching psychology-of-women courses in two conservative communities in two Midwestern states. Hence, the reader should be aware that my views of change evolved out of those experiences and may not be held by women's studies instructors in more progressive communities.

Overall, women are ambivalent about having taken a women's studies course. Women students have commented that course content made them very anxious and uncomfortable, *but* they were glad they took the course because it made them "think about things they never thought about before." In a class I taught recently, thirty out of thirty-five students answered "yes" to the question, "Were you at anytime during the semester frustrated by the subject matter for the course?" Students taking their second course from me (an advanced course involving field studies) stated that ideas about feminism were "invading our lives" and they sought to develop C-R groups outside the small class to deal with their discomforts. Likewise, Carter (1975) observed that three out of four small discussion groups sought to continue meeting after her course was completed. I also noted that two out of three persons in a course with leaderless groups expressed interest in continuing in a group, even though it would be a different and new group. It does seem that, despite anxieties, women have positive experiences with these courses.

Positive Aspects

What, then, are these positive experiences? Most important of all, women have the exhilarating experience of learning to think for themselves. This can be scary, but liberating.

Very important is the realization that what they formerly thought were their "unique" problems are shared by almost every woman! For years women have blamed themselves for lack of achievement, lack of motivation, discord in marriage, problems with sexuality, and the like. They discover that some of their "shortcomings" are due to cultural conditioning rather than to personal inadequacies. They become aware that they have been "ripped off" by a sexist society which makes unrealistic and contradictory demands on them.

With the realization that experiences are universally shared by women, women are able to externalize blame for the first time in their lives. Women characteristically assume blame for their failures and fail to assume responsibility for their successes. They tend to blame themselves while men tend to blame others. Also, women characteristically tend to feel guilty or selfish for caring about themselves and for not caring about others enough. With the insights that they each have a right to be a complete person and that their humanity is diminished by too much concern for others, women can shed their great burden of self-abnegation and habitual guilt.

Another positive experience is reduced alienation brought about by a new respect for other women and by the development of a group-consciousness. Feminist writers (especially sociologists) have pointed out that women are alienated from other women by the nuclear family. Men have camaraderie outside the home, but a woman's first (and often sole) concern is her family or husband. Women wash, cook, and care for children alone; hence, marriage tends to segregate women from one another.

This segregation is reinforced by the distrust and disrespect they acquire for other women. [Lionel Tiger (1969) has gone so far as to theorize that women have no "group instinct!"] With the development of a group-consciousness, women begin to discover they have much to share with other women. As they do this, they become less alienated from other women, and concomitantly, less alienated from themselves.

Of direct value to women is the development of a more objective and realistic approach to career, marriage, education, and motherhood. A women's studies course equips them with a more cautious attitude toward society's sacred institutions. Myths about the fulfilling nature of marriage and motherhood are discounted. Realities about marriage-career conflicts are brought to the fore, and difficulties attendant to career ambitions in light of discrimination and sexism in the society are faced. I think this knowledge prepares women to deal more adequately with the roles in which they find themselves with husband, children, and employers. Brodsky (1973) found that thirty out of thirty-six in one women's studies class, and thirteen out of eighteen in another, were optimistic about women's roles in the future. In a perverted way a few women may experience a sense of loss in learning that men are not Prince Charmings who carry them off into the sunset, that the real Prince Charming may have a drooping lance and human frailty. Nevertheless, a more realistic attitude about sex roles and institutions makes women feel stronger and gives them good preparation for the future.

Negative Aspects

Why are women ambivalent about women's studies courses? It happens that concomitant with positive changes are experiences which may be perceived as negative. Carter (1974b) has theorized that there are five stages of feminist consciousness, each marked by changes in women's attitudes and in behaviors towards themselves and other women and men. According to Carter, attitudes towards men change from confusion and despair in the first stage, to distrust, intolerance, dislike and anger in the second stage, developing into trust, tolerance, and liking in the final stages. Appreciation among women increases in a women's studies course, although hostility between the sexes may increase; it is not likely that many women can achieve a successful development through all five stages in any one course. There is not sufficient time over the course of one semester to reach the final stages; so many women report discomfort, anxiety, and a need for continuing interaction with a W.S. group.

This hypothesis is consistent with others' observations. Marlowe and Shapiro (1972) noted that some students taking women's studies courses find the analysis of sex roles threatening. Developers of a women's studies minor at a California university, recognizing the needs of students enrolled in large introductory courses, provide one day each week for small discussion groups.

I have observed that women who are actively involved in the women's liberation movement go through six stages of consciousness: First, there is consciousness-raising, which provides an ever-increasing awareness of discrimination against women and awareness of how this relates to each woman personally. Second, anger increases to the point at which participants feel something must be done to promote equality. Third, anger is channeled into political and organized action in a feminist group. Fourth, the newly politicized women are enchanted with their power, their new self-esteem, and the "beauty" of women comrades (often called the honeymoon stage by politicos). Fifth, a disenchantment occurs when women experience political and personal conflicts with other women and disappointments with inevitable failures of some of their group's important political efforts. In the final stage, participants who remained after the fifth stage experience a decrease in emotional intensity, but an increase in awareness of and commitment to the hard and frequently ungratifying work involved in maintaining a political-action group. Even strong, aware, and self-assertive women in political groups find themselves in despair at times and require continuous group support. The majority of women who take a women's studies course or who get involved in group consciousness-raising do not participate in political groups, but the changes that occur in all women are parallel. And the course of change seldom runs smoothly.

Empirical Findings

Joesting, Joesting, and Guzell (1974) conducted an exploratory study of mood and attitude change in two women's studies courses. The Profile of Mood states, POMS, (McNair, Lorr, Droppelman, 1971) and the Woman and Man attitude scale (Tavris, 1971) were employed. Group I consisted of students in a Southern university who elected the course because they had been interested in feminism. Group II consisted of students in a conservative Midwestern university who elected the course naively, that is, the course was titled "Current Problems in Psychology," and they did not know prior to taking the course that problems of women were the focus. The Control group was a developmental psychology class at the Southern university. Both Experimental groups evidenced statistically significant change toward more liberal attitudes about women's roles, while the Control group showed no attitude change. On the POMS, Group II, showed statistically significant increases in Tension-Anxiety ($P = <.01$), Depression-Defection ($P = <.05$), and Anger-hostility ($P = <$

.05), while they evidenced a significant decrease in Vigor-Activity (P = < .01). Group I and the Control group showed no mood changes. These findings could have been due to chance, but, because students in Group II reported anxieties and frustrations in open discussion at the end of the semester, my colleagues and I favor the view that the course experience produced mood changes in this group.

Another study may have bearing on the above findings. Miller and Guzell (1973) investigated the self-concept and ideal self-concept of liberated and nonliberated women. The liberated group included eight members of a women's caucus on campus and ten members of an advanced women's studies class; the nonliberated groups included fifteen women from a college home economics class and nine housewives in the community. Seventy-five "favorable" and seventy-five "unfavorable" adjectives were employed from two scales on the Adjective Check List (ACL)

TABLE 17 - I

"FAVOURABLE" ADJECTIVES CHECKED MORE
FREQUENTLY BY LIBERATED WOMEN*

Adjective	LW	NLW	Chi Square	Level of Significance
Assertive	13	5	11.091	< .001
Curious	14	10	5.777	< .05
Determined	13	9	4.972	< .05
Frank	13	8	6.222	< .02
Insightful	12	2	15.750	< .001
Inventive	14	6	14.032	< .001
Rational	12	7	5.839	< .05
Resourceful	14	11	4.356	< .05
Spontaneous	12	4	10.904	< .01
Strong	14	11	4.356	< .05
	N=18	N=24		

*(Miller and Guzell, 1973)
LW = Liberated Women
NLW = Nonliberated Women

TABLE 17 - II

"UNFAVOURABLE" ADJECTIVES CHECKED MORE
FREQUENTLY BY LIBERATED WOMEN*

Adjective	LW	NLW	Chi Square	Level of Significance
Aloof	8	4	3.889	< .05
Argumentative	13	7	7.644	< .01
Arrogant	6	1	6.300	< .02
Careless	6	2	4.169	< .05
Cynical	9	1	11.911	< .001
Disorderly	9	3	7.088	< .01
Egotistical	9	0	15.273	< .001
Opinionated	11	8	3.204	< .05
Self-centered	7	2	5.704	< .02
	N=18	N=24		

*(Miller and Guzell, 1973)
LW = Liberated Women
NLW = Nonliberated Women

(Gough and Heilbrun, 1965). The scales had been combined and rearranged in random order. Subjects completed the scale twice, first with instructions to "describe yourself as you are", and second, to "describe how you would like to be — your ideal self."

The investigators found no significant differences between the groups of women in their "real" and "ideal" self. However, the liberated women (LW) more frequently checked both "favorable" and "unfavorable" adjectives. (See Tables 17-I and 17-II). Favorable adjectives checked significantly more often by liberated women are: assertive, curious, determined, frank, insightful, inventive, rational, resourceful, spontaneous, and strong. Unfavorable adjectives checked significantly more by liberated women are: aloof, argumentative, arrogant, careless, cynical, disorderly, egotistical, opinionated, and self-centered. The only adjective checked significantly more by nonliberated women was "patient." So it would be a fair interpretation to say that non-liberated women are generally the same as liberated women in the adjectives that they checked, but that liberated women differentiated themselves by checking additional adjectives significantly more.

When the favorable adjectives checked significantly more by liberated women are subjected to a clinical analysis, it does appear that these are characteristics of a healthy, self-actualizing male in our society. A superficial clinical analysis of the unfavorable adjectives is suggestive of an unhealthy adjustment. However, other evidence suggests a different interpretation. Seven of the ten favorable adjectives and seven of the nine unfavorable adjectives checked significantly more by the liberated women comprise about one fourth of a well-researched fifty-nine item Creativity Scale adapted from the Adjective Check List (Domino, 1970). Creativity researchers have observed that highly creative persons are both sicker and healthier than noncreative persons, or that at least they may appear to be sicker due to great honesty in self-report or greater self-awareness. Perhaps, after all, the unfavorable adjectives are not so unfavorable in certain contexts.

I have stated earlier in this paper that liberated women may be more androgynous than traditional women. Creative persons, also, have been described as androgynous, as "bisexual" in their personality traits. Creative men are dominant and independent, yet are not without a high degree of emotional sensitivity. Creative women are sensitive, but are also assertive and independent. Creative persons in general and liberated women in particular tend to be liberated from stereotyped sex roles and personality traits associated with stereotyped sex roles. I might add, also, that highly creative men and women do not differ in personality traits associated with creativity.

More light is shed on the adjectives checked by liberated women when these are compared with those on the Counseling Readiness Scale (CRS) of the Adjective Check List (ACL).

> The high-scorer on (the) CRS is worried about (her)/himself and ambivalent about (her)/his status. (S)/he feels left out of things, unable to enjoy life to the full, and unduly anxious. (S)/he tends to be preoccupied with (her)/his problems and pessimistic about (her)/his ability to resolve them constructively. The lower-scorer is more or less free of these concerns. (S)/he is self-confident, poised, sure of (her)/himself and outgoing. (S)/he seeks the company of others, less activity, and enjoys life in an uncomplicated way (Heilbrun and Sullivan, 1962).

Two categories are of interest here, the low-scoring male and the high-scoring female, that is, males who *do not* perceive they are in need of counseling, and females who *do* perceive they are in need of counseling. Twenty-one adjectives from the ACL Creativity Scale (Domino, 1970) fall into these two categories (low-scoring males, 12; high-scoring females, 9). Cashdan and Welsh (1966) found that highly creative adolescents scored significantly higher on Liability, Change, and Counseling Readiness Scales of the ACL. Further, the Miller and Guzell (1973) findings indicate that liberated women checked six adjectives in the low scoring male and

TABLE 17 - III

ADJECTIVES COMPRISING THE COUNSELING READINESS SCALE (CRS)
OF THE ADJECTIVE CHECK LIST (ACL) PERSONALITY SCALE.*

Men		Women	
High Scorers	Low Scorers	High Scorers	Low Scorers
Awkward	Active (C)	Aggressive	Energetic (C)
Cautious	Adventurous (C)	Assertive (C) (LW)	Honest
Cold	Affectionate	Autocratic (C)	Jolly
Commonplace	Ambitious (C)	Bossy	Patient (NLW)
Complicated (C)	Boastful	Cold	Peaceable
Dull	Capable (C)	Cynical	Slow
Fussy	Cheerful	Dignified	Sociable
Inhibited	Clever (C)	Discreet	Suggestible
Meek	Confident (C)	Effeminate	Trusting
Moderate	Courageous	Enterprising	Wholesome
Peculiar	Determined (LW)	Formal	
Quiet	Egotistical (C) (LW)	Independent (C)	
Rigid	Emotional	Individualistic (C)	
Self-seeking	Energetic	Inhibited	
Sensitive	Enthusiastic (C)	Intelligent (C)	
Shy	Headstrong	Moody (C)	
Silent	Humorous (C)	Noisy	
Slow	Initiative	Opportunistic	
Spineless	Jolly	Painstaking	
Timid	Original (C)	Rigid	
Unrealistic	Robust	Self-centered (C) (LW)	
Withdrawn	Snobbish	Serious (C)	
	Spontaneous (C) (LW)	Soft-hearted	
	Temperamental	Stingy	
	Tough	Tense	
	Uninhibited	Thorough	
	Witty	Unaffected	
		Unemotional	
		Unrealistic	

*Adapted from Heilbrun and Sullivan, *Personnel and Guidance Journal,* 41, 112-117, 1962.
(C) = adjectives also appearing on the Creativity Scale of the Adjective Check List (Domino, 1970)
(LW) = adjectives checked by "liberated" women (Miller & Guzell, 1973)
(NLW) = adjectives checked by "nonliberated" women (Miller & Guzell, 1973)

high scoring female categories, whereas nonliberated women did not
check any. Not a strong finding certainly, but suggestive that liberated
women see themselves in need of counseling. More suggestive, perhaps,
are the creativity scale comparisons, which indicate that females with
creative characteristics may perceive that they are in need of counseling.*

Considering only the category for women who perceived themselves in
need of counseling, Dianne Carter (1974a) suggested that by most standards of mental health people checking these adjectives would be perceived
to be high functioning. However, these adjectives do not meet society's
rules for appropriate sex-role behavior for females. Therefore, women
who describe themselves with these adjectives fail to meet societal expectations, and so such women apparently do not consider themselves emotionally sound. Carter concluded that from a feminist standpoint, these
women are actually healthier than traditional women.

It appears that the Creativity Scale of the ACL and a feminist analysis
of the Counseling Readiness Scale present a complex picture of self-concept in women who seek liberation. The self-concept of liberated women
may be seen as negative or positive, depending upon one's values regarding "appropriate" behavior for women, as well as one's definition of
mental health in general.

It should be pointed out that the liberated women studied by Miller
and Guzell represent a more advanced stage of feminist consciousness
than is achieved in any one women's studies course. Also, women who
become feminist may have been less traditional and stronger to begin
with. My personal experiences with feminist women are that they are
more androgynous (having more characteristics of both men and women)
than traditional women.

Anger and Self-Assertion

I think that the two most important problems that women begin to
confront in a women's studies course are *anger* and *self-assertion*. Since
most women are accustomed to being passive, kind, patient, loving, and
self-sacrificing with men, they have difficulty in handling anger towards
men. A woman fears becoming a "bitch" or a "man-hater." Worse yet,
her heterosexuality may be at stake in her eyes. The reasoning goes something like this: (1) Men have oppressed women. (2) I hate men. (3) George
is a man. (4) I hate George ... and Harry, and Bob, and Mike ... Anger
becomes ego-alien and threatening, and some women cannot deal with

---

*Barron (1969) reported that creative women were more subjectively unhappy than either creative
males or noncreative females. They cry more often, report overwhelming feelings of emptiness,
aloneness, and desolation, and are quite commonly preoccupied with thoughts of death and suicide.
Barron attributes this to their "existential reality".

the internal conflict, let alone tackle problems of self-assertion.

Now suppose a woman is able to face anger in herself and seeks to channel that anger into healthy self-assertion. She proceeds to overtly challenge her boyfriend, husband and/or employer. She may ask her boyfriend to be less protective, her husband to do more housework and care for children, or her employer to give her a raise. In short, she acts in ways that threaten men. Now, the threatened male will retaliate with anger, guilt-inducing mechanisms, and threats to withdraw his love. Her attempts to carry out self-assertive behaviors are continually thwarted by males! She becomes more angry with males than she was before she attempted to assert herself. This is a crucial stage. She can persist in efforts at self-assertion (which is easier where there is feminist support), or, feeling defeated, she can turn her hostility against herself. Her old ego defense is intropunitiveness, and now with newly felt hostilities, the resulting self-hate can be especially intense and stressful. Successful self-assertions promote growth while unsuccessful self-assertions may increase self-doubts and anxieties.

In summary, women experience various degrees of change in women's studies courses depending upon the initial personality characteristics of the individual woman and the social support in her daily subcultural milieu. Feminist women, who may have started out as nontraditional and who subject themselves to more intense feminist influences outside women's studies courses, may represent the "success stories" of positive personality change via feminism. In them, change consists of healthy self-doubt, self-assertion, effectively channeled anger, and personality growth. But for many women this not the case. Many women are traditional to begin with, have only limited experience with feminist ideology in women's studies course, and have very little social support from their primary group of local community. For these women, personality change is more problematic. For women who guard their femininity tenaciously, a women's course may either accomplish nothing, or stir-up trouble for such individuals. It is little wonder that many women are ambivalent about the potential attitude and behavior changes stimulated by women' studies courses.

Probably all psychotherapists would concur that personality change is difficult to achieve. Desirable personality changes in women, from a feminist standpoint, are especially difficult to achieve because women are expected to change in ways that are not consistent with the traditional "healthy female personality" (Broverman, Broverman, Clarkson, Rosenkrantz, and Vogel, 1970; Carter, 1974a).

The seed for change can be planted in a women's studies course, and the women's studies instructor has the responsibility of being a change agent. The women's studies classroom is limited by its structure; however, certain procedures can be employed to increase change potentials and reduce confusions and anxieties of women in such courses.

RECOMMENDATIONS FOR INCREASING THERAPEUTIC POTENTIALS IN WOMEN'S STUDIES COURSES

Perhaps I should predicate my remarks here by pointing out that all women's studies courses do not necessarily have change potentials. The writer knows of courses taught by nonfeminists who manage to make the subject just "interesting," but those courses are in the minority. The majority of women's studies courses (especially introductory ones) are oriented towards personal and social change and are at least moderately upsetting. For courses in which growth and social change are goals, I make the following suggestions:

1. The most important recommendation I would make is that there be opportunities provided for persons to express themselves about personal, but relevant matters. Sometimes this is possible in a small class of twenty-five when openness and honesty are encouraged and valued by the instructor. Still better is a method suggested by Dianne Carter and Edna Rawlings*, wherein classes are divided into permanent small same-sex discussion groups of seven to nine persons. When this method is employed, participants are instructed in basic principles of small group dynamics (confidentiality, tolerance, group pressures to conformity, avoidance of scapegoating, openness, equality of opportunity to speak). If necessary, students can be given a topic to lend structure to the groups for each session in order to encourage participants to make more meaningful and personally responsible communications. The initial topic may be developed around discussion of family backgrounds. Value-clarification exercises relevant to aspirations for self and sex-roles may also be developed for initial small group meetings.* I am currently using the topic method in a women's studies course, and, although the groups are leaderless, they are meeting with success.

Referrals to consciousness-raising groups can be made, as those are implicitly, if not explicitly, therapeutic. Students may be encouraged to begin their own C-R groups: in dormitories, co-ops, or other places. There can be groups for males as well as for females. If forming C-R groups is suggested, guidelines for consciousness-raising should be provided as well as guidelines for conducting small discussion groups.

One may argue that it is sexism-in-reverse to insist upon same-sex groups initially; however, there is support for more learning in same-sex

*Dianne Carter and Edna Rawlings, Personal Communication, January, 1975.

groups. Lockheed (1975), in her study of mixed- same-sex adolescent groups engaged in game-playing, found that: (1) women in same sex-groups participated more than women in mixed-sex groups; (2) women in same-sex groups were more democratic than men; (3) nondominant males in all-male groups experienced failure and subsequently partici-pated less than women in mixed-sex groups. Hence, same-sex groups may initially benefit women more than men, but males, also, need to learn how to communicate with other males in a supportive and noncompeti-tive manner. Mixed-sex groups reflect the male dominance in the society; females tend to defer to males and to try to please them. Ultimately such mixed groups achieve conflict-free, but superficial concordance between the sexes. In other words, mixed groups tend to seek adjustment rather than change. Probably, mixed-sex groups would function more construc-tively *only after* both sexes have improved their communications within their own sex group.

2. Timing in teaching is just as important as it is in therapy. There should not be too much explosive reading material in too little time without opportunities to digest it. Topics evolving around irritating sexism may be interspersed with success stories about women or male-female relationships that are favorable. "This is what women *cannot* do" should be monitored by "this is what women *can* do" or "this is what women *have* done." If an instructor puts too much emphasis on the crippling effects of sexism and misogyny, women may begin to inter-nalize an unhealthy sense of actually being a psychological cripple. Pro-viding positive role models in biographies of great women, for example, may help prevent this.

3. Excessive stereotyping about men may be a problem in women's studies courses. Overgeneralizing insights about men may lead women to greater discontent in their personal relationships with men. This is a constant danger to be avoided.

4. To avoid guilt and potential anger in male students from snow-balling, the subject of men's roles in the class and in societal (structural) oppression should be discussed at the beginning of the course. This can be approached in numerous ways depending upon the instructor's ideolo-gies. In my own classes I say something to the effect that no individual man is responsible for all sexism; that the goal of feminism is, not only to change society for women's benefit, but also for men's (who are likewise oppressed by sexism); that the goal is not to make men feel guilty, but to change people; that both men and women are perpetrators and victims of sexism; and sexism is structural. Hopefully, such statements will discour-age men from making remarks which anger the women, and also take the edge off the personal anger any of the women carry with them. It almost always happens, however, that an unsuspecting and unaware

male will betray his stereotypes and will be attacked by the female members. He will feel at a loss to defend the whole race of men by himself, though he may unwisely try. Attacks on male members, even though provoked by them should usually be minimized. Otherwise, tension will increase and morale will decrease.

5. Dianne Carter* suggests that the small discussion group is a good place to discharge anger that gets generated from classroom discussions or current personal transactions. Simply encouraging an animated discussion of a particular anger-provoking incident should be sufficient for catharsis to occur. If these groups have skillful leaders, role-playing is also useful for processing current anger; assertion training is effective for preventing more anger from building up. Old anger, which has been building up over the years, can be processed under the guidance of a trained facilitator using bioenergetics and gestalt therapy.

6. Social action is another means of redirecting the anger and helplessness felt toward men in the classroom. Instructors can bring in newspaper clippings on legal and political issues to which interested women students can address themselves. Almost all current popular political issues can be harnessed for course topics. A speaker on the Equal Rights Amendment could talk in a class discussing female stereotypes on "arguments used to defeat the ERA for four decades". Instructors need not fear bringing politics into the classroom; politics is a form of reality testing to women students as well as a constructive outlet for aggression or anger. In one of my classes I assigned students interested in political and community issues to the same discussion group so that they could communicate with like-minded students. Another interest group was formed on the basis of women's interest in carrying out research projects on women. These are two forms of channeling emotional reactions constructively and in a manner which has therapeutic potential for the person and for society.

7. Men should be discouraged from dominating a women's studies class. Therapeutic potentials will be limited when males dominate. More self-assertion among women is one of the therapeutic goals of a women's studies course. A women's studies classroom may be the first mixed-sex classroom in which females assert themselves. Females can be encouraged to speak more and males less by directly talking about how men and women behave in groups and classrooms. Merely bringing in some relevant research in the area is effective. This, too, should be done as near to the beginning of the course as possible to prevent a pattern from developing.

8. It may sometimes be necessary for instructors to refer students for

---

*Personal Communication, May, 1975.

psychological treatment or legal services. It is very useful if referral services congruent with the goals of feminism are available. This greatly increases the probability of sympathetic treatment. In most communities a reserve of appropriate treatment resources will have to be built up. The easiest way is to find out through word-of-mouth who the sympathetic professional people are. Often a women's studies instructor may have to assist directly in creating such services. She can do this by providing workshops, limited courses, or lectures on feminism and women's studies for practicing psychologists and other professionals. The primary goal would be to raise the professionals' awareness about sex-role problems.

9. Anxieties can be lessened by preparing students for the uncertainties they will experience when they question traditional sex roles. This can be done by merely telling them that women in such courses often experience emotional problems and anxieties when they relate the material to their own lives. Also, one might bring in research as described in this article, suggesting that sometimes during changes women feel depressed, angry, and anxious. Just as in therapy where clients are prepared for what to expect, so students in a women's studies course can be taught to anticipate some anxiety and anger. They should be told (as are therapy clients) that anxiety is a normal part of growth and is not abnormal (the same with anger). Students may look at you with disbelief, but later they will remember your words with some comfort.

10. One of the greatest fears of women in women's studies courses is loss of femininity. A graphic experiment wherein students take androgyny tests can be performed in the classroom (Bem, 1972). Naturally, the results will show that a large number of men and women are androgynous, and that it is more healthy to be androgynous than it is to be either entirely masculine or feminine. This test is the most effective way I have found to deal with the loss-of-femininity fear.

11. Another fear of both men and women is that if they relinquish stereotypic notions of masculinity and femininity, they risk losing their sexuality. We know that masculinity-femininity affects sexuality, but sex roles and sexual potential are not causally connected. The instructor must continually point out that the two are separate; otherwise, students' sexuality fears may obstruct any experimentation with new interpersonal roles. Genitals tends to be overcathected, but when the difference between sex roles and sexuality is confronted directly, potential sexual problems in students may be prevented.

12. My final recommendation is a reading list. To promote understanding between women students and their male significant others not enrolled in the course, it is helpful to assign a feminist work written by a man and to recommend that students encourage their husbands, boyfriends, and/or father to read it. Especially helpful are, Gene Marine's *A*

Male Guide to Women's Liberation, (1972), John Stuart Mill's *On the Subjection of Women,* (1869), and H. R. Hay's *The Dangerous Sex,* (1966). Marine's book is very straightforward and is favored by men and women students alike. In fact, some cautious and traditional female students at first appear to be more comfortable reading a book by a man, than they are with female authors. An interesting and useful book written by a man about males is Harvey E. Kaye's *Male Survival,* (1974).

SUMMARY

A women's study course is unlike many other college courses in that it grew out of the Women's Liberation Movement and implicitly encourages personal and social growth toward greater female equality. As a college course it represents an efficient vehicle for the transmission of feminist ideas. No matter how much it resembles a C-R or therapy group, structural characteristics of college classrooms usually preclude possibilities for it becoming either.

Students bring their "whole" selves to class because the subject matter invites it. Traditional sex roles are challenged, and women begin to reevaluate traditional values and beliefs as well as to experiment with new assertive behaviors. Women already involved in feminism will experience growth; a majority of more traditional women experience threat and anxiety. The handling of *anger* and *self-assertion* is especially difficult for some women.

Social support from friends, family, associates, and the local community is very important in aiding changes that are generated by feminist ideology. Often this support is lacking and women bear burdens alone. If that is the case, a women's studies course can create problems that it is not ordinarily equipped to solve. To avoid creating self-doubt and confusion and to promote constructive change in women, procedures for conducting women's studies courses have been recommended.

REFERENCES

Barron, Frank: *Creative Person and Creative Process.* New York, Holt, Rinehart, and Winston, 1969.

Bem, Sandra L.: The measurement of psychological androgyny. *Journal of Consulting and Clinical Psychology, 42:*155, 1974.

Brodsky, Annette M.: The psychologist's role in women's studies. Paper presented at the Southeastern Psychological Association, New Orleans, Louisiana, April 6, 1973.

Broverman, Inge K., Broverman, Donald M., Clarkson, Frank E., Rosenkrantz, Paul S., and Vogel, Susan R.: Sex-role stereotypes and clinical judgments of mental health. *Journal of Consulting and Clinical Psychology, 34:*1, 1970.

Carter, Dianne: Ego defenses of women: Consequence of minority status. Keynote address presented at the University of Tennessee conference, Innovations in Counseling Women, November 1974a.

Carter, Dianne: Stages of Feminism. Paper presented at the University of Tennessee conference, Innovations in Counseling Women, November 1974b.

Cashdan, Sheldon, and Welsh, George S.: Personality correlates of creative potential in talented high school students. *Journal of Personality, 34*:445, 1966.

Domino, George: Identification of potentially creative persons from the Adjective Check List. *Journal of Consulting and Clinical Psychology, 35*:48, 1970.

Gough, Harrison, and Heilbrun, Jr., Alfred B.: *The Adjective Check List Manual.* Palo Alto, Consulting Psychologists Press, 1965.

Hays, Hoffman R.: *The Dangerous Sex.* New York, Putnam, 1964.

Heilbrun, Alfred B., and Sullivan, Donald J.: The prediction of counseling readiness. *Personnel and Guidance Journal, 41*:112, 1962.

Joesting, Joan, Joesting, Robert, and Guzell, Marie: Mood and attitude changes in students enrolled in women's studies courses. Unpublished paper, 1974.

Kaye, Harvey E.: *Male Survival.* New York, Grosset and Dunlap, 1974.

Lockheed, Marlene: Deferring to the male. *Human Behavior, 4*:33, February, 1975.

Marine, Gene: *A Male Guide to Women's Liberation.* New York, Avon Books, 1972.

Marlowe, Lee, and Shapiro, L.: An institutional case study report on female studies. Paper presented at the Annual Meeting of the American Psychological Association, Honolulu, September, 1972.

Mill, John Stuart: *On Liberty, Representative Government; The Subjection of Women.* London, Oxford University Press, 1973.

Miller, Lise, and Guzell, Marie: Self-concept in women's liberationists as measured by the Favorable-Unfavorable scales of the Adjective Check List. Unpublished paper, 1973.

McNair, Douglas M., Lorr, Maurice, and Droppelman, Leo F.: *Profile of Mood States Manual.* San Diego, Educational and Industrial Testing Service, 1971.

Tavris, Carol: Woman and Man — A *Psychology Today* questionnaire. *Psychology Today 4*:82, 1971.

Tiger, Lionel: *Men in Groups.* New York, Random House, 1969.

—— Chapter 18 ——

FEMINIST BIBLIOTHERAPY — PRESCRIPTION FOR CHANGE: A SELECTED AND ANNOTATED BIBLIOGRAPHY

C. JANE SANDERS AND DOROTHY COX STEWART

THE influence of media begins in early childhood, is perpetuated in the school years, and is exacerbated in adulthood. In advertising, textbooks, and fiction women see their sex portrayed as drudges or sexpots. Such images undermine their self-esteem and personality development. The woman who declares herself ready for therapy has probably been prepared by the media only for self-defeat. The attitudes, values and concommitant behaviors which are a part of her inadequate arsenal for survival have been assimilated from a culture which portrays her as helpless and rather dull. Therapy for women, then, must concern itself with the resocialization and reeducation of those who perceive themselves as powerless.

Through feminist bibliotherapy, therapists can redefine the traditional image of women by using the printed word as a constructive training instrument. It seems both logical and ironically satisfying to transcend the negative influences of traditional writing by using the positive aspects of the same medium.

Popularly, bibliotherapy consists of providing fictional characters and situations with which persons can identify, thus experiencing catharsis. There is a great deal of this literature available, and it is often effective. The focus of the selections in this annotated bibliography, however, will be *cognitive* in nature, the content *nonfictional*. In many instances an emotional response occurs as a result of cognitive insight. For example, insight into the dynamics of discrimination often results in confusion and anger. Relief comes with the recognition that feelings of isolation and inadequacy are caused by internalized values. Becoming aware, through bibliotherapy, that other women share similar feelings and that many of these women have made changes in their lives conducive to self-respect and integration can be therapeutic to the client.

Feminist bibliotherapy can be used in several ways. Literature given to a woman early in the therapeutic relationship can help the client define for herself the meaning of feminism and can enable her to share the responsibility for her own therapy. Articles can provide information on subjects about which clients express concern or can simply serve as a bridge of communication between the therapist and client. The most important outcome of reading, however, is that it enables clients to identify the main source of stress as environmental and cultural, not personal. This awareness is crucial to the process of feminist therapy.

Women often enter therapy with problems that are caused by the constraints of the feminine role. Many of these women will claim that they have chosen their role and are happy in it. Suggesting appropriate reading selections for such women can introduce them to sources of unrecognized conflict. Identifying the processes of socialization and sharing in the experiences of other women who have struggled against these influences is therapeutic for the client who must reject old values in order to grow to independence and autonomy. Some women come to the counseling relationship facing special problems or crisis situations. Feelings of fear and of isolation can be attenuated by the awareness through bibliotherapy that many women have had similar experiences.

In organizing the following bibliography, the reading material has been grouped under four major headings: *Societal Values, Therapist Values, Client Values, and Future Values.* Since feminist therapy is a philosophy and not a collection of techniques, values have been emphasized in the bibliography. In the first section, *Societal Values,* the general areas of socialization that have negative effects on women are included. These selections are appropriate for clients who need to develop a general awareness of the way in which cultural values have shaped their attitudes toward themselves. Awareness of these influences is the first step in feminist therapy.

The second section, *Therapist Values,* assumes that the feminist therapist has already acquainted her/himself with societal values. This section contains materials which will help the therapist become knowledgeable about how general attitudes toward women are expressed in psychotherapy. The importance of the therapist as a role-model and the evidence that values are transmitted from therapist to client without conscious effort make therapists' awareness of values a factor of incalculable weight in the process and outcome of therapy for women.

Readings for clients with particular problems or different life-styles are presented in the section entitled *Client Values.* Although this area is third in order of presentation, it is by no means of reduced importance. These selections represent typical client concerns and serve as a basic therapeutic library.

The final section, *Future Values,* focuses on personal growth for all women. It is a potpourri of anthologies, bibliographies, and primary sources for additional readings. This section also includes suggested readings covering positive options for women from assertive behavior to body work. Beginning with the negative influences of socialization in the first part of the bibliography there was a conscious attempt to end the concluding selections on an optimistic note.

Remembering that this bibliography supplements but does not replace therapy, each therapist must decide how best to put the materials to use. Each item should be carefully read by the therapist before recommending it to clients. Those who find a particular article or book especially useful for many of their clients may wish to keep a number of copies on hand in order to facilitate introducing the reading at the appropriate time. Relevant literature is being published periodically, and the ambitious therapist will no doubt locate other helpful resources.

The following bibliography provides a current and basic supplement to therapy. The tools of feminist bibliotherapy will provide not only hope to clients but also opportunities for therapists to grow as professionals.

SOCIETAL VALUES

Achievement

Hoffman, Lois Wladis: Early childhood experiences and women's achievement motives. *Journal of Social Issues, 28*:129, 1972.

Demonstrates the effects of sex-role socialization during early years on adult achievement motivation. Expresses recognition of the conflict involved if women strive to reach their intellectual potential.

Horner, Matina S.: Toward an understanding of achievement-related conflicts in women. *Journal of Social Issues, 28*:157, 1972.

Focuses on the result of the prevalent belief that "femininity and individual achievements which reflect intellectual competence or leadership potential are desirable but mutually exclusive goals." Explains the "motive to avoid success" found in many young women and the effects of this fear on their choices and attitudes.

Appearance

Harmon, Lenore W.: . . . and Soma. *The Counseling Psychologist, 4*:87, 1973.

Outlines the effect of externally imposed and artificially contrived standards of appearance on women. A more wholesome approach to attitudes towards one's own body is suggested.

Language

Densmore, Dana: *Speech is the Form of Thought.* Pittsburg, Know,

Inc.

Consciousness-raising demonstration of the subtle oppression to women by the use of pronouns and nouns in ordinary speech. Alternatives are suggested and defended.

Literature

Ellman, Mary: *Thinking about Women.* New York, Harcourt Brace, Jovanovich, Inc., 1968.

Investigates the characterizations of woman in literature from passivity to formlessness, from Freud to Mailer. A serious resource for students of stereotypes. The section on feminine stereotypes is a specific help in shedding any vestiges of your own stereotypes. Thoughtful, literary, subtle. Ellman writes with humor as well as depth.

Psychology

Heide, Wilma Scott: *The Reality and Challenge of Double Standard in Mental Health and Society.* Pittsburgh, Know, Inc.

Explores the development and functioning of a double standard in sex-role expectations and rights. Good consciousness-raising instrument, especially for women still convinced by their socialization that inequality does not exist.

Rape

Griffin, Susan: Rape: The all-American crime. In Freeman, Jo (Ed.): *A Feminist Perspective.* Palo Alto, Mayfield, 1975.

An excellent discussion of the incidence and indignity of rape. Makes a particularly telling case for the interrelation of the cultural attitudes of males toward women and this crime against women.

Religion

Scanzone, Letha, and Hardesty, Nancy: *All We're Meant To Be: A Biblical Approach to Women's Liberation.* Waco, Word Books, 1974.

An excellent book for women who are committed to Christianity and fear that feminism will disrupt their faith. Although we cannot endorse all aspects of the book, e.g. references to homosexuality, it nevertheless clearly differentiates between Biblical law and cultural custom in a way which will be freeing to many women.

Sex-Roles

Bem, Sandra L., and Bem, Daryl J.: Case Study of a nonconscious ideology: Training the woman to know her place. In Bem, Daryl J. (Ed.): *Beliefs, Attitudes and Human Affairs*, revised, March, 1971. Belmont, Brooks/Cole, 1970.

Telling revelation of the homogenization of America's women by the values and dictates imposed upon them at an early age. Answers the arguments of free-will, biology, and complementarity. Useful consciousness-raising tool.

Freeman, Jo: *The Social Construction of the Second Sex.* Pittsburg, Know, Inc., 1970.

An excellent brief summary of many of the recent studies and conclusions concerning the results of socialization on women. Clearly written. Could be really helpful to women trying to understand the origin of some of their beliefs and also to those making decisions about child-rearing.

Schools

Howe, Florence: Sexual stereotypes start early. *Saturday Review,* October 16, 1971.

Concentrates on the role of schools in reinforcing sexist roles via attitudes, books, and practices. Some of the experiences mentioned are now illegal, but, until challenged in local schools, may still be continuing. Helps a woman see where to begin if she chooses to use her energy in fighting early socialization of stereotypes.

THERAPIST VALUES

Broverman, Inge, K., Broverman, Donald M., and Clarkson, Frank E.: Sex-role stereotypes and clinical judgments of mental health. *Journal of Counseling and Clinical Psychology, 34*:1, 1970.

Using bipolar items, active clinicians described a healthy, mature, competent (1) adult, sex unspecified, (2) male, (3) female. Findings were: (1) Clinical judgments differ as a function of sex; differences parallel stereotypic sex-role differences. (2) Characteristics judged healthy for adults parallel those judged healthy for men but differ from those judged healthy for women. Expresses concern that because clinicians are reflecting stereotypic attitudes, they are responsible for perpetuating them. Emphasizes a need for an optimal functioning approach rather than an adjustment approach. A must for mental health professionals, students in women's studies, and for women clients.

Chesler, Phyllis: Patient and patriarch: Women in the psychotherapeutic relationship. In Gornick, Vivian, and Moran, Barbara (Eds.): *Woman in Sexist Society*. New York, Basic Books, 1971. (Also available in Signet paperback).

Discusses the implications of social role (stereotype) in terms of the fact that more women than men "go crazy." Explores social institutions, marriage, and psychotherapy as reinforcers of a dependent role for women. The author proposes that women should seek female rather than male therapists, and of the females, feminist therapists, rather than women who have never realized their oppression as women. Good introduction for your clients to you as a feminist therapist.

Deckard, Barbara: Theories of women's liberation. *The Women's Movement*. New York, Harper & Row, 1975.

Sketches the ideas prevalent in the three major ideological positions within the women's movement: moderate or women's rights feminists, radical feminists, and socialist feminists. Since these distinctions get extended into feminist therapy, this selection is particularly appropriate for therapists.

Freedman, Mark: *Homosexuality and Psychological Functioning*. Belmont, Brooks/Cole, 1971.

Freedman makes the point that gays are no different from heterosexuals in psychological functioning. He backs up his argument with a review of the *research* and an explication of his dissertation on Lesbians. He found Lesbians to be different from heterosexual women in some positive respects. For instance, Lesbians tended to be more independent. Lesbians and mental health professionals need this book when confronting practitioners who believe in the disease model of homosexuality.

Keller, Suzanne: The female role: Constants and change. In Franks, Violet, and Burtle, Vasanti (Eds.): *Women in Therapy*. New York, Bruner/Mazel, 1974.

Keller describes a conceptual model of the female role. She identifies basic components and variations (social class, educational level, age, and life-style) in an effort to delineate the complex realities of womanhood. Addressed to "those concerned with theory and practice in the healing arts".

Neuhring, Elane M., Fein, Sarah Beck, and Tyler, Mary: The gay college student: Perspectives for mental health professionals. *The Counseling Psychologist*, *4*:64-72, 1974.

If you are a counselor in a university setting or in any facility which might serve gay clients (and most do - if you think yours doesn't, you are probably serving them badly), then you need this. Appropriate not only for the mental health professional but for the gay student seeking information about the counter-culture. Based on a field study in a college community and other pertinent literature on a nonclinical gay population.

Polk, Barbara Bovee: Male power and the women's movement. *Journal of Applied Behavioral Science, 10*:415, 1974.

Socially-defined sex roles, differences between "masculine" and "feminine" values and cultures, analysis of the power differential between males and females, and the socialist perspective of economic relationships are examined as four major approaches to the understanding of the power imbalance between men and women. Useful in recognizing how male oppression is institutionalized and enforced, and how it is experienced by women. A good background for the therapist in clarifying basic issues of male power, and in examining the political impact of the Women's Movement on that power.

Rice, Joy and Rice, David G.: Implications of the women's liberation movement for psychotherapy. *American Journal of Psychiatry, 130*:191, 1973.

Criticizes psychotherapy in terms of its antifeminine, Freudian position; predominance of male therapists; its characterization of role unhappiness as pathological; and its need for social power in the therapist.

Weisstein, Naomi: Psychology constructs the female. In Gornick, Vivian, and Moran, Barbara (Eds.): *Women in Sexist Society.*

Outlines reasons for inaccurate concepts about women. Conclusion: Failing to accurately construe the nature of women, psychology constricts their behavior by promulgating narrow social expectations. Excellent for researcher, clinician, student, and for the client who needs to see the environmental/historical nature of "her" problems.

CLIENT VALUES

Adolescents

Macleod, Jennifer S. and Silberman, Sandra T.: *You Won't Do!* Pittsburg, Know, Inc., 1973.

A carefully documented study revealing "what textbooks on U. S. Government teach high school girls". Examples and illustrations are powerful. Also includes "Sexism in Textbooks: An annotated Source List of 150+ Studies and Remedies." This is for the woman whose consciousness is raised to the point where she is concerned about what the schools are covertly and overtly passing on to her sons and daughters (or those of her neighbor).

Mitchell, Joyce Slayton: *Other Choices for Becoming A Woman.* Pittsburg, Know, Inc., 1974.

A feminist handbook for high school women. The chapters vary somewhat in their usefulness, but there is enough good material over a wide range of areas to be exceedingly helpful to young women trying to escape stereotypes.

Children

Feminists on Children's Media: *Little Miss Muffet Fights Back.* New York, Feminists on Children's Media, 1974.

A rationale for compiling a bibliography of nonsexist books about girls for young readers followed by a carefully annotated and extensive list of books for all ages.

Graham, Alma: The making of a nonsexist dictionary. *Ms. Magazine,* December, 1973.

A telling demonstration of the sexist brain-washing encountered by girls and boys in schoolbooks. Centers especially on what our classroom dictionaries teach children. Shows that in quantity and quality of items listed, females rate much lower than males.

Divorce

Fuller, Jan: *Space, The Scrapbook of My Divorce.* New York, Arthur Fields, 1973.

Excerpts from the personal diary of the first three months of a woman's life following her divorce. Sensitive and honest. Recommended, not to imply that other women's lives will or should be identical, but rather to suggest that each journey is important and worthy of being recorded. This book could encourage a woman to keep her own journal, a therapeutic exercise in itself.

Krantzler, Mel: *Creative Divorce.* New York, M. Evans, 1973.

A well-rounded and realistic appraisal of the emotional process experienced by most divorced persons. Readers will be reassured that the trauma they are enduring is neither unique nor permanent. They will be challenged to use the experience in creative, growth-producing ways.

Women's Survival Manual: A Feminist Handbook on Separation and Divorce. Philadelphia, Women in Transition, 1972.

In spite of occasional references to practices specific to the state of

Pennsylvania, this is a priceless manual of moral support, legal advice, and useful suggestions for women considering or getting a divorce or separation. Written seriously, yet simply and humorously, it will appeal to a wide range of women facing the painful experience of withdrawal from an intimate relationship.

Lesbian

Abbot, Sidney and Love, Barbara: Is women's liberation a lesbian plot? In Gornick, Vivian and Moran, Barbara (Eds.): *Women in Sexist Society*. New York, Basic Books, 1971 (also available in paperback).

Addresses the political aspects of lesbianism and its relationship to the Women's Movement as a whole. Emphasizes the "relationship of equals" epitomized by lesbians. Essentially a fair presentation of what is simply an alternative life-style with something to offer to the Movement. Recommended for clinicians and lesbians.

Brown, Rita Mae: *Ruby Fruit Jungle*. Plainfield, Daughters, 1973.

Growing up gay and surviving is part of the message that Brown gives us. She is vital, funny, and has the credible recommendation that lesbians love to read what she writes. Highly readable and pertinent to anyone with a sense of justice/humor/curiosity. Fiction, but heavily autobiographical.

Jay, Karla and Young, Allen: Lesbians and the women's liberation movement. In Jay, Karla and Young, Allen (Eds.): *Out of the Closets - Voices of Gay Liberation*. Lakewood, Douglas, 1972.

A handful of pungent offerings from several lesbian organizations and two essays from Rita Mae Brown. Excellent material for the lesbian trying to increase her political consciousness and for the feminist attempting to raise her lesbian consciousness. This is a collection of radical experiences and philosophies. *Not* an introductory reader. Gay bibliography. International Directory of Gay Organizations.

Martin, Del and Lyon, Phyllis: *Lesbian/Women*. San Francisco, Glide Publications, 1972 (also in paperback, Bantam Books).

A personal and social history which has broad appeal. Highly recommended as an introduction to understanding and respecting the lesbian life-style. For clients who are exploring their sexuality and for therapists who are attempting to aid them.

Marriage and Equal Relationships

Bernard, Jesse: *The Future of Marriage*. New York, World Publishing

Company, 1972.

A statistically supported and startling description of "his marriage" and "her marriage;" points out that marriage for men is healthier emotionally and physically than being single, while the reverse is true for women. Good support for women who fear that they are "sick" because they are not finding happiness in their marriage relationship. There is also a look at alternate patterns of relationships and a glance into the future.

Burton, Gabrielle: *I'm Running Away From Home But I'm Not Allowed to Cross the Street*. Pittsburgh, Know, Inc., 1972.

A quick-reading, excellent consciousness-raiser. Many situations with which housewife-mothers will identify. Written with humor as well as some solid statistics. Highly recommended for men or women who want to know about the Women's Liberation Movement.

Burton, Gabrielle: *You, Too, Can Walk on Water*. Pittsburgh, Know, Inc., 1973.

In a speech at a NOW National Convention, one feminist sorts through her priorities and experiences in a way which encourages others to believe that (a) it is possible to do so, and (b) each person will find individual answers to her own situation. This could be especially helpful to feminists who choose to remain married and sometimes wonder if it is possible.

Friedan, Betty: *The Feminine Mystique*. New York, Dell, 1963.

A well-documented exploration exploding the myth of the happy housewife; a forerunner of many more current books. Especially useful for two audiences: (1) women who were young adults in the late forties and the fifties and who are now asking themselves, "How did I let that happen to me?" and (2) their daughters who, surrounded now by much that contradicts the mystique, cannot understand what their mothers faced.

Miller, Jean Baker and Mothner, Ira: Psychological consequences of sexual inequality. In Wortis, Helen and Rabinowitz, Clara (Eds.): *Women's Movement: Social and Psychological Perspectives*. New York, John Wiley, 1972.

Demonstrates the effects of male dominance and female subordination upon the relationships between the sexes. Benefits of open confrontation in place of covert conflict are pointed out. Good reading for women ready to make significant changes in their relationships with the opposite sex.

Symonds, Alexandra: Phobias after marriage. In Miller, Jean Baker (Ed.): *Psychoanalysis and Women*. Baltimore, Penguin, 1973 (hardcover professional edition is available from Brunner/Mazel, Inc., New York, N. Y.).

Presents a discussion of three case studies of women afflicted with phobias and constriction of self after marriage. These extreme cases provide a thought-provoking picture of those who see marriage as an absolute necessity for achievement of personhood and who give up all prior interests. Relationship and marriage counselors, therapists, and leaders of divorced women's groups can use this for their own edification and as stimulus material.

Widmer, Kingsley: *Reflections of a Male Housewife: On Being a Feminist Fellow-Traveller.* Pittsburg, Know, Inc., 1971.

Humorous, pointed, and candid thoughts of a man who is living a role reversal situation. Reinforces the realization that many "typical" reactions of housewives are not due to sex-related traits but to role-induced frustrations. Could be helpful to men or to women who have trouble making this distinction.

Middle Age

Bart, Pauline, B.: Depression in Middle-Aged Women. In Gornick, Vivian and Moran, Barbara (Eds.): *Women in Sexist Society.* New York, Basic Books (also available in Signet paperback).

A study involving middle-aged women suffering from depressions of various types. Subjects were shown to be restricted in their roles of homemaker and mother. They were overprotective of their children and overinvolved in relationships to them. Depression tended to be precipitated by role-loss, particularly maternal role-loss. As supermothers, obsessive-compulsive housekeepers, and martyrs to the family, the subjects became depressed when superabundance was not returned in kind. For young women with a "supermother" syndrome and for middle-aged displaced housewives.

Sontag, Susan: The double standard of aging. *Saturday Review,* October, 1972.

The title spells out the problem; the article documents it. Sontag offers women another option. They can age naturally, disobeying the social convention which progressively destroys women. Women and men of any age are the appropriate audience for this consciousness-raiser.

McBride, Angela Barron: *The Growth and Development of Mothers.* New York, Harper & Row, 1973.

In a lively and personal manner, the myths and realities of motherhood are explored. The heavy toll of social expectations and the bright glimpse of a sex-role-free future are included. Would be helpful to and accepted by many women including those just beginning to understand feminism.

Mintz, Ellen: *The Prejudice of Parents*. Paper presented at 80th Convention American Psychological Association. Pittsburgh, Know, Inc., 1972.

Interesting and very complete description of the ways in which our social system creates two distinctly "different" kinds of people out of males and females. Not only shows how we got where we are, but also clearly specifies some practices of parents which contribute strongly to the perpetuation of the same situation. Hence, useful for parents who wish to change.

Single

Adams, Margaret: The single woman in today's society: A reappraisal. In Wortis, Helen, and Rabinowitz, Clara (Eds.): *The Women's Movement: Social and Psychological Perspectives*. New York, John Wiley, 1972.

An overview of the position of single women today with suggestions of how society has reinforced some of the negative connotations. A view of the radical feminist movement and how the single woman will be helped by the movement. Includes a suggestion of what the future might look like.

FUTURE VALUES

Resources*

Adams, Elsie and Briscoe, Elsie (Eds.): *Up Against the Wall, Mother ... On Women's Liberation*. Beverly Hills, Glencoe Press, 1971.

This extensive anthology can serve as a basic text in women's studies or as a source of stimulus materials for C-R groups. The appeal flows across age groups and the political spectrum. The editors examine the establishment of sexual stereotypes and the reasons for revolt through the use of such diverse sources as Matina Horner, S.C.U.M. Manifesto, and the U.S. Dept. of Labor. There is a nice bonus for the novice teacher/therapist — discussion guides following each article.

EVERYWOMAN FEMINIST BOOK SERVICE. Offers a wide choice of titles ranging over diverse areas. Human relationships, sexuality, literature, and history are represented as well as categories for children of various

---

*See end of this Section for addresses of feminist literature resources.

ages. Old and new titles at reasonable prices.

THE FEMINIST PRESS. Publications include fiction, nonfiction, and poetry for adults and children. Educational projects, however, are a large part of their purpose. These include the Clearinghouse on Women's Studies, the Women's Studies Newsletter, and nonsexist teaching packets.

KNOW, INC. A feminist press printing originals and reprints of books and articles at modest prices. A wide range of topics pertinent to feminism is available.

Maccoby, Eleanor M. and Jacklin, Carol N.: *The Psychology of Sex Differences.* Stanford, Stanford University Press, 1974.

This volume is *the* resource on the origins and current status of sex differences (and similarities) in intellect, achievement, and social behavior. The interpretation of a massive body of research and an exhaustive annotated bibliography of research studies published since 1965 pertinent to the area make this a necessary resource for therapists, teachers, vocational and school counselors. The authors include a section on the social implications of their findings. Note: The authors are feminists and state their bias in the introduction.

Safilios-Rothschild, Constantina: *Toward a Sociology of Women.* Lexington, Xerox College Publishing, 1972.

A collection with the avowed purpose of influencing a wide public of women and men, students and laypersons. Chapters on the possibilities of women combining "deviant" (occupational) and conventional (marriage) options speak to the timely problems of many women (and men). Good for the women experiencing role conflict in anything from student vocational indecision to dual career problems. For graduate and professional women. Helpful to couples, also. Slightly conservative but a much needed resource.

Task Force on Gay Liberation: *A Gay Bibliography.* Philadelphia, American Library Association, 1974.

This is the primary resource for nonfiction materials which support a positive view of homosexuality. Includes books, articles, pamphlets, periodicals, audio-visual, and directories.

WOMEN'S STUDIES ABSTRACTS. Published quarterly, it contains abstracts from an extensive list of periodicals plus book reviews and biographical articles. Categories explored include education and socialization, sex roles, employment, sexuality, family, society and government, religion, mental and physical health, history, literature and the arts, and women's liberation movement.

Action

Alberti, Robert E. and Emmons, Michael E.: *Your Perfect Right: A Guide to Assertive Behavior*. 2nd ed. San Luis Obispo, Impact, 1974.

A paperback primer for assertive training. Very good for clients and helpful to the therapist who wants a quick and readable introduction to the area.

Boston Women's Health Book Collective: *Our Bodies, Ourselves*. New York, Simon and Schuster, 1971.

Demythologized, clear, common sense discussions of many areas related to the physical and mental well-being of women. Excellent counteraction to elitist professionals who leave the impression that women cannot learn to take care of and love themselves sensibly.

Rush, Anne Kent: *Getting Clear, Body Work for Women*. New York, Random House, and Berkley, The Bookworks, 1973.

Especially good for a woman making a new start in understanding and loving her own body and her relationship with herself, and significant others. Lots of practical applications.

Jakubowski-Spector, Patricia: Facilitating the growth of women through assertive training. *The Counseling Psychologist*, 4:75, 1973.

Although written for therapists, selected clients could find this article useful for a quick grasp of the concept of assertive behavior. It may motivate a woman to seek assertion training therapy.

Whitely, Rita M.: Women in groups. *The Counseling Psychologist*, 4:27, 1973.

Demonstrates the value of consciousness-raising groups; useful for enlightening men or encouraging women. Most women would be able to identify with some of the personal situations reported in the verbatim excerpts.

ADDRESSES OF FEMINIST LITERATURE RESOURCES*

Every Woman Feminist Book Service
7426 Orion Avenue
Van Nuys, California 91406

The Feminist Press
SUNY/College at Old Westbury
Box 334
Old Westbury, New York 11568

---

*Descriptions in alphabetical listings under Resources.

KNOW, Inc.
P.O. Box 86031
Pittsburgh, Pennsylvania 15221

Women's Studies Abstracts
P.O. Box 1
Rush, New York 14543
(Issued quarterly, indexed annually.)

RADICAL FEMINISM:*
A CHALLENGE TO
PROFESSIONAL PSYCHOTHERAPY

*Radical feminism as used in the title should not be confused with *radical feminism* which is an ideological position within the women's movement (See Deckard, 1975).

INTRODUCTION

WEBSTER'S SEVENTH NEW COLLEGIATE DIC-
TIONARY (1965) defines *radical* as "tending or disposed to make extreme changes in existing views, habits, conditions, or institutions"; and
"of relating to or constituting a political group associated with views,
practices, and policies of extreme change." Both Ardelle Schultz and
Hogie Wyckoff, whose papers appear in this section, are radical in the
sense of the first definition, and, in addition, Wyckoff meets the criterion
of association with a political group. Schultz and Wyckoff are both
feminist therapists who practice therapy in groups and who use sex-role
analysis as part of their treatment of women.

The treatment and philosophy of both authors challenge professional
psychotherapy. Schultz works with addicted women. Her analysis of
therapy reveals that they have conflicts because of an overinvestment in
the traditional feminine role. They have tried to deny valid parts of their
nontraditional selves. Her treatment is a challenge to traditional therapy
which decreases the self-esteem of addicted women by emphasizing the
traditional feminine role. Likewise, in "Radical Psychiatry for Women,"
Wyckoff issues a radical challenge:

> We (radical psychiatrists) are a counter-institution with the intention of
> bringing the practice of soul-healing back into the hands of the people
> ... while putting expensive, individualistic "professionals" out of bus-
> iness.

Both women issue their challenges out of their own personal experiences.

Ardelle Schultz's credentials for writing "Radical Feminism: A Treatment for Addicted Women," include being a former alcoholic and having
six years experience in leading therapy groups for addicted women.
Schultz demands separate treatment for women and encourages female
addicts to release their suppressed anger and strengths. Hogie Wyckoff
has had five years of experience facilitating Radical Psychiatry problem-
solving groups for women. In "Radical Psychiatry for Women," Wyckoff
discusses the theory of radical psychiatry and also describes her use of
transactional analysis in sex-role analysis with women. In her second
chapter, "Radical Psychiatry Techniques for Solving Women's Problems," she gives a complete description of the techniques she uses.

In "Radical Feminism — A Treatment Modality for Addicted Women," Schultz observes that addicted women have intense conflicts and doubts concerning their adequacy as women because of strong masculine components, e.g. anger, aggressiveness, competitiveness, power strivings, existing at the unconscious level of personality. They experience their masculine characteristics as threatening to their identity as women. In attempts to feel more "womanly" they may adopt an exaggerated sex-object image or seek validation of feminine identity in motherhood. They learn that alcohol and drugs help them blot out masculine traits. However, in advanced stages of addiction, alcohol or drug dependence is self-defeating in that it does not enhance "feminine" qualities nor aid repression of "masculine" traits. The addict begins to neglect her appearance and her family responsibilities and has greater difficulty controlling her anger. Addiction leads to rejection by significant others and the destruction of an already fragile self-esteem. By the time these women reach rehabilitation centers they are full of self-hate and loathing.

Treatment by male therapists in either all women or mixed-sex groups is oppressive and damaging to addicted women because it exacerbates the dynamics that led to the original addiction. Male therapists punish anger and aggression in women and pressure them to behave in a ladylike fashion. The approval and acceptance by male therapists and male group members is conditional on a woman's denial of part of her being. Often, a woman will be the only female group member. In some instances she may be exploited as a female identification object for the male members or she may receive a false sense of self-worth by being treated as "special" by the group. In either case, no lasting changes will be made because of the sex-role playing being reinforced by the group; the probability of recidivism is high.

Schultz's treatment "challenges the accepted methods of treatment and seeks the right for women to be treated for what they are — not what male-dominated institutions and professions think they should be." Her recommendations include all-women groups led by a female therapist. In these groups women are encouraged to accept their "masculine" side. They are also urged to get in touch with their anger, express it, and learn its power once they have it under control. The leader should be a model of a strong woman who can demonstrate how to use anger constructively. By identifying with a powerful female role model, these women overcome their self-hate. They develop honesty, integrity, independence and self-confidence — characteristics which legitimately earn the respect of other group members. Thus, their growing feelings of self-worth have a genuine basis.

The recovery statistics for women treated by Schultz's approach suggest that this type of treatment is exceptionally effective with addicted women.

In one program for which figures are available, 59 percent of the women beginning Schultz's treatment program completed it compared to 35 percent completion rate before she came and after she left.

Despite the effectiveness of this program, it is difficult to implement in male-dominated institutions because the separate-sex treatment and the encouragement to women to be strong and to express their anger is threatening to male authority. So threatening was this approach to the male authorities in one rehabilitation center that despite her effectiveness, Schultz was fired.

Although Schultz is primarily concerned with the treatment of addicted women, she suggests that men can also benefit from a feminist treatment philosophy. Men need more freedom of expression than the male sex-role allows. By discarding artificial sex-roles, both sexes have a better chance to find an authentic sense of self.

In "Radical Psychiatry for Women" Hogie Wyckoff supports the view that psychotherapy is a political activity. People are oppressed, not sick. Diagnostic labels and medicines have no place in radical psychiatry. The practitioners of radical psychiatry are community organizers who teach people problem-solving skills and political awareness, provide protection while people make changes, and put people in touch with their power as full and potent human beings. Since one-to-one psychotherapy results in only a few people receiving help, radical psychiatrists work with groups. Their theories represent a synthesis of theories from R. D. Laing, Fritz Perls, and Claude Steiner who all believe that people are born "OK" and are made unhappy because of what they do to each other. Radical psychiatrists insist that the language of psychiatry be simple and be communicated to group members, eliminating secrets and the one-up ploys of professional psychotherapists.

Wyckoff believes that women need more help than men because they endure more subtle "mind-rape" than men and "mind-rape" causes break-downs. Professional elitist sexist men cannot help women. Women can and must free themselves. When women's well-developed skills in intuition and insight are coupled with the permission to be strong, to take care of business, to think rationally, and to talk straight, the result is a skillful and powerful people's psychiatrist. Training collectives teach women who have been members of women's radical therapy groups to be facilitators for other women's groups.

The basic tenets of radical psychiatry are expressed in the following equations:

Mystification + Oppression = Alienation. People feel there is something wrong with *them* rather than society. An example is sexual alienation which is an index of personal alienation. Many women, alienated from their sexuality, do not love themselves but rather hate themselves and other women. When mystification is removed through radical psychiatry, women feel OK about themselves and other women.

Oppression + Awareness = Anger. Anger helps motivate women to action using rational power and reclaimed energy to move against the real culprit.

Awareness + Contact = Action →Liberation. Strokes (positive attention and support) give contact. Contact gives us support to overcome oppression. Cooperative hard work is necessary to achieve liberation which comes only when *all* are free.

Wyckoff uses the language of Transactional Analysis in groups because the terms are easy to communicate and the oppression that comes from mystified transactions can readily be diagrammed for group members. According to Transactional Analysis, people act in one of three ego states: Parent (knows right from wrong, "how to," and nurtures); Child (plays, creates, feels) and Adult (processes information). In the Child ego state, people act as Natural Child (spontaneous, free, creative), Intuitive Child (Little Professor), or Pig Parent (love is conditional on Child obeying Pig's demands).

Women, according to Wyckoff are oppressed in all ego states. The most destructive part of a women's psyche is the Pig Parent which carries all the oppressive messages which tell a woman what she should do and be and terrorizes the Child when she tries to be free. Destroying the Pig Parent ("Offing" the Pig) is one of the most significant and difficult aspects of group work.

An important component of T.A. analysis is *scripting*. Scripts are life-plays embarked upon at an early age which result in stilted, determined behavior. Scripts are induced by powerful injunctions and attributions from parents and are another example of mystification. The scripting of women shapes them to complement the incomplete halves which men are scripted to be. Men and women are supposed to fit together in a beautiful relationship. However, complementary sex-roles are a myth. This myth conspires against genuine communication. In her first chapter, Wyckoff gives a thorough analysis of the following scripts for women: Mother Hubbard, Plastic Women, Poor Little Me, Nurse, and Fat Woman.

In "Radical Psychiatry Techniques for Solving Women's Problems," her second chapter, Wyckoff details an application of her approach in women's groups. The groups are composed of all women and one or two facilitators. The therapeutic concepts are the *contract, homework, equalizing power, group collusions, Rescue, strokes, stamps*, and *group exercises*.

Each woman who joins the group makes a *contract* which is a work agreement between the woman and the whole group. It clearly states, in observable behavior, what the woman would like to change. One benefit of contracts is that they prevent women from being oppressed by the facilitator. *Homework* is self-assigned projects to be carried out during the week. Responsibility for oneself is also emphasized. Before each group session women who want to work sign up on a blackboard. This insures their taking responsibility for asking for what they want from the group.

Facilitators *equalize power* by sharing themselves as persons, being emotionally available and vulnerable, expecting confidentiality from all participants, and sharing responsibility for group work. Facilitators must be willing to demystify group collusions such as Rescue attempts, i.e. taking the responsibility for someone else and to confront members who are not talking straight about touchy subjects. Facilitators also give *strokes* (reinforcement) for hard work.

Other group techniques include setting aside a time for giving *stamps* (expressing resentments) and expressing paranoid fantasies about other group members. A frequent outcome of the stamps and paranoid fantasies exercises is a freeing of the warm feelings members have for one another.

Wyckoff describes the following group exercises: emotional release (bioenergetics is an example); permission (helping people get what they want but feel is prohibited); Nurturing Parent (taking care of oneself); "Offing" the Pig; and bragging (noncompetitive appreciation of oneself). Insight into what is happening during the exercises is important so that women are not merely discharging energy but are also learning new understandings and new ways to act.

Wyckoff observes that healthy groups are characterized by high and prompt attendance. Members make sure that they share the group's time, talk straight, work hard, keep no secrets, avoid Rescue, and give strokes to women who work hard.

REFERENCES

Deckard, Barbara: *The Women's Movement: Political, Socioeconomic, and Psychological Issues.* New York, Harper and Row, 1975.

Webster's Seventh New Collegiate Dictionary. Springfield, Massachusetts, G. and G. Merriam, 1965.

Chapter 19

RADICAL FEMINISM: A TREATMENT MODALITY FOR ADDICTED WOMEN*

ARDELLE POLETTI SCHULTZ

RADICAL feminist therapy recognizes the oppression of women as clients. It challenges the accepted methods of treatment and seeks the right for women to be treated for what they are — not for what male-dominated institutions and professions think women should be.

This paper does not claim to be an objective, scientific research study, although I shall incorporate some statistics and factual data at times. Rather, I propose to state the case for a Radical Feminist approach to addicted women by drawing on three different experiences; first, my own life experience; second, my first attempt to gain treatment rights for women in a rehabilitation center; and, third, my current two-year experience in a drug rehabilitation program for young adults, where I am the Director of Therapy. Finally, I will submit the conclusions I have drawn as to how the Radical Feminist approach for women can be translated into a Nonsexist approach for addicted people.

MY OWN LIFE EXPERIENCE

I grew up in a male-oriented family, i.e. the boys went to college, and the girls went to business school *until they got married.* The family ethic was that we were all *smart* and *athletic.* I competed scholastically and athletically in high school, and could not see myself becoming a secretary or housewife. I was, therefore, at a loss to decide how or where I could find a career or identity.

Modeling seemed to have all the right answers for me. It had prestige and it was a permissible — indeed, downright desirable — profession for a young woman in the 1950's. On the surface, I was doing very well. Had you asked anyone who knew me in those years, "Who is Ardelle Poletti? What is she like?" the answer probably would have been, "She is a nice girl, very quiet, very sweet." Beneath the surface, however, the fragile ego was already crumbling. It was a very narrow door through which I had been permitted to seek a recognizable and worthwhile identity. My conditioning did not permit me to act out sexually. My image of the mother-role had been heavily damaged by my own mother's martyrish

---

*Revised and expanded version of paper presented at the Ohio Bureau of Drug Abuse, Cleveland, Ohio, June, 1974.

representation. I had been discouraged in the intellectual area: "You're rather bright, for a woman." Therefore, I opted for the exploitation of my most marketable talent: looking pretty. But even that did not come easily. In America, pretty is slim, very slim. The agony of trying to stay skinny enough to fulfill the Madison Avenue fantasies of women began taking its toll in my emotional and physical health. For example, once when I was 105 lbs., 5'6" height, I was told to lose ten pounds in two weeks if I wanted to gain admission to one of the bigger agencies in New York.

... Enter starvation diets, diet pills ... and the genteel nervous break-downs. Also enter psychiatrists (male), mental hospitals, suicide attempts, and drugs: nice legal, male-doctor-administered, ups and downs. Over the next seven years, the *nice girl, very quiet, very sweet* became a poor, sad, tragic, nice, sweet, pretty girl.

In 1960, held together with psychiatric insights into my Oedipal Electra complex, packaged with falsies, false eyelashes, and newly bleached hair, I was on the verge of commercial success and the realization of every American girl's dream: the beautiful blonde, whom men admire and who really has more fun. The myth suddenly exploded, however, when I lost my hair through a mistake in a highly sensitive bleaching process. Along with my hair went every vestige of my fragile identity.

... Enter alcoholism ... For a time, I was able to maintain the "sophisticated drunk" image. Rapidly, though, I reached bottom with my drinking; in eighteen months I ended up in a drying-out clinic for alcoholics. Here I met my future husband, and with his support I managed to get enough of a sense of self-worth to begin to recover.

My identity for the next few years, then, was that of a sober, loving housewife. While my husband acted on his decision to continue schooling and prepare for a career in the field of alcohol and drug rehabilitation, I worked selling cosmetics to help him accomplish his goal. After five and one-half years of sobriety, stability, and increasing boredom with my housewife-helpmate role, I dared to think of myself as having something more to offer. My husband was now a skilled therapist, working at a rehabilitation center for alcoholics and addicts. I began working with him as a cotherapist in marathon experiences for Alcoholics Anonymous members looking for further growth.

It was during these marathon experiences that I found my first point of identity with other women alcoholics: we were *overly aggressive and angry*. I knew a lot about anger. It had come very close to killing me. Even before I saw the relationship of repressed anger to women's repression in society, I felt the need to accept my own anger and learn ways in which to express it. Looking back, it seems somewhat short of miraculous that I was able to do it. Society does not like angry little girls! Men despise and fear angry women.

During a period of active alcoholism in 1963, I was in treatment with a male psychiatrist in New York. I was not aware that I was alcoholic. Being totally indoctrinated in the male psychiatric model, I viewed my drinking as symptomatic and sought help. A close male friend had offered to finance treatment, paying $125 a week for five sessions. I was an honest patient, telling my psychiatrist openly about my drinking. Often I was drunk during the sessions. Since drinking released some of my inner feelings, I was often angry, if not belligerent, in his presence. I felt strongly that he did not like me. He refused to talk about my drinking and kept probing for causes. One day I brought my modeling portfolio to his office and he asked to see it. The pictures reflected my commercial womanhood — a sweet, pretty girl: a seductive woman; loveliness and serenity; femininity personified — what I got paid to project. His response was animated and positive for the first time. He said he now saw a completely different person.

Shortly after that the psychiatrist told me that my friend had called and said he was tired of paying the bill for such a hopeless case. I later learned this was a lie to facilitate the involvement of my family. Although I had been trying to become independent of them, out of desperation I finally agreed to their participation in my treatment, but only if any discussion of me with them took place in my presence. The psychiatrist agreed. When my brother arrived, however, they closeted themselves in his office, leaving me out in the waiting room like a sick little girl that the responsible daddies would take care of. I exploded, told the psychiatrist I was through, and stomped out of the office.

That night I had trouble sleeping, which was not unusual. I took several sleeping pills which finally took effect at 6 AM. At 9 AM (having taken the phone off the hook to ensure a few hours of sleep), I was awakened by four of "New York's finest" standing over my bed. They said they had gotten a call from my psychiatrist that I was killing myself. I said it was obviously not true as I was talking to them. They replied they heard that I was a model and asked to see my portfolio, and when they asked to see "the dirty pictures," I reacted angrily. They knocked me out and took me to an uptown hospital emergency ward. There six interns surrounded me and tried to induce me to drink an emetic to "save my life." No amount of protest would persuade them that I was not in imminent danger from an overload of barbituates. I was suffering from thirst and asked for a coke. Someone brought in a coke from a machine, and I was told I could have it if I drank the emetic, so I did. They then poured the coke into the sink.

Obediently, I threw up a lot of liquid emetic. Then papers were signed, and I was taken to Bellevue Psychiatric Ward. I had induced one of the interns to telephone a friend of mine to come to the hospital. He arrived after I was taken away and was told by the charge nurse, "I don't know what they were doing to that girl. There was nothing in her stomach." Nevertheless, for nine days I was suspended in acute isolation and anxiety at Bellevue. I was interviewed dozens of times by different psychiatrists who tried to "break my story". Labels of schizophrenic, manic-depressive, and psychotic, were thrown at me. My Park Avenue psychiatrist refused to talk to me on the phone. Plans were being made to have me committed to a New York State Mental Hospital. Finally, on the ninth day, a nurse took me aside and said, "Look, hon, I don't know what went on between you and this doctor, but if you're smart you'll tell him you're sorry." To lie to a psychiatrist at that point in my life seemed like a gross sin, but moralizing and philosophizing are luxuries in a mental hospital. I called him, and in my best little girl manner, told him I was sorry, that I needed him, and to please help me. He said he was glad I had learned my lesson. I was released the next day.

The message women get from male doctors is clear: "If you want my help, you will have to be what I want you to be. You will have to get rid of your anger elsewhere. It is not feminine. It is ugly; you are ugly." Male psychiatrists play St. George killing the Dragon with angry female patients. Phyllis Chesler (1972) suggests in *Women and Madness* that women practice with male therapists at learning appropriate feminine behavior to get a husband — seeking safety in the arms of the right husband on the couch of the right therapist. A woman is expected to cooperate with Dr. St. George and help him to kill her Dragon. One problem, when the Dragon is an essential part of you, he would be asking you to kill yourself.

A lot of women obey the command. I am not sure about women in general, but I do know about addicted women. We have these so-called "masculine" traits of aggressiveness, competitiveness, anger, and desire for power. Accordingly, we have been disliked, rejected, and forced to repress any traits which are not "feminine" and, therefore, acceptable to males. Shulamith Firestone illustrated this in the *Dialectics of Sex*:

> A woman seems incapable of expressing her strong negative feelings and explains her incapacity in a psychoanalytic session: "I am afraid to show these emotions because if I did it would be like opening Pandora's box. I am afraid my aggressiveness would destroy all." — a female patient of Theodore Reik (Firestone, 1970, p. 66).

Was she paranoid? Or rather, was she having an appropriate response to Reik's male message?

My identification with women and their problem with anger led me to a job in a rehabilitation center where I worked with over 100 women who were both drug- and alcohol-dependent, both black and white, from all socioeconomic backgrounds, in an age range from fifteen to seventy-five. Let me quote some descriptions of their underlying dynamics from the psychological and psychiatric examinations:*

Twenty-year-old white drug addict —
  Passive-aggressive,
  depressive, suspicious
  and hostile, dependent
  problems.
Thirty-year-old black alcohol-dependent woman —
  Passive-aggressive
  suspicious, depressive
  identity conflicts.
Forty-year-old white alcohol-dependent woman —
  Passive-aggressive,
  acting-out, depressive
  features, repressed rage.
Fifty-year-old black alcohol-dependent woman —
  Passive-aggressive,
  acting out, depressive
  features, repressed rage.
Sixty-year-old white, skid-row alcohol-dependent woman —
  Passive-aggressive,
  hypomaniac, schizoid
  features.

It was a rare woman, no matter what age, color, social status, or addiction, who did not have elements of aggressiveness and anger which she had learned to repress carefully. It is not suprising that psychiatric diagnosis should be passive-aggressive, depressive, suspicious, suicidal, identity problems, etc.

It is beyond me how any woman could avoid having identity problems with the "identity establishment," Erikson et al., defining and redefining our identity. It is not necessary to go back to Freud and his Dora to uncover the male psychiatrist's dislike and rejection of women who are aggressive and angry. I quote from a psychiatric evaluation of a forty-nine-year-old drug- and alcohol-dependent woman who later killed herself:

> Despite the patient's history being clouded by denials, rationalizations and intellectualization, it is clear that the patient has great problems centering about unresolved Oedipal feelings. Because the mother was the dominant figure in the family, the patient has confusion as to sexual

---

*Medical Records, Eagleville Treatment and Rehabilitation Center, Eagleville, Pennsylvania, 1971.

role, identification, and fears of inadequacy. She fears separation from her husband during hospitalization because he will leave her when he finds out she is unworthy. The depths of the patient's low self-esteem and depression is measured by the extreme amount of defenses that she employs. Her infantile complaining, demanding, and aggressive demeanor is strikingly similar to the description of her mother and probably represents identification with an aggressor.*

I saw this woman as attractive, competent, talented, aggressive, angry, but warm and giving. That I loved her for what she was, was too late and by then irrelevant to the messages she had gotten for forty-nine years. Women in their humanity, cannot survive without love from significant others in their lives. When that love is conditional on denying part of their very being, and when they are left feeling inadequate, unsupported, undefined, and without confirmation, they cannot survive.

As the women's movement grows, women professionals are beginning to ask some of the right questions. A recent study of women alcoholics reported in *Psychology Today* indicated that heavy drinkers tended to write more "masculine" stories (Wilsnack, 1973). Alcoholic women tended to have more unconscious masculine traits than nonalcoholic women. On a conscious level, the alcoholic woman values traditional female roles and is significantly more feminine, particularly in attitudes toward motherhood.

The alcoholic woman's conflicts and the doubts about her adequacy as a woman, may stem from the existence of so-called masculine traits in the unconscious levels of her personality. For example, a woman who is very assertive or aggressive in her personal style and whose unconscious sex-role identity is more masculine than the average woman probably senses that she somehow does not act and feel like a "real woman". The life-crises that are more significantly a cause of female alcoholism are usually centered around the death of or divorce from a husband, a husband's extramarital affairs, obstetrical or gynecological problems, the death of a parent, or children's growing older and leaving home. These crises seem to threaten her fragile sense of femininity, and she drinks to gain artificial feelings of womanliness. This is obviously a losing battle. The loss of control of the drinking brings on neglect of appearance, reduced ability to cope with demands of home and family, disapproval of family and friends, and eventually feelings of being even less of a woman.

In a measured, male-logical, research-minded tone, this woman professional asks if the women's movement will have any impact on female drinking. She suggests that, perhaps, if women learn to accept in themselves certain traditional "masculine traits" they will feel less of the

*Medical Records, Eagleville Treatment and Rehabilitation Center, Eagleville, Pennsylvania, 1971.

conflict that drugs soothe. And finally, she asks if liberation from sex-role stereotypes is in anyway an antidote for alcoholism.

Not having an academic-professional reputation to uphold, and no longer caring to prove myself logically and reasonably to the male professional establishment, I say that my empirical experience makes the question rhetorical. Slowly and painfully, over a period of time, I have, therefore, come to believe that a Radical Feminist approach is the appropriate treatment modality for addicted women.

MY FIRST ATTEMPT TO GAIN TREATMENT RIGHTS FOR WOMEN

Another dramatic awakening took place in the eighteen months I worked with women in the rehabilitation center previously mentioned. I arrived there in November of 1969, with very few preconceived ideas of what women needed to recover from alcoholism and drug addiction. I knew they needed a sense of self-worth and an opportunity to express their anger. I felt that their self-worth should not be too dependent on their feminine/sexual identity.

There were thirteen women in treatment in a community of 110 men. The minority problem was obvious. There was tremendous pressure to split the women up, and I had difficulty comprehending why. As time went by, however, the reasons became more apparent. Women had been "prostituted" in every conceivable way during the six months they had been members of the community. They were being used for sex itself, for acting as hostesses at community gatherings, for kitchen work, and mostly, for role play for the men in therapy groups. If a male group was planning an extended therapy session, women were included to act out the mother, sister, lover role for the male residents. This was blatantly stated in one of the funding proposals written at that time:

> ... Women have recently been added to our community, both as staff and as residents, as we are aware that alcoholics and addicts have many problems in their lives with women, as mothers, wives, sisters, lovers, etc...*

My first point of resistance to the community was to insist that the women not be split up into eight other groups. This creates what I call the "Elizabeth Taylor syndrome," i.e. the only woman in a group of ten or eleven men will be seen as sexually special so she will rely on the artificial sense of self-worth that such a group dynamic produces. While my initial motive for keeping the women together was to avoid the "Elizabeth Taylor syndrome," a more important reason began to

---

*Grant Proposal, Eagleville Treatment and Rehabilitation Center, Eagleville, Pennsylvania, 1970.

emerge. If self-worth was necessary for successful recovery, then caring about oneself as a human being and as a woman became crucial. How could a woman see herself as worthy if she could not identify with other women in a positive way? Society has kept women isolated from each other through competition and superficiality. Women themselves do not trust each other; they see other women as dangerous to their own search for male approval. Older women are threatened by the unlined faces and nubile bodies of younger women. Younger women do not want to be reminded of aging by the presence of sagging breasts and varicose veins. The moralistic suburban alcoholic decries the immorality of the young, promiscuous drug addict. The younger drug addict attacks the phoney value system of the older married alcoholic, seeing her as the biggest prostitute of all.

Carl Rogers (1969) states that there is no way to move forward until you first confront yourself where you are. Therefore, one of the therapeutic thrusts in an all-women's therapy group is to get women to confront their self-hate. As long as women avoid seeing themselves in the eyes and behavior of other women, they cannot reach their moment of truth. If a woman is afraid to stand beside another woman and say, "I am with you, I am like you, I identify with you," for fear that she will be exposed to her own self-perceived evil or that the other woman may be the one chosen by a man, then she is unable to really trust herself, believe in herself, and love herself. An example is a forty-five year old woman alcoholic who talks about her experience in a women's therapy group:

> After eighteen years of addiction to drugs and alcohol, I desperately clung to the only identity I thought I had — that of an "intellectual lady." The men in my life had always apologized for using four-letter words in my presence — and I reveled in my ladyhood. I refused to lower myself in the group to the level of the young junkie whores and use their street language ... until that day when I was confronted by twelve other women, junkies and alkies, who joyously chanted the numbers while they made me say "fuck" fifty times. My choked voice gradually rose to a triumphant yell, and I was free. This was the beginning of the end of my lonely, self-loathing. When twenty-four arms reached out to hold me, I wept for all that I had missed. For the first time I shared, communicated with, and trusted my own sex.*

WOMAN THERAPIST AS ROLE MODEL

Just as essential as an all-women's therapy group is the need that it be led by a woman therapist. Phyllis Chesler warns in *Patient and Patriarch*:

---

*M.H., former patient of Woman's Group, Eagleville Hospital and Rehabilitation Center, 1971.

Male psychologists, psychiatrists, and social workers must realize that as scientists they know nothing about women; their diagnoses, even their sympathy, is damaging and oppressive to women .... (Chesler, 1971, p. 384).

An example of Chesler's warning is illustrated by a male psychiatrist who directs a program for women on one of the larger drug treatment centers in this country. He made this statement in a paper delivered at a conference for Women and Drug Concerns:

Five years of experience in treating addicts indicates that a female who takes drugs, and especially one who violates her body by the use of a needle, indicating poor body and self-image concept, has more severe psychopathology than a male drug user ...*

A women's therapy group that is led by a male, especially a male doctor, sees itself, and is seen, as a *doll's house*. Daddy is in charge and keeps his girls together, so long as they give him the sense of "benevolent authority" that his experience and conditioning expect.

A women's group should be led by a woman who is able to be a role model, providing strength, compassion, and competence: A woman who can say that the primary ingredient of therapy is the capacity of the therapist to love her patient and to say to her,

Here is a second chance to organize your life. If you are angry and aggressive, that's okay. If you must ventilate your anger, use me. I can take it. If you must cry, I will not treat you as a little girl, but as a woman in pain who needs nuturing and acceptance. If you are afraid of being alone, I will share my own loneliness with you and, together we will support each other's solitude. If you want to use your aggressiveness, your talents, your competence, DO! It will not threaten me. I will do anything to help you be what you want to be and can be. My love for you is such an order.

A twenty-four year old woman drug addict talked about the effect of such a woman role model:

I had seen her before on the grounds of the therapeutic community where I was trying to recover from my addiction to heroin ... I knew she was the Director's wife, a recovered alcoholic, and a qualified therapist in her own right.

One day I happened to overhear her having a loud verbal argument with her husband, the Director. Her voice clear and distinct, angry and unwilling not to be heard, stating her demands, taking a stand, telling him where it was at, and what she was worth. To me, this was unheard of, practically unlawful, from the kind of suburban background I had come from. No woman dared to speak to her husband like that. As I

---

*Domantay, Antonio, M. D. Medical Director of Psychiatric and Treatment Services, Odyssey House. Paper presented at National Convention, Chicago, Illinois, May, 1973.

came to know her in the coming months, she did dare to speak ...

A woman therapist in an all-female group has a tremendous amount of power and influence, and it is eminently crucial as to who assumes that responsibility. When this woman took over our group, it was like an end to a spiritual famine. She gave to myself and the other women a very real conception of what a successful, self-directed woman is, something none of us had ever seen in the flesh. Our groups were now an inspiration, a vast reservoir for learning about oneself and the dream of self-involvement became a reality ...*

SPECIAL PROBLEMS OF WOMEN

Other problems had to be faced regarding the special concerns of women. This was particularly true with black and other minority women who have experienced the double oppression of racism and sexism. In a therapeutic community, minority men, both staff and residents, put tremendous pressure on the minority women to identify with the minority struggle only, and to see the women's issues as relevant just to the upper- and middle-class white woman.

Ideally, a minority woman therapist who has dealt with these conflicts is best equipped to work with and help women caught in this sociocultural double bind. As a white woman, I have tried to use the empathy involved in our womanhood and to be sensitive and open to the experiences I could not share specifically. Most importantly, a white woman therapist should not become an instrument of conflict for the minority woman by creating more pressure, by pressuring her to identify entirely with the women's movement. She should be free to seek her sense of worth at her own pace and in her own way.

Motherhood also presents special psychological, social, and economic concerns for women that are not comparable to men's roles as fathers. Motherhood is one of the only career identities open to women in our society that promises power, prestige, and prominence. Addicted women quite naturally seek that role, probably more than most women, as some insurance against their feelings of inadequacy and self-hate. As a twenty-three-year-old woman addict says:

> Even though I met my husband over a drug deal, and even though we married while still on methadone, for the first time in my life I felt respectable. My feelings of being a woman blossomed in marriage, and then I was desperate to have a baby. Now that I was truly a woman, motherhood would be the ultimate fulfillment.†

This drug-blinded search for fulfillment as a mother leads all too often

---

*R.J.S., former resident, TODAY, Inc., 1972.
†E.M., former female resident, TODAY, Inc., 1972.

to further disgrace for a woman. As an addict, it is quite impossible to fulfill the mother role, and children are either left to fend for themselves or given over to relatives or public agencies.

When an addicted mother reaches a point of sobriety, after physical withdrawal from the drug, she is overwhelmed with feelings of shame and guilt about her children. The feelings must be dealt with therapeutically. However, this cannot be done successfully in a vacuum of inaction, for you must also be able to assure her that the children are being cared for in an appropriate and acceptable way. Few programs have addressed themselves to this need for temporary foster homes and child-care facilities. One solution we found was to place the children in foster homes near the treatment center so that the women could visit their children. They could then move in steps toward accepting the full responsibility of motherhood.

Older women, with grown children, face different problems with their motherhood. Often their drinking and drug use has taken place over the years of their children's adolescence and young adulthood, and in many cases the children have turned away in disillusionment and hostility. Sometimes reconciliation can be effected and sometimes not. Nevertheless, the issue for the addicted woman is still learning how to forgive herself for one of society's biggest crimes: failure at motherhood.

"GUILTY" BY ASSOCIATION WITH FEMINISM

As the months went by in the rehabilitation center, much was happening to the women being treated and to me as a woman and as a therapist. I had begun this job with only casual attention to what was going on in the world with women's liberation movement. If anything, I avoided identification with it. Glib remarks, such as "I'm not a joiner," and "I'll not give up my false eyelashes for anyone," kept me safe from looking at the larger issues. But I could not work day in and day out with women who exposed themselves to me in all their pain and not see a commonality among us all. I could not be honest with myself, or with them without beginning to see the relevance of their problems to my problems and to the problems of women everywhere. I had to face my fear of being labeled *Women's Libber*, with all the possible sublabels — *Man-Hater, Aggressive Bitch, Lesbian* — because although I did not identiy with IT, IT was identified with me. Because I took a stand on how the women were being treated, because I demanded certain treatment rights for women, because I dared to keep the women together in a group, because I withheld their "favors" from the male community, and finally, because I became successful, I was identified with feminism.

Women began staying in treatment longer. Women began asking for their own rights. More women came for treatment. From the thirteen beds for women in November 1969, there were thirty-three beds for women in June of 1971. Treatment completed rates for women went from 35 percent to 59 percent.

In June of 1971, the male community reacted. Caucuses were held. All kinds of charges were leveled against me. To avoid further chaos, I was asked to leave.

Research figures obtained from the Director of Research at this center show that, in the eighteen months following my departure, the treatment-completed rate for women dropped from 59 percent to 38 percent.*

The Women's Unit was taken over after my departure by a male coordinator and male therapists were included in the women's therapy groups. A current check of females in treatment show the number to be fourteen as of March, 1974 (Barr, 1974).

MY CURRENT EXPERIENCE AT GAINING
TREATMENT RIGHTS FOR WOMEN

I came to my current work situation, TODAY, Inc., in October, 1971. The status of women was typical of most treatment programs. While there were women drug addicts in treatment, there were no women on the staff, nor on the Board of Directors. Initially, my status was "wife of the Director." It took several months to convince the Board that I was a professional in my own right. Women were being taught a new set of behaviors to please males. They were told to give up their sleazy bitch street ways, and stop using their cunts to attract men. If a woman happened to be naturally sexy and sensuous, she was accused of seducing the men. If she was unfemininely aggressive and angry, she was told she was treacherous and that she was losing her sensitivity and her humanity. If she was Lesbian, she was accused of being a man-hater and "sick." She was learning, again, to repress part of herself and to become an "honest paper doll" cut out for man's satisfaction.

The Director, my husband, had become awakened by some of our prior experiences in regard to women and a woman therapist was hired. Separate male and female therapy groups were established, and TODAY became embroiled in the Male-Female issue. I found myself panicking at times when I saw this happening. However, I had survived the other experience and, in the meantime, had fully identified myself with the women's movement.

I had done a great deal of reading during the previous six months and

---

*Barr, Harriet, Ph.D., Director of Research & Evaluation, Eagleville Hospital and Rehabilitation Center, 1974.

had begun to feel myself a part of the history of women. The long, sometimes glorious, but mostly painful, struggle of women over thousands of years lifted me from my isolation and fear and gave me inspiration and support. Losing some of the fear and defensiveness allowed me to think more clearly, and to be more aware of the overall view. If anything I was more firmly committed to the concepts of treatment I had developed over the prior two years. However, I began to see that, if the male part of the community did not see that there was something for them to gain as well, being "right" would be useless.

When I became part of the staff, I spent time with the male staff and residents talking to them about women's problems. Usually, men, both staff and residents, agree that women need "special treatment." They do not have to give up much of their power status to say that women are different, or that they have more needs. Patronizingly, they agree it is all right if women have a group of their own. Perhaps they see it as analogous to woman's bridge clubs or sororities. That a very different thing is taking place in the group is not apparent at first.

SELF-HELP TECHNIQUES APPLIED TO THE SPECIAL PROBLEMS OF WOMEN

The self-help concept of TODAY has several components that are of particular benefit to women.

Slip Groups

Slip groups emerged from the Synanon/Daytop encounter model of treatment and are based on the Hold-and-Dump theory. We make no moral judgments on feelings, but we believe that it is what you do with your feelings that is important. Hence, residents may not dump their feelings within the course of the day, but are strongly encouraged to deal with them in a Slip Group. "Slip" refers to the slip of paper on which residents write their name, name of the person they are "dropping a slip" on, and the reason. There are many advantages to this technique. People learn that anger can be controlled. They learn that anger does not have to destroy, but can be used in a positive way to defend oneself. They also learn that they can survive other people's anger and not be destroyed.

For women, Slip Groups offer one of the most important learning experiences. For the first time in their lives, many are in an atmosphere where they are allowed to be angry. Many more find, for the first time, that they can survive anger directed at them, especially male anger. Slip Groups provide women with the awareness of the power that anger can generate. They see how it has been used to keep them frightened and in their place, and they also see how they have used their own anger against themselves. With the support of other women, they learn to survive the charges of *aggressive, angry bitch,* and to believe that their womanhood is not dependent on sweet passivity. It is in the Slip Groups that men begin to perceive that something very different is happening with women.

It is also in the Slip Groups that our attempt to develop a single standard of mental health can be most dramatically observed, contrary to the cultural double standard of mental health. In an investigation by Broverman et al. (Broverman, Broverman, Clarkson, Rosenkrantz, & Vogel, 1970) entitled "Sex-Role Stereotypes and Clinical Judgments of Mental Health", it was found that the mental health standard for the healthy male correlates with the standard for the healthy adult. However, the standard for the healthy female differs significantly from the healthy adult. This places a woman in the conflictual position of having to decide whether to exhibit those positive characteristics considered desirable for males and adults but not for females and so have her femininity questioned or to behave in the prescribed feminine manner and accept second-class status.

Isn't it possible that women who abuse drugs and alcohol, a "male disease," are making a strong statement about their need to find an outlet for their "male traits?" I leave the answer to that to the scientific researchers. For treatment purposes, it is enough for me to know that women must learn to develop honesty and integrity in order to feel the self-worth necessary to live sober lives. For most addicted women, that means learning to be independent and self-confident. To do this they must have an environment which does not question their femininity or call them deviant, but one which will support their right to first-class adulthood.

In the Slip Group, women confront others with their anger. They risk the rejection inherent in showing their bitchy selves to men. Twice a week they practice with anger, something most men have been doing all their lives. To a woman, a successful encounter is worth a hundred psychotherapy sessions, for in the slip chair everyone is equal. Men of course, do not like this at first, but as they change and grow, and as they see that they are given equal opportunity to express feelings of tenderness, tears and trepidations that society has not allowed them to express, they begin to prefer the "honest" women to the game-players they have known most of their lives.

The Work Structure

Another aspect of the program that offers women, and men too, vast opportunity for growth is the work structure. The professional staff directs the therapy, but the day-to-day operation of the house is taken care of by the residents themselves. Four departments, Kitchen, Housekeeping, Maintenance, and Public Relations, are maintained and run by a status structure. From Toddy, where a resident has little responsibility and few privileges, through three worker stages, to leadership, and to the top resident job, that of Facilitator, residents experience all aspects of each department in the house. People are assigned and promoted on their abilities rather than on their sex. Therefore, there may be a male resident in charge of housekeeping and a female in charge of maintenance.

A twenty-three-year-old recovering heroin addict said of her experience:

> It was necessary to step out of my old feminine role as I began to run the maintenance department rather than the kitchen. The experience of learning about such mysterious things as plumbing and boilers brought an increased sense of independence, but also more rejection from the men. The position not only meant power, but a chance to test my newly found convictions.
>
> I relied heavily on the solidarity we had built as a group of women. The women gave me the message that it was all right to be aggressive, angry at times, and independent that I was still a woman.*

The Learning Experience

In the role of sex object, a woman becomes overly concerned with her looks. When a woman has a poorly defined ego, as well as low self-image, she relates to her sex-object image in an exaggerated way. Many found temporary self-worth and power in the drug world on basis of this identity. A nineteen-year-old heroin addict related:

> I met a heroin wheeler-dealer from Philadelphia. He took me on as His Girl. He wined me and dined me, and dressed me up in pretty clothes, and most importantly, he supplied me with junk. Of all my identities, it gave me the most reward. I had status, a sense of power, I was adored by an important person and any conflicts that even started to surface could be easily deadened with heroin.†

Even when the sex-object identity fails and they find themselves alone, helpless, and without hope, and even after they have come to a program for help, they have trouble giving up that which has worked even partially or temporarily. A woman resident recalled:

---

*E.M., former female resident, TODAY, Inc., 1972.
†M.C., former female resident, TODAY, Inc., 1972.

I arrived at TODAY in rolled up jeans, four-inch platforms, a long curly shag, red lipstick, and rhinestone earrings, bracelets and belt. I was scared and needed help, but I didn't know why. I entered the house as a very sexy broad and continued to be a very sexy broad for the first two weeks. My behavior was upsetting to the rest of the women who began to confront me about my relationships with men.*

Here was a young woman who for twenty-three years had drawn her sense of herself and value from being a "sexy broad." As she herself said, she never thought of developing traits of honesty, courage, and integrity. Her job was to find a man who possessed these qualities. Beneath her sexy front, she felt she had nothing. When she realized this, she agreed to accept a learning experience, which involved wearing a stocking cap to cover her hair, baggy shirts to cover her figure, using no make-up, and having a communication ban with all the males in the house.

This learning experience is another kind of withdrawal experience for a woman. In the search for herself, she must systematically eliminate the destructive ways she has attempted to solve her identity/worth problems. Without her *sexy* looks, and her seductive maneuvers to gain male attention, she is forced to develop other ways to feel good about herself. As she discovers that she does have some strength, she has a brain that works and a body that is utilitarian for something other than sex, and most importantly that she has a soul that reflects all that she is, she is applauded and supported.

THE PROBLEMS OF WOMEN WHO ARE ALSO LESBIAN

If women have problems in this hetereosexual society being treated as second-class citizens, what happens to a woman who happens also to be Lesbian? Many turn to drugs and alcohol in order to be able to express their homosexuality. Usually they have never lived openly as gay women. When they come to treatment for addiction they are very sensitive to the issue of their sexual identity. A twenty-five-year-old Lesbian spoke of her fears:

Upon entering TODAY, Inc., I was much more afraid of being discovered homosexual than I was of dealing with my addiction. By this time "straight" women were the last people on earth I wanted to live with.†

A therapeutic community does not differ from the outside world in being comfortable with homosexuality. In a community that segregates male and female therapy groups and does not allow sexual acting out, the

---

*E.M., former female resident, TODAY, Inc., 1972.
†R.J.S., former female resident, TODAY, Inc., 1972.

homosexual anxiety level is very high. Staff avoidance of the homosexual issue is common. When it becomes unavoidable the average therapist hides behind a "liberal" attitude. I was guilty of this for the first couple of years that I called myself a therapist. But along with other areas of growth, and with a great deal of help from the Lesbian women residents at TODAY, I was able to break through my own fears and deal with my own homosexuality. Isn't that what is really on the line with all of us? It is only if we can look at our own homosexuality with some measure of ease that we can be authentic in helping people who are homosexual.

The Lesbian has particular problems in an all-female group. She has trouble identifying with some of the issues that hetereosexual woman have to deal with in relationship to men. In addition, the therapist tends to see her as different, perhaps even as having an advantage in not needing male approval. However, I learned that the ego problems of addicted Lesbians do not differ significantly from those of addicted heterosexual women. The need for a woman/lover to confirm and fulfill her ego identity is equally strong. Addicted Lesbians are as prone to personal compromise, loss of self-respect and dignity within their love relationships as are addicted heterosexual women. To be a homosexual sex object is no better than to be a heterosexual sex object. And it is only if we acknowledge that, that we can deal with the problems that surface within the therapy group.

> I was rejected and scrutinized for a period of time after exposing my homosexuality. My gestures were misinterpreted and some of the women hurled accusations of my attempted seductions. In actuality, it was never that exciting. A few women did attract me physically, but I managed very well to abide by the rules of no sex while in residential treatment (R.J.S., 1972).

And within the community, there were problems:

> A female staff member made heavy accusations to the Director of the program as to my overt attempt to "put the make" on her in the third floor bathroom. I was verbally crucified in front of the entire residential community on my irrational, self-gratifying homosexual instincts. The story, graphically and angrily conveyed, was a total fantasy on the part of this dangerously corrupt female staff member. (She was later dismissed for other inappropriate behavior.) But at the time, I suffered again those horrible, petty, silent thoughts from people who believe that all lesbians are raving maniacs.*

The nature of the involvement between therapist and resident is the crucial ingredient of therapeutic success. A therapist must be authentic.

Months later I was able to deal confrontatively with this injustice with

---

*R.J.S., former female resident, TODAY, Inc., 1972.

the help of my new therapist, a woman who was authentic, whose presence commanded respect, and, above all, who accepted me for myself.*

The needs of Lesbian women for a sense of self-worth, for self-confidence, and self-direction, are much the same as for other women with addiction problems.

A NONSEXIST APPROACH FOR ALL ADDICTED PEOPLE

If men are at fault for defending the power base of a sexist world, women must hold themselves accountable for accepting and, in fact, encouraging men's will to power. It is often convenient for women to avoid risk and responsibility by allowing men to play their superior roles. By supporting society's shallow definition of femininity, women force men into the typical masculine role to feel sex-role security.

At TODAY, as our attention to women's needs began to produce results, as a new breed of women began to emerge who were strong, assured, and self-reliant, we began to question the equality of our treatment for men. A twenty-five-year-old recovering male addict raised some questions:

> While I was going through the program I got two messages — one, that men should have "healthy" attitudes toward women; and, two, men should not have hostility for women. But to me it did not seem possible to develop healthy attitudes without dealing with the hostility, and there was no opportunity.†

As we searched ourselves for the answers, we found some interesting things. We had all, men and women staff alike, accepted the therapeutic tradition that one does not tamper with a man's sexual identity too early in his recovery. It seemed logical that since man's social-sexual role was "superior," we would be wise to use the feelings of worth emanating from that to build sobriety time. Later, when he had some stability, we could raise questions surrounding his sexuality.

Looking back, I can see that in accepting this tradition without question, the women were holding on to the last vestige of the old law: To feel like women, men must be men. And the men, well, as John Stuart Mill said more than a century ago, "Was there ever any domination which did not appear natural to those who possessed it?" (Mill, 1971, p. 27).

As we opened our attitudes, we became aware of some of the ways in which we were depriving man of the freedom of expression we were

---

*R.J.S., former female resident, TODAY, Inc., 1972.
†W.S., former male resident, TODAY, Inc., 1971.

giving women. In the women's groups led by a woman therapist, no male staff participated on a regular basis. We had felt justified in this because many men felt threatened in all-women's groups and some women were so intimidated by the presence of a male that they were unable to express their negative feelings, particularly those toward men. However, in the all-male group led by a male therapist, a female cotherapist was always present. One might argue that the hierarchical structure of leader and coleader made this all right, that women are used to being second in command, and hence, it was easier to get an appropriate woman cotherapist than to find a qualified, competent male who was willing to work in a secondary position in the women's groups. No doubt it was a combination of factors that had produced the situation, but the situation was inhibiting the expression of the men's negative feelings, especially toward women.

When the change was made, and women were no longer participating regularly in the male groups, the therapist noted more openness about women, and especially more free expression of hostility. And so we moved forward in our struggle to create a community that is freeing itself of the sex-role stereotypes.

Periodically, the Male-Female issue reaches a peak of conflict, and staff and residents wage battle. Inevitably someone feels that if we mixed the males and females in the therapy groups we would have less trouble. My answer to that is that *less trouble* is not good therapy. We could also use tranquilizers and we would have a much more peaceful community. However, "peace is not the absence of conflict but the ability to cope with it." If repressed rage between the sexes causes much of the havoc of sexual relationships, and if addicted people in particular have trouble with their sexual identities, then an environment in which men and women both can express their hostilities, cope with their conflicts, and question their conditioning, has a better chance of helping them find an authentic sense of selfhood.

Does a Radical Feminist approach work? Research statistics gathered for the two-year period between March, 1972 and March, 1974, show that our success with males compares favorably with other programs. Our success with females is exceptional. Of the women who have come to TODAY for treatment, 68 percent are doing well, i.e. free of drugs and living responsible lives. Of the women who completed the entire residential program, 88 percent are successful.*

REFERENCES

Broverman, Inge K., Broverman, Donald M., Clarkson, Frank, Rosenkrantz, Paul S.,

---

*McBrearty, John, Ph.D., Director of Research and Evaluation, TODAY, Inc., 1974.

and Vogel, Susan R.: Sex role stereotypes and clinical judgments of mental health. *Journal of Consulting and Clinical Psychology*, 34:1, 1970.

Chesler, Phyllis: Patient and patriarch: Women in the psychotherapeutic relationship. In Gornick, Vivian, and Moran, Barbara (Eds.): *Women In Sexist Society.* New York, Basic Books, 1971, p. 384.

Chesler, Phyllis: *Women and Madness.* New York, Avon, 1972.

Firestone, Shulamith: *The Dialectic of Sex: The Case for Feminist Revolution.* New York, William Morrow, 1970.

Mill, John Stuart: *On the Subjection of Women*, Fawcett, 1971.

Rogers, Carl: The group comes of age. *Psychology Today*, 3:27, 1969.

Wilsnack, Sharon C.: Femininity by the bottle. *Psychology Today*, 6:39, 1973.

Chapter 20

RADICAL PSYCHIATRY FOR WOMEN

Hogie Wyckoff

POLITICS AND WOMEN'S PROBLEM SOLVING GROUPS

WE in radical psychiatry begin with a definite radical political perspective. We are not interested in being *hip shrinks* who service counter-culture people. We are community organizers; we want to teach people problem-solving skills and political awareness. We want to provide protection to people while they make the changes they want in their lives. We desire to put people in touch with their power because we are interested in people reclaiming themselves as full and potent human beings.

The radical psychiatry problem-solving group model has been developed through a synthesis of psychiatric theories borrowed from R. D. Laing, Fritz Perls, and Claude Steiner. Radical Psychiatry theory incorporates some basic transactional analysis (T.A.) assumptions about psychiatry and people. We assume, as Eric Berne did, that people are born OK and that they are made unhappy because of what they do to each other (Steiner, 1974b). We agree with Berne that the language of psychiatry should be simple and that people who practice psychiatry should communicate their opinions to group members rather than keep secrets and thus maintain a one-up stance.

Women

The majority of people who seek psychiatric help are women. This is the result of the gross, yet subtle, oppression of women as a class. They have been denied full development of their power as human beings. Rather than expressing their righteous anger about this violation, they have too often come to view themselves and each other as somehow deficient. Because of the stress of this mind-rape, women break down more often than men. Furthermore, due to sex-role programming, women more often than men admit their need for psychiatric help. The problem is that most of the "help" women receive is from psychiatrists whose values are ultimately anti-women's liberation.

As radical feminist psychiatrists, we believe that psychiatry is a political activity. Psychiatrists cannot be neutral; they insert their personal values, either blatantly or passively. By not taking a clear stand they support the *status quo* through what Marcuse (1965) termed "repressive tolerance." Therefore, at this point in history we feel that men, particularly professional, elitist, and sexist men, cannot help free women.

We, as women, *can* and *must* free ourselves. We can effectively take care of our own and one another's heads and souls. We should seize the means of producing and preserving our own mental health. Women already have well-developed skills in intuition and insight; as oppressed people we are accustomed to adapting and compromising to the desires of others, to tuning in scrupulously to other people's feelings, and to taking care of their unspoken needs. When these skills are coupled with permission and training to be strong, to take care of business, to think rationally, and to talk straight, the result is a skillful and powerful people's psychiatrist.

We call ourselves "psychiatrists" (soul-healers in the original Greek) in order to communicate the competency of our work and the coopting of power from the medical establishment. This reclamation has been happening for over four years in Berkeley; women have started reclaiming their own mental well-being. Women who have themselves worked in problem-solving groups are learning to facilitate women's groups in training collectives.

We do not see ourselves as providing alternative services to coexist with psychiatry based on the medical model and dominated by the psychiatric establishment. We are a counter-institution with the intention of bringing the practice of psychiatry as *soul healing* back into the hands of the people. We intend to make high-quality, powerful psychiatry available to all who want it while putting expensive, individualistic "professionals" out of business. We refuse to "diagnose" "patients" as "sick," label them with such terms as "schizophrenic," or "treat" them with "medicines." We are convinced that people are basically good and powerful and, given the right conditions, can live cooperatively together. Therefore, when people are troubled, they are oppressed rather than sick. Since people are socially oppressed, we believe in social solutions achieved in group settings. We do *not* believe in one-to-one psychotherapy for an extended period of time; that only concentrates the talents of a few on helping a few. Furthermore, because we believe that people must have the right to choose when, how, and with whom they wish to change, we work with people contractually by providing mutually agreed upon services.

Alienation

We believe that people have the wish, and the desire, and the capacity to live in peace and harmony with themselves, each other, and the earth. We believe that *alienation* is the result of deceptive or mystified oppression (Steiner, 1971b). By alienation we mean a sense of not being right with oneself, the world, or humankind. It is a feeling of being not OK because something is wrong with you (Steiner, 1974a).

The alienation that most women experience daily as a result of their oppression is enormous. It is shocking, for instance, to consider how many women are alienated from their own sexuality. Sound data is not readily available, but a survey in *Psychology Today* (Athanasiou, Shaver, & Tavis, 1970) reporting on a very select, relatively-enlightened and sexually-free audience, related that 20 percent of the women responding said that during intercourse they reached orgasm never or almost never, and an additional 10 percent said they reached it only one fourth of the time. In other words, 30 percent of these women achieve orgasm less than once every four times they make love.

A woman's sexual alienation causes her to feel she is not OK. If her oppression is made clear to her, a "frigid" woman can view herself compassionately as a victim of prejudices concerning women's sexuality and can begin to fight back. Women have the right to have orgasm at least as often as men. But this realization will not occur if psychiatrists continue to listen to sexist Freudian theories which demean women's sexuality with accusations of penis envy or inadequacy. Sexist theories promote women's sexual alienation.

Another form of alienation can be found in older women who are slandered as being "bitchy" or menopausally depressed when in actuality they are feeling the full thrust of their oppressive role in society. Because they have not pursued careers or been recognized as producers within the system, they have received little in the way of recognition for their work. Due to media prejudice in behalf of youthful sexual beauty, they are not considered viable sex objects. In their roles as homemakers and mothers, they receive scant thanks for spending their lives sacrificing and caring for their families. When they become depressed about this unjust payoff they often receive the outrageous punishment of electric shock therapy and/or stupefying drugs.

Further examples of alienated women would include those who do not accept and love themselves, those who feel hatred and contempt for themselves and other women, and those who hate their bodies and see themselves as ugly. Some alienated women feel crazy because, while their intuition tells them certain things are happening, no one around them agrees.

Radical Psychiatry Equations*

Alienation = Oppression + Mystification

Women are deceived or mystified into colluding with their oppression;

---

*Steiner, 1971b.

they are deceived into believing there is something wrong with *them* rather than in this exploitive society. Once mystification is removed, a woman can realize that she actually has been oppressed. She will now feel she is OK.

Oppression + Awareness = Anger

Awareness is the opposite of mystification. Awareness or conscious thought incorporates an understanding of the necessity for action. To be able to make her life better, a woman must take control over it; she must act. Conscious thought is alienated when it excludes action, when it is disconnected from real-life experience. Consciousness must be grounded in action. An example of alienated thought is traditional psychoanalysis; people experience themselves as growing in self-understanding, but they are unable to make actual changes in their behavior.

The anger that comes from awareness is very useful in motivating women to use their rational power and to focus their energy on fighting for and reclaiming their full humanity. Once she is aware of her injury and becomes angry, a woman can move against the real culprit.

Awareness + Contact = Action ➤ Liberation

To overcome our oppression we need support from others. This is called *contact*. *Contact* can be in the form of *strokes*. *Strokes* are positive human recognition, such as warm smiles, sincere compliments, hugs, caresses, or credit for hard work. The antithesis to Alienation or Mystified Oppression is *Liberation*. But liberation will not come until we are *all* free and this will require much collective, cooperative hard work (action).

STRUCTURAL ANALYSIS OF EGO STATES

Radical psychiatry incorporates some basic tools of Eric Berne's transactional analysis (T.A.) (Berne, 1972). Berne observed that people act in three distinctive modes called *ego states*. They act like *parents*, people who know without questioning what is right and wrong and how things should be done; they act like *adults*, who process information and make predictions from the data like a computer; and they act like *children*, who can play, be creative, open, and in touch with their feelings and what they want. Using these three ego states, the Parent, the Adult, and the Child, we can explain what is going on with people and help them demystify what is happening within themselves, and in their transactions with others.

People act in three different ways when they are behaving in the ego state we call their Child. First, they act as the *Natural Child*, who is free and creative, in touch with feelings and acts on them spontaneously. Second, people act as an *Intuitive Child*. Berne called this the "Little Professor," whose intellect is intuitive rather than rational and logical. Third, they act as the *Pig Parent*. This is the Parent in the Child, who loves and cares for the Child only as long as the Child adapts to what the Pig demands. If the Child does not adapt, the Pig Parent withdraws its love and protective support.

By discussing ego states, it is possible to explain to a woman why she feels resentment when her husband repeatedly tells her how to do things. The transaction is supposedly Adult=Adult (overt communication), but because of the repetition, she experiences it as his Parent giving orders to and dominating her Child (covert communication). In Radical Psychiatry we feel that it is vital to be able to explain in easily understood language what goes on between people. A blackboard can be used to diagram and explain these transactions.

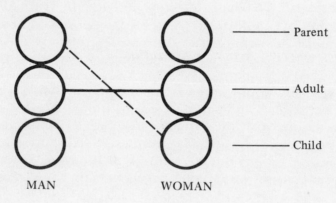

Figure 20-1.

Sex Role Oppression

Women and men are socialized to develop some parts of their personalities while suppressing the development of other parts. This programming, which Claude Steiner (1974b) has called *banal scripting*, promotes a stilted, predetermined and repetitive way of acting in life. Banal sex-role scripts invade the fiber of our day-to-day lives. Let me begin with a general explanation.

Definitions of female and male roles are intensively socialized from

birth on and are constantly reinforced throughout life. Since these definitions are dependent upon one another, I will contrast men's programming with women's. Traditionally, a man is supposed to be productive,
rational, and hardworking, but he is not supposed to be emotional, in
touch with his feelings, or overtly loving. On the other hand, a woman is
not supposed to think rationally, be productive, or be powerful. She
supplies the man she relates to with the emotion that is missing in him,
and he is rational and takes care of business for her. These, of course, are
the extreme characteristics of male/female sex roles. Obviously all people
do not fit neatly into them. In general, however, there is a tendency for
people to define themselves in their society's masculine and feminine
terms.

One particularly unhealthy result of our male/female sex-role training
is that limits have been placed on the development of women and men as
whole human beings. Like two halves of a puzzle, people feel incomplete
when they lack a partner of the opposite sex who would fulfill them;
when they are not in a relationship they feel not-OK. Consequently, they
put their energy into looking for someone to match up with or they cling
desperately to an already-established dependency relationship, even if it is
unhealthy.

When looking at people in terms of their ego functions, it becomes
evident that males are pressured to conform to certain scripts. They develop their Adult so that they will be rational, good at math and science,
and generally able to think logically. They are dissuaded from developing
their Nurturing Parent for others or for themselves. Most boys, for instance, do not include in their self-image the ability to nurture children
or the ability to take care of and comfort others. A boy's OK self-image
depends more on his ability to take care of business and be strong, so that
if he were needed to take care of people it would only be indirectly
through his Adult performance. He is taught that it is important to have
a well-developed Adult, while it is not necessary or even all right to have
a strong Nurturing Parent. Sometimes men are told they *should* be nurturing, *should* take care of other people. They feel guilty if they do not
want to, so they Rescue, that is, they do things for others that they really
do not want to do, because their Pig Parent tells them they should. An
example is a man who works at a job he hates to support a family he does
not really want.

Men are also enjoined not to be in touch with their Natural Child.
They are given messages not to feel, and to discount their feelings; they
are told it's best if they are not "too soft" or "too emotional." It would be
difficult, for instance, for a boy to compete and to be willing to get hurt
in a football game if he were in touch with his fear of competition and of
being hurt. If men were tuned in to their feelings, they would not only be

unable to exploit others, but they would also be unable to exploit themselves and their bodies; they would not do unpleasant and boring labor or risk their lives or kill others in military service.

A man is also told that it is not important to be in touch with his intuition (Little Professor). If Mr. Jones, making a business deal, is using his Intuitive Child he might understand that Mr. Brown is scared and worried about the negotiations. Further, if Mr. Jones has a clear pipeline to his Nurturing Parent, he might feel empathetic, feel compelled to be fair, and want to give Brown a break. He would have trouble being competitive and "successful," he would want to be cooperative and understanding.

The male Pig Parent's main job is to police men into always having their Adults turned on, to do what their Pigs say they should to be "real men," that is, to be out of touch with their nurturing, intuitive, or fun-loving feelings. The following is a diagram of the ego development of men under banal sex-role scripting:

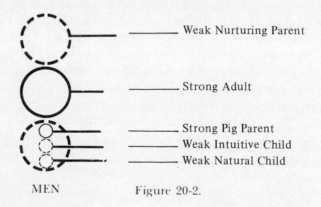

MEN   Figure 20-2.

Under banal scripts women are the male's complementary other half. More precisely, men are incomplete halves which women are supposed to complete. Women are programmed to be adaptable. They are enjoined to have a strong Nurturing Parent: It is their job to bring up children, to take care of people, especially "their" men, and to be nurturing. They are not programmed to have a strong Adult. It is understandable and OK if a woman cannot figure out her income tax forms, or if she does not understand math or mechanics. She does not have to think rationally and logically. Actually, for her to fulfill her functions as assistant, girl-Friday, volunteer, and/or unpaid houseworker, it is important that a woman *not* develop her Adult. But it is necessary for her, as it is for men, to have a Pig Parent to enforce the *laws* of her script, and to keep her in her inferior status.

Society's general script for women is designed to make them feel powerless. In terms of a structural analysis of the ego states, that means that they do not have Adult power, that they tend to be irrational and have difficulty taking responsibility for their decisions and actions. When they are following the usual basic script, they look for others, especially men, to Rescue them and they do not trust themselves or other women to take care of the business of the world.

On the other hand, it is OK for a woman to have a well-developed Little Professor, to be intuitive and know what is going on with other people (Rosenthal, Archer, Di Matteo, Koivumaki & Rogers, 1974) so that she knows when and how to nuture them. When women are tuned in, they take care of people's wishes without even being asked (the usual female role in the Rescue game). But a woman does not have permission to have a Natural Child, because if she did, she would be tuned in to her own desires and would not be willing to settle for less.

The common body script for women is to meet the media image of beauty, to look good from the outside in — not to feel good from the inside out. The "ideal" woman (Barbie Doll®) in our culture tends to have weak arms, long fingernails that make for inefficient use of the hands, a small waist with a tight, flat stomach, long slender legs that look good but are not particularly strong, narrow, pointed feet that are not well-planted on the ground, and large breasts that are not full of feeling.

The following is a diagram of the ego development in women which depicts the effects of banal sex-role scripting:

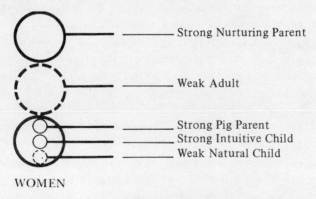

WOMEN

Figure 20-3.

The Sex-Role Conspiracy

Men and women are mystified into believing that they are scripted to go together like sweet and sour sauce, hot and cold, or Yin and Yang. It is supposedly a "groovy" and "beautiful thing". But the problem is that people really *do not* fit together very well that way. This is grotesquely exemplified by TV's Archie and Edith Bunker. Actually, men and women become puzzles to each other, rather than complements. Men often say they can not understand the way women think; women say they do not understand the way men think. The relationship between them breaks down because the myth of complementary sex-roles conspires against genuine communication.

The way in which communication is defeated can be easily seen in the following diagram illustrating the possible transactions between banally scripted man and women:

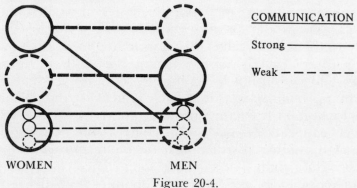

COMMUNICATION

Strong ——————

Weak — — — — —

WOMEN   MEN

Figure 20-4.

As the diagram shows, communication is possible from her Nurturing Parent to his Child, but rarely vice versa. And because there is weak communication between their Adults, it is difficult for them to develop the intimacy of a cooperative and efficient working relationship. The potential bond between Nurturing Parents is also lacking because he is not scripted to develop in that area, while she is taught to assume the entire responsibility for bringing up their children. The communication between Little Professors is also weak, causing a lack of shared intuition. Lacking effective communication, men and women are unable to be intimate and loving and to have satisfying and equal working relationships.

When we put these two people together and they "become one," we find that they are indeed little more than one whole person. The composite of their two personalities equals one Nurturing Parent, one Adult, one Little Professor, two halves of a Natural Child and two Pig Parents. A paltry human being indeed! (see Fig. 20-5.)

Women's Ego State Oppression

Women are oppressed in all their ego states. First of all, they are oppressed as Nurturing Parents because they are enjoined to Rescue others and to give all their nurturing away, especially to their husbands and

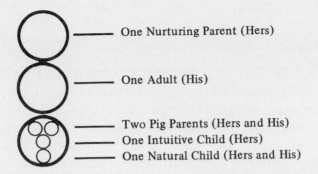

One Nurturing Parent (Hers)

One Adult (His)

Two Pig Parents (Hers and His)
One Intuitive Child (Hers)
One Natural Child (Hers and His)

Figure 20-5. A woman and man join together and "become one."

children. If a woman is a living, nurturing parent to herself she is seen as selfish, cold, and uncaring because she will not be self-sacrificing. Our goal in women's groups is to stop this absurd altruism and allow women to love themselves *first*.

Women are oppressed in their Natural Child when they do not feel safe enough in the world to do what they feel like doing. They are other-directed: They look to others rather than trusting their own feelings and doing what feels good.

Women are made to feel crazy when men do not validate their Intuitive Child perceptions. Because men are not usually in touch with this ego state, they discount many of the things women are aware of intuitively. For instance, a husband may discredit his wife's sense that he is loving her less because he feels so guilty and scared about those feelings. Women also discount their own intuitive feelings in order to Rescue themselves from the truth.

In women's groups, women can become familiar with what insidiously keeps them down, not only the obvious, overt sexism but also internalized oppression which turns a woman against herself, making her her own worst enemy rather than her own loving best friend.

Women's groups are an excellent place for women to feel safe enough to use their Adults in a potent way. They receive support to use their intelligence, to think about things they have never thought about before, and to take the power to make decisions based on knowledge they had not previously given themselves credit for having. They are given an opportunity to experience and respect the intelligence of other women.

When women nurture themselves, use their intelligence, and trust their intuitions, they can act in behalf of their true core, the Natural Child. We can only be truly powerful when we are in touch with this part of ourselves. Only then can we know what feels good and what does not, what hurts and oppresses us, what causes us joy, fulfillment, or righteous anger.

The Pig Parent

The internalized oppressor I call the Pig Parent. I use the term *Pig Parent* rather than Berne's term *Critical Parent* because I want to dramatize to women that this part of their psyches is truly bad for them and may wish them harm. The Pig Parent is the incorporation of all the messages which keep women subordinate: She must not outdo a man, she must be humble and not love herself, she must take care of others first, she must not be angry or "bitchy." These messages terrorize the Child in her when she tries to be free.

The oppression of the Pig Parent can be easily illustrated by a technique we call *bragging*. Children who feel OK about themselves love to tell how fine and wonderful they are until their parents and other grown-ups teach them that they are bad (conceited, narcissistic) to truly like themselves. Children believe this lie and grow up unable to love themselves.

It is regrettably easy for women to be controlled by their Pigs. They merely need to stand up in front of friends and tell them what they like about themselves, especially such forbidden subjects as the way they look, their delight in their bodies, or they way they make love; they will experience anxiety and qualify what they believe. The Pig in their heads tells them to be humble; its messages are like these: "You'll make a fool of yourself because nobody believes that about you," or "Shut up, you're boring them."

When women are acting in their Pig Parent ego state they are always measuring their performance and productiveness. Their attitude toward themselves is demanding, not accepting; things are never good enough. This internalized form of oppression can be devastating. In women's groups we are very interested in helping women "off" (destroy) their Pigs. It is important for a woman to become aware of her Pig messages as a powerful element of her oppression. To overcome her Pig a woman can be sensitized to it. It is helpful to anticipate when the Pig may become active. It usually expresses itself most strongly when the Child wants expression or when a woman has been feeling fine, or when someone else's Pig is colluding with hers. It is helpful to become familiar with the Pig's language: "must, should, ought, better, best, bad, stupid, ugly, crazy, or sick."

The Pig has a program which should be understood. An example might be a woman's being so afraid all the time that she can not get in touch with her real feelings and what she wants in life. The Pig Parent would enforce this program by making threats about frightening things that might happen to her if she asked for what she wanted.

A Pig Program sets up a vicious circle which is difficult to escape once it is set in motion. For example, suppose that a woman does not ask for what she wants, but only asks for what she thinks people have for her to avoid putting anyone on the spot. In other words, she Rescues people from knowing how she really feels and what she wants. When she finally does ask for something she really wants, she applies a lot of pressure to get it. If she does not get it, she feels very bad and her Pig wins a victory. It can then say, "See, it does not pay to ask for what you want." Consequently, she asks even less often for what she wants and feels even worse when she does not get it.

The only way out of this cycle is for her to make a decision to ask for what she wants 100 percent of the time. She thus stops Rescuing people from her desires, letting them take care of themselves; she accepts a *no* answer without acting the Victim. Because she will be getting a lot more of what she wants, she will not be so disappointed about things she does not get. To be sure, some people will sometimes do things for her which they do not want to do, that is, they will Rescue her. And since Rescuers inevitably become Persecutors, she will have to absorb some anger from some people. But the benefits of asking for what one wants far outweigh the problems that accompany the requests; the Pig Program is defeated.

Women's Banal Scripts*

A script is a life-play embarked upon at any early age. It is induced by powerful injunctions (Don't) and attributions (Do), which are transmitted by parents and society (Steiner, 1971). Banal scripts do not lead to tragic endings as do the hamartic scripts described by Steiner (1971a), but rather they result in restrictions of autonomy and spontaneity.

Women are not only scripted by their parents and encouraged in their roles by the mass media, but also by the history of role models including the Greek mythological goddesses: Athene can be seen as the prototype of the "Woman behind the Man;" Hera as "Mother Hubbard;" and Aphrodite as "Plastic Woman." Similar sex roles have been reified by psychiatrists, for example, the Anima and Animus archetypes of Carl Jung.

In the following sections I will present some women's scripts to show how women are trained to accept the mystification that they are incomplete, inadequate, and dependent. The scripts that I will describe have been chosen because of their common occurrence. It is possible for a woman to have a blend of two or three scripts. Specifics within a

---

*These scripts and others are explained in greater detail in my chapter on women's scripts in Claude Steiner's book, *Scripts People Live* (Wyckoff, 1974).

common theme stand for a general occurrence and will differ between individuals. For example, the Nurse script can represent any helping profession and an alcoholic husband can indicate a passive-dependent nonalcoholic husband as well.

In describing these banal scripts I will first describe the Thesis, the way in which intimacy, spontaneity, and awareness are oppressed. Next I will relate some of the injunctions or attributions the woman received, her mythical heroines, and the sad ending called for by her script. I will indicate how a therapist might collude with the script. Finally, I will present the Antithesis, the way out of the script.

Mother Hubbard (or Woman Behind the Family) Thesis

A Mother Hubbard spends her life nurturing and taking care of everyone but herself. She chronically gives much more than she receives and accepts the imbalance, because she feels she is the least important member of her family and that her worth is measurable only in terms of how much she supplies to others. This life-style is constantly legitimized by mass media promotion of the housewife and mother role. Meaning and strokes in life do not come to her for herself and her labors, but rather for her family, her husband, and her children. She chooses this script because it is safe and allows her to avoid taking on the enormous struggle involved in confronting how scary it is to try to be an independent and whole woman in a sexist society. Whenever she rebels and does what she really wants, her husband and children get angry with her.

Although she plays all roles in the Rescue Triangle (see Rescue Triangle section for explanation), she is most familiar with the one of Rescuer. In an effort to get something back from her family, she often talks too much (for attention), or she creates guilt in her husband and children for not loving her enough or giving her what she wants, even though she does not ask. Additionally, she refuses to make love with her husband, using excuses like "I'm too tired," or "I have a headache," in the hope that he will give her some nurturing strokes instead of sexual ones.

When she reads women's magazines, she envies the slender models in fancy clothes and in comparison feels not-OK. She is caught in a vicious cycle of cooking delicious recipes and going on diets. The more she feels not-OK, the more she wants to rebel, cook fancy recipes, and overeat.

Later in life she ends up depressed and lonely, appreciated by no one. Her children dislike her and her husband no longer finds her interesting. She has been used up and discarded by them. Like Portnoy's mother, she is despised as the cause of her children's problems. When her usefulness to others ends, often coincidental with menopause, she may undergo psychic death (labelled involutional melancholia) and be dealt a rude shock (electroshock) in return for her long hard life of labor.

Injunctions and Attributions:

Be a good mom

Be kind

Sacrifice yourself for others

HER MYTHICAL HEROINES. She always loved the old-time TV show called "I Remember Mama," likes Betty Crocker commercials, and enjoys "Mother Earth" imagery.

THERAPIST'S COLLUSION IN THE SCRIPT. He tells her not to get angry, but to adapt. He gives her tranquilizers to keep her comfortable and in her "place." He tells her she must diet and prescribes various pills, some to keep her thin and others to keep her happy and calm. When these fail, he may finish her off with electric therapy.

ANTITHESIS. She begins to listen to and respect her own inner desires; she starts getting strokes for who she herself is and not for what she can give to others. She absolutely refuses to Rescue, and starts demanding that people ask for what they want from her. She does not give more than she receives. It is essential that she put herself and her needs before those of others. She pays attention to her body — not to be beautiful in media terms — but because she loves herself and wants to feel good. She exercises regularly, takes up women's studies, and learns history, auto mechanics and akido. She makes her psychic and physical health a priority.

Once under way, the Mother Hubbard script is difficult to overcome because of the lack of viable alternatives available to an overweight mother of four. But women who really want to change can take power over their lives, they can fight to make their lives the way *they want* them to be by cooperating with and getting support from other women. They can cooperate in raising children or in exchanging child care. They can organize themselves in action groups to work for improved day care and welfare rights.

Plastic Woman Thesis

In an effort to obtain approval and sexy strokes, the Plastic Woman encases herself in plastic: bright jewelry, platform heels, "foxy" clothes, intriguing perfumes and dramatic makeup. She attempts to buy beauty and OK-ness, but never really succeeds. She constantly feels inferior to the beautiful women she idolizes in women's magazines and the movies. Her strokes come (mostly from store clerks) for being a fancy dresser and a clever shopper. These are the activities to which she devotes all her off-the-job hours. She feels safe in the role of consumer and experiences herself as having power when she makes consumer decisions and when she can buy the things she thinks she wants. On the other hand, she does not feel she has much power over what happens in her life outside the department store. Thus, she becomes accustomed to the role of Victim in the game of Rescue. She spends her time shopping, putting on makeup, trying on different outfits at home, and reading movie star and fashion magazines. Over and over she proves the validity of her script by sensing that she is ignored by people when she is not dressed up. Because she does not get what she really wants out of her life (what she wants can not be bought), she may begin to fight back by shoplifting. When she's angry with her husband, she may overspend to beat him to death with a plastic charge plate or she may use his money to buy time and attention from a psychoanalyst.

When she realizes that superficial beauty can no longer be bought and pasted on, she ends up depressed: She does not get any strokes that she truly values, either from herself or from others. She may attempt to fill the void with alcohol, tranquilizers, or other drugs. As an older woman she will often fill her life with trivia and her house with knick-knacks and gimmicks.

Injunctions and Attributions:

Do not be yourself

Be cute

Stay young

Her Mythical Heroines. She is enchanted by Doris Day and other such movie stars and amused by the style of Phyllis Diller, Joan Rivers, and Carol Channing.

Therapist's Collusion in the Script. He readily prescribes drugs and engages her in an extended course of psychotherapy. His "diagnosis" precludes group psychotherapy because she is *so* "neurotic." He sees her individually three or four times a week.

Antithesis. She decides to like and enjoy her natural self. She discovers that her "power" as a consumer is an illusion and decides to reclaim actual power and responsibility for her life. She no longer takes drugs to blur what's unsatisfactory about her life but joins a women's problem-solving group and learns how to make real changes. She works on developing aspects of herself besides her appearance. She begins to enjoy exercising and gets into a hiking club to meet new people. She involves herself in feminist body therapies and commits herself to caring about how she feels on the inside rather than just how she looks from the outside.

Poor-Little-Me Thesis

Poor-Little-Me is a Victim looking for a Rescuer. Her parents did everything for her because she was a *girl* (girls are supposed to be helpless), debilitating her, and making her completely dependent upon them. After struggling against their control, she gives up and concludes they are right: She is helpless. So she marries a prominent man, often a doctor, who plays Rescuing Daddy to her helpless little girl. She does not get strokes when she shows her strength but only when she is down. Thus, the strokes she gets are bittersweet and unnourishing.

Because she has permission to be spontaneous in a childlike and help-less way, she does experience some intimacy in her Child ego state with the Parent ego state of others. She rarely experiences the intimacy of equals. She learns she can get what she wants more easily if she tells people about her troubles; thus she becomes attached to a defective self-image. She spends much of her time complaining about how awful things are and trying to get others to do something about it. She keeps proving that she is a Victim by creating situations in which she first manipulates people into doing things for her that they really do not want to do, and then gets persecuted by them when they feel resentful towards her. Her husband gets sexual and other strokes from her for being a good Daddy to her weak Child; when she totally falls apart he gets strokes from others for being the martyred husband. She may fight back by "going crazy," making public scenes to embarrass her husband, and creating doubts in the community about his competence. She ends up not being able to function adequately. She is either locked into an oppressive, dependency relationship with a man or is institutionalized.

Injunctions and Attributions:
　　Do not grow up
　　Do not think
　　Do what your parents say

Her Mythical Heroines. As a child this woman loved reading about Cinderella and Little Orphan Annie.

Therapist's Collusion in the Script. He plays Rescuer until she relapses after a brief period of progress. Then he switches to Persecutor and calls her names like "unmotivated" or "schizophrenic."

Antithesis. She stops taking the easy way out by acting like a Victim or playing "Do Me Something." She decides that it is worth it for her to grow up, to develop her Adult and to take care of business for herself. She begins to get strokes for being OK when she shows her strength and does not accept strokes for being a Victim. She no longer enjoys the injured inferior self-image. She becomes keenly aware of how oppressive and condescending it is when others Rescue her. She commits herself to doing 50 percent of the work all the time, knowing that Rescue does her about as much good as heroin. She starts getting high off her own power. She does body work to release the scared energy that is blocked in her body and learns karate so that she can feel safe and strong on the street. She asks people to call her by her middle name, Joan, instead of her first name, Susy.

Nurse Life Thesis

The Nurse is a professional Rescuer, who works in an institution that exploits her and pushes her to her physical limits. Initially, her motivation to help others comes from caring, but caring soon becomes oppressive to her. She is taught to skillfully intuit other people's needs and meet them. Therefore, she expects others to read her mind the way she reads theirs and to take care of her the way she takes care of them. But it does not happen and she does not ask for what she wants so she does not get it. What she does get are "candy strokes" from appreciative patients and their families. Finally, after too much Rescuing, she becomes hurt and angry. She is not getting what she wants, so she adopts the role of Persecutor in the guise of so-called "professional detachment" which often takes the form of "I'm not giving anything that isn't asked for!"

She spends a lot of time complaining about how terrible the doctors and her supervisor are but she does not have the time or energy to confront them. Perhaps this is impossible because of potential recriminations. She may also feel she has to adapt for bread-and-butter survival since she is the economic mainstay of her family, either because she is Rescuing her alcoholic husband or because she is a single parent. When things don't work out in her love relationships she thinks she should have done more (Rescuing).

Ironically, when she's older, she ends up spending a lot of time as a patient in the hospital as a result of how she has been forced to exploit her body in the service of saving others. She may have injured her back moving a patient or taken too many "uppers" to keep going during the day or too much alcohol to cool out at night.

Injunctions and Attributions:

   Work hard

   Take care of others first

   Do not ask for what you want

HER MYTHICAL HEROINES. When she was young she had fantasies of being a long-suffering and ever-listening woman like Jane Adams or Florence Nightingale.

THERAPIST'S COLLUSION IN THE SCRIPT. He tells her to keep doing her job, taking care of others and, of course, supporting doctors in their patriarchal role. He willingly prescribed drugs for her so she can do it: uppers during the day, downers at night. He may tell her about *his* troubles since she's such an understanding listener.

ANTITHESIS. She learns to put her own needs first and to ask for what she wants. She makes a decision to stop Rescuing others and learns how to have Rescue-free relationships by working with people in groups. She may quit her hospital job and start working part-time or doing private work so that she can have some time for herself. She learns to respect her body and her own needs. Later, it will be useful for her to organize other Nurses to accomplish reforms so that their work is not so exploitative. With other Nurses she can eliminate her Rescue role and can talk with patients about patients' rights and responsibilities.

Fat Woman Life Thesis

The Fat Woman spends most of her life worrying about what her scale says and going on endless diets to obtain OK-ness through self-deprivation. She has been labeled *Fat* for as long as she can remember and told she has no self-control. Like most of us, as a child, she was encouraged to eat carbohydrates and was given sweets as rewards for "good" behavior. She also was told to eat everything on her plate, since "it is a sin to waste food." "Think about the starving people in China," (not about your own full stomach).

She has trouble letting her anger out and difficulty saying "no," so she literally swallows things she does not really want. One thing she gets out of being overweight is feeling solid and substantial. Because she has difficulty saying "no" or getting angry, her fat also serves to keep away men whom she wants to repel. Her fat is a *Wooden Leg*, a handy cop-out for not doing things she wants in life. She longs for strokes about her appearance yet never gets them. The bulk of her spontaneity is centered around what, when and how she eats. She feels victimized by her own body, her alleged lack of self-control, and other people's opinions about her weight. She is caught in a vicious circle of rebellious food binges after she has starved herself on cruel, self-punishing diets. She is convinced that she is not OK because of her weight. Her repeated failure in torturous dieting proves to her that she has no self-control, that she is a helpless Victim to her addiction.

Because she worries about her weight and is heart-broken from not getting the kind of loving she wants, she ends up having heart trouble, which is what the doctors threatened would happen to her anyway.

Injunctions and Attributions:

    You overeat

    Do not love yourself

    Swallow your anger

HER MYTHICAL HEROINES. She likes Rubens's paintings and follows the adventures of Elizabeth Taylor and *her* weight problems.

THERAPIST'S COLLUSION IN THE SCRIPT. He says that she has to learn to adapt better, that is, to cope with her "problem," and he prescribes diet pills and painfully boring diets. He is physically repelled by her body, and subtly communicates this to her.

ANTITHESIS. She gives up her self-hate: She decides that her body is OK just the way it is and learns to love and take care of it. She learns to enjoy food again without fear or guilt and eats what tastes and feels good to her body. She learns to relax and feel good without anesthetizing herself with food and stops torturing herself with diets.

In loving her body she tunes into it, listens to it and, therefore, stops abusing it. Centering on her own inner feelings puts her in touch with her body's messages about what it needs and does not need for nourishment and what she wants and does not want from others. Since she at times was overeating for comfort from a stroke deficit, she does not give more strokes than she gets. She is tuned into the oppression that is foisted on fat people and makes contact with other Fats to fight back (Aldebaran, 1973). She may never be thin in media terms, but she will enjoy her body and feel good from the inside out, rather than feeling constantly hungry and guilty.

WOMEN'S OPPRESSION

How Rescue Oppresses Women

We feel it is vital that women understand the sources of their oppression. In our problem-solving groups, we constantly build awareness of how sex roles and capitalist society oppress women. Our most crucial point is that in order for women to feel better, to get what they want, and to *take care of business*, they must act. They must stop colluding with things *outside* themselves that are oppressive. People have to work to get what they want, both in their groups and between meetings. A contract with the group helps a woman accomplish her goal. The group cannot do a woman's work for her; it can only encourage her to work on improving her life and protect her when she gets scared. The ultimate responsibility for a decision to change lies with her.

We can not Rescue people who are oppressed. In this case, Rescue is an attempt to save someone who views herself powerless and unable to help herself. To Rescue someone is oppressive and presumptuous, since it colludes with her apathy and sense of impotence. Instead of resulting in women's taking power and asking for what they want, Rescuing reinforces women's passivity. The image Rescue evokes is that of a world full of helpless consumers, powerless victims aching for visitation from powerful rescuers.

When two people play the Rescue game, they each take on one of three roles in the Drama Triangle, (Karpman, 1968) which they then proceed to exchange. The three roles are Victim, Rescuer, and Persecutor. They are capitalized to distinguish them from the real-life role of a person who is a victim of circumstances such as an old person caught in a fire and a person who assumes an active rescuer role such as a fireperson.

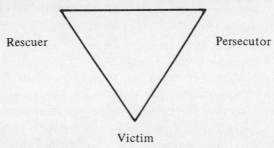

Rescuer   Persecutor

Victim

Figure 20-6. The Drama Triangle.

For example, Frances felt very sorry for her roommate, Sarah, whose lover was killed in an accident. She had a lot of sympathy for her and wanted to console her. But Sarah never seemed to feel better and always told Frances how hard it was not to have a man. After a while, Frances began to dread talking to Sarah, but she would listen, playing the Rescuer role, because she felt guilty that her own relationships with lovers were fine.

Frances could not tell her friend she did not want to hear her complaints anymore. Finally, Frances began to get angry and to think about moving out. She felt that Sarah was persecuting her by not working to make things better for herself. The group advised Frances to take responsibility for not talking straight from the start and to stop being angry (her Persecutor role). They suggested she act in her Adult and have her Nurturing Parent available for her friend. Frances decided to talk frankly to Sarah; she told her how she felt about her playing the Victim role and that she wanted Sarah to start taking care of herself. Frances reported to the group that although it was hard for Sarah to take this feedback, after a while Sarah felt a lot better and told Frances how much she appreciated her stopping the Rescue that might have destroyed their friendship and prolonged Sarah's period of mourning and self-pity.

I think we do women a great disservice when we Rescue them and provide them with a consumable, feel-better therapy. We can help women by showing them new options and teaching them problem-solving skills, but it is really up to them to make the leap of faith and get support to work through fears of changing and taking power over their own lives. Women must also learn to work cooperatively in a group so that everyone can get what she wants.

Lack of Strokes and Intimacy

Women who come to a group seeking help experience themselves as being oppressed in many ways. The most common oppression reported is feeling a lack of strokes and intimacy. Women are exploited in their strokes; they are taught to be givers not getters, particularly in their relationships with men and children. The dependency exchange between men and women parallels their dependent scripting. Men are supposed to take care of business, and, in exchange, women are supposed to be tuned in, loving, and nurturing. Women are supposed to give to children, not make demands on them or ask for things for themselves.

As for intimacy, women are taught to be intimate only with the right person at the right time in the right place, and that if these conditions are not met, intimacy does not happen. If a woman does not find the man of her dreams, which is often the case, she loses all chance for intimacy. But this does not have to be so. There are many opportunities for intimacy which could satisfy a woman's desires, although the opportunities do not fit the script program which has been laid on women. Romantic fantasies can keep women from dealing with the nitty-gritty reality of what is happening in a relationship. The awakening from such fantasies can be painful and abrupt.

Most women are caught between the banal script rules that inhibit intimacy and the lack of permission to use their Adults to think, to talk straight, and to plan a strategy for getting exactly what they want. The inhibiting rules about strokes are: Do not ask; do not give; do not accept; do not reject ones you do not want; and do not stroke yourself.

Sexuality is a topic that many groups avoid, but more and more it is being discussed. I consider a woman's sexuality an important expression of her identity and power as a woman. Gay and straight issues are crucial to confront. I like to have women expose any Pigs they have about gayness and to help gay women overcome any sense of isolation they might experience working with straight women.

We believe that to overcome oppression and gain liberation people need support and impetus from others; that is, people need contact. Women working in groups need strokes from other women.

REFERENCES

Aldebaran, Mayer: Fat liberation. *Issues in Radical Therapy*, I:3, 1973.
Athanasiou, Robert, Shaver, Phillip, and Tavis, Carol: Sex. *Psychology Today*, July 1970.
Berne, Eric: *What Do You Say After You Say "Hello."* New York, Grove Press, Inc., 1972.
Karpman, Steven: Script Drama Analysis. *Transactional Analysis Bulletin*, 7:26, 1968.
Marcuse, Herbert: Repressive tolerance. *A Critique of Pure Tolerance*. Boston, Beacon

Press, 1965.

Rosenthal, Robert; Archer, Dave; DiMatteo, M. Robin; Koivumaki, Judith Hall, and Rogers, Peter L.: Body talk and tone of voice: The language without words. *Psychology Today*, Sept.:64, 1974.

Steiner, Claude, and Wyckoff, Hogie: Alienation. In Steiner, Claude (Ed.): *Readings in Radical Psychiatry*. New York, Grove Press, 1974a.

Steiner, Claude: *Games Alcoholics Play*. New York, Grove Press, Inc., 1971a.

Steiner, Claude: *Scripts People Live*. New York, Grove Press, 1974b.

Steiner, Claude: Radical psychiatry principles. In Agel, Jerome (Ed.): *The Radical Therapist*. New York, Ballantine, 1971b.

Wyckoff, Hogie: Banal scripts of women. In Steiner, Claude (Ed.): *Scripts People Live*. New York, Grove Press, 1974.

Chapter 21

RADICAL PSYCHIATRY TECHNIQUES FOR SOLVING WOMEN'S PROBLEMS IN GROUPS

HOGIE WYCKOFF

CONTRACTS

OUR basic working structure is a group of eight women with one or two leaders which meets once a week for two hours. To facilitate the work, contracts are used. We consider contracts absolutely vital so that the responsibility for the work between the person, the group and the group facilitator is equally shared.

A contract is a work agreement between each person and the whole group in which a member states simply and clearly what she would like to work on. The desired goal must involve some easily observable behavioral change. This is essential because if there were no overt behavioral change, there would be no way for the group to be certain if the contract had been fulfilled. "I want to be able to love myself," would involve overt behavior change. The group could tell if this were happening by how the woman talks about heself, how she takes care of herself, and what the group members' intuition tells them she feels about herself.

The contract guards the facilitator against imposing her own values on any member and allows her to decide if she can work with each woman. If a facilitator and a member cannot agree on a contract, they cannot work together. An example of a contract I would not agree to is: "I want to learn to be satisfied with being a housewife."

The contract keeps the work emphasis in the here and now and provides motivation for a member to work on her problem. It protects her from being manipulated by the facilitator or other members and gives her a sense of her own potency in being able to act effectively as an agent to produce changes in her life.

Homework

A useful tool in promoting problem-solving efficiency is homework. After a woman makes a contract she can be assigned or can assign herself homework for the week. Good homework for the woman who wants to work on loving herself is to ask others for strokes and to give herself strokes. Homework is used to work on the long-range goal of the contract on a step-by-step basis. Women make changes in their lives by moving in stages they feel they can handle rather than in frightening leaps.

Before each group session women can sign up on a blackboard for the amount of time they want to work. Signing up helps the group work efficiently: It lets the members of the group know who wants to work so that the entire group rather than the facilitator can take cooperative responsibility for time.

EQUALIZING POWER

As group facilitator, I want to be real and intimate with the people in the group and not hold myself back or be *professionally cool*. I want to share myself as a person and answer any questions that people have about my life, assuming, of course, that I have the same right to confidentiality that everyone else in the group has.

I think it is an error for psychiatric workers to discount any strong feelings they might have when they walk into a work setting. To do so is a mind-rape and confuses group members. One woman reported a dream in which I came into group feeling very sad and that I turned my head away and started crying. I did not say why I felt bad and then I got up and left. I clearly saw the point and told her that I definitely did not want to be overdisciplined and nonhuman. I made an agreement with the group to share any strong feelings I might have when I come in.

I explain to group members that I want to struggle with them in the same manner I do with people with whom I am intimate. I tell them how I feel about them and what they are doing: I do not hold back or censor, and I am as emotionally available with them as I am with the people with whom I live. I let them know I want to do away with unnecessary barriers, and that I care about them deeply. I also share the changes I am going through and tell briefly about any important new things I am working out. My writing has helped me to share myself. The articles on "Bisexuality" and "Me-My body," give a good sense of who I am (Wyckoff, 1973, 1974).

I have found that I can get the maximum productiveness out of group interactions by talking openly. For example, I tell potentially suicidal women that I do not want them to kill themselves and ask them to give up that option. If they are not willing to give it up, I do not want to work with them; I do not want any responsibility for their deaths.

I also have talked openly to women who have scared me because their Pig hooks me. I ask those women to realize their power and use it well. I also ask them to work to expose and separate themselves from their Pig, and not to protect or to keep secrets with it.

It is necessary that each woman take responsibility for what happens in the group. The goal is not to build dependency relationships or admiration for the facilitator's skills, but rather to work on a constant transfer of power and expertise in the process of self-transformation. Therefore, I encourage women to challenge me in group. I welcome constructive criticism and feedback and work hard to respond to it. I do not work on my own problems in the group, but I do talk about relevant experiences so the women know I am fighting the same oppression that they are up against.

I work in my Adult to give information, my Nurturing Parent to give support and strokes, my Little Professor tuned into intuitions, and my Child ready for a good laugh or joyous smile at someone's latest victory.

GROUP COLLUSIONS

One of the pitfalls of women's groups is that group collusions may develop. Unconscious agreements can be made among group members not to talk straight about certain touchy subjects or not to press each other about certain kinds of problems. This keeping of secrets can become part of the group culture or *Karma*. One example is a group that encourages its members to look for a Rescue. In such groups, women are encouraged to be Victims, to be powerless, and to feel sorry for themselves and each other; they are discouraged from using their Adults, talking straight, being potent, taking care of business, and getting what they want. In a group like this the facilitator must demystify what her Little Professor senses is going on. She should encourage people to talk about solutions, rather than about how bad things are. She also should give people strokes for working and encourage others to give a woman strokes for being powerful and taking care of business.

A useful tool for demystifying what is going on in a group is the process of letting go of held resentments, or "stamps." The process, as worked out in Radical Psychiatry, is executed in the following manner; It may be decided, usually at the beginning of a group, to "do stamps." People will say to each other, "I have a stamp for you, will you accept it?" The other person says "yes" or "no" depending on whether she feels strong enough to accept critical feedback. It is understood that a stamp may be quite paranoid, that it can be *off the wall*, and that it is usually generated by a misunderstanding; therefore, no discussion or disagreement is allowed to follow stamp-giving. This is how it is done: "I was angry at you when you didn't talk to me at the party Saturday." The person receiving this may say "thank you," or "I hear you," or nothing, and the exchange is ended at that. Time is given for the resentment to sink in, and if further discussion is needed it can be taken care of at a later time. No one is given more than one stamp in a row.

In the same manner, paranoid fantasies can be expressed. An example is, "I think you've got a secret you're not telling the group." The person receiving the paranoid fantasy will then answer; often there is at least a grain of truth in the paranoia.

People in the group are always urged to talk straight about the present and encouraged not to hold resentments or paranoid fantasies. The above techniques are an efficient way to work things out between people in groups when they have not been straight.

After all the stamps and paranoias have been given out, people then give strokes; often when people are holding stamps they are also holding strokes they have not felt free to give. Stamps, paranoias, and strokes are powerful antidotes against collusions in groups.

I also think it is vital that the facilitator make herself as emotionally available as she can to the group. If she is in touch with herself and sensitive to group dynamics, she can prevent heavy collusions by saying how she feels about the group as it is in proess. She thus sets an example for others to take care of themselves and the group in that manner.

EXERCISES

Emotional Release

I have found emotional-release work in conjunction with problem-solving work to be very useful. For example, one woman who had done a lot of analyzing in her head about her life and had gotten in touch with her Adult power, felt stuck emotionally. She could not seem to get her Child working. One night in the group she lay on the mattress and did some deep bioenergetic breathing while the rest of the group sat around her and supported her work. I helped her to get into her feelings by staying close with her emotionally and by using my intuition to make suggestions to use or not use as she thought best.

The breathing charged her with energy and helped her to get in touch with strong feelings she had been clamping down on. She released some sadness and anger and then began to feel really wonderful, loving herself, and feeling reborn. It was a very high experience for her. One woman in the group said she was amazed by this kind of work; another said it was like a "religious experience."

Emotional catharsis fits well with the ongoing problem-solving work, although working on contracts and keeping things open between group members composes the bulk of the work we do. Nurturing and giving each other strokes oils the gears and keeps us running smoothly together.

Permission Exercises

Permission exercises are ancillary to Adult work in a problem solving group. They are designed to help people do things they want to do but can not because they are filled with prohibitive and inhibitive Parental messages. To do Permission exercises each member of the group has a contract arrived at ahead of time. The contract should state simply and clearly what her Child wants. It must be capable of being fulfilled here and now. People who change their minds are free to terminate the contract.

In conducting permission exercises the group facilitator must provide three P's: *Permission, Protection,* and *Potency* (Steiner, 1968). Permission is approval given to the Child to do what she wants. Protection is safety provided by the leader's Nurturing Parent. (It is absolutely necessary that the person facilitating the exercise be nurturing to the people working.) Potency is the strength to back up what the group member says, carry it through, and deal head on with someone else's Pig 'Parent.

For an example, a woman's Natural, Free Child may want to be able to ask for the strokes she wants (a hug, a kiss) but her Critical or Pig Parent says "No! Don't you dare!"* I would say, "OK, I want you to ask someone here for a stroke." I would insist that the person do this, assuming we had a contract between us specifying that she wanted to work on this. If she got frightened, I would reassure her; if someone else tried to pig her, I would protect her; and if her own Pig intruded, I would help her get rid of it. I would not back down, yet I would be very sensitive to her feelings and be supportive and responsive to her individual needs while teaching her a new way to be.

Permission in Radical Psychiatry is not just giving people contact or pacifying their alienation as many "touchy-feely," "good-vibe" therapy techniques do. Radical Psychiatry involves awareness as well. Therefore, we talk about what is happening in order to provide the necessary consciousness-raising for true liberation. We do not want to co-opt a woman's potential to discover how she is oppressed, because with awareness of her oppression, she can become angry enough to do something about it. Neither do we have angry women beat on pillows, pacifying them temporarily, and mystifying them with an unexplained good-feeling experience. Instead, we help them learn new ways of being and help them learn how to get what they want. Thus, it is important to ask women how they are feeling when doing exercises. To keep communication open, we encourage women to talk about their experiences, to get

---

*Such parental values force on us an artificial scarcity of strokes. In effect, a scarcity stroke economy is created, putting a premium on strokes that we believe are in short supply.

and to give feedback.

It is important to note that in doing permission exercises, no one is giving anyone anything they did not originally have. People are born OK but oppressed and denied their full human potential.

Nurturing Parent for Oneself

The following are directions for an exercise to help women develop the Nurturing Parent (N.P.) in themselves. Using the *other hand* (left if right-handed or vice versa), have each woman write with large crayons on one side of a big sheet of paper, words or phrases that describe what her Child would like its N.P. to be like. The words should be child-type words, like "loves me, gentle, holds me". On the other side of the paper have each woman write what her Child would like her N.P. to say to her, for example, "I love you, you're beautiful." Then have all the women describe what they would like their N.P. to be like. (Have each woman keep these lists to use for herself when she needs them.) When all the descriptions are finished have them say the things they would like to hear from their N.P. Everyone should say the words the way she wants to hear them in a warm and loving way. In a group, everyone will feel warm and good when the things are said. Some may even get homesick and cry.

This is a way to learn what other women's N.P.'s are like. We can also learn not to be embarrassed to use nurturing, loving words.

Now have each member give her words to someone she likes. Have the other person say the words while she holds the woman on her lap or cuddles her. This gives women practice in being N.P. to others who need it and in learning to accept the N.P. that they want from others. It also gets women in touch with their basic goodness and with caring for one another. People should touch each other and not be afraid to be comforting. They should say the words slowly, letting them soak in. People can ask to hear their nurturing words again.

For a group experience, have people close their eyes and mill around the room. When people come in contact with each other, have them be nurturing and loving to the Child in the other woman, touching them in a nurturing way and saying N.P. words. Appropriate music is very helpful.

After the members have been N.P. to each other, have them be N.P. to themselves. For example, have them give themselves a hug and say good things to themselves. This teaches women to be self-nurturing. It also helps break down the artificial *stroke economy* between people and within each woman. It gets people in touch with the basic OK-ness of the group.

Off the Pig Exercise

This is a powerful exercise requiring skill and great care. Expertise in working with people is necessary to do it well. You must have a contract with the person to *Off the Pig*. It should come after the N.P. exercise. In some ways it is similar to it. Only three to five people should do it at the same group meeting with the people preparing their words and masks together and then *Offing their Pigs* one after the other. The rest of the group should remain in their N.P. for support. It is a struggle to *off* the Pig Parent, and when a facilitator agrees to help someone do it, she has to be potent, aware of what is going on, and persistent about carrying through.

Using her *other hand* have each woman who wants to *off* her Pig write on one side of large sheets of paper Child words or phrases to describe what her Pig is like — "mean, stupid, sneaky," and on the other side what the Pig tells her — "You're crazy," "No one likes you." Next, have her draw a face mask depicting her Pig on a smaller sheet of paper. Then she should read the descriptions and the words of the Pig. She should act out her Pig nonverbally, using both body movements and sounds, with her mask held to her face to show what her Pig is like. Also, have her use the words her Pig uses. Then have her give the facilitator the list of her pig's words to refer to while she works on destroying her Pig in the form of the mask.

This exercise teaches a woman how to get her Pig off her back by demystifying it. She learns what her Pig is like; what words it uses, how it acts and the emotion it uses to oppress. She learns how to answer the Pig, how to stop it, and how to neutralize it in the future. A woman can learn a strategy for fighting the Pig by knowing it as the enemy. This shows her she can do it and that people will back her up. She should get encouragement from others while she is doing this exercise.

To do this exercise effectively each person must combine three important elements into one forceful act: the right words, emotions, and action. All three must be present at the same time or the Pig will not leave. Leaving one out would be like trying to get rid of a tricky person by just being angry or like trying to get rid of a bully with words alone. While leading this exercise, the facilitator should trust her guts to know if the Pig has really been *offed*. Let the energy build up. It will feel obvious and definite when the Pig has been defeated and the exercise will end with a flourish of finality. People feel good after they successfully Off the Pig, not sad or afraid or doubtful.

Throughout, others in the room should give all the nurturing and support needed. The leader should allow no Pig Parent behavior by others during this exercise. Do not let anyone Pig the person working by trying to goad them into action or anger. After people off their Pigs they should be given all the strokes they want from whomever they want. A celebration usually follows this exercise because it is scary and feels like a real victory when it is done well.

Offing the Pig can be an alienating experience if people do not really want to do it. If someone realizes she does not, let her out of her contract because it definitely will not work unless all three parts of the offing are there. The right emotion and action without the right words will not do it. People have to be able to answer their Pigs to shut them up. Words and emotion without action or any other combination of two will be ineffectual.

Bragging

Bragging is a good way for someone to work on loving herself and destroying her Pig. She should stand where everyone can see her and say all the good things she can think of about herself. Not only things she does but also things she is. She should say what things she likes about her body and about how she looks. Since it is not a competitive situation, it is not proper to use comparisons like *better*. This exercise teaches people that although the word "bragging" has a bad connotation in our society, it is not a bad thing to do as long as it is not competitive. Bragging trashes the scarcity stroke economy and allows women to apprciate themselves publicly and see that others like them when they like themselves. People should cheer each other on and generally be supportive to and appreciative of someone who brags. Be sure to let people know if they use inverted pig messages on themselves like "I look pretty good for someone this fat."

HEALTHY GROUP ACTION

In healthy groups women cooperate in making sure they share the group's time, work hard on each other's contracts, talk straight, keep no secrets, and do not Rescue each other. A healthy group has high and prompt attendance. Members who are interested in working sign up immediately. Anyone in crisis says so and puts a circle around her name.

An example of a healthy group interaction might be the following situation: Jane wants to work. Her contract has been established as "I want to be able to know what I want, and be myself with others." All her life she has adapted to the values and desires of other people. She has acted on the basis of what others want her to be, rather than what she wants herself to be. Today she reports that she's having trouble at work.

She feels that she has lost touch with her coworkers. Her job is oppressive and working conditions are dehumanizing. The group is sympathetic and advises her not to take action alone, but to try to organize her co-workers so that they can all make demands and get satisfaction as a group. Jane works hard giving and getting feedback from the group. She talks about how she can take power in this situation, and the group gives her strokes for her work. She asks for homework, and the group recommends that she work at talking openly to people at work and getting their support to improve conditions. The woman is well-liked. Members of the group care deeply about her, and she gets the strokes that she wants. Overall, Jane has worked well in the group and done much to transform herself and her life. She has struggled against things that were inhibiting her and has done much to make her political awareness a part of her everyday actions.

A recurrent discussion in women's groups is the issue of women Rescuing their children. In the stereotypic program of the nuclear family it is Mom's job to take care of everyone. The assumption is that she is supposed to do things for her kids for gratis. In return they should obey her, love her, and so on. This sets up a Rescue triangle. Mom is the Rescuer doing good things for the kids; they are helpless Victims who supposedly can not take care of themselves. Thus, her children are kept dependent and basically experience themselves as not having power. But as they fail to do what they are told to do, Mom eventually feels unloved and victimized by them and she comes to view them as persecuting her.

Once she has accumulated enough held resentments she can cash them in by pigging the children. She then becomes the Persecutor to their Victim. They feel guilty and Rescue her and on and on it goes. The only way out for her is to use her Adult and completely reappraise her living situation. She has to give up the fairytale of the happy nuclear family and begin living collectively, that is, act as if she were living in a commune where all members are expected to work cooperatively and take responsibility for making the collective function. Living collectively gives the children an opportunity to use their power and to ask for what they want; it enables parents to give only what they want to give and to get things in return from their children.

Here is an example of how this problem was worked on in a healthy group by one woman. This woman is divorced and has two adolescent children. Her contract was "I want to know what I want and how to get it." She complained to the group that after working at her boring and poorly paid job all week, she had to spend Saturday cleaning her house with little or no help from her kids or the man who lives with her. Because she felt ripped-off, she pigged everybody on Saturday, and by Sunday everyone was feeling unhappy and her weekend was shot. The group gave her feedback about how she was playing Rescue. The members gave her homework to take care of herself and ask her family clearly and strongly for the help she wanted. They pointed out to her that her family may not have understood what she wanted from them or the benefits if they cooperated. The group's feedback sunk in, and soon the woman announced to the group that things were much better. During the week she had come home from work and found a sink full of dishes. She refused to cook dinner until the dishes were done; she sat in the living room just taking care of herself. This sit-down strike was a good object lesson for her lover and children. They let her know the next day that they wanted to have a house meeting and figure out how to work together.

The women in the group were really pleased that she had taken care of herself and gave her lots of strokes. The following week she told us that by working together the house had gotten clean on Saturday morning and the afternoon had been open to play and enjoy each other for a change.

Another example of good group interaction comes from the story of a woman who had been in the group for a little over a year. When she came into the group she was frightened and felt unable to take care of herself and get what she wanted in life. She was constantly playing the role of a Victim looking for a Rescuer. She would engage in playing "Ain't it Awful?" which is a futile game of complaining about oppression but never working to do anything about it; it co-opted her energy and kept her passive. She would describe how much of a Victim she was, and when group members would make suggestions about what she could do to help herself she would make excuses and play "Yes, but ..." A year ago she had been "diagnosed" at a clinic as in a state of "agitated depression." Her general stance in the group was that she wanted other people to do something for her and take care of her rather than encourage her to do something for herself and take responsibility over her own life. We will describe briefly the dialectical process of her contracts with the group, that is, the different stages by which her work in group proceeded.

She started with a contract to get her Pig off her back. This contract was vague and served only to help the members get a sense of what her Pig program was. This contract evolved into a contract to talk straight. For the first time in her life, she told people how she really felt about them and began getting in touch with her true feelings. The contract then changed into being able to say what she thought or felt at any given time. This helped her to be spontaneously in touch with herself. Her final contract was to be powerful for herself.

In the first six months of her work with the group this woman would repeatedly make phone calls to me which she attempted to stretch into twenty or thirty minutes. She would be looking for a Rescue and showed little interest in taking care of herself. With the awareness that she has gotten in the group and the support from group members, she has slowly learned to take care of herself and assume responsibility for her own life. Now, when she calls, she asks for something specific like information, reassurance, or strokes which can usually be given in five minutes. She is interested in getting support and information from others as to what she can do to take care of herself. She comes to the group and works hard and assigns herself homework rather than having it assigned to her. She no longer expects people to Rescue her and she resents people who try to. She understands that the game of Rescue is vicious and debilitating, and that it robs people of their power.

I believe that she will soon be leaving the group. She will then have completed her contract and have a sense of closure. She will feel that she has gotten what she wanted and will take away the ability to solve her own problems and take power over her own life. It will also be evident to her that she cannot get everything she wants in life as an individual, but that solutions will have to come through working with others. She knows if she gets confused or scared she can ask some friend who has been in the group who knows how to do problem-solving to get together with her and help her. If she gets into hassles with another person she can ask someone to mediate the difficulties.

CONCLUSION

The group situation is the most auspicious for women since the group process demonstrates that when we work together we have strength. One of the most important aspects of group work is to teach women to work cooperatively together. Our Pig programming instructs women to compete with each other. It is essential for women to interact with other women and develop a feeling for sisterhood. Loving and respecting other women helps a woman love and respect herself.

Complete human liberation is not possible in our present capitalist society. Women and men cannot be free from sex-role oppression in a society where such oppression is an integral part of how the corporate economy maintains itself. For individuals to be free, society must be free. Women cannot overcome social and cultural oppression as individuals. Only by working cooperatively together can we become powerful enough to make substantive changes in our world.

REFERENCES

Steiner, Claude: Transactional analysis as a treatment philosophy. *Transactional Analysis Bulletin, 7:27*, 1968.

Wyckoff, Hogie: In behalf of bisexuality. *Issues in Radical Therapy,* I:3, 1973.
Wyckoff, Hogie: Me-my body. *Issues in Radical Therapy,* 2:1, 1974.

Section IX

SOCIAL ACTIVISM AS THERAPY

INTRODUCTION

AS long as social institutions remain oppressive to women, feminists see no individual solutions to women's problems. Consequently, feminist therapists recommend political action to their clients and sometimes join them in that activity.

The interconnection between personal change and social activism is reflected in two papers in this section. In the first paper, "A Dialectical Base for an Activist Approach to Counseling", Harold J. Adams and Leona Durham describe dialectical counseling. This is counseling which leads a client through personal change into social action. The dialectical counselor uses the client's personal contradictions or conflicts to help the client become aware of related root contradictions in society. Often, awareness of root contradictions motivates the client to join a political action group or to fight (with the counselor) against the basic contradictions in society. Adams and Durham identify capitalism as being at the root of society's contradictions, a position similar to the ideology of socialist feminists (Deckard, 1975).

"Beyond Therapy: A Personal and Institutional Perspective" is written from a different point of view. Norma Gluckstern approaches social action as a counselor who has rejected one-to-one counseling in favor of social activism as her way of fighting the oppression of women. From her personal experience, she observed that social activism led to personal changes in women. When women overcame their acculturated passivity and self-doubts and collectively engaged in social action, they developed new competencies, new roles and new options in their lives. The institutional changes they effected provided growth opportunities for large numbers of women. In the process of social action, women developed a new model for society: one which was more supportive, caring and cooperative. Gluckstern seems optimistic that women can bring about sufficient reform within the existing institutional structures to achieve a society that will be more responsive to human needs.

In "A Dialectical Base for an Activist Approach to Counseling" Adams and Durham define counseling in a way that "will allow it to relate to large social movements and to change". These authors apply the dialectical model (which has been used by Marx, Engels and others to explain social change) to an understanding of individual change in counseling and to the relationship between individuals and social change. These authors take the position that political education in counseling and therapy and social activism by counselors and therapists are legitimate, even essential, aspects of counseling and psychotherapy.

Dialectical counseling begins with the recognition of the existence of opposing forces or contradictions within all people (as within all social systems). A manifest observable characteristic is called the *thesis;* suppressed opposite characteristic is the *antithesis.* The interactions of these opposite create a *synthesis,* a new whole greater than the sum of the original parts. A dialectical approach in counseling aims at total change in clients and in society. Thus, behavior cannot be linearly predicted from past performance. Counselors generally work with the personal aspects of their clients lives, but they must be aware of the close relationship existing between personal and societal conditioning. Counselors should prepare clients to ultimately deal with societal contradictions.

Dialectical models are materialistic. Adams and Durham are socialists, as are many feminists. They view capitalism as being full of fundamental contradications. They argue that an emphasis on abstract values supports the *status quo* and is characteristic of *mechanistic counseling.*

Most counseling and therapy today fit the mechanistic model. Mechanistic counselors look at people and behavior in a one-sided way. Sex-role stereotyping is an example of looking at people unidimensionally. By stereotyping themselves, men and women deny half of themselves. Only women who adopt certain masculine traits are permitted career success and that is at the cost of relinquishing their identity as women. Men, who hold institutional power, define women as "the other," an inferior being whose purpose is to serve them.

Mechanistic counselors view the world as constant and unchanging. They limit their interventions to personal contradictions and deal with these in a one-sided way rather than taking all elements into consideration. They encourage clients to make their behaviors consistent with past, previously successful values and behaviors. Large changes are discouraged so that only minor and incremental change can occur in mechanistic counseling.

Adams and Durham distinguish two phases of dialectical counseling. In Phase I the counselors deal with secondary contradictions by developing new alliances, attitudes, behaviors, and skills. Mechanistic counseling stops at Phase I. The authors feel that counseling which ends at Phase I is worse than no counseling at all since it temporarily relieves the client's pain without correcting larger problems. In Phase II the counselor teaches the client to apply what s/he has learned to combat the intolerable contradictions in her/his life.

Dialectical counselors view the client's suffering as the result of contradictions which have arisen from being forced to view a multidimensional world in a unidimensional way. The dialectical counselor questions nondecisions, i.e. behaviors dictated by conventional wisdom or institutionalized ways of living one's life. Periods of intense discomfort experienced in times of personal upheavals, e.g. death, divorce, need to be worked through to a creative resolution rather than smoothed over by institutionalized processes.

The dialectical counselor is concerned with involving the client in social change. Dialectical counselors must be willing to make their political biases known to their clients and, if necessary, to join with their clients in political action to finish the job which therapy begins.

In "Beyond Therapy: Personal and Institutional Change," Gluckstern describes the personal changes she and other women experienced when they became involved in a social action group of the women's movement. The women's movement, unlike other movements of the 1960's which primarily emphasized institutional change, legitimated the need for attention to both personal growth and institutional change. Out of mutual support, experiential understanding, and a developing political consciousness, the women's movement has grown and been effective.

The development of a center for women, Everywoman's Center (EWC), at the University of Massachusetts is an example of the process and problems involved in effecting joint institutional and personal change. A "community-action nucleus" formed the basis of action which evolved into an organization with a broad and varied constituency. New political consciousness, commitment, strategy for action, and cooperation emerged.

Difficulties in the establishment of EWC reflected both the institutional and personal problems the women were attempting to confront. The values and goals of the male-dominated university were replaced with new values and goals. A major problem for the group involved moving from their "feminine" inactivity and passivity to an assertive stance. The experience of risking their professional status and privileges developed the participants' confidence in themselves and in their task. As a result, the women experienced changes in opportunities and responsibilities and the university experienced changes in administrative policies and greater awareness of women's problems.

Gluckstern insists that C-R groups stagnate if they do not move beyond the group's initial emphasis on personal analysis and discussion to working on common political goals and issues. In action groups, new roles, ideas, sources of support, and responsibilities are actively tried out. Rather than merely talking, women begin to take action on important issues. In the process, women develop a new model for society which is more supportive, caring, and cooperative.

Through their mutual support, women learn to differentiate between individual constraints and external structural constraints. In developing a political consciousness, blame and self-guilt are replaced by personal responsibility and collective action. Women also see new alternatives open to them, in using new skills and roles and in seeing other women in action. As a consequence, women begin to see needed institutional reform and develop effective change strategy. Gluckstern notes the interaction between personal change and institutional change. The process of being involved in institutional change produces change and that change in turn opens new opportunities of growth for large numbers of women.

Gluckstern observes that the women's movement has implications for all women which cross class, race, and ethnic divisions. Middle-class women can provide the means and impetus to social action while working class and Third World women can provide the political consciousness and the orientation to action. Each can benefit by affirming the importance of the other group's experiences, advantages, skills, and liabilities. Each can learn from the other while affecting major institutional changes collectively.

Gluckstern recommends that counselors learn to look for structural causes of personal problems: that they present themselves as women (people) first, counselors second; and that they face their own tendencies to be passive and ambivalent toward taking social action.

REFERENCES

Deckard, Barbara Sinclair: *The Women's Movement: Political, Socioeconomic, and Psychological Issues.* New York, Harper and Row, 1975.

—— *Chapter 22* ——

A DIALECTICAL BASE FOR AN ACTIVIST APPROACH TO COUNSELING*

HAROLD J. ADAMS AND LEONA DURHAM

COUNSELING needs to be defined in a way that will allow it to relate to large social movements and to change. On a societal level there is a demonstrated need for significant change, a need made apparent by the increasing gap between the *haves* and the *have-nots* and by the friction created by the demands of women, ethnic, and Third World groups for increased participation in world affairs. Just as many radical social movements are grounded in dialectical thinking, so should radical approaches to counseling include more investigation into dialectical models of personal change.

There is in humanistic literature a basis for viewing people from a dialectical perspective. However, practicing counselors, regardless of theoretical orientation, do not generally assume strong dialectical postures. Rather, counseling practice typically grows from a mechanistic perspective. A counseling approach based on a dialectical view of the world is fundamentally different from one based on a mechanistic view. One cannot logically view the world from a dialectical perspective when considering social change, then when counseling an individual turn about and act as if the world is mechanical.

The theories of social change which propose that radical change is necessary and beneficial to society must be considered on the level of personal change, for it is at least in part through personal change that these larger societal changes are effected. Because of this need for societal change through personal change, the dialectical approach to counseling, which accommodates change on a large scale, is an obvious and preferable direction for counseling to take.

This paper will describe the dialectical and mechanistic models of change, then contrast these two approaches.

DIALECTICAL CHANGE

The essence of dialectical change is found in Engels' words:

---

*This chapter is an expansion of a paper entitled, "Toward a Dialectical Approach to Counseling", by H. J. Adams which originally appeared in the *Journal of Humanistic Psychology*.

> ... For dialectical philosophy nothing is final, absolute, sacred. It reveals the transitory character of everything and in everything; nothing can endure before it except the uninterrupted process of becoming and of passing away, of endless ascendency from the lower to the higher (Quoted in Lenin, 1970, p. 36).

Nothing is final, absolute or sacred because all things contain conflicting elements. The conflicting elements are called *contradictions*. Any person, any situation, is full of contradictions which sets up a dialectical process. It is through dialectical interaction that all fundamental changes ultimately occur.

The existence of opposites within individuals is discussed by several authors. Slater, for instance, explains that people possess a full range of emotions:

> The emotional repertory of human beings is limited and standard. We are built to feel warm, happy, and contented when caressed. To feel angry when frustrated, frightened when attacked, offended when insulted, jealous when excluded, and so on. But every culture holds some of the human reactions to be unacceptable and attempts to warp its participants into some peculiar specialization. Since human beings are malleable within limits, the warping is for the most part successfully achieved, so that some learn not to laugh, some not to cry, and some not to hate in situations where these reactions might appropriately be expressed (Slater, 1970, p. 3).

People are not naturally emotionally one-sided. The point Slater makes is that while all people have the potential for all the emotions, they express only a small range. They develop some emotions and retard others because of training and socialization.

Dialectical change assumes that the process of integrating opposites results in a product that is greater than the original parts. Hampden-Turner (1971) in *Radical Man* refers to the *synergy* achieved through the dialectical approach to a problem of situation.

> (Synergy) consists of an affective and intellectual synthesis which is *more* than the sum of its parts, so that each party to the interaction can win a "return on investment" that is greater than the competence risked (Hampden-Turner, 1971, p. 55).

Dialectical interaction is difficult for the participants because results of the interaction are not known beforehand. The process requires a risk or a suspension of oneself. Since the result will be more than the sum of the parts, the result cannot be known ahead of time. It is this dimension of unpredictability which makes the dialectical process both frightening and exciting. It also accounts for creativity and totality in change rather than mere reformism. Change is not a balancing or compromise situation between two contradictions, although on occasion balances and compromises are made in preparation for a dialectical resolution. Dialectical change is a viable explanation for revolutary developments in the world and in the individuals of the world.

A dialectical change model assumes the possibility of great personal changes. This is because of the existence of opposing forces (contradictions) within all people. The dialectical perspective assumes that all persons possess characteristics which are opposite the characteristics which are usually evident in their behavior. For example, a highly socialized man, one who is aggressive, manipulative and in control of his emotions also has the capacity to be passive, manipulated and controlled by his emotions. Likewise, a highly socialized woman, one who is passive, manipulated and controlled by her emotions can be aggressive, manipulating and in control of her emotions. The side of a person evident at a given time is the result largely of situational variables or of the socialization process.

The personal characteristic which is dominant in a person at a given time is called the *thesis*. The opposite hidden characteristic is the *antithesis*. Under the proper conditions, the interaction of these opposites results in a *synthesis*. In the case of the above examples, the man and the woman originally had only the options of behaving in socially acceptable masculine ways (tough, aggressive, emotionally controlled) or in socially acceptable feminine ways (soft, manipulated, victimized by emotion). In dialectical interaction the thesis and the antithesis evolve into a synthesis. The man and the woman are capable of evolving new behaviors (a synthesis) which are neither traditionally masculine nor feminine. Rather, the new behaviors can be loving, thoughtful and purposeful, behaviors perhaps not previously exhibited.

Feminine-Masculine

One of the clearest examples of how human beings come to deny half of themselves and thus inhibit the operation of the dialectical process is through sex-role stereotyping. The system under which we live is served by having groups of people in categories which are narrowly defined. Therefore, personal identity is learned through a process in which men and women are socialized into rigidly masculine and rigidly feminine behavior modes. But the absolutes produced by this process belong more to myth than reality. It is nonsense to say that men are: assertive, unemotional, logical, ambitious, seeking, adventurous, risk-taking, strong, independent, intelligent, sexually aggressive, stable, dependable, courageous, athletic. It is equally nonsensical to say that women are: passive, emotional, illogical, lacking in ambition, risk-avoiding, weak, dependent, less intelligent, romantic, sexually nonaggressive, unstable, undependable, noncourageous, nonathletic. Obviously every individual, male or female, can, under certain circumstances, exhibit any of these characteristics.

However, masculine-feminine socialization creates a more fundamental problem than myths about what is masculine or feminine behavior. The more difficult problem is that one group (males) are socialized into seeing another group (females) as *the other*, as somehow different from themselves as they relate to the world (de Beauvoir, 1952). This could be said in reverse, of course, that one group (females) are socialized into seeing another group (males) as *the other*. But the singularly important fact is that, because men hold institutional power over women, it is they who are permitted to define what is *other*.

Many have suggested that men suffer as much from this rigid stereotyping as women. Unquestionably they pay a high price in terms of personal mental health; they continue to pay the price because they are afforded the illusion of power which makes their lack of it more palatable. However, because they hold institutional power, men have not been willing or are unable to voluntarily give up the illusion of personal power. But ultimately an unearned sense of superiority is as costly to an individual as an unearned sense of inferiority. Because few men measure up (or down, depending on your perspective) to the standards of behavior inflicted upon their role as human beings, they cannot fail to feel inadequate and this sense of inadequacy is no less important for the fact of their rarely confessing it.

Women, on the other hand, taught to feel inferior and encouraged to acknowledge that inferiority, have fewer compunctions about seeking help. And because few women measure down to the standards inflicted upon them by their role, women often have something to hang on to when put to an emotional test because of a hidden awareness of their own adequacy.

At its most fundamental level, the basic problem for men and women in terms of their socialization is that men are encouraged to equate their unearned superiority with a sense of being, if not *more-than-human*, at least human; women are encouraged to see themselves, through men, as inferior, even *less-than-human*. The experience of both groups denies the validity of this view of themselves. Therapists devoted to the mental health of all persons, not just her/his clients, would emphasize these contradictions, would help their clients deal with them. Because the definition of *other* is left to those holding institutional power, the questions raised by these contradictions are essentially political in nature. That means if the contradictions are to be resolved, political activity to that end must be encouraged.

The dialectical concept makes for a fluid world full of people who are capable of making major changes in themselves. A dialectical world is not full of constants. People's behavior, therefore, cannot be predicted from their past performance. Rather, predictions must be made upon analysis of the contradictory forces in their lives and upon the potential of the dialectical process to work for the resolution of those contradictions into new behaviors. Prediction based upon past behavior considers only that part of the dialectic which has been evident in behavior. The suppressed half of the dialectic must be examined to provide a whole picture.

Primary vs. Secondary Contradictions

All contradictions in the world, while related, are not considered to be of equal importance. Some contradictions are considered to be *primary* while others are *secondary*. The primary contradictions are the ones which, if eliminated, would resolve a host of secondary contractions with them. For instance, eliminating racism would automatically eliminate job discrimination against racial minorities. Eliminating job discrimination would not, however, necessarily eliminate racism. Racism is, therefore, a primary contradiction while job discrimination is a secondary contradiction. Receiving even less priority might be the contradictions within a person which emanate from the race contradiction. Where to buy a house or who to pick up hitch-hiking might be examples of personal questions which arise from the race contradiction. Clearly, resolving these personal contradictions does not resolve the larger racism questions, but resolving the racism contradiction would resolve the personal dilemmas.*

This is not to argue that secondary contradictions are not important. On the contrary, because of their less threatening nature we understand secondary contradictions more readily than primary contradictions and because of this we are often faced with no alternative other than to work on secondary contradictions. Counseling is, on the whole, concerned with the resolution of secondary contradictions. This can be justified because the dialectical approach to change implies that every contradiction is related to every other contradiction.

By helping a female student to take a dialectical approach to the feel-

---

*Marxism views the primary contradiction of the world as between the owners of the means of production (the bourgeoisie) and the workers (the proletariat). In this view, other large contradictions, such as race and sex are important, but not primary. The use here of the terms *primary* and *secondary* are for convenience and are not a rejection of the marxian notion of the primacy of the class contradiction.

ings of inadequacy brought on by a sexist attitude of a teacher (a secondary contradiction), a counselor can help sharpen the contradictions of sexism in general (the primary contradiction). By developing an understanding of the dialectical conditions leading to the situation, the student may be able to make the necessary synthesis to temporarily resolve the dilemma while at the same time heighten her awareness of the primary contradictions. This understanding permits the student to make a more permanent dialectical analysis and to take action on the primary contradictions of sexism at a later time.

Materialism

All dialectical models are not materialistic models. However, an approach to counseling which is consistent with Marxist-Leninist views of social change will by definition be materialistic. This means that the important factors in the change process are related to economics. A broad definition of economics includes factors such as income, housing, food availability, matters of physical comfort, and the power position one has relative to others. Nonmaterial factors are such things as dreams, far-off goals, religious considerations and abstract value systems. Many humanistic counselors, of course, feel that metaphysical considerations are crucial in individual decision-making. It is at this point, perhaps, where humanists and social revolutionaries part company. A materialist argues that emphasis on metaphysical considerations simply maintains the *status quo* by diverting attention away from conditions rooted in the political and economic conditions of the society.

A materialistic approach says that change is the inevitable result of the contradictions in the objective conditions in a person's life. Lenin, however, made it quite clear that the direction of the historical process could be influenced by actions based upon analysis of the contradictions within the society. This is not to argue, as Lenin did, for a revolutionary party to influence such changes. Rather, it is to point out that one can be a materialist, believing in the important effects of such *objective* factors as class, sex, and race, and yet not be constrained from interjecting individual initiative into the historical change process. Repression in this country (even though it is, for the most part, subtle) is great enough to suppress the dialectical interaction of the system's contradictions for long periods of time. Denying material considerations and emphasizing abstract values, is one way this suppression is accomplished.

As a revolutionary, a dialectical counselor must surface those contradictions with individuals in pain. Part of that process is helping people to see the confining effect that traditional values and theories have had upon them. The problem that must be made clear to people is that their difficulties do not stem from their inability to live up to far-off goals and abstract values. The difficulties can be explained, in large part, through understanding the political and economic conditions of their lives. It is in this area that counseling often fails.

MECHANISTIC CHANGE

The mechanistic view sees the world as a relatively constant place; it assumes that the essential nature of things is highly established and fundamentally unchangeable. Predictions about the future can be made based upon the way things have occurred in the past or upon the particular theory, values, philosophy or attitudes a person has about life. It assumes that goals for people can be determined from analysis of these theories, values, philosophies and attitudes. This point of view holds that individuals can make adjustments consistent with larger values.

Counseling approaches can be called mechanistic if they either (1) assume a great deal of predictability in the process of human development (in which case they attempt to facilitate the individual's growth by adjusting behavior to accepted developmental patterns) or (2) rely to a great extent upon the individual's value system or goals as the guide for individual decisions (in which case the approach involves helping the person make adjustments in behavior that will lessen the discrepancy between values and behavior). In the one case, it is a generally accepted view of human development which determines how people should make decisions. In the other, individuals make decisions based upon their own internalized goal systems. In both cases, however, it is a preestablished value against which individuals test their behavior and make adjustments.

A typical decision faced by many young people serves to demonstrate the point. A young woman facing high school graduation must decide what to do next. The mechanistic way of approaching this situation has the woman consider her goals and values. Also considered are skills and interests she has developed. Depending upon the orientation of the counselor, she may be encouraged to explore her past, feelings, self-concept, test scores, past grades and so on. All of these considerations assume that whatever the young woman *is* is basically determined by factors which have developed within her through her life. The task becomes one of figuring out how her interests, abilities, feelings, values, etc., will effect the next step. The next step is seen to be natural and predictable because it is viewed as a logical progression which is based upon her growth to the present. This new phase must not differ too much from the past. The decision she makes should be consistent with her growth and development to this point as well as being consistent with the values and goals that have become a part of her over the years.

Any decision which does not consider the factors mentioned above is considered by the mechanistic approach to be inadequate or even dangerous for a person. A mechanistic view of change emphasizes the unities or "positive" aspects of a person's life. Those parts of a person which have in the past facilitated success are accentuated. A mechanistic counselor encourages a person to recognize strengths, unities and ways of working creatively within the structure. These goals of counseling are often stated as fulfilling one's potential, finding one's niche and so on. Responding slowly, making sure, considering alternatives are very important to the mechanist. There is fear and avoidance of large change and distrust of sudden change. A mechanistic counselor, therefore, will often refer to past records of a person having difficulty with identification of behaviors which demonstrate dramatic shifts. For the most part, the mechanistic approach is blind to the potentially positive aspects of radical change.

DIFFERENCES BETWEEN THE APPROACHES

In contrast to the mechanistic model, the dialectical approach views emphasis on the positive aspects of a person's life, the "success factors," as an example of looking at things *one-sidedly* rather than dialectically. A dialectical change model encourages a person to examine and to heighten contradictions in order that the most clear and multidimensional view of a situation may be established. According to the dialectical view, mechanistic change is contrary to the nature of real change. This is because the effect of viewing things *one-sidedly* is to reduce rather than to heighten the contradictions within a person. Adjusting to one side of the dialectic of self serves to entrench the *status quo* position rather than allowing the natural dialectical process to occur. One purpose of helping, dialectically speaking, is to assist individuals to heighten the contradictions within their lives and to help them realize that the existence of these contradictions is a natural state which will eventually cause them to change their behavior or their situation.

As an example let us look at the typical case of a woman who is asking for help in her decision to return to school after her children are grown. She is voicing the usual fears which include such questions as: "Will I be able to compete academically after all these years?" "Will my husband cooperate?" "What will my friends think?" "Can I keep up my responsibilities around the house?" and so on.

A one-sided (mechanistic) approach to the situation includes assessing the woman's past success and failure in school, discussing her feelings about the proposed decision, listing alternatives with respect to the schools or programs available, analyzing her values and determining how the decision to return to school fits with these values. A multidimensional (dialectical) approach may include some of the above, but the emphasis is clearly different. For instance, the counselor striving to expose the dialectical relationships will often take an adversary position in the interview which will serve to highlight elements of the problem which the woman may not have considered. The very heart of the decision will be challenged. Those societal values which reinforce returning to school will be questioned. The role of universities in the perpetuation of traditional women's roles will be emphasized. The woman will be encouraged to examine the dialectical nature of her experience. The *good* and the *bad*, the *joy* and the *hurt*, the feelings of oppression and the feelings of freedom will be central to the counseling process because only through the total airing of her experience can she see the right decision clearly.

The counselor constantly attempts to help her expose opposite sides of issues or of personality characteristics. The counselor must make certain that decisions are not made without understanding the politics of being a woman in a sexist and capitalist society. The roots and manifestations of her oppression must be understood both by the woman herself and by her counselor. The goal of this process is more than reaching a decision about the immediate question of returning to school. The counseling goal is to view this particular and immediate problem as part of a complex of contradictions existing in her life and in the entire society.

Extent of Change

Change for the mechanist is typically small. The end result may be very important for the individual but the adjustment in the behavior or value system will be a relatively small choice or action. Mechanists are often called reformers because they believe that the best way to make changes is by building on the strengths of a situation. They strive to preserve the "best" part of what exists and to adjust those parts which are causing the problem. The implicit hypothesis is that the core of what is already there is all right, but that reforms are necessary to make things work better. The mechanistic approach to change, therefore, predicts incremental change.

Change for the dialectical person is ultimately total. This is clear from the assumption the dialectical method makes regarding the existence of opposites within all things. The dialectical approach holds that radical change is natural and good. Change is the process of growth itself. However, while radical change is at the center of a dialectical approach, it is recognized that all change does not occur in sudden great leaps. Rather, dialectical change occurs in two phases. The first phase is characterized by harmony, searching, agreements, rationality, caution, planning and gathering data. The second phase is marked by struggle, emotion, disagreement, risk taking, action, and recognizable movement in a new direction.

The fundamental difference between the dialectical and mechanistic models is that the mechanists stop after step one of the process, while the dialectical model assumes that after the individual forms alliances with others or learns new skills or behaviors, larger contradictions become sharper and more recognizable (Phase 1). The individual is then ready to use the new alliances, skills or behaviors to change the situation radically in order to remove the intolerable root contradictions within her/his life (Phase 2).

As an example we can consider the case of a young women possessing certain professional skills. In acquiring those skills she successfully dodged, ignored, or outmaneuvered those who would deny professional training to women. But once out of school and on the job market, she finds she can no longer cope successfully with the sexist attitudes she encounters. The confidence she possessed which was sufficient to get her through school begins to erode. Asked to "take off your jacket so I can get a look at you" often enough by those to whom she must apply for work causes her to begin to question the competencies she developed in school.

The mechanistic counselor would begin to help her modify her behavior and aspirations in such a way as to permit her to better deal with the realities with which she is faced and would seek to help her redevelop her confidence. Confidence on the upswing and behavior modified, the mechanist would view the counseling as successful.

The dialectical counselor also would see the redevelopment of confidence as a desirable first step and might very well use the same techniques as the mechanist in helping the client to recover these skills. Overcoming the initial difficulty for the dialectical counselor, however, is only the first step. Understanding both the contradictions which led to the difficulty and the actions necessary to begin the elimination of the contradictions is the second step. In the case of the young woman, the contradictions could be, on the one hand, the traditional value placed on productive work in this culture and, on the other hand, the generally held belief that women are inferior beings, incapable of successfully handling professional responsibilities.

For the most part, only women able to adapt to certain "masculine" behaviors are permitted success. The contradictions are obvious. To be "successful," the woman must relinquish her identity as woman. Not a very reasonable situation, and one fraught with danger both for those unable to make the transition at all and for those who, on the surface, seem to succeed. Living with such a contradiction would easily create a situation where self-confidence is eroded. This contradiction would be at the core of any effort at dialectical counseling.

If the confidence that both the mechanistic and the dialectical counselor wish to help her develop is to be used only to maintain the system that put her in the situation in the first place, in the long run the woman will gain little from the counseling. To use her rediscovered self-confidence as a tool to become more like men merely perpetuates the conditions which led to the original contradictions. On the other hand, her self-confidence can be used to combat the contradictions. Learning to say, "NO! I cannot participate in my own exploitation," begins to get at the roots of the problem. Counselors should not try to resolve a problem by only changing some personality deficiency, i.e. lack of self confidence. Fundamental external causes must not be ignored.

Of course, merely opting not to participate in a life-style does not eliminate the contradictions brought about by an entire economic system. It does, however, serve as a necessary step in the continual raising of awareness of fundamental contradictions. Heightened awareness can lead to more and more actions which, if taken in concert with others experiencing the same alienation, can be an effective tool in resolving contradictions.

Helping young men or women develop self-confidence *can* have the effect of adjusting them to one side of the dialectic of self, thereby limiting the amount and quality of change. It must be remembered that the dialectical approach assumes that every contradiction is related to every other contradiction. Counseling, on the whole, is concerned with secondary contradictions (dealing with lack of confidence, for example). From a dialectical perspective, treating secondary contradictions is acceptable *as long as* the new skill and attitudes can be used in combating primary contradictions. Counseling which treats only the secondary contradictions involved is worse than no counseling at all because it only serves to relieve the pain and in that manner serves to perpetuate the existence of the primary contradictions.

Pain

Another difference between the two approaches lies in the way the source of individual pain is perceived. Pain is caused, the mechanists say, by alienation from one's values or environment. When working with a person in pain, the objective for the mechanist is to achieve harmony between the person's behavior, values, and environment. If there is conflict among these factors the counselor helps the individual achieve consistency by adjusting her value system, her behavior, or, occasionally, the environment.

A danger here is that the pervasive value system of the culture will be used by the counselor aš a base for the individual's value system. For example, someone must take responsibility for the care of children and men have tended not to want that responsibilty, or to feel that to want it would be symptomatic of "unmasculine" behavior. Therefore, it has been held that the general welfare is best served if women assume that responsibility. Alternatives such as shared responsibility or men taking the primary responsibility are not only not seen as viable, they are not seen at all. Thus, a woman who feels resentment at being cooped up with a three-year-old child all day would be viewed by the mechanist as a person whose behavior needed altering, rather than as a person suffering from a contradiction which needed sharpening.

Some social critics such as Marcuse (1964) have stated that the culture is presently so one-dimensional that people do not have the chance to examine the dialectics of an issue. In a one-dimensional society people do not have an adequate opportunity to develop independent value systems. However, mechanists *act as if* people *do* have this opportunity. This is one of the major weaknesses of the mechanistic approach to change on an individual level. The result of the harmonizing process (Phase 1) in which mechanists engage is to create a relatively placid, unfluid, situation for a person where the potential for large change is dissipated. The goal is to help the person attain a state of consonance and be relatively free of pain.

A dialectical model assumes that the natural state for human beings is one in which the individual is in a constant state of disruption (though not necessarily in pain). This model assumes that it is natural for individuals to be full of contradictions and in a constant process of synthesizing these contradictions into new behavior and attitudes. Pain is caused by the alienation of the individual from this synthesizing process.

Poverty is a source of great pain in this culture but the degree of pain is in large measure determined by the approach of the economically deprived person. If the particular individual suffering from poverty has accepted the American myth that anyone can *make it* in America, then her/his pain is going to be greater than that experienced by those who have adopted a multidimensional view of the situation. Those in the first group must take on themselves a sense of guilt and inferiority for what, from a one-dimensional point of view, must be *their* problem and *their* failure. For those able to view the situation from more than one perspective, the immediate pain of poverty may be no less difficult to deal with, the problems no less real and frustrating, but they will not have to add to the burdens of poverty by taking on themselves total responsibility for the situation.

For women, the problems created when value systems and behavior come into conflict can be particularly acute. Few women, or men, for that matter, are able to escape to any significant degree the internalization of this culture's value system as it relates to women. Told they must act in certain rigidly defined ways or risk the loss of that which is held to be essential to their being — femininity — women are caught between their own needs, which they are told they must not have, and the lesser valued role society gives them. Many women find themselves at odds both with themselves and the culture.

The primary role women are socializing into playing is that of wife and mother — servants, however esteemed, of others. The media has recently begun a campaign, in the fact of the women's movement, which acknowledges that women can play roles, even valuable ones, outside the home. The thrust of that campaign, however, has been an attempt to convince women that roles outside the home can be had only by those who can successfully manage two jobs, one inside, one outside the home. The value placed on women playing the housewife role is rarely questioned in the media; that women must play this role amounts to a fact held nearly sacred by those who have power positions and intend to maintain them.

When a woman appeals to a therapist because she is racked with guilt feelings she does not understand or feels resentment she cannot control, because she has headaches and suffers from constant fatigue or cannot respond sexually to her lover any more, the mechanist seeks to understand the relationship between her behavior and values. The values she has internalized are often values the therapist has also internalized. Consequently, they are rarely questioned. Instead the mechanist begins to seek to adjust her behavior in ways which will make it more consistent with her (and his) values. The strategy for change is to provide her with the support she needs to "adjust" to the situation.

The dialectical approach would commence a thorough examination of the contradictions of both values and behaviors (Rokeach, 1973). The possibility that the values themselves might be the problem would be considered (See Ch. 1). Values are not held inviolate. The process of a thorough examination of values and behaviors would not be the same for any two women, nor would the consequences; but the dialectical approach assumes that with awareness of the contradictions, large changes will occur and that these changes, whatever their magnitude, will provide a sense of relief not afforded by those who insist on a one-dimensional view of the situation. It is not upheaval, but an absence of upheaval which is the main source of pain in this culture; it is being forced to view a multidimensional world through one-dimensional glasses that afflicts us.

Scope of Perspective

Part of the difference in the way the two views look at change and growth can be accounted for by the scope of their perspectives. Mechanists are likely to view things narrowly, in terms of their own life space, close environment or individual client. A dialectical counselor takes a more global view. For instance, mechanists seldom refer to the social consequences of a given client's action while dialectical counselors would always consider the impact of an individual's action on the society.

This difference in outlook can be accounted for, in part, by the assumptions in the dialectical model regarding the universality of contradiction. Contradictions can be found in everything and all contradictions are interdependent. No one contradiction can be separate from all others.

A mechanist is concerned with the pain of the moment, has implicit faith that "basically, all is well," and believes that changes are personal and individual matters. A mechanist would view power hierarchies in interpersonal relationships, for instance, as individual problems that should be resolved only by the parties involved. The dialectical counselor would view individual power struggles as mere symptoms of broader societal contradictions. Therefore, eliminating the domination that a given husband has over "his" wife, for example, becomes a question of eliminating the whole socialization process which leads to sexist behaviors and unfair power relationships. Individual acts of oppression, the dialectical perspective would say, are only part of large oppressive systems and the two cannot be separated from each other.

This is not to say that mechanists are uninterested in society as a whole. As a matter of fact, to the extent that their values derive from the system, they have a vested interest in preserving that system. The point is that mechanists *do* actively preserve the *status quo* by tapping off potential revolutionary energy, generated by alienation and oppression, into "harmless" introspective, isolationist and individualistic efforts.

This difference in world view between the two approaches also accounts for the differences in the way individual growth is seen. Developing the belief that a person's influence is limited is viewed by mechanists as growth. Developing awareness of the limits of one's sphere of influence is a sign of health. "Give me the strength to change what I can change, the tolerance to accept what I cannot change, and the wisdom to know the difference," is a slogan which captures the essence of this thinking. This view can be accounted for, in some measure, by the middle-class bias of the counseling movement. Only those in a comfortable position can afford to buy this "leave-well-enough-alone" attitude.

A dialectical approach requires that each person search deeply into a problem, making all the connections possible. Not the limits of one's influence, but the far-reaching impact of one's influence is stressed. A dialectical solution to a situation requires a person to explore many more ramifications than the mechanistic attitude requires. A mechanist is basically interested in the decision of a client as it affects her/his well-being, with little regard for social consequences. A dialectical counselor is interested in the decision not only as it affects the client but also as it affects institutions, the society and the world.

Decisions and Nondecisions

One way of opening up the dialectic is to prevent people from making nondecisions. A nondecision is a choice that is made by virtue of *not* taking action. It is letting tradition, momentum, or someone else decide. In a culture that is one-dimensional, there is great opportunity for nondecisions to occur. This is because one side of the dialectic is elevated to apparent respectability by the conventional wisdom while the other side is either repressed or reduced to apparent absurdity. Nondecisions are important because they can lead to deeper and deeper involvement in contradictions and have long-range consequences for people.

A good example of nondecisions that have long-range effects on people are economic behaviors. In certain subcultures there are strong, obvious, and subtle pressures for people to involve themselves in huge investment projects such as home ownership, life insurance, and all the other trappings of the idealized *young family*. Large debts usually have a conservative effect upon the attitudes of the debtor towards political and social policy. Marriage and having children are other examples of nondecisions with enormous implications.

These behaviors regarding finances, marriage, child raising, and so on are viewed as natural and expected. The truth is that many of these culturally expected behaviors are by no means actually *universally* human. Such behaviors should be analyzed in depth from a dialectical position with the contradictions made clear. However, the momentum is so strong and the involvement is so deep with many culturally expected behaviors that they are beyond analysis.

Once such large nondecisions are made they have the effect of tying individuals even more deeply into the system which continually and with increasing effectiveness inhibits examination of the dialectic. People with huge payments of one kind or another have special sets of fears which prevent serious exploration of the system which got them there and, more importantly, can punish them for not keeping commitments. There is also the need on the part of persons having made these nondecisions to save face by twisting their thinking to let their behavior seem to have been consistent and wise. In brief, nondecisions almost always more deeply embroil the individual in the system. Embroilment in the system then has the effect of limiting the awareness of the contradictions so necessary for dialectical interaction.

Mechanists do not, of course, view drifting into decisions as desirable. The "good" mechanistic counselor helps the client to recognize dimensions of the decision. The overriding concern of the mechanist is, however, that the decision not differ too much from the client's past behaviors and values. The effect of such an attitude is that values of the past are emphasized. The decision reached is in concert with past values and, hence, with the values of the established order. What this means is that traditionally accepted behaviors, such as marriage or large financial investments, are placed in a particularly favorable light by the mechanist. Despite the fact that the mechanistic counselor may have encouraged the client to explore various dimensions of the decision, bias is, perhaps unintentionally, toward socially acceptable decisions. Such decisions are nondecisions.

The only way that nondecisions can be avoided is to have a total reexamination of "acceptable" behaviors; not superficial adjustment which makes the old behaviors more efficient or more palatable. Any process which does not actively expose traditional behaviors to serious examination *at the core* is going to result in nondecisions. The established order has momentum and nondecisions are one of the ways it perpetuates itself. Surfacing the dialectical relationships within such an order requires that we seek ways to help people stop making "acceptable" decisions. People need to examine things at the core.

Institutionalizing Change

Periods of rather intense discomfort are expected in the dialectical model of change. And in fact, this seems to be the way life proceeds. Most people report being besieged from time to time with such difficult periods. Creative individuals report that these events occur frequently in their lives. Despite the desirability of these periods, since real change requires such periods of upheaval, there are serious attempts by society to deprive us of them. The unidimensional character of the culture has created structures which function to institutionalize our difficult periods where qualitative change might occur. Institutionalized functions which serve to relieve the pain often serve to deny the very occurrence of the event.

An example is the procedures the society has developed for handling the trauma of divorce. The sticky details like child custody and property settlements are turned over to lawyers. The process is removed from the hands of the participants by the court. The parties involved are then free to return to a state of "normalcy" as quickly as possible. One gets the impression that the final decision is the result of legal procedures rather than the result of genuine human conflict resolution, and decision-making.

While the legal wheels are turning in an attempt to deny the *human* upheaval, other less-formalized but equally effective institutions, such as neighborhood bridge clubs, function to further the "normalizing" process by reinforcing traditional values. A time ripe for dialectical change is diffused.

Other examples are the attempts to institutionalize the human suffering which accompany unemployment, sickness, and death. By placing unemployed people on welfare, a bureaucracy handles the details. The agony of unemployment is removed from the view of the community. The unemployed themselves are given just enough to put the lid on any real expression of rage at their situation. Sickness is removed from sight by the establishment of private hospital rooms (for the rich). For the poor, there are drugs available to suppress action which could lead to radical changes in the delivery of health care.

The handling of death is, perhaps, the best and most familiar example of the institutionalizing of human experience. Funeral directors are charged with the responsibility of setting a stage which will deny that death ever occurred. The body is made to look alive, the music is soothing and grief is muffled. The "messy" details are handled by a dispassionate third party. A quick return to "normalcy" is facilitated.

The agonies of human experience, which traditionally concern the counseling function, *can* be a time of great personal growth. A dialectical view of change insists that resolution of agony is best accomplished by working through the agony. A return to the situation which existed before the agony occurred is the worst possible solution. A new synthesis needs to evolve. This synthesis cannot be born unless the person in pain examines things in a dialectical manner. In the interest of preserving the *status quo*, the institutionalization of human experience denies that examination.

One counselor working with one client cannot combat the forces of institutionalization. Only an activist position by the counselor can help make life more dialectical and, therefore, more genuine.

The Activist Position

Traditional counseling often holds that the relationship between counseling and institutional change lies in the hope that clients, having received counseling, will take more initiative in the change process. There is the assumption that someone who has learned a skill, changed an attitude or improved their self-concept through counseling will be better prepared to change their environment. Involvement of counseling in societal change efforts is usually indirect and incidental at best. In the interest of "freedom of choice" political action is left entirely up to the individual client during or after counseling.

In contrast, a dialectical view does not accept the separation between the person and the environment. In fact, the dialectical position holds that all the contradictions of the world are related. This means that individual or group counseling, not directly associated with action toward the institutions and society, will be ineffective. Secondary contradictions in the lives of people who come for counseling can only be effectively addressed in the context of larger (primary) contradictions which have given rise to personal concerns. Another way of saying this is that the environment to which clients return after counseling is biased and oppressive enough that clients must either adjust to the environment or the environment will render them as unhappy or neurotic as before counseling. Counseling and therapy cannot be separated from social concerns.

The question at this point is, "How can one counselor working alone in a school, agency, or hospital hope to promote the social changes usually indicated by a dialectical analysis?" One counselor working alone *cannot* promote this change. This is not to say that individual or small group therapy is useless. It is to say that individual efforts are usually not helpful unless taken in conjunction with united political action. It is senseless to send a woman client back into a system that systematically discriminates against her. No one, alone, can withstand the cultural pressures. However, helping a woman find political groups or, better yet, joining with her in political action is a viable way to finish the job that therapy begins. This means, of course, that the counselor's political biases must be identifiable and presented openly. It also means that the counselor needs to educate the client to the dialectical notion that contradictions in our lives are related. That is, political education is part of therapy and counseling.

REFERENCES

de Beauvoir, Simone: *The Second Sex*. New York, Knopf, 1952.
Hampden-Turner, Charles: *Radical Man*. Garden City, Anchor Books, 1971.
Lenin, Nikolai: *Lenin: Selected Works Vol. I*. Moscow, Progress Press, 1970.
Marcuse, Herbert: *One-Dimensional Man*. Boston, Beacon Press, 1964.
Rokeach, Milton: *The Nature of Human Values*. New York, The Free Press, 1973.
Slater, Philip E.: *The Pursuit of Loneliness*. Boston, Beacon Press, 1970.

—— *Chapter 23* ——

BEYOND THERAPY: PERSONAL AND INSTITUTIONAL CHANGE

Norma B. Gluckstern

THIS article will consider social and political action as a means of addressing problems both in institutions that need change and in individuals that need support to free themselves from old patterns of behavior. These two goals can go hand in hand, and simultaneous attention to them improves the chances of achieving both.

This approach is not new. In the 1960's a number of programs showed that fighting for social change brings about personal growth in the participants. This approach applied to community mental health problems was strongly endorsed by Pearl and Reissman (1965) under the name of "the new careerists." A classic study in this area was conducted by J.

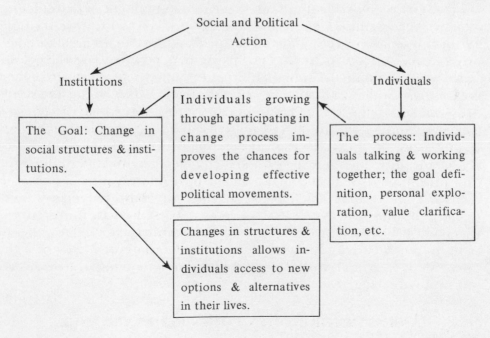

Figure 23-1. Interaction of process and goal to bring about institutional and individual change.

429

Douglas Grant (1967) in which eighteen hard-core felons participated in a self-study, social-change oriented program. Grant pointed out in his study the difficulty of changing the behavior of large groups of people without at the same time changing the operations of organizations and institutions in which these people have to function.

The following diagram suggests one way of conceptualizing how process and goal intermix to bring change to both institutions and individuals:

Participation in social action in the 1960's did have a significant impact on the personal lives of those who got involved. They were expected to and, indeed, did reevaluate personal goals, clarify values, and change life-styles. However, rarely did these programs and groups deliberately intend to focus both on individual and institutional change. Most often, the movements of the 1960's emphasized institutional change.

One reason for the stress on institutional change was a reaction against the influence of Freud and psychology which had placed the burden of change primarily on the individual. Another reason was the desire to counter the American belief in "survival of the fittest" which encouraged people to blame themselves; in reaction, the groups stressed the importance of looking at the structural reasons behind the situations in which people found themselves.

The women's movement was an exceptional movement in that it legitimized giving attention *both* to the need for personal growth and the need for institutional change. Many women recognized their need to come together and support each other by talking over personal experiences. By perceiving the commonality of their situations, they were able to go beyond the feeling that they individually were to blame. By developing an experiential understanding of the institutional sources of personal oppression, they developed a political consciousness. Though this consciousness-raising aspect of the women's movement may at first seem extraneous in the broader movement for institutional change, it seems to have been the very reason why the women's movement has endured, grown, and been effective even into the 1970's when other groups have retrenched.

The following discussion describes the process by which a group of women at the University of Massachusetts in Amherst worked together to bring into existence a center for women on the campus. It tells how the group developed and will illustrate how both individual growth and institutional change were fostered in the process.

A CENTER FOR WOMEN COMES INTO EXISTENCE

My first contact with the women who were to become the nucleus in the creation of the Everywomen's Center at the University of Massachusetts came when they approached me about teaching a workshop in life-planning as part of Project Self — a self-help education project for women. At that time, I was working in a university office in charge of resolving differences among faculty, students, and administration. Even though my training was in counseling and I had spent a number of years counseling students on an individual basis, I had begun to feel that my role should be more geared toward addressing institutional causes of problems.

I approached the life-planning workshop thinking of myself as a professional, intending to help other women explore their lives, roles, and needs. As the workshop got underway, I quickly came to realize that I was still facing many of the same frustrations and personal difficulties as the women I was supposed to be "teaching." Even though these problems were not new to me, I had never before dealt with them in terms of the social and cultural situation of being a woman. Leading this workshop gave me a new political consciousness.

With this consciousness came a new commitment to the cause of women, but I still had to choose an approach to that cause. With my counseling background, the most obvious format for me would have been to work with women one at a time in a fairly traditional therapy format. This might have helped a few women to face adversity, but I realized that it would not have addressed the realities of the environment in which both they and I were trying to function.

A second strategy I considered was attacking one specific problem: counseling. However, I decided that working to bring about improved counseling might help individual women, but would inevitably be rendered useless because of other situational determinants.

My decision to work at developing a base for bringing about institutional change came at a time when I discovered two other women working toward that end in the university. Joan Hemmer, Lois Phillips and I joined forces to begin the work of bringing together a constituency of women who would take political action to change the situation of women.

The three of us became what Biddle and Biddle (1965) describe as a "community-action nucleus." Our first task together was to find a common goal and a basis for commitment to collective action. We met together regularly to consider what we could do. We visited a number of other women's centers to compare ideas. Then we enlisted the help of women from the Project Self Workshops who had identified themselves as wanting to get more involved. At this point we realized we needed more space, money, supplies, and assistantships for a few people who could commit more time to the center. As the political base widened, we got space for a larger office and Everywomen's Center grew quickly into the focal point for a variety of women's groups and activities on campus. Many subgroups formed as new people came into the center with specific needs. By the second year Everywomen's Center was well-established and had a dependable base of support. Women had a constituency which could come together politically around specific issues as they arose.

In retrospect, our work together as a community-action nucleus approximates Biddle's six stages of community action (Biddle and Biddle, 1965):

1. *Exploration* — preliminary study of the problem and an invitation to others to join in the exploration.
2. *Organizational* — informal meetings, getting structures set up, establishing commitments.
3. *Discussion* — alternative solutions to the problems, setting limits, choosing appropriate action.
4. *Action* — work projects, reporting and analysis, evaluation of the work done.
5. *New Projects* — broadening contacts, dealing with controversies that arise, considering new alternatives, the need for coalition with outside groups.
6. *Continuation* — commitment to indefinite continuation of the nucleus, frequent withdrawal by initiators, problems increase in complexity, increasing responsibility to deal with more complex problems.

Figure 23-2 also adapted from Biddle and Biddle, shows the evolution of our organization that came as a result of these six stages.

The action that resulted as subgroups got underway included such projects as a Poor Women's Task Force that got women on welfare into the University, secured a $70,000 operating budget and organized a highly successful midterm study program for women. Other plans of action were conceived to meet the needs of all women in the university — students, faculty, staff, and administration. Workshops were held for university secretaries to help them think about their particular problems. Everywomen's Center brought together a mixture of women — young and old, poor and middle-class, students and staff.

Though both of the following diagrams look relatively simple on paper, in reality we experienced difficulties all along the way. We had disagreements over needs and goals, had problems in creating new structures for ourselves, were faced with a constantly evolving and changing leadership and struggled to overcome the effects of our long histories of functioning in dependent and passive roles.

These difficulties reflected the very institutional and personal problems we were trying to address. For example, we worked within the context of

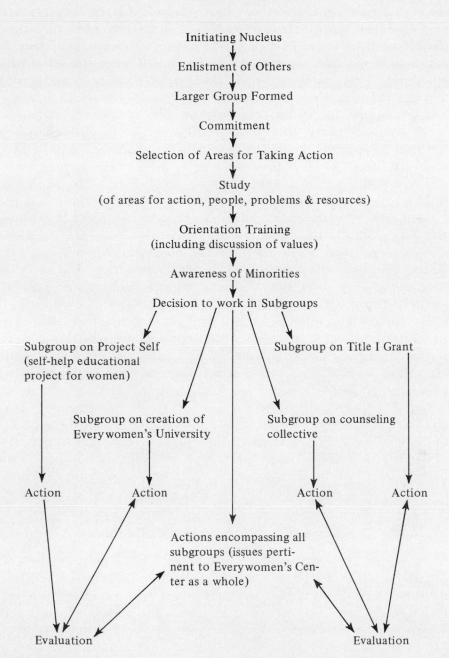

Figure 23-2. Stages of community action and change. (Adapted from Biddle and Biddle, 1965.)

a university that was oriented to departmentalization, competitiveness, and professional isolation and jealousies. The three of us in the original nucleus came from different departments. We had to overcome the values within which we had learned to operate and relinquish some of the things that had given us professional security. We had to move out of the traditional individualistic orientation to personal success and accept in its place the promotion of a collective good.

In the course of facing this conflict within ourselves, each of us began to see changes coming about in our values and in the conduct of our professional lives. We had previously accepted a male-oriented style of achievement and personal success. Now we began to reconsider and search for a style more truly our own. We began to care about new goals and about each other in a way we had not previously and we began to feel a sense of belonging to a wider community of women. Our feelings of alienation were eased and we felt better about ourselves.

Our efforts were most seriously endangered when we had to move from the discussion stage to taking specific actions. Could we somehow overcome our acculturated stance of inaction and passivity? We were all good at talk. Our socialization as women had emphasized that. Action was another matter. In spite of the fact that we were all professional women who had seemingly overcome that "fear of success" of which Matina Horner (1970) writes, we still carried the fears that are attached to growing up female.

There were also some very real risks involved in what we were doing. We had stepped into the forefront and made demands on the university, claiming that we spoke for a wide constituency of women in proposing what needed to be done. We put ourselves on the line, and, if our judgement had been wrong, we would have hindered the cause of women's rights in the long run. On a professional level, we risked losing credibility in our university roles and faced the possibility of being ostracized in our respective departments and of losing access to professional opportunities.

Yet, the process of taking these risks helped us to gain greater confidence in ourselves. In perceiving the risks and forming our collective goals to override them, we began to take ourselves, our lives, our goals, and each other more seriously than we had in the past. Working together in a group as well as our personal investment, helped us move beyond our fears to initiate action. The group provided support, pressure, and impetus to act. Our commitment to the cause of women provided our motivation.

Everywomen's Center had an impact on the women who brought it into existence as well as on the university within which it now functions. It brings women from all over the university together for mutual support.

Many women who got involved have gained a new certainty that something can be done. Some have chosen to go back to school. Others are more politically sophisticated after negotiating endlessly with university administrators.

EWC provides opportunities to many women looking to change the basis of their lives and to take on new responsibilities. It provides support for individual women and groups by collective pressure. It also provides an important structural change in the university; it has repeatedly challenged the administration on its policies. It has opened up new and specific opportunities for women. It has brought a number of new populations into the university, especially poor and older women. It has helped place women in significant faculty and administrative positions of power. And, finally, it has created a watchful presence in the university which has made people at all levels more aware of sexism and its results.

SOCIAL ACTION: INDIVIDUAL AND
INSTITUTIONAL CHANGE

It is appropriate at this point to examine the process that takes place in women's political action groups that change the lives of participants. What is it about the change process that fosters personal growth, and what is the nature of the growth that takes place? Clearly, political action can become a substitute for addressing one's own personal issues. Like caring for children, it can become another means of avoiding a hard look at one's own life. What is it about the women's movement in particular with its attention to consciousness-raising that made political action for many not an avoidance of personal issues, but a mechanism to more effectively bring about both institutional and personal change?

Working in Groups

An *action* group of women working together to bring about institutional change is not primarily a support group. However, many action groups have emerged out of groups initially developed for group support. The difference to be emphasized between a consciousness-raising group and a political action one is that the political action group moves from working toward common political goals to a consideration of personal issues. In contrast, "the ideal course for a C-R group is from discussion of feelings and experiences, to analysis, and then to action" (Deckard, 1975, p. 413).

The action group is a growth-producing mechanism *in combination* with the experience of taking action. It is a place for touching base, getting ideas and support, comparing experiences, and understanding the difference between the limitations of individuals and the limits imposed by social structures. The group provides a challenge. There is pressure from peers and the pressure of accountability to assigned responsibilities. It is a place to test one's potential for leadership. It is a safe environment in which to try on new roles and begin to break away from the constraints of what a woman is "supposed to be." The existence of the group can help an individual woman take risks she would not have felt able to do on her own.

The readiness to use political action groups as a forum for discussing personal issues came both from the proliferation of women's consciousness-raising groups and from women's acculturated inclination in that direction. One danger in C-R groups is that they stagnate when they do not go beyond the discussion of feelings and experiences. Women's support groups which turn toward interpersonal conflict within their groups as a way of getting to deeper personal issues are operating along the lines of the traditional encounter group. These groups reflect the difficulty that women have in learning to take action. However, some groups have transcended the discussion stage and moved into taking action around specific issues. One support group in Boston that included a number of women studying to be doctors and workers in health fields wrote a self-help education guide for women, the well-known book, *Our Bodies Ourselves* (Boston Women's Health Book Collective, 1971). Another support group of rape victims moved into learning karate and teaching it to other women. Consciousness-raising groups provide legitimacy and an orientation for looking at personal issues, but unless they move beyond the discussion stage, C-R groups perpetuate the cycle of passivity.

Women who work within a collective model to bring about political change provide a communitarian alternative to the prevalent authoritarian way in which most institutions in this society are structured. Our collective style of leadership in the EWC forced the University to make accommodations in its usual procedures. By working in these groups, women not only grow individually, but they grow in their ability to relate to one another. This provides a model for a new society: less individualistic and competitive, and more supportive and caring. The best of the experiences of being women are incorporated into the style of institutional and social change.

Political Consciousness:
Internal vs. External Restraints

The use of the group as a supportive mechanism forces those involved to differentiate between the individual factors that limit them and those which are clearly constraints in structures that have historically treated women as second-class citizens. The feeling of internal restraint is operating in the woman who insists somebody else in the group would be better at negotiating with the university administration and in the woman who uses imagined repercussions from her husband as a way to avoid taking on responsibilities. Of course, the repercussions from husbands are often very real, but many times an individual woman will speculate on the repercussions rather than deal with them in order to avoid facing issues about herself.

External restraints are well-known. In the university setting faculty women are constrained by the threat of losing tenure for being politically active, the difficulty of getting hired as a woman professor, the difficulty of getting moved from assistant to full professor. Students are also constrained by the attitude that women are less important to educate since they will only go on to family life.

The process of differentiating internal and external restraints is the process of developing a political consciousness. Women begin to see the specific needs for institutional reform and become more effective in developing strategies for bringing pressure to bear. At the same time the emergence of a political consciousness directly contradicts the debilitating habit many women have of blaming themselves for the situations of their lives. Since Eve, women have been blamed for the problems of man, mankind, and themselves. The pressure to internalize feelings of guilt is enormous. Everytime a woman locates an external source of a restraint, she comes further out from under a cloud of confusion and isolation. When women talking together see that they feel the same limitations, there is the new feeling, "Oh, it's not just me. It's something I can change. It's something we can do something about."

This both enables and, in a sense, *requires* women to take action. It forces the issue of personal responsibility. Neither can women blame all problems on themselves, nor can they blame all problems on institutions. They can see more clearly where they have avoided taking responsibility for their own lives, and where they have used obligations to children, husband and home as an excuse for not coming to terms with themselves as people. They also see more clearly what the issues are and where only collective action can be effective.

New Alternatives and Options

Women who become involved in social and political action begin to see many new options and alternatives open to them. They may also begin to think anew about things that they had long ago wanted to do with their lives. The commitment to the political group requires women to adjust their life-styles to allow for more time away from home. Patterns which they may have previously considered inviolate now are considered. The woman who has never left her children with a babysitter has to ask herself if that behavior is rational. She is forced to make decisions according to her own personal values rather than unthinkingly accepting old traditions.

Political action requires new skills. Women who are committed to taking an action are motivated to acquire the skills and information they will need. Political action also encourages women to recognize the skills they already have and did not appreciate or value. In both these instances, the group helps by providing support for trying out new endeavors and giving respect and validation for achievement.

In my own experience working for the creation of the women's center, I recognized skills I had which I had not previously acknowledged. I saw I had an ability to conceptualize programs and integrate disparate parts into a workable plan. I also got a chance to try on a leadership role. Though leadership had appealed to me in the past, I had been intimidated from trying it because of my feeling it was inappropriate for a woman. Now I found I enjoyed it and received respect from my peers for the way I was able to carry it out. I learned many new skills in the course of our actions: I had to write proposals; I had to learn to cope with bureaucracies. The motivation of working for the cause of women and feeling the support of the group enabled me to push ahead where alone, or in a different area, I would have held back.

Another way in which new options and alternatives are opened to women is through the example of other women in action. Seeing women in leadership positions, going back to school, negotiating with university administrators, trying out new skills, meeting together and affirming their rights, and fulfilling themselves in roles outside their families and homes creates an inspiration for others. Women face the realization that they, too, can establish a direction in their lives.

Access to new options comes through addressing external constraints. One woman who wanted to become more involved in the Center was told by her husband that if she did he would leave her. This made the realities of her situation crystal clear. A proportion of women who get involved in political action do end up getting divorced. This is an example of how taking action affects both the institutions of society and the individuals. The way marriage has been structured in our society has been restrictive to the lives of many women. When women want to get involved outside of their homes, these patterns get challenged. Something has to change or give. For many, the marriage undergos a basic reevaluation and change. For others it ends. An increasingly widespread reconsideration of the style of marriage in the society as a whole has resulted.

Clearly, institutional change will have a therapeutic impact on more women, but involvement in the process of institutional change creates personal change. The following diagram illustrates the process by which social action by women changes their lives and the institutions that affect them.

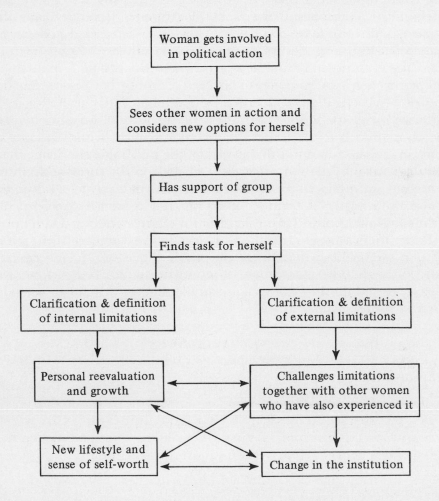

Figure 23-3. Personal and institutional change interaction.

The Danger of Creating New Dependencies
and the Issue of Interdependency

One problem with this model is the danger of creating new dependencies by fostering dependency on the support/action group or on the active members that keep it moving. Many women slide readily into dependent positions. This form of dependency is seductive because of the illusion of independence. The important thing that mitigates against such a dependence is the group's commitment to action and attending to that personal growth which facilitates getting tasks done. The group should not hold discussion of personal issues as an end in itself. This does not mean that discussion of personal issues is not legitimate. It only means that as women, with our long acculturation of passivity and dependency, sole attention to personal issues can provide yet another detour from doing what needs to be done and acting on our own behalf.

There is a critical distinction between a group that fosters dependency and one that encourages interdependency. The latter does not reject or ostracize its members when they grow to the point of wanting to move on to other areas and challenges. In fact it encourages and welcomes new members because it is not threatened by the inevitable challenge that new members bring. Allowing members to leave with support and encouraging new members to bring their ideas and goals creates a self-renewing group and counters the danger of too much dependency. Interdependency means that the group is a mechanism for change and not an end in itself.

There are two other crucial advantages to the interdependent structure. First, it establishes a model for the whole movement which can reverberate through other movements and institutions. And second, women who leave and go into other areas can model interdependent behavior for other women.

NEW ALLIANCES

The experience I have described and my own participation in it is basically a middle-class one. The three of us who started Everywoman's Center were all of middle-class backgrounds with substantial professional credentials already established. We worked within a university which was in a middle-class area and, at first, the women who came to join us were middle-class as well. The women's movement is one political movement that has the potential to cross class divisions; it is important to note that the models and experiences I have described above have important implications for all women — working-class, middle- and upper-class and Third World women alike.

One of the liabilities of the women's movement in its early days was that many Third World and working-class women did not see their part in it. Though there was a basis for building a movement across class and racial lines, many were suspicious and felt their first alliance was with their ethnic or class group. Some of the reasons for this lack of trust are described in an article by Consuelo Nieto, a woman active both in the women's movement and on behalf of her own people, the Chicanos. She explains,

> For a Chicana allied with the struggle of her people, such a simplistic approach to her identity is not acceptable. Furthermore, it is difficult for the Chicana to forget that some Anglo women have oppressed her people within this society, and are still not sensitive to minorities or their needs. With Anglo women the Chicana may share a commitment to equality, yet it is very seldom that she will find with them the camaraderie, the understanding, the sensitivity that she finds with her own people.
>
> Anglo women sensitive to Chicanas as members of a minority must guard against a very basic conceptual mistake. All minorities are not alike. To understand the black woman is not to understand the Chicana. To espouse the cause of minority women, Anglos must recognize our distinctiveness as separate ethnic groups ... (The Chicana women's) approaches to feminism must be drawn from her own world, and not be shadowy replicas drawn from Anglo society (1974).

Despite these complexities, many women accept and value the need for alliances across racial and class lines. One important way in which the alliances can be built is through an emphasis on what particular strengths and resources each of the groups has to contribute. By demonstrating that each group will learn and benefit from the others, the problems of lack of trust may be overcome. Rather than denying the differences, we can affirm the importance of each group's particular experience.

Middle-class women bring certain advantages to the women's movement. Generally, they have more free time to work for institutional change. They are less likely to be busy supporting their families financially. They are better able to make provisions for child care. In addition they bring their "middle-class skills" to the movement. They are more likely to know how to deal with bureaucrats and to write proposals, for example. Also, they are more likely to have money to contribute to their work, or be free to volunteer their time. The liability that middle-class women, the largest consumers of therapy, bring is their long history of believing traditional therapists who say their problems are all personal in nature.

Third World women have not accepted the Freudian litany in the same way. Their influence in the feminist movement is to counter the Freudian orientation with an aggressive political consciousness. Because they are more oppressed than middle-class women by society — oppressed not only as women, but also for their social, economic backgrounds and the color of their skin — they more clearly see the institutional oppression around them. Third World and working-class women bring not only their political consciousness, but also their personal histories to counter the passivity of the middle-class women. Third World and working-class women cannot afford to be passive in the way that middle-class women can. ADC women have to learn to be aggressive on their own behalf, or they will not survive.

By referring back to Figure 23-1, we can see that it is possible to fit different class experiences into the model of how institutional and individual change work in concert. Third World and working-class women obviously come more strongly from the left-hand side of the chart. They come to the women's movement less from a feeling of personal dissatisfaction within their lives than from a feeling of the oppression of the institutions around them. Middle-class women tend to come to the women's movement more from a sense of personal anxiety and a desire to grow beyond their old restrictive identities. Since effective change means attending to the personal and the institutional at the same time, allying groups that represent each of these two orientations will produce a more powerful and effective political base.

The creation of the Poor Women's Task Force at Everywomen's Center is an example of how this alliance can work to the benefit of both groups. Originally, the Task Force developed as an advocate group, helping women on welfare to find ways to get past bureaucratic red tape involved in becoming students at the university. Eventually, the Task Force was taken over by the welfare women themselves who renamed it "Advocacy for Welfare Mothers" and now offer counseling and guidance to new women on welfare trying to go back to school.

Middle-class skills, free time, money, and contacts can provide the means and the impetus; working-class and Third World political consciousness, and orientation toward action can provide the dimensions and the reality. In the course of creating this alliance, middle-class women can gain a better appreciation of political reality and the reality of oppression. Simultaneously, with group support, the Third World and working-class women can learn to look more closely at who they are as individual people. Both groups have a significant amount to learn from one another. An alliance of the political with the personal produces the most effective and long lasting institutional change.

CONCLUSION

In conclusion I would like to return briefly to the nature of the role I played in the development of the Everywomen's Center, and specifically to my decision to become a counselor/activist instead of a traditional one-to-one counselor.

Counseling is traditionally a feminine position in society. It calls upon the socially conditioned skills (in women) of listening, being supportive, talking and nurturing. It is a comfortable role for many women since it allows for lots of talk and does not require action outside the office. It is another area in which the pattern of passivity can be frequently spotted.

One particular aspect in the training of counselors mitigates against being effective activists in a political arena. Our training encourages us to look for and focus on factors *within* the individual which restrict growth. Most counselor training delegitimizes attention to structural causes of personal problems. Many women have heard psychiatrists say, "Yes, it's all fine and interesting, this business about your being a woman, but why don't we get back to the things that are bothering you ..." Counselors who allow political consciousness to grow, enable women to break out of the debilitating cycle of self-blame and inaction.

Furthermore, counselors must realize the importance of being a peer and not setting up false distinctions between themselves and the women with whom they work. By presenting themselves as women first and counselors second, they will avoid that dependence on professionals that has encouraged women not to take responsibility for their own lives.

In order to be an effective counselor/activist working in the women's movement, I had to face my own tendency toward passivity and the ambivalence I felt about taking action. It meant becoming a role model, and learning to take risks and assume leadership. For me, breaking out of the traditional constraints of the counselor role led to breaking out of the limitations of being a socialized woman. I experienced growth as I moved away from seeing only my particular needs to identifying with the needs of all women. In taking action, I found within myself abilities I had not recognized before and I began to challenge the limits I had previously felt imposed on me. I saw new alternatives open to me and I began to seek them. When I succeeded, I gained a new feeling of pride and satisfaction.

My personal experiences and my observations in this paper on the possibilities for individual and institutional change demonstrate, I believe, the tremendous potential of political and social action as a therapeutic form.

REFERENCES

Biddle, William & Biddle, Loureide: *The Community Development Process: The Rediscovery of Local Initiative*. New York, Holt, Rinehart and Winston, 1965.

Boston Women's Health Book Collective: *Our Bodies, Ourselves*. New York, Simon and Schuster, 1971.

Deckard, Barbara S.: *The Women's Movement: Political, Socioeconomic, and Psychological Issues*. New York, Harper and Row, 1975.

Grant, J. Douglas: New Careers development project. Final report. National Institute of Mental Health project OM-01616, sponsored by the Institute for the Study of Crime and Delinquency, 1967.

Horner, Matina S.: Toward An Understanding of Achievement-Related Conflicts in Women. *Journal of Social Issues, 28,* 1972.

Nieto, Consuelo: Chicanas and the Women's right movement: A perspective by Consuelo Nieto. *Civil Rights Digest, 6,* 1974.

Pearl, Arthur & Reissman, Frank: *New Careers for the Poor: The Non-professional in Human Service.* New York, Free Press, 1965.

Section X
EPILOGUE

Chapter 24

PSYCHOTHERAPY FOR
<u>SOCIAL CHANGE</u>

PSYCHOTHERAPISTS who confine their activities to contacts with clients in their offices often fail to see a connection between their professional activities and social change. In the concluding section of this book we would like to explore the ways psychotherapists' activities facilitate or impede social change. Beit-Hallahmi (1974) has said: "Most psychologists see themselves as part of a movement toward positive social change and will be terribly offended if we suggest to them that they are part of a social control mechanism" (p. 126). That statement could be aptly applied to psychotherapists as well.

DEFINING SOCIAL PROBLEMS

The helping profession has been given a mandate by society to define who is deviant, ill, needy, and entitled to their services. In this sense, the mental health profession defines a significant aspect of social reality, and, as a consequence, exerts social control. In return for exerting social control, society accords the members of the profession high status, high income, and autonomy over their professional conduct (Reiff, 1974).

Bart (1971) blamed Freud for the tradition of "quietism" among psychotherapists. Freud focused his attentions on the "inner person" and condemned radicalism in any form as a neurosis. He was pessimistic about the possibility of social change. Civilization, he believed, was antagonistic to human happiness and psychotherapy was a course in resignation. Bart found similar attitudes in private psychotherapists who, feeling they are not in a position to change the environment of their private patients, emphasize the dogma of "its what's inside that counts."

How psychotherapists conceptualize their patients' problems is highly relevant to and has implications for social change. Caplan and Nelson (1974) suggested that, "what is done about a problem depends on how it is defined" (p. 200). Likewise, Argyris (1975) observed:

> One of the most powerful ways to control others is to control the meaning of what is valid information. The basic act of creating a concept whose meaning is given by us to others and whose validity is defined by us for others is a powerful control over others (p. 469).

447

Definitions of social problems are based on assumptions concerning the causes of the problems. Two basic types of definitions of social problems were identified by Caplan and Nelson as: (1) person-centered interpretations and (2) situation-centered explanations.* Person-centered interpretations of social problems imply that external factors can be ignored because they presumably have little etiological significance for the problem. In contrast, situation-centered explanations lead to a *system-change* orientation. These authors observed: "Train a person in psychological theory and research, and suddenly a world disastrously out of tune with human needs is explained as a state of mind" (Caplan and Nelson, 1974, p. 202). Since psychotherapists have a tradition of "looking between the ears" for causes of social problems, they add legitimacy to person-centered definitions of social problems (Bart, 1971). Caplan and Nelson (1973) warned that psychologists should be cautious of person-blame explanations of social problems, since such definitions potentially reinforce established stereotypes and thus perpetuate the conditions of the problem group. In addition, person-centered definitions distract attention from possible abuses in the social system itself.

WHO SHOULD DEFINE THE PROBLEM?

A group that has "the problem" is in the best position to define or diagnose the problem and to suggest remedies. Accurate diagnosis is essential to effective action, yet, due to their lack of power, the problem group is seldom consulted. Caplan and Nelson (1973) explain this by quoting Becker on the hierarchy of credibility: "In any system of ranked groups, participants take it as given that members of the highest group have the right to define the way things really are" (Becker, 1970, p. 18). To question established definitions is a radical act; it challenges institutions and belief systems anchored in such definitions (Caplan and Nelson, 1973). Similarly, Beit-Hallahmi (1972) suggested that "serious challenges to the traditional model of the person in psychology come from those who attack the basic definition of deviance" (p. 127).

One group which has challenged the definition of deviance is feminist. Feminists have usurped the prerogative of defining the mental health problems of women. They have jarred the complacency of "experts" who treat women's emotional problems as evidence of personal inadequacies rather than as evidence of social and political conditions. Beit-Hallahmi summarized the feminist position as follows:

The feminist viewpoint implies that there are external forces and neces-

---

*Compare with the mental illness and environmental models of psychotherapy discussed in Chapter 1.

sities that shape women's behavior into forms that are then regarded as deviant or pathological. The external social forces are those that determine what appears to be prevalent forms of psychopathology. The hysterical, depressed housewife has some pretty good reasons to be depressed and identity conflicts in college women are a result of reality pressures (1972, p. 128).

Without the impetus from feminist groups and feminist therapists, many traditional psychotherapists, wedded to the power establishment, would not have taken a fresh look at women's problems.

Blaming the victim for her/his own predicament is one of the insidious results of person-centered definitions of social problems. Victims are most likely to accept inequitable treatment when they believe they possess personal defects that make them unworthy of societal rewards (cf. Bandura, 1974; Caplan and Nelson, 1973). Those who challenge person-centered definitions are themselves often labelled "sick," e.g. feminists, ghetto rioters, war protesters, etc.; this definition discredits the dissenting persons and, in extreme cases, can lead to their incarceration in mental hospitals for "rehabilitation" (Erlich and Abraham-Magdamo, 1974).

Accepting situation-centered definitions of problems is not a cop-out for individual responsibility. Indeed, person-centered definitions such as "mental illness," "sick," and "genetically inferior" are ways of robbing persons of responsibility for their behavior. Showing persons how society has placed them in the position of victim is a way of returning their personal power to them. With this knowledge they are free to become self-defining and self-directing by taking action on their own behalf and on behalf of their minority groups to increase their political, social, and economic power.

CONFLICTING INTERESTS

Brickman (1970) discussed the difficulties faced by a psychiatrist in a mental health center attempting to reconcile her/his roles as both an agent of social control (of deviant behavior) and as an agent of social change. According to Brickman: "The goal of treatment of a socially victimized client cannot realistically be total reintegration into her/his alienating milieu. This is even more true of community consultation and educational efforts" (p. 60). He gave an example of social intervention or advocacy on behalf of a client in which he promoted an open dialogue between members of a minority group who objected to an arbitrary school policy and school officials. In that particular case, the school personnel were pleased to have the support of members of the community (most of whom belonged to the minority group) in opposing the nonfunctional rule handed down by the central school authority. Brickman expressed concern for assisting his socially disadvantaged clients "without subverting duly constituted governmental functions in the community" (1970, p. 418).

However, he did not address himself to instances in which a compromise between minority group members and community institutions was not readily forthcoming nor to the issue of the existence of other nonfunctional rules which may be however duly constituted. Thus, he evaded the important issue of conflict of interest in psychotherapist-assisted confrontation of widely divergent minority and community values. Unless members of the helping profession can truly serve as advocates for the individuals and groups she/he proposes to assist, she/he will continue to operate with a conflict of interest.

Members of the helping profession must understand their own values and priorities when conflicts exist between their disadvantaged client and powerful social institutions. Otherwise, out of ignorance rather than malice, helpers will end up serving the *status quo*. Psychotherapists must determine the source of their basic allegiance: the institutions that provide them jobs and income, their profession which accords them status and promotes their welfare, or the target population which depends upon their services.

Morgan (1974), addressing agency counselors, suggested that members of the mental health profession stop feeling sorry for themselves and start taking some responsibility for their own professional activities within an agency. As professionals they should write their own job descriptions, reorder their priorities so that helping clients comes first, and, finally, be willing to take risks by initiating social action programs to benefit their clients.

Unfortunately, one important reason mental health professionals do not take many risks in initiating meaningful social action programs is that programs that would benefit disadvantaged groups often do not promote self-serving professional needs. As Caplan and Nelson (1973) so aptly phrased it: "There is no chance for a career-conscious psychologist to become successful by helping people who are not" (p. 205). This is also true of career-conscious psychotherapists. Too often members of the mental health profession are more concerned with obtaining the approval of their superiors and colleagues than of the population affected by their activities. To put it crudely, psychotherapists are not apt "to bite the hands that feed them."

It is not only the promise of reward but also the fear of sanctions that keep career-conscious mental health professionals following the institutional line. O'Day (1974) described *intimidation rituals* (nullification, isolation, defamation and, if necessary, expulsion) employed by institutions to discourage zealous reformers within the ranks. Gluckstern (cf.

Chapter 23) observed that in academic settings, threats of not achieving tenure and losing credibility in one's professional field were everpresent realities that operated to prevent academicians from challenging certain university practices. Schultz (cf. Chapter 19) explained the loss of her position in a rehabilitation center for addicts by showing that she met disfavor with male authorities for setting up sex-segregated treatment programs for female addicts which promoted behavior in the women that the male authorities found threatening.

Presumably, the mental health profession serves the public good or social welfare; in reality, it more often serves the dominant classes, identified by Chesler and Worden (1974) as WAMAP (White-Anglo, Affluent, Male, Adult, and Protestant). According to Reiff (1974), at least one half of the members of the mental health profession work in institutions and agencies which have sufficient financial resources to purchase professional expertise. As a rule, the professionals have little control and input into the bureaucratic structure and the policies of such institutions and agencies. Ignorant of the reality of social power, these professionals serve established power without taking responsibility for doing so. As Bandura (1974) observed:

> People will perform behavior they normally repudiate if a legitimate authority sanctions it and acknowledges responsibility for its consequences ... Exemption from self-censure can be facilitated by diffusing responsibility for culpable behavior. Through division of labor, division of decision-making, and collective action, people can contribute to detrimental practices without feeling personal responsibility or self-disapproval (p. 861).

Any significant social change involves the redistribution of social power. Those already in power have as much interest in retaining their power as those attempting to wrest power have in gaining it. In general, changes acceptable to those in power are those that do not in fact alter existing power arrangements; hence, changes are more apt to be superficial than meaningful in terms of power alterations (Chesler and Worden, 1974).

Social action programs are supported by power holders as long as they do not present serious challenges to the system. Some social action programs are useful to power groups. Caplan and Nelson (1973) discuss the political advantages obtained by power groups when they help "problem" groups. Control of troublesome sections of the population is maintained by obstensibly being "helpful." Caplan and Nelson explain this political advantage.

> Normally one would expect that those who control power and resources would be unrelentingly noncooperative with system-anatagonistic "problem" groups. "Cooperation" with such groups is possible, however, if a person-blame rather than system-blame action program can be

negotiated. Thus they can be "helpful" as long as the way in which the target group is helped serves the interests of those offering assistance (p. 208).

For example, in response to the delinquency problem, youth rehabilitation centers, job retraining programs and psychotherapy programs have been developed; our economic and political systems which spawn slums and poverty go unexamined. Concern over family disorganization has produced a proliferation of marital and family counseling programs; the institution of marriage and our patterns of child-rearing remain unchallenged.

GIVING PSYCHOTHERAPY AWAY

The power of the mental health profession itself rests on its monopoly of skills and knowledge. It is through controlling skills and knowledge — not mere possession of them — that the power of this profession is maintained (Reiff, 1974). Actually, psychotherapy and helping skills are more art than science, more faith than fact, more ritual than established procedure. The refusal to share whatever skills and knowledge are available with the public gives the profession the appearance of possessing a greater range of knowledge and skills than actually exists.

The word to consumers of mental health services should be *Caveat Emptor!* — "Let the buyer beware!" The consumer is not given sufficient information to make intelligent choices concerning the need for help, the type of help needed or the ability of the helper. The client is considered unable to judge the competence of the help she/he receives. Presumably only colleagues are qualified to render such judgements. Therefore, if therapeutic errors are made, it is the client and not the helper who suffers the consequences.

Ironically, as techniques for altering behavior and personalities become more effective, the danger the techniques pose as instruments of social repression and control becomes greater. Reiff writes: "The only assurance that knowledge will be used in the promotion of human welfare is the assurance that knowledge has no guardians, that it is available to all, and that the professions be held publicly accountable for making it so" (p. 459).

As Miller (1969) said of psychologists, psychotherapists should be giving away their knowledge and skills to the public as fast as possible. One significant way psychotherapists can distribute their knowledge and skills is by training paraprofessionals.

PARAPROFESSIONALS

Some oppressed groups prefer to use mental health professionals as consultants rather than as helpers. The professionals teach paraprofessionals in the oppressed groups to become the helpers of their own group. This model is used in rape crisis centers and in abortion clinics to train women to help other women.

Paraprofessionals have proven themselves effective helpers in a variety of mental health settings (Sobey, 1970). Some professionals have questioned whether the use of paraprofessionals from the ranks of the poor and disadvantaged would result in less adequate services to those groups, but there is no evidence that this occurs. On the contrary, there is some evidence that in many cases the paraprofessionals' service is actually better (Sobey, 1970).

An innovative role for paraprofessionals is that of client advocate described by Felton, Wallach and Gallo:

> Acting as the patient's advocate is one of the major responsibilities of the human services worker. For no other staff member has this been an explicit assignment. [She]he will listen to complaints, know basic patients rights, and be familiar with eligibility structures. [She]he will be responsible for a selected, somewhat limited caseload and will be readily available to [her]his patients for lengthy contacts. Hopefully, [she]he will be able more effectively to obtain a job, leave the hospital, or to do something more meaningful within the hospital structure if a staff member is able to devote several hours or even entire days to support [her]him actively in [her]his progress. The human services worker will be free to offer this kind of support (1974, p. 59). (Brackets [ ] added.)

Reiff (1974) believes that "the introduction of the paraprofessional into human services has added a new dimension to the power struggle. For the first time the client has resources to draw on inside the professional institution" (p. 460).*

Since paraprofessionals have proved themselves to be skillful clinicians and valuable resources for the community, the reluctance and, in some instances, antagonism of professionals to their presence can be interpreted as fear of losing power. This fear is not without foundation. Paraprofessionals have been known to demand equal pay for equal work and other professional prerogatives. Sobey (1970) described a situation in which paraprofessionals were able to exert sufficient power to obtain a change in professional leadership in an institution. Reiff (1974) is concerned that paraprofessionals will identify too strongly with professionals

---

*Competencies would become as important as academic credentials in determining career opportunities if the following recommendation from the Vail Conference on professional psychology were implemented:

> Personal competencies, skills, and related experiences should be applied as equivalents in lieu of specific academic requirements in meeting formal requisites for the performance of certain activities and for salary levels associated with designed positions in a functional career ladder (Ivey and Leppoluate, 1975, p. 751).

and will be seduced by their power and prestige. If this occurs, the para-professional will become absorbed into the existing power structure and will not provide leverage for disenfranchised clients.

COUNTER-INSTITUTIONS

A possible buffer against the co-opting of paraprofessionals by the existing power structure is the formation of counter-institutions. Lacking institutional power, such counter-institutions are set up independent of established agencies in the form of self-help groups or clinics. A number of feminist groups have set up such self-help clinics in the form of therapy collectives. These collectives usually involve a few professional female therapists working on an equal (low) pay basis with lay volunteers (Elias, 1975). The philosophy of these collectives resembles the philosophy of social intervention articulated by Vallance (1972).

Vallance (1972) summarized his philosophy of social intervention as follows:

> Regarding the intervention process and its management, my suggestions stem from the proposition that the quality of human life is improved in proportion to the number of things that people know how to do for themselves and have the open opportunity to do. An associated and perhaps more basic proposition is a humanistic one which asserts that the quality of community life is in important ways related to the degree of mutual support and confidence — or if you prefer, love and trust — which members of a community can give and receive from one another (p. 108).

Because they work outside of an institutional framework, feminist therapy collectives are able to implement social action programs consistent with the philosophy described by Vallance. The collectives provide both an alternative to institutional care and a new model of mental health services to women. "Made aware that there are better alternatives, women will question the way Establishment institutions treat women" (Deckard, 1975, p. 434). Hopefully, the feminist experiment will raise both the consciousness of women and of mental health professionals, leading to better professional treatment of women.

The contributions that feminists have made to the understanding of the mental health needs of women and the appropriate therapy for them demonstrate that the sharing of knowledge is not a one-way street with the professionals giving and the public taking. Professionals can learn from nonprofessionals and paraprofessionals because these people are more closely in touch with minority persons' experience and are not prejudiced by theoretical precepts. By participating in the consciousness-raising groups of the women's movement, many female mental health professionals were converted to feminist therapy.*

Radical therapists such as Wyckoff (See Ch. 20) are understandably suspicious of professionalism in psychotherapy. Their goal is to seize the means of mental health and return psychiatry ("soul healing") to the people. They do not plan to set up an alternative to professional psychotherapy but to replace it with their counter-institution. Actually, the replacement of the mental health profession by counter-institutions appears remote at this time. Deckard notes that:

> However great the need for the services provided, our present society will limit the growth of feminist institutions and will not allow them to become a threat to the system. Constrained by lack of money, harassed by Establishment groups who see them as a threat to their monopoly position, feminist counter-institutions will be able to fill only a fraction of the need for their services (1975, p. 434-435).

NEW ROLES FOR MENTAL HEALTH PROFESSIONALS

Militant feminists take the position that professional psychotherapists (especially male therapists) who want to help women overcome oppression can be most helpful in educating members of their own profession on sexism and by raising the consciousness of male clients. Furthermore, radical feminists exhort mental health professionals who express concern for the plight of women to use their power and prestige to challenge the institutions primarily responsible for the oppression of women in our society, e.g. the educational system, the institution of marriage (See Seidenberg, Ch. 7), churches, and the economic system (See Adams and Durham, Ch. 22).

Still another way professional mental health workers can assist disadvantaged groups is by sharing with them their expert knowledge and understanding of "how the system works" to develop what Iscoe (1974) called a *competent community* — a community able to challenge the existing power structure. Fostering a competent community would be another way of giving psychotherapy away. Iscoe's suggestions closely parallel a portion of the mental health community itself, the 1973 Vail Conference of professional psychology, which made the following recommendations: "The public should be incorporated into the evaluation process. A mechanism is needed for incorporating community and public objectives. The aim is to produce change, not merely to set standards (Ivey and Leppaluoto, 1975, p. 750). Ivey and Leppaluoto interpreted the above recommendation as follows:

---

*See Ch. 3 for a description of feminist therapy.

The spirit of these recommendations is that client populations ought to be involved in helping determine what is "done to them" by professionals; and clients should be equal and active participants in evaluating the effectiveness of professionals who deliver these services (1975, p. 750).

Vallance (1972) has suggested steps that professional mental health workers might take to set up a competent community:

1. Clarify awareness of problems and the possibility of improvements in conditions;
2. Describe problems in detail with respect to seriousness and the number of people affected;
3. Formulate and select possible problem-solving approaches;
4. Identify community resources needed and potentially available;
5. Specify additional resources needed and acceptable to the community;
6. Implement approaches selected and evaluate the results; and
7. Teach community members how to use and extend the desirable effects.

Iscoe warns that as these groups develop competence and independence they will inevitably make more trouble for the existing power structure. Iscoe gives the following example of a challenge to the establishment by a group that had had some prior success participating in a social action program:

Imagine, if you will, a group of Chicano parents asking for a meeting with the school principal to discuss plans for the coming year. They have had rather good experiences with Head Start or day care programs; they have participated in various ways. They have taken responsibilities; they have a feeling of just a little more hope that their children may get a better break in school. The principal is unsympathetic and outraged. How dare these "Messcans" even ask about the curriculum! He has told them it is the same for all first graders in the public school system (nondiscrimination is one of the ways of keeping the system as it is). The parents have had contact with persons who are interested in the situation. The parents obtain expert advice about the discriminatory effects of intelligence testing, grade placement, and the like, from various sources including the community psychologist who was available to them in Head Start days. A million-dollar suit is threatened against the principal, the teachers, the superintendent, and the school board, seeking exemplary damages as well as remediation of the current situation. The case is expertly worked up by a high-powered conservative lawyer, socially prominent, with political ambitions. He uses consultants skilled in community action and cognizant of the deleterious effects of inferior education on children. The complaint stresses the lack of validity of standard intelligent tests, the physical inadequacies of the school building, the lack of experience of the teachers compared to a school in a better part of town, the absence of a Spanish-speaking secretary, and the rudimentary bilingual program, etc. The school board capitulates in a hurry. Genuine changes are instituted. Parents are involved in planning a new school. Loud rumbles are heard about outside interference and agitators (1974, p. 612-613).

However, Iscoe warns that as these groups develop greater competency and independence they "will predictably begin to ask questions of professionals, even about professionalism itself" (p. 612). The competent community will demand an active role in setting the objectives of social programs and evaluating these programs, perhaps even taking over the programs themselves. At the very least this would enforce more accountability from mental health professionals.

PROBABLE FUTURES

Our point of power, the center from which we act, is the present (Roberts, 1974). But, our concept of the present affects the future. Bell and Mau write that, "As one copes with present realities as well as with attitudes and beliefs about them, one's images of the future can change" (1971, p. 12).

The key explanatory concept in Bell and Mau's (1971) theory of social changes is the present "image of the future." The pessimism or optimism with which we forecast the future can become a self-fulfilling prophecy (Bell and Mau, 1971). Facts do not speak for themselves, they must be interpreted. How they are interpreted in terms of the possible consequences for the future is a factor in shaping that future. For example, psychotherapists who interpret the current identity crisis in youth and in women as evidence of growing societal alienation predict disorganization and doom for the future. Conversely, psychotherapists who view such crises as opportunities for women and youth to develop new, creative ways of relating to others and in society predict reduced alienation and a more cohesive, humane society. The significance of the difference between the two viewpoints is not merely rhetorical; our collective present image of the future influences which of many probable futures will materialize.

One of our most potent present beliefs shaping the future is our image of [woman]man. Bandura observed that: "What we believe [woman]man to be affects which aspects of human functioning we study most thoroughly and which we disregard ... As knowledge gained through study is put into practice, the images of [woman]man on which social technologies rest have even vaster implications" (1974, p. 859).

Nineteenth-century feminists who demanded that women be allowed to control their own lives, demanded in vain because women had no control over their reproductive systems. Women have recently gained control over their reproductive systems through reliable, inexpensive contraception and abortion techniques. However, the development of abortion techniques is not recent, but has been known for many many years. Logic suggests that the current legal availability of this service for women is not due to unforeseen technological advance nor to sudden humane concern for the self-determination of women, but rather to the previously unforeseen circumstance of overpopulation. Fear of overpopulation is the major impetus behind society's increased willingness to accept a new image of "what we believe [woman]man to be," and to sanction other roles for woman beyond motherhood for achieving self-identity, self-esteem and satisfaction.

Another important source of present beliefs which shape the future is society's philosophy of what constitutes a good life. Reiff (1974) is critical of the mental health profession for its failure to develop models of mental health and a vision of a good society. He complains that: "No better example of organized irresponsibility exists than the mental health profession, which not only presumes to tell people what is mentally healthy without an established notion of mental health, but lately has begun to tell people how to bring about social change that will make us all healthier and happier (1974, p. 452).

Creating a model of mental health requires a vision of the future. Granted that we have limited vision and that projecting the future will have imperfect results, must we therefore ignore the future? Psychotherapists should no more excuse their own lack of social responsibility toward the future on the grounds that they cannot predict it than they are willing to excuse their clients' reluctance to invest energy in self-change because there are no guarantees of favorable outcomes.

Feminists do have a view of the future. Their view can be summarized as follows (Palme, 1972): Personality differences and role differences based on sex will be eliminated. Thus, both men and women will be given more freedom in expressing individual differences based on individual temperament, talent, and ability. Both men and women will receive the same education and career opportunities. Role-sharing will replace role-division along sex lines. More options in career and family combinations will be available to both sexes. The role of the father in his children's development and socialization will be recognized as essential as the mother's role; both parents will assume equal responsibility for their children. In place of concern only for working mothers, society will be concerned for working parents. Either or both parents may opt to work halftime, especially if their children are young. Greater variety in lifestyles will be available to people. Each person, regardless of her/his interpersonal relationship or commitments, will be recognized as an autonomous person by the state. Marriage will be a contractual arrangement between two or more persons (of either sex).

All citizens will have equal rights and equal protection under the law. The economic system will be more socialistic; there will be less income disparities between groups of people. Social security will be extended to include men or women who chose to work in the home. All citizens will be guaranteed adequate medical care, education, housing, and leisure. There will be greater experimentation with many forms of community and communal living. For example, apartment complexes will provide food, laundry and cleaning services to enable individuals and families to have more leisure time.

It is, of course, impossible to change the role of one sex without changing the role of the other. The liberation of women must of necessity involve men's liberation. The feminists' vision of the future is one of human liberation.

This feminist view of the future has grown out of their interpretation of the present.

BUILDING THE FUTURE

Not only does our view of the present shape the future, but our image of the future shapes the present. Bell and Mau (1971) point out that "the emerging future also affects the realities of the present as well as our perceptions and evaluations of them" (p. 13). Our personal and professional activities are continually affected by our expectations of the future. We are constantly attempting to block anticipated undesirable outcomes or facilitate desirable ones. Bell and Mau (1971) quote Waskow who discusses one way the future can be imported into the present: "One of the most powerful ways of achieving social change is to imagine in vivid detail a desirable and achievable future and then *build* a part of that future in the present — rather than merely pleading for it to be built (1969, p. 35-36). Counter-institutions such as the feminist therapy collectives described above are examples of building part of the future in the present. Dissatisfied with the quality of mental health services women were receiving, feminists in the collectives have set up their own model of the mental health care they felt women should receive.

A way in which psychotherapists can build part of the future in the present is to make their present work with clients relevant to the basic values they hold for the emerging future of both the client and society. One way to make present therapy relevant to a client's future was introduced by Lessee (1971): future-oriented psychotherapy. After his clients recover from crises and can function with an adequate degree of maturity,

Lessee begins to introduce the notion "that the present should be viewed as a functional or logical increment leading toward a tentative future" (p. 189). In describing his approach he says:

> My concepts of the future are never presented with any dogmatic certainty, but solely as tentative probings, and the patient is encouraged to disagree and to develop his or her own ideas with regard to the broad scope of possible futures. Having done so, the patient is encouraged to project himself or herself into the world that he or she has conceptualized. The therapist must be prepared to guide the patient with pertinent questions and observations (p. 190).

Clients are encouraged to deal with such issues as professional or vocational decisions, plans for changes in family relationships, parent-child relationships, and retirement. The following descriptions of some future issues involving his women clients are paraphrased from Lessee:

1. Ambitious young women who were junior executives were encouraged to evaluate their professional potentialities in anticipation of lessening prejudices against women in particular fields.
2. Women were asked to explore long-range expectations concerning the quality of relationships they expected to have with men, concepts of future marriage if they choose to marry, future role relationships in marriage (or in male-female relationships), and marriage with and without children.
3. Mothers were asked to consider what their world is likely to be like when their children are older or no longer at home, what activities will then bring them pleasure as well as satisfaction, how they planned to direct their lives now in order to be able to arrive at flexible goals in the tenative future.

Lessee's future-oriented psychotherapy is compatible with Harmon's approach to career counseling (see Ch. 10). Harmon suggests that vocational counselors not only help women to identify skills they can develop to meet their current needs but also take a broad developmental approach and suggest women use their lower-level skills as stepping stones to future goals and higher need fulfillment. Radical therapists would criticize the future-oriented approach because the therapist or counselor is involving the client in changes related only to an anticipated personal future rather than involving her/him as a change agent in shaping her/his social as well as personal future.

Bugental (1971) insists that once a client has been exposed to humanistic values through therapy she/he is less tolerant of dehumanizing and antitherapeutic aspects in the environment. According to Bugental, providing the client with a mutual relationship and encouragement in self-development is in itself a radical act and will ultimately pose a threat to the *status quo*. Having discovered that she/he can change what she/he does not like about her/himself, the client would be more optimistic about changing what she/he does not like in the environment.

Adams and Durham would (see Ch. 22) agree that social change begins with personal change. These authors would argue, however, that Bugental's position is politically naive. Regardless of philosophy, values and skills developed in therapy, one person alone cannot stand up against a whole society. She/he would either regress to her/his former level of neurotic adjustment or become cynical and disillusioned. These authors insist that political education is a legitimate and necessary part of psychotherapy. In addition to dealing with her/his individual conflicts ("secondary contradictions"), the client must become aware of the root contradictions in society ("primary contradictions") which are related to the individual conflicts. In addition to making the client aware of political realities and power relationships in society, the therapist must also aid her/him in locating a group of people she/he can join for political action. In some cases, the therapist her/himself may join the client in political activity.

Gluckstern (see Ch. 23) also suggests a way therapists can build part of the future in the present. Instead of confining their activities to the consulting room, therapists can give first priority to social action in order to make oppressive institutions more egalitarian and humanistic. Gluckstern's experience provides optimism for the usefulness of "on the job training." "Learning by doing" would be necessary because, at the present time, few therapists have adequate training in functioning as social-change agents.

However, many do not have the interest in becoming change agents. Roe (1959) cites a talk by Halpern who reported a survey which showed that an overwhelming number of young psychologists were interested only in the practice of therapy. Halpern is quoted as follows:

> It seems to me that there is something a bit amiss with a group of scientists who are overwhelmingly service-oriented and who, recognizing that life adjustment is increasingly complex and difficult, offer to cure the ills resulting from the present state of affairs, but do little or nothing to help society learn how best to meet their interpersonal, emotional and social problems so that the present seemingly all-pervasive disturbances may be avoided (p. 264).

We hope that young women and men in the mental health professional training programs of today will have more interest in the societal ills which produce personal disturbance and limit personal growth. Such students would require their training programs to take a broad (external) societal view of the cause of behavior in addition to the present narrow (internal) individual view. This broad view will not be diagnostic and reactive, but will contain a vision of individual mental health and of a good society. The recommendations of the 1973 Vail Conference on professional psychology echo a similar view.

> Professional psychology training program at all levels (continuing professional development, doctoral, master, prebachelors) should provide information on the potential nature of the practice of psychology. This does not imply that a "right" answer is to be suggested; rather the very serious implications of practice on society become part of the awareness of every psychologist (Ivey and Leppaluoto, 1975, p. 748-749).

The women and men who contributed to this book are building part of the future through their current professional activities. The approaches they describe not only enable women to better cope with the present realities in their lives but also prepare them to function in a possible future in which women will be equal members of a more humane society. The very diversity of ideas in these contributions is exciting and bodes well for the future direction of psychotherapy.

Social change is a slow process and those who now hold power, including members of the mental health profession, will not easily relinquish it. While working for social change, we take courage from Miller's statement: "Vested interests, however powerful, cannot withstand the gradual encroachment of new ideas" (1969, p. 1074). We invite all members of the helping professions to join us in deliberately developing and distributing ideas which will increase the probability of an egalitarian society in the future.

REFERENCES

Argyris, Chris: Dangers in applying results from experimental social psychology. *American Psychologist, 30*:469, 1975.

Bandura, Albert: Behavior theory and the models of man. *American Psychologist, 29*:859, 1974.

Bart, Pauline B.: The myth of a value-free psychotherapy. In Bell, Wendell and Mau, James A. (Eds.): *The Sociology of the Future*. New York, Russell Sage Foundation, 1971.

Becker, H. S.: Whose side are we on? In Filstead, W. J. (Ed.): *Qualitative Methodology: Firsthand Involvement with the Social World*. Chicago, Markham, 1970, p. 18.

Beit-Hallahmi, Benjamin: Salvation and its vicissitudes: Clinical psychology and political values. *American Psychologist, 29*:124, 1974.

Bell, Wendell & Mau, James A.: Images of the future: theory and research strategies. *The Sociology of the Future*. New York, Russell Sage Foundation, 1971.

Brickman, Harry R.: Mental health and social change: An ecological perspective. *American Journal of Psychiatry, 127*:413, 1970.

Bugental, James F. T.: The Humanistic ethic — the individual in psychotherapy as a societal change agent. *Journal of Humanistic Psychology, 11*:11, 1971.

Caplan, Nathan & Nelson, Stephen D.: On being useful: The nature and consequences of psychological research on social problems. *American Psychologist, 28*:199, 1973.

Chesler, Mark A. & Worden, Orian: Persistent problems in "power and social change." *The Journal of Applied Behavioral Science, 10*:463, 1974.

Deckard, Barbara S.: *The Women's Movement: Political, Socioeconomics, and Psychological Issues.* New York, Harper & Row, 1975.

Ehrlich, Annette & Abraham-Magdamo, Fred: Caution: mental health may be hazardous. *Human Behavior, 3*:64, 1974.

Elias, Marilyn: Sisterhood therapy. *Human Behavior, 4*:56, 1975.

Felton, Gary S., Wallach, Howard F. & Gallo, Charla L.: New roles for new professional mental health workers: training the patient advocate, the integrator, and the therapist. *Community Mental Health Journal, 10*:52, 1974.

Iscoe, Ira: Community psychology and the competent community. *American Psychologist, 29*:607, 1974.

Ivey, Allen E. & Leppaluoto, Jean R.: Changes ahead! Implications of the Vail Conference. *Personnel and Guidance Journal, 53*:747, 1975.

Lessee, Stanley: Future oriented psychotherapy. *American Journal of Psychotherapy, 25*:180, 1971.

Miller, George: Psychology as a means of promoting human welfare. *American Psychologist, 24*:1063, 1969.

Morgan, L. B.: Counseling for future shock. *Personnel and Guidance Journal, 52*:283, 1974.

O'Day, Rory: Intimidation Rituals: Reactions to Reform. *Journal of Applied Behavioral Science, 10*:373, 1974.

Palme, Olof: The emancipation of man. *The Journal of Social Issues: New Perspectives on Women, 28*:237, 1972.

Reiff, Robert: The control of knowledge: The power of the helping professions. *The Journal of Applied Behavioral Science, 10*:451, 1974.

Roe, Anne: Man's forgotten weapon. *American Psychologist, 14*:260, 1959.

Sobey, Francine: *The Nonprofessional Revolution in Mental Health.* New York, Columbia University Press, 1970.

Vallance, Theodore R.: Social Science and Social Policy: Amoral methodology in a matrix of values. *American Psychologist, 27*:107, 1972.

Waskow, Arthur I.: Looking forward: 1999 in Jungk, Robert and Galtung, Johan (Eds.), *Mankind 2000.* Oslo: Universitets-forlaget, 1969.

INDEX*

*Additional authors and books will be found listed in the annotated bibliography that is a part of the chapter on bibliotherapy (pp. 328-342).